Handbook of Cognitive Semantics

Volume 1

Brill's Handbooks
in Linguistics

VOLUME 4

The titles published in this series are listed at *brill.com/bhl*

Handbook of Cognitive Semantics

With a Foreword by Leonard Talmy

VOLUME 1

Edited by

Fuyin Thomas Li

BRILL

LEIDEN | BOSTON

Library of Congress Cataloging-in-Publication Data

Names: Li, Fuyin, editor.
Title: Handbook of cognitive semantics / edited by Fuyin Thomas Li ;
    with a foreword by Leonard Talmy.
Description: Leiden ; Boston : Brill, [2023]- | Series: Brill's handbooks in linguistics,
    1879-629X ; volume 4 | Includes bibliographical references.
Identifiers: LCCN 2022050816 | ISBN 9789004468207 (v. 1 ; hardback ; acid-free
    paper)
Subjects: LCSH: Semantics–Psychological aspects. | Cognitive grammar. |
    LCGFT: Essays.
Classification: LCC P325.5.P78 H366 2023 | DDC 401/.4301835–dc23/eng/20221215
LC record available at https://lccn.loc.gov/2022050816

Typeface for the Latin, Greek, and Cyrillic scripts: "Brill". See and download: brill.com/brill-typeface.

ISSN 1879-629X
ISBN 978-90-04-46820-7 (hardback)

This book is printed on acid-free paper and produced in a sustainable manner.

Printed by Printforce, United Kingdom

Contents

VOLUME 1

PART 1
Conceptual Semantics

PART 2
Basic Issues

Preface

Cognitive semantics has developed into an interdisciplinary approach to the study of meaning and mind. To date, there has been no other handbook or similar type of publication to provide a practical guide for research in the field. With 46 chapters contributed by the experts, this handbook aims to provide a comprehensive coverage of the field, from basic concepts to major theories, methodologies, and applications.

I thank the publisher, Brill; its department manager, Uri Tadmor, for his initiative and insightfulness in commissioning this reference work; and its responsible editor, Elisa Perotti, for all her subsequent work in production and revisions. The overall design and organization of the book, the selection of the topics and experts, revisions of its contents were aided by Leonard Talmy. In addition, Talmy provided the Taxonomy of Cognitive Semantics (Chapter 1) and contributed another chapter on his latest theory (Chapter 44).

I particularly thank the authors for their chapters. The chapters were written by the authors, reviewed by the authors, and revised by the authors. If the handbook proves itself as an authoritative work of the most significant topics in cognitive semantics, it is due to the professional work of the authors.

My last thanks go to my three editorial assistants. They are Jing DU, Na LIU, and Shan ZUO. They were responsible for all the correspondence, especially during the review process.

Fuyin Thomas Li

Figures and Tables

Figures

Tables

Notes on Contributors

Esra' M. ABDELZAHER
(MA 2017) is an ABD-PhD candidate of linguistics at the University of Debrecen, where she started her research on computational lexicography at the Institute of English and American Studies. Her main research interests include Frame semantics, FrameNet, cognitive semantics and corpus linguistics. Esra' Abdelzaher is now exploring the new potentials provided by Bert in lexicographic practice. She published research articles addressing the possibility of applying FrameNet to the user-generated content for granular detection of social or political phenomena. Esra' Abdelzaher investigates the plausible interoperability between FrameNet and other language resources for improving the output of modern lexicography. She has contributed recently to the *Routledge Handbook of Cognitive Linguistics*. Esra' Abdelzaher can be contacted at esra.abdelzaher@arts.unideb.hu and esraa.abdelzaher@alsun.asu.edu.eg

Mira ARIEL
is professor emerita of linguistics at Tel Aviv University. She is the author of *Accessing NP Antecedents* (Routledge, 1990), *Pragmatics and Grammar* (Cambridge University Press, 2008) and *Defining Pragmatics* (Cambridge University Press, 2010), as well as numerous articles. Her main areas of research are reference, specifically, Accessibility theory, the grammar/pragmatics interface, particularly in connection with connectives and quantifiers, and grammaticization. Mira Ariel can be reached at mariel@tauex.tau.ac.il.

Daniel CASASANTO
is associate professor of psychology at Cornell University and director of the Experience and Cognition Laboratory. He studies how the diversity of human experience is reflected in our brains and minds. To study cognitive diversity across cultures, his lab conducts research on five continents, using methods that range from watching children at play to brain imaging and neurostimulation. A former opera singer, Casasanto received a graduate diploma in voice from the Peabody Conservatory before earning a doctorate from the department of brain and cognitive sciences at MIT in 2005. Casasanto's awards include a National Research Service Award, the James S. McDonnell Foundation's Scholar Award, the Association for Psychological Science's Award for Transformative Early Career Contributions, the American Psychological Association's Fantz Memorial Award for Young Psychologists, and the Psychonomic Society's Early Career Award for Exceptional Research Contributions to Scien-

tific Psychology. Casasanto has authored over 100 scientific publications. He serves on the editorial board of seven journals and was a founding editor of Cambridge University Press's interdisciplinary journal *Language and Cognition*. Daniel Casasanto can be reached at casasanto@cornell.edu.

Patrick DUFFLEY

is professor of English Linguistics at Université Laval in Quebec City. He has published monographs on linguistic semantics, syntax and English verbal categories (mainly the infinitive and the gerund-participle), as well as articles on modal auxiliaries, *wh-* words, negative polarity items and indefinite determiners. His work utilizes concepts inspired by cognitive grammar and Guillaumian psychomechanical theory in order to develop a properly semantic approach to grammar and syntax. In particular, his research is inspired by Langacker's semiological principle, according to which the fundamental role of language is to allow the symbolization of conceptualizations by means of phonological sequences, and takes the fundamental task of linguistics to be deducing the nature of the cognitive content stably attached to the linguistic sign. In 2014 he published a monograph with John Benjamins proposing a semantico-pragmatic explanation of the syntactic phenomenon of subject vs. non-subject control with non-finite verbal forms in English (*Reclaiming Control as a Semantic and Pragmatic Phenomenon*). In 2020 Oxford University Press published an introduction to semantics intitled *Linguistic Meaning Meets Linguistic Form* authored by him predicated on the non-autonomy of syntax from semantics. Patrick Duffley can be reached at Patrick.Duffley@lli.ulaval.ca.

Cliff GODDARD

is professor of linguistics at Griffith University. He is a leading proponent of the Natural Semantic Metalanguage approach to semantics. He has published widely in descriptive, theoretical, and applied semantics, language description and typology, ethnopragmatics, and intercultural communication. His most recent monograph is *Ten Lectures on Natural Semantic Metalanguage: Exploring Language, Thought and Culture Using Simple, Translatable Words* (2018, Brill). Cliff Goddard can be reached at c.goddard@griffith.edu.au.

Peter HARDER

is professor emeritus of English linguistics at the University of Copenhagen. His research interests include core linguistic areas like grammaticalization theory as well as macro-linguistic areas such as linguistic normativity and the societal role of conceptualization. A common thread is the interest in the interplay between functional and conceptual factors in shaping relations both between linguistic facts and between language and broader conceptual and societal processes. His main books are *Functional Semantics: A Theory of Meaning, Structure and Tense in English* (1996) and *Meaning in Mind and Society; A Functional Contribution to the Social Turn in Cognitive Linguistics* (2010). Peter Harder can be reached at harder@hum.ku.dk.

Ronald W. LANGACKER

(PhD 1966) was professor of linguistics at the University of California, San Diego, until his retirement in 2003. His early research dealt with generative syntax and the comparative-historical grammar of the Uto-Aztecan family of Native American languages. Since 1976 he has been developing an innovative theoretical framework which has come to be known as cognitive grammar. Monographs presenting this model include *Foundations of Cognitive Grammar* (1987, 1991), *Concept, Image, and Symbol* (1990), *Grammar and Conceptualization* (1999), *Cognitive Grammar: A Basic Introduction* (2008), and *Investigations in Cognitive Grammar* (2009). He has also published numerous articles dealing with a broad array of issues in cognitive linguistics. He was a founding member of the International Cognitive Linguistics Association and served as its president from 1997 to 1999. He was an original co-editor of the monograph series Cognitive Linguistics Research and is a member of numerous editorial and advisory boards. Ronald Langacker can be reached at rlangacker@ucsd.edu.

Fuyin Thomas LI

(PhD 2002) is professor of linguistics at Beihang University and organizer of the China International Forum on Cognitive Linguistics (cifcl.buaa.edu.cn). He is the founding editor of the *Cognitive Semantics* (brill.com/cose) journal, series editor of *Distinguished Lectures in Cognitive Linguistics* (brill.com/dlcl), and organizer of ICLC-11. His main research interests involve Talmyan cognitive semantics, overlapping systems model, event grammar, causality, and related topics, with a focus on synchronic and diachronic perspectives on Chinese data with a strong commitment to usage-based models. His representative works include the *Handbook of Cognitive Semantics* (2023), *An Introduction to Event Grammar* (2021, in Chinese), *Semantic Typology of Events* (2019, in Chinese), *Toward a Cognitive Semantics I & II* (2017 and 2019, in Chinese—both originally by Leonard Talmy, MIT, 2000), *Metaphor, Image, and Image Schemas in Second Language Pedagogy* (2009), *Semantics: A Course Book* (1999), *An Introduction to Cognitive Linguistics* (2008, in Chinese), *Semantics: An Introduction* (2007, in Chinese). Other publications include journal articles in *Cognitive Linguistics*, *Review of Cognitive Linguistics*, *Cognitive Semantics*, and *Foreign Language Teaching and Research*, among others. Thomas Fuyin Li can be reached at thomasli@buaa.edu.cn; thomaslifuyin@hotmail.com.

Nian LIU

is associate professor and chair of the Department of Modern Languages, Literatures, and Linguistics at University of Oklahoma, where she conducts interdisciplinary research on cognitive linguistics and Chinese humanities. Her research interests cover diverse topics including simulation semantics, linguistic relativity, bilingualism, and Chinese language processing. Her main research projects explore the relationship between language, culture and cognition using behavioral and neuroimaging experimentations. Several of her research projects have been supported by the National Science Foundation (NSF), Ministry of Education of China, and University of Oklahoma Research Council. She was a visiting scholar at University of California San Diego, University of Latvia, Peking University, and Chinese University of Hong Kong working on several cross-linguistic comparison projects. Her publication appeared in high-impact journals including *Cognitive Linguistics*, *Brain Research*, and *Journal of Neurolinguistics*. She currently serves as review editor of *Cognitive Semantics*. Nian Liu can be reached at nian.liu@ou.edu.

Magdalena RYBARCZYK

is a tutor in linguistics and literature at the University of Nottingham Ningbo China. She holds a doctoral degree in cognitive linguistics from the University of Warsaw, Poland. Her research interests lie primarily in cognitive linguistics, an approach to language and mind which places central importance on meaning and its grounding in bodily and social experience. She is the author of the research monograph *Demonstratives and Possessives with Attitude: An Intersubjectively-Oriented Empirical Study* (2015). Her work explores the subtle semantics of grammar and conceptual structuring, which give access to studying human intersubjective disposition and coordination. She aims to continue to offer accounts of linguistic phenomena in light of human shared social experience and non-dualistic body/mind. Not unrelated to this line of research is Rybarczyk's keen interest in mental health and meditative practices. Magdalena Rybarczyk can be reached at Magdalena.Rybarczyk@nottingham.edu.cn.

Michael STEVENS PÉREZ

is currently a PhD candidate at the University of Nottingham Ningbo China, in the School of Education and English. His research focuses on gesture and cognition in interaction at the level of concept development, specifically within learning environments that use a foreign language as academic lingua franca. His approach brings together methods in cognitive linguistics, conversation analysis, and enactive cognition to the study of gesture and embodied actions in learning, and seeks to promote local, human-centered approaches to *mind*. His interests lie at the interfaces between individual, interactional, and socio-cultural process of meaning-making. He is also a participant in the multi-modal project, the corpus of Chinese Academic Written and Spoken English (CAWSE). Michael Stevens Pérez can be reached at michaelpaul.stevens@nottingham.edu.cn.

Leonard TALMY

is professor emeritus of linguistics, director emeritus of the Center for Cognitive Science, and affiliate professor emeritus of philosophy at the University at Buffalo, State University of New York. His research interests cover cognitive semantics, the properties of conceptual organization, and cognitive theory. Within linguistics, his interests center on natural-language semantics, including typologies and universals of semantic structure; the relationship between semantic structure and formal linguistic structures—lexical, morphological, and syntactic; and the relation of this material to diachrony, discourse, development, impairment, culture, and evolution. He is the author of a two-volume set, *Toward a Cognitive Semantics* (2000) and of a single volume, *The Targeting System of Language* (2018), both with MIT Press. He is the recipient of the 2012 Gutenberg Research Award. Leonard Talmy can be reached at talmy@buffalo.edu.

Anna WIERZBICKA

is professor emerita of linguistics at the Australian National University. She is the founder of the Natural Semantic Metalanguage approach to semantics. Her work spans a number of disciplines, including anthropology, cognitive science, philosophy, and religious studies, as well as linguistics. She is author of many books, most recently *What Christians Believe: The Story of God and People in Minimal English* (2018, Oxford University Press). Anna Wierzbicka can be reached at Anna.Wierzbicka@anu.edu.au.

Zhengdao YE

is senior lecturer in linguistics and translation at the Australian National University. She specialises in semantics, pragmatics, translation studies, and intercultural communication. She is editor of *The Semantics of Nouns* (2017, Oxford University Press). Zhengdao Ye can be reached at zhengdao.ye@anu.edu.au.

CHAPTER 1

Foreword: A Taxonomy of Cognitive Semantics

Leonard Talmy

1   Introduction

The central concern of cognitive semantics is how language structures conceptual content. That is, it concerns the patterns in which and processes by which
a conceptual range that includes ideation and affect is organized in language.
This concern distinguishes it from such other areas of linguistic research as
phonology and syntax when undertaken without consideration of meaning.

Cognitive semantics, further, treats the conceptual structuring that it
observes in language not as a research end in itself, but as a window onto cognitive organization in general—that is, how the mind works. It thus allies with
such other approaches as cognitive psychology and forms part of cognitive science. This larger concern is what distinguishes it from traditional semantics.

Since its origins, cognitive semantics has grown greatly in the range and
depth of its research on conceptual structure in language. This expansion now
calls for the present Handbook to document it. The forty-five other chapters in
this volume provide overviews of portions of the field that together map out its
present extent.

In the spirit of this undertaking, this Foreword presents a taxonomy of cognitive semantics. The intention is to approach the field comprehensively and
outline its main contours. But the taxonomy is only heuristic—it is an initial
endeavor to survey the field and is meant to be developed. It inevitably has
omissions that could be filled and analyses that could be structured otherwise.
The aim, though, is to provide a basis for discussion.

The taxonomy is organized in terms of categories and subcategories into
which conceptual structure in language or research on it can fall. The focus
and methodology of a cognitive-semantic study may then largely represent a
particular selection from these entries. In fact, a potential advantage of the taxonomy might be to reveal combinations of the entries that are understudied.

In the remainder of this Foreword, the taxonomy is first presented in table
form and is then discussed.

© KONINKLIJKE BRILL NV, LEIDEN, 2023 | DOI:10.1163/_002

2 The Taxonomy in Table Form

Our taxonomy of cognitive semantics is presented below in table form. The table represents up to three levels, marked from high to low by upper-case letters, numbers, and lower-case letters. Each level appears with increasing indentation. If the entries at a given level are short, they are placed on the same line to save space, rather than each on a separate line. The discussion after section 3 often presents distinctions still more granular than the lowest level indicated in the table (with the fourth level indicated again by numbers).

TABLE 1.1   Taxonomy of cognitive semantics

A. Major language divisions—The three main compartments of language
  1. Form; 2. Grammar; 3. Meaning (semantics/pragmatics)
B. Participant structure—the sending vs. receiving of a communication
  1. Participant types; 2. Participant numbers; 3. Participant directionality
C. Arenas of assembly—the venues in which meaning-associated units come together
  1. Inventory; 2. Expression; 3. Part inventory part expression
D. Content structuring mechanisms—the major systems by which language structures conceptual content
  1. Closed-class semantics—the conceptual "schematic systems" represented by explicit or implicit elementsof grammar
    a. Configurational structure; b. Perspective; c. Attention; d. Force dynamics; e. Cognitive state f. Reality status; g. Communicative purpose; h. Ontology; i. Role semantics.; j. Quantity
  2. Content patterning—the patterns in which the conceptual continuum is partitioned and arranged
    a. In the morpheme; b. In the lexicon.; c. In expression
  3. Content selection—whether/which content is expressed by a speaker
    a. Inclusion vs. omission; b. Alternatives for inclusion; c. Constraints on selection
  4. Content inference—The hearer infers conceptual content additional to what is explicit
  5. Context—constraints from,e.g., linguistic/thematic/physical/interlocutory/epistemic/social circumstances
  6. Interaction—the structuring of content through cross- participant accommodation
    a. Cross-consideration; b. Turn taking
E. Combination—the patterns in which linguistic elements can combine
  1. Additive; 2. Operational; 3. Idiomatic; 4. Constructively discrepant

TABLE 1.1   Taxonomy of cognitive semantics (*cont.*)

F. Diachronic comparison—comparing conceptual structures in a single
   language across different points of its temporal continuum
   1. Long time scale; 2. Medium time scale; 3. Short time scale
G. Crosslinguistic comparison—comparing conceptual structures across
   different (varieties of) languages
   1. Absolutely universal; 2. Typological; 3. Repertorial; 4. Indefinitely
   diverse
H. Quantity of manifestation—(changes in) the amount of conceptual content that is represented or occurs
   1. Elaboratedness—the comprehensiveness and granularity of conceptual
   content
      a. In a communication system; b. In a language user; c. In a lexicon;
      d. In expression
   2. Prevalence—the frequency of occurrence of conceptual content
      a. Compared across languages; b. In a single language
I. Communication systems—the use of different channels based on the
   mode of the sender's production and the receiver's perception
   1. Co-speech gesture; 2. Signed language
J. Research characteristics—the methodologies and other aspects of
   approach that shape a language study

3   Discussion of the Taxonomy: Introduction

The aim of the discussion that follows is to balance the overview character of
the table above with enough detail and illustration to make its categories recognizable. To this end, each section below generally presents a variety of linguistic
phenomena to show the range of application of the category it is describing.
Where the description in one section relates to that in another section, the latter is indicated within parentheses. A speaker is referred to as "she" and the
hearer as "he."

The fact that the taxonomy is an overview of an entire field prevents citing
most work in the area, so that only a small subset of relevant references is provided. However, a personal advantage of the taxonomy is that it has provided
a grid over which elements of my own work can be located, and some of these
are indicated at pertinent points. The letter T followed by a number from 1 to 14
gives the publication (this number is shown as well in the references section),

the letter "c" plus a number gives the chapter, and the letter "s" plus a number gives the section.

The ten main categories of the taxonomy are presented in the next ten sections of this Foreword. Space limitations have required the omission of several further categories, but two of these—evolution and the relation of language to other cognitive systems—are addressed respectively in T11 and T8.

4   A. Major Language Divisions

In accord with linguistic tradition, language as a whole can be partitioned into three main divisions or compartments: form, grammar, and meaning. These divisions are not wholly independent but in part interrelate. Accordingly, though cognitive semantics focuses on meaning, it readily brings in the other divisions where they relate to meaning.

4.1   *A1. Form*

Form in spoken language rests at base on vocally produced sound. Five types of form might be recognized. One type, "vocal dynamics," is wholly gradient and includes pitch, loudness, speed, timbre, and precision of articulation (T12 s2.2.1). In any given language, three further types consist of discrete elements in specific arrangements and conform to certain constraints universally. These are phonetic distinctive features, phonology, and morphemic shape. And a fifth type of form—intonation—within any given language is a closed class of sentence-spanning sequential patterns consisting mainly of different relative pitches and loudnesses, themselves in part gradient and in part discrete.

4.2   *A2. Grammar*

To characterize it in a first-approximation, grammar consists of all closed-class morphemes. Excluded from grammar then are both open-class morphemes and closed-classed linguistic phenomena other than morphemes, for example, such phonological phenomena as distinctive features and phonemes. Because of their significance in this taxonomy, the notions of morpheme, closed class, and open class are expanded on next.

4.2.1   A2a. Morpheme

The term "morpheme" here refers to any minimal linguistic construct that is associated with a concept—its "meaning." "Minimal" here indicates that the construct's overall meaning is not a combination of meanings associated with any components the construct may have. Because our analysis bases grammar on morphemes and morphemes on meaning, the division of grammar cannot be fully characterized apart from that of meaning.

The linguistic construct here considered to be a morpheme can be divided into three groups, each with its own types. In the first group, a morpheme has phonological substance. In one type within this group, the morpheme is a particular segmental sequence (potentially with suprasegmental tone or stress), like that in *flask* expressing the concept of a kind of bottle. In another type, it is an intonation pattern, like the singsong contour expressing the concept of mock threat in *I'm gonna tickle you!* In yet another type, it is a suprasegmental element, like heightened stress on a constituent (indicated throughout this Foreword by an exclamation point before the constituent), representing the concept and operation of a correction, as in *No, I was in !-Paris, not !-London.* And in a still further type, it is an idiom, like *have it in for* which expresses the concept 'nurse a grudge against'. A complex like this, though composed of what would otherwise be morphemes themselves, is a morpheme in its own right because its meaning cannot be derived from their meanings.

In the second group, a morpheme does not itself have phonological substance but is a pattern involving phonological morphemes, a pattern largely based on affordances or constraints on their co-occurrence. As with all morphemes, such a pattern morpheme is associated with a concept. In one type within this group, the morpheme is a particular constituent order (i.e., word order), such as auxiliary before subject, as in *had I known*, expressing the concept 'if'. In another type, it is a constituent category (a term used here as a generalization over the more traditional "lexical category") like that of adjective, such as *blue*, expressing the concept 'attribute'. In a further type, it is a particular phrase structure, like that of adjective-noun, as in *blue hat*, expressing the relationship of attribute to substrate. And in a still further type, it is a grammatical relation like that of direct object, exhibited by *plum* in *I ate the plum*, expressing the concept 'affected Patient'.

The third group has one type, that of complex construction, where a morpheme is a composite that generally includes both phonological morphemes and morphemic patterns but that has an overall meaning not derivable from those of its components. An example is the construction seen in *Could you pass the salt?*, expressing a request by the speaker to the hearer (8.3).[1]

---

1 In the wide application it has here, our term "morpheme" is close to the "construction" of construction grammar. In turn, the term "construction" is here mainly used for the kind of complex described in the text.

4.2.2   A2b. Closed Class

A closed class in any given language is a formally distinguishable set with few members that it is difficult to add to. Our concern here is with those closed classes whose members are (largely) concept-associated morphemes.

Within the first group, two of the morpheme types are closed-class. Thus, perhaps every language has a small and relatively fixed set of intonation contours over a sentence, each with an associated concept or polysemous set of concepts. And any concept-associated suprasegmental morphemes in a language like that of heightened stress constitute a closed class, sometimes with just one member. Further, the segmental and idiomatic morphemes in perhaps every language include closed classes, whether free like prepositions and conjunctions or bound like inflections and derivations. But the remainder of these two types consists of one or more open classes.

Within the second group, seemingly every language's set of constituent categories, of phrase structures, of grammatical relations, or of constituent orders (where these are not wholly free) constitutes a closed class. A further supposition here is that every member within each of these second-group closed classes is itself a morpheme with an associated concept or polysemous set of concepts, however general. For example, within German's closed class of constituent orders, the final positioning of the tensed verb in a syntactically subordinate clause can be interpreted as a morpheme associated with the concept that the clause's event is conceptually subordinated to a main event. This supposition would be faulted, however, if it is determined that a particular language has certain constituent categories, phrase structures, grammatical relations, or constituent orders that simply lack all conceptual associations. In that case, though, the original characterization of grammar as consisting of all closed-class morphemes would be shifted to its consisting of all closed classes with some (concept-associated) morphemes.

In the third group, finally, every language has complex constructions that can incorporate members from any of the preceding types of closed classes as well as particular open-class morphemes. Suppositionally, each such construction is itself a morpheme associated with a concept. But it may well be that, in every language, such complex constructions constitute a closed class.

4.2.3   A2c. Open Class

An open class in any given language is a formally distinguishable set with many members that can be readily added to. Though possibly applicable to other phenomena such as a polysemous range, the term mainly applies to segmental morphemes and idioms. Within the former of these, an open class can consist of the roots of nouns, verbs, adjectives, or mimetics, where a language includes such distinctions. Open-class morphemes can be associated with certain closed classes such as that of constituent category but, apart from this, they are not in themselves part of grammar.

4.2.4 A2d. Morpheme Types within Multimorphemic Words

The morphemic types in the first two groups of (4.2.1) were mainly characterized in terms of free forms, but their adaptation under morphology to word-internal morphemes can be considered. While syntax mainly addresses the combination of mono- and multimorphemic words into phrases, clauses, and sentences, morphology addresses the combination of morphemes into multimorphemic words in the languages that have them. A multimorphemic word commonly consists of an open-class morpheme as the root and one or more closed-class morphemes as bound affixes.

Within the first group, morphemes of the segmental type clearly occur for both root and affix, as in *retest*. Idioms also occur, whether involving root and affix as in English *considerable* 'fairly great in amount' or involving just affixes, as where Atsugewi *-tip* 'out of a container' and *-u·* 'along an extended path' together in sequence mean 'into a pit'. But it is unclear whether the morpheme types consisting of an intonation contour and a suprasegmental element have counterparts within multimorphemic words.

For the second group of morpheme types we look at the morphological pattern of Atsugewi, whose polysynthetic verb consists of a "slot" for the verb root surrounded by up to some dozen prefixal and suffixal slots in a fixed order. The constituent category type of morpheme carries over here in that each slot is a distinct constituent representing its own semantic category. Thus, the slot immediately before that of the verb root is the "instrumental constituent" expressing a causal event. The phrase structure morpheme type also has a counterpart—thus, the instrumental constituent and the verb root together form a structure that expresses the relation of cause to result. But there are no counterparts for grammatical relations or constituent order—the latter since the fixed-order slots allow no morphemes consisting of alternative sequences with distinct semantic correlates.

4.3 *A3. Meaning*

Meaning in language consists of conceptual content associated with form or grammar. Such meaning can then be divided into semantics and pragmatics.

By one analysis, semantics in the first instance refers to those associations that are pre-established in a language. In such associations, elements of form and/or grammar are lexicalized to represent particular concepts and appear as such in the lexicon. Semantic meaning here is thus the conceptual complex associated with a morpheme of any of the types presented in (4.2). In addition, semantics refers to combinations of such associations in a multimorphemic word or an expression.

Pragmatics, on the other hand, refers to conceptual content that a hearer—through world knowledge, association, or inference—adds to what is present explicitly—that is, semantically—in a speaker's expression.

To illustrate (T11 s1.6.1), a hearer might process the sentence *The goblet of wine slowly went around the banquet table* to form first a semantic conception of a goblet moving along a closed circuit path near a table's perimeter; then an "immediate pragmatic" conception of the goblet successively passed from hand to hand by diners adjacently seated at the table's perimeter; and then a "further pragmatic" conception of the event as the custom of a social order that the diners are members of, each in turn sipping the wine as part of a ritual.

Cognitive-semantic research largely focuses on the meaning division of language and brings in form and grammar mainly for their relation to meaning—a balance reflected in this taxonomy.

5   B. Participant Structure

A communication has certain participants in its execution—a sender that produces it and a receiver that interprets it. Such production (7.3) and interpretation (7.4) engage different cognitive processes in the structuring of conceptual content. A cognitive-semantic study can involve the one, the other, or both participants—or neither if the subject of analysis is judged to be neutral to the distinction. A study can also focus on any of the alternatives distinguished next.

5.1   B1. Participant Types

A communication can occur in different modalities (12), and the terms for its participants can vary accordingly. Thus in English, the sender can be a speaker, signer, gesturer, or writer, while the corresponding receiver is a hearer, sign viewer, gesture viewer, or reader. For ease, though, the discussion here largely refers only to speakers and hearers.

Receivers can be divided along a further parameter. An addressee is one to whom the speaker has overtly directed her communication, while a bystander has perceived the communication otherwise. And a bystander can be further subdivided into an incidental type and an "indirect addressee," where the speaker tailors her communication to function as a message to him.

5.2   *B2. Participant Numbers*

A communication may prototypically have one sender and one receiver but can readily diverge from this pattern. Thus, a producer can lack an addressee, as with internal speech. Two individuals can function as a single speaker as when completing each other's sentences while addressing a third person. And a sender can have multiple receivers, as in public speaking or published writing.

5.3   *B3. Participant Directionality*

A communication can proceed in just one direction, as in the last two cases. Or it can proceed in both directions with the participants alternating their roles, as in written correspondence or in verbal turn taking (7.6.2).

6   C. Arenas of Assembly

A cognitive-semantic study can address a language's basic meaning-associated units individually or as they are assembled in either of two arenas: the inventory or the expression. An inventory consists of pre-established elements in the language in a structured atemporal collection, while an expression consists of elements selected from the inventory by a speaker and placed in a structured temporal sequence.

6.1   *C1. Inventory*

At any given time in a language's history, its morphemes—that is, its minimal concept-associated constructs (4.2)—numbering in the thousands, constitute a fixed inventory. As a whole, this inventory is the language's lexicon or construction.

A research study might address this whole. Or it might address any of the innumerable subinventories within the whole, themselves formally and/or semantically characterized. A formally based subinventory could vary quantitatively with greater or lesser size, like that of open-class morphemes and that of mass nouns, respectively. Or it could vary qualitatively like the set of affixes that make up an inflectional paradigm. A semantically based subinventory in turn might consist of those morphemes whose meanings include a semantic component of path or negation, or of those whose meanings are judged to be universal. And a subinventory defined both formally and semantically might consist of Manner verbs or topicalizing constructions.

6.2   *C2. Expression*

In the arena of expression, a speaker selects elements from her language's lexicon and joins them temporally in a nonce formation. This process can occur
over the scope of a single multimorphemic word, as with the six morpholog-
ically assembled morphemes in the word *unredirtiably*, or over the scope of
a syntactically assembled sentence, as in *This high-tech polish has made my
counter unredirtiably clean*.

6.3   *C3. Part Inventory, Part Expression*

A language generally has numerous temporal assemblies of morphemes that
are not idioms—their overall meanings arise compositionally from their components—but that occur so frequently that they, as it were, have honorary
status as members of the lexicon. Such "collocations" straddle both the arenas
of expression and inventory. They can occur over the scope of a single multimorphemic word like *unforgettable*; over that of a phrase like *every last vestige
of*; over that of a clause like *I never cease to be amazed (that S/at NP)*; or over that
of a complex sentence, like the formulation *just because S1, (it) doesn't mean S2*,
as in *Just because their lights are on, (it) doesn't mean they're home*.

The effect at work in such lexicalizing is called "entrenchment" by Langacker
(1987) and "unitization," "routinization," or "automatization" in the psychological literature.

7   D. Content Structuring Mechanisms

Language has certain major mechanisms, that is, extensive organized systems,
that function to structure conceptual content. Six such mechanisms are proposed next.

7.1   *D1. Closed-Class Semantics*

A principal mechanism by which language structures conceptual content is
closed-class semantics. The closed-class morphemes that occur across languages, as they were characterized in (4.2), largely represent conceptual com-
plexes that function to structure conceptual content.[2] These conceptual com-
plexes can in turn be analyzed into basic semantic components.

---

2   My work has systematically used the term "conceptual content" at two different levels. At
    the lower level, it refers to the semantic contribution only of open-class morphemes within
    an expression or the lexicon and contrasts with that of closed-class forms, characterized as

Gathered crosslinguistically, these basic semantic components constitute a certain set. In turn, they can be grouped into a smaller set of conceptual categories, and those into a still smaller set of large-scale "schematic systems." At each level, the units are under strong semantic constraints so that the sets are mostly closed, each constituting a universally available "repertory" (10.3). This entire three-level mechanism is one of language's most fundamental conceptual structuring systems.

From this hierarchy, every language draws a representative sample of semantic components that it assembles into the meanings of its own particular closed set of closed-class morphemes. These together provide the language with a local conceptual structuring system of its own.

The following discussion is organized in terms of the large-scale schematic systems that have been reliably determined. The first four were proposed in T1, while the remaining six are newly proposed here.

7.1.1   D1a. Configurational Structure

In the schematic system of configurational structure, closed-class morphemes represent or form delineations—often geometric-like structures or schemas—in space, time, quality, or other ontological domains.

7.1.1.1   *D1a1. In Space*

In space, configurational structure is seen in the scene partitioning of a closed-class preposition like *above*, as in *The lamp is above the radio*, which requires a division of the referent scene into three components and their relations. The components are a Figure object (the lamp), a Ground object (the radio), and the "secondary reference entity," here the vertical axis of the earth-based grid—where the Figure must be on the same vertical axis as the Ground and in a positive direction from it.

Due to the semantic constraints on the closed-class mechanism, closed-class forms can represent space only with respect to certain conceptual categories, and those categories can include only a certain few basic semantic components (T4). To illustrate, the conceptual category of "number" includes only the four semantic components of one, two, several, and many (never: even, odd, dozen), and there are English prepositions requiring a particular one of those components for the Ground, as seen respectively in *The basketball lay near the boulder/between the boulders/among the boulders/ amidst the cornstalks*. The category of "motility" has two components, stationary and moving

---

providing "conceptual structure." At the higher level, it refers quite generally to all linguistic meaning. This Foreword mainly invokes the latter sense.

(never: fixedly vs. temporarily stationary), as represented by the prepositions in *I stayed at / went into the library*. The category of bounding has two components, unbounded and bounded (never: gradient transitional zone), as in *I walked along the shore / the-length-of the pier*. And the conceptual category of "contour" has only four semantic components, straight, arced, circular, and meandering (never: spiral, zigzag, square), as in *I walked across the plain / over the hill / around the flagpole/ about the town*.

7.1.1.2   *Dia2. In Time*
In time, configurational structure is seen in the episode-partitioning of a closed-class conjunction like *after*, as in *I went home after I shopped*. This form requires that an episode be divided into a Figure event (going home), a Ground event (shopping), and the time line, where the figure must lie on the time line in a positive direction from the Ground without overlap (T1 c6).

It is also seen in the closed-class morpheme marking tense, which represents the timeline relation of an event not to another event, as in the preceding example, but to the moment at which the morpheme is uttered (T11 c11).

7.1.1.3   *Dia3. In Quality*
In the qualitative domain, configurational structure is seen in the "axial" properties of closed-class forms like *somewhat* and *almost* in construction with adjectives like *sick* and *well* as against the inadmissible **He is somewhat well / almost sick*. A single qualitative configurational structure underlies the meanings of all four forms. This structure is: a point and an unbounded line extending from it. *Sick* refers structurally to the line and *well* to the point. Then *somewhat* indicates a fictive path from the point to a location along the line a short distance away, while *almost* indicates a fictive path from further along the line back to the closer location (T1 c1 s5.7).

7.1.1.4   *Dia4. Across Domains*
A number of conceptual categories within configurational structure apply to more than one domain, thus showing a commonality of conceptual structuring. For example, the category of "plexity" with its two main members "uniplex" and "multiplex" is in play where certain closed-class forms represent either the pluralization of a noun's reference to a uniplex object in space while others represent the iteration of a verb's reference to a uniplex action in time. And the category of bounding with its two main members "bounded" and "unbounded" is at work where certain closed-class forms respectively represent the count or mass status of a noun's reference while others represent the telicity or atelicity in the aspect of a verb's reference.

7.1.2 D1b. Perspective

In the schematic system of perspective, closed-class morphemes determine the location, distance, or motility of a perspective point from which a referent scene is to be conceptualized (T1 c1).

For example, the location of the perspective point within the scene represented by *The lunchroom door opened and two men walked in* must be inside the lunchroom but is outside it or neutral in *Two men opened the lunchroom door and walked in.* In accord with certain English rules, the difference arises from the closed-class factor of whether the initial verb's subject is its Patient (the door) or its Agent (the men).

With regard to distance and motility, the perspective point is distal and stationary in the scene represented by *There were some houses in the valley*, whereas it is proximal and moving for the same scene when represented by *There was a house every now and then through the valley.* This distinction is effected by the following closed-class differences: plural vs. singular subject number, a construction representing spatial vs. temporal distribution, and a static vs. dynamic preposition.

7.1.3 D1c. Attention

In the schematic system of attention, closed-class elements direct greater and lesser degrees of attention to different aspects of a referent situation (T14 s1.2.1).

For example, in referring to a multiplexity of entities, English has numerous pairs of closed-class constructions that direct greater attention either to the full complement of the entities en masse or to a single exemplar representative of the set (T1 c1). Where the entities are doctors, these constructions include: doctors/a doctor (generic); all doctors/every doctor; all the doctors/each doctor; many doctors/many a doctor; some doctors here and there/a doctor here and there; doctors one after another/one doctor after another; hardly any doctors/hardly a (single) doctor; no doctors/no (nary a) doctor.

For another example (T14 s7.1.3), the closed-class grammatical relation of subjecthood generally directs greater attention to the referent with that status than to other such referents. Thus, in *The landlord rented the apartment to the tenant*, the owner as subject is more salient than the user as oblique object, and as such may evoke thoughts of collateral actions by him such as preparing the apartment for new occupancy, advertising it, and interviewing interested parties. But in *The tenant rented the apartment from the landlord*, the user as subject is now more salient, and as such may evoke thoughts of collateral actions like checking publicized listings and visiting other vacancies.

7.1.4   D1d. Force Dynamics

In the schematic system of force dynamics, closed-class morphemes represent the patterns in which one entity exerts force on another. These patterns include the exertion of force, resistance to such exertion, the overcoming of such resistance, the prevention of a force effect, and the removal of such prevention, and hence can represent causing, letting, helping, hindering, blocking, and unblocking (T1 c7).

Two of the basic steady-state patterns, the extended causing or hindering of motion, are seen in *The ball rolled on because of the wind/despite the stiff grass*, where the closed-class forms representing force dynamics are *on, because of*, and *despite*.[3] The ball in the first case has a tendency toward rest which the stronger wind overcomes, but in the second case has a tendency toward motion that overcomes weaker opposition from the grass.

The closed class of modals largely represents force-dynamic patterns as well. Thus, *should*, as in *She should lock her door*, pits the speaker's values as to what is good and beliefs as to what is beneficial against the subject's contrary behavior. And *dare*, as in *He dare not leave the house*, opposes the subject's courage against external threat.

7.1.5   D1e. Cognitive State

In the schematic system of cognitive state, closed-class forms represent certain psychological conditions in a sentient individual. Such states largely fall into four categories: knowledge, expectation, intention, and affect.

7.1.5.1   D1e1. Knowledge

A major grammatically represented category of cognitive state is an individual's state of knowledge. One example of it is a speaker's choice between a definite and an indefinite determiner to represent her assessment of the hearer's state of knowledge. Thus, in saying *I fed the cat*, the speaker judges that the hearer knows (can readily identify) the particular cat. But in saying *I fed a cat*, she judges that the hearer does not know the particular cat.

Or again, in using a question construction, as in *Who was at the party?*, a speaker indicates a lack of knowledge on her part that she wants the hearer to fill in. And some epistemic modals indicate the speaker's lack of definite knowledge about the proposition, as in *The tower may have collapsed in the earthquake*.

---

3   Force dynamics in the predicate can be represented not only by the satellite *on* but also by the verb *keep* (*keep rolling*), which is presently open-class but seems amenable to grammaticalization.

Further, some disjunctions represent a certain pattern of both knowing and not knowing. An example is *Either Wayne or Rose spoke next*, where the speaker knows that one of those two spoke but does not know which one. A comparable pattern is represented by some conditional constructions, as in *If Lynne presided, then the meeting ended on time*. Here, the speaker does not know who in fact presided, but does know that, of the alternative possibilities, the one in which Lynne presides finishes punctually.

7.1.5.2   *D1e2. Expectation*

Another grammatically represented category of cognitive state is expectation. This is an individual's relatively strong belief that a certain outcome was or is to occur. Constructions expressing expectation can present the outcome as either known or unknown.

A construction with a known outcome can further evoke a sense of confirmation or surprise if the outcome respectively does or does not conform with the expectation. To illustrate, the closed-class conjunctions *and* and *but* mark their clause as being confirmingly in or surprisingly out of accord with prior expectation. A possible example is *He knocked on her door and/but her husband answered*. This distinction is an English realization of the general expectational category of "mirativity."

An expectation regarding a known outcome can also concern an aspect of it rather than its overall occurrence. Thus, the closed-class particle *only* as in *Sue read only one poem*, concerns quantity within an outcome and can be glossed as 'surprisingly less than expected'. Comparably, the particle *even*, as in *Even Trent sang*, ranks a set of entities along an expectational hierarchy and indicates the participation of the least expected one in addition to that of the others.

For the case where the outcome is unknown, the expectation can concern the occurrence of a future event. This holds for the closed-class particle *yet*, as in *The governor is not implicated in the scandal yet*. It also holds for the conjunction *when*—unlike the expectationally neutral *if*—as in *We'll watch the movie when/if they come*. In some constructions, an unknown outcome can take place at any time, including the present. Thus, in contrast with a simple yes/no question like *Is she in college now?*, a tag question indicates the speaker's expectation that the polarity of the main clause is correct, as seen in *She's in college now, isn't she?* as against *She isn't in college now, is she?*

7.1.5.3   *D1e3. Intention*

Closed-class morphemes can further represent the cognitive state of intention —an Agent's aim that certain actions she performs lead to a desired outcome. For example, the particle *to* with an infinitive can introduce the intended result, as in *She broke open the bone to get at the marrow*. And the grammatical relation of indirect object status as well as the preposition *for*—as in *I bought Jane a cake/a cake for Jane*—indicate the subject's intention to give, while the preposition, as in *I bought a cake for the party*, indicates the intention to provide.

Further, a deictic demonstrative, like the *there* in *You can hang your coat over there*—accompanied by a targeting gesture (T11 c5)—expresses the speaker's intention that the hearer join his attention with her own on a particular target (here, a certain location). And unlike English, as in *I broke my arm*, many languages e.g., Spanish, have different constructions or inflections indicating whether the outcome was intentional or accidental.

7.1.5.4   *D1e4. Affect*
Closed-class morphemes can also represent certain types of affect, another category within cognitive state. For example, a speaker's desire or wish is expressed by the desiderative or optative inflections of some languages as well as by the English constructions in *May she succeed!* and *Would that she succeeds!* The particle *so*, as in *That sequoia is so wide!*, expresses the speaker's amazement at the extremeness of the indicated quality. And the subordinating conjunction *lest*, as in *They cleared the path lest she trip*, represents the main-clause subject's concern or worry over the potential occurrence of an undesired event.

While closed-class representation of affect is limited in English, it is broader and more extensively used in other languages. Thus, to the three types of affect just cited, Yiddish adds endearedness with its noun suffix *-ele*, impatience with its verbal clitic *-zhe*, and pity and willfulness with its verb phrase particles *nebekh* and *dafke*.

7.1.6   Dif. Reality Status
In the schematic system of reality status, closed-class morphemes represent or determine the state or degree of a referent's realization. This schematic system interacts closely with the preceding one, specifically with state of knowledge. Thus, certain types of reality status are known to be realized or unrealized, while others are unknown.

7.1.6.1   *D1fi. Known as Realized*
The main type of known realization—the factual or actual—is largely represented across languages by their indicative declarative constructions with positive polarity in either the past or present, as in English *He danced/is dancing*.

Further, realization can largely be conceptualized as a gradient, achieved only to some degree along a one-dimensional scale, and some closed-class forms can specify that degree and indicate that it is known. An example is *almost* as in *This peach is almost ripe.*

And in a performative construction, the speaker causes the specified proposition to become realized by the act of uttering the construction, and thus knows that it is in fact realized. This construction is grammatically indicated in English by the simple present and by the closed-class form *hereby*, as in *I hereby declare this meeting adjourned.*

7.1.6.2   *Dif2. Known as Unrealized*

As for known nonrealization, one main type is simply indicated by a negative, as in *I didn't dance.* Another type appears in a counterfactual construction, as in *I should have danced,* or *I would have danced if I'd had the time*—which express the known fact that I did not dance.

A third type is represented by a future tense construction, as in *I'll bake the apple,* where it is known that the referent event is not (yet) realized. Languages can have different future constructions based on where the potential event is located on a scale from prediction to a commitment to bring it about.

And the referents of all tropes are known not to be realized as represented literally. However, this fact fits the present schematic system only where closed-class elements signal the presence of the trope. This can be the case with sarcasm, as in *Here comes Mr. Sure-footed,* where the singsong intonation, and the "Mr." before an adjective are the indicators that the stated attribute must be conceptually reversed (8.4.2).

7.1.6.3   *Dif3. Unknown State of Realization*

As for unknown reality status, one main type is a yes/no question construction, as in *Did she swallow the pill,* where the speaker does not know a referent event's state of realization and wants the addressee to provide information specifically on that issue.

Further, without knowing the state of a referent's realization, a speaker can still estimate its probability, indicating this value from lesser to greater with closed-class elements like *just maybe, perhaps* or the epistemic modal *may,* and *likely,* as in *It may have/It likely rained there last night.* In fact, seemingly all epistemic modals represent the speaker's lack of knowledge about the referent's actual realization while providing an estimate of its probability. Thus, the *should* in *Bess should be home by now* indicates that the speaker does not know specifically whether or not Bess is home but estimates it as probable on the basis of other knowledge.

Comparably, evidentials other than the factive kind seem to indicate that the speaker does not know the referent's state of realization but infers that it is probable on the basis of certain types of evidence. For example, the Atsugewi verb suffix -*it*, an "aftereffect evidential," indicates that the action of its verb can be surmised as having taken place from currently perceivable consequences of it. Thus, on seeing dirty dishes on a table, a speaker might add it to the verb for 'eat' to indicate the likelihood that people had eaten there based on the residue.

7.1.7   Dıg. Communicative Purpose

In the schematic system of communicative purpose, closed-class morphemes indicate the effect that a speaker intends to have on the hearer by communicating with him. Among these effects, the speaker can inform, order, request, question, suggest, warn, and correct—all expanded on next.

7.1.7.1   *Dıgı. Informing*

The speaker's seemingly most frequent communicative purpose is to inform the hearer of the proposition being represented—that is, to present certain information to the hearer with the aim that he store it at least in working memory, available for reference in the immediate discourse. This purpose is represented crosslinguistically by declarative constructions, as in English *They signed the petition.*

7.1.7.2   *Dıg2. Ordering*

In ordering, the communicative purpose of the speaker is, through her socially based influence, to induce the hearer, through his own volitional activities, to perform the specified action. Ordering is largely represented by imperative constructions, like the subjectless English construction in *Sign the petition!*

7.1.7.3   *Dıg3. Requesting*

In requesting, the speaker's communicative purpose is to let the hearer know of some action that she would like the hearer to perform voluntarily. English can represent requesting with what might be called the "modal-request construction," which consists of the interrogative construction with certain modal forms and optionally the particle *please* (8.3). An example is *Could you (please) sign the petition?*

7.1.7.4   *Dıg4. Questioning*

In questioning—represented by closed-class interrogative words and constructions, as in English *Did they dance?* and *Who danced?*, the speaker lacks certain information and her purpose in communicating is to fill that lack by requesting the hearer to provide it verbally. Questioning is thus a subtype of requesting, where the hearer's response is to be verbal. Its effect can accordingly be equaled by a request construction that specifies such a verbal response, as in *Could you please tell me if they danced / who danced?*

7.1.7.5   Dıg5. Suggesting

In suggesting, as when represented by specialized constructions like those in *Why not go to Hawaii* and *How about going to Hawaii?*, the speaker's purpose is to present or advocate for an action that the hearer can consider undertaking as his choice among alternatives.

7.1.7.6   Dıg6. Warning

In warning, a speaker's communicative purpose is to inform the hearer of a potential risk to him that he might therefore want to avoid. Atsugewi has an entire "admonitive" verb conjugation expressing warning, a conceptual area that can extend to mock threat and teasing. An example is *tamlawilcahki*, a verb inflected for 'I' as subject and 'you' as object, that, serving as a mock threat, can be glossed as *I'm going to tickle you*. As seen in (4.2), English has closed-class representation of just such mock threat—a certain singsong intonation contour—which could, for example, be used with the gloss just cited.

7.1.7.7   Dıg7. Correcting

In correcting, the speaker, who believes she has noticed a mistaken reference in the hearer's preceding utterance, provides the correct reference and her purpose is that the hearer substitute the latter for the former in his cognitive representation (T11 s13.1.2). One closed-class element that English uses for this purpose is heightened stress on a constituent. It here appears on the replacement constituent, as where the hearer first says *I heard you were in London last year* and the speaker responds *No, I was in !-Paris.*

As another example, beside the ordinary closed-class morpheme in French for 'yes', *oui*, is the alternative morpheme *si*, which is lexicalized to correct a mistaken negative polarity in the hearer's prior utterance and replace it with a positive one.[4]

7.1.8   Dıh. Ontology

In the schematic system of ontology, closed classes indicate which category a referent belongs to within an ontology, that is, a classification of phenomena

---

4 We have analyzed cognitive state, reality status, and communicative purpose as distinct schematic systems on semantic grounds. But the traditional linguistic term "mood" has generally covered all three, and indeed languages often use the same closed-class elements to represent more than one of, or combinations of, those systems.

into basic categories—another respect in which language structures conceptual content. Different linguistic closed classes commonly divide their respective conceptual areas differently, though the resulting ontologies can share certain features, such as a distinction between the domains of space and time.

The closed class of triggers (deictics and anaphors, including all pro-forms) can be analyzed crosslinguistically as distinguishing twelve ontological categories for their targets (T11 s2.2.1). Five such categories are seen in the English monomorphemic triggers *that* 'that entity', *there* 'at that location', *then* 'at that time', *thus* 'in this/that manner', and *such* 'of this/that kind'.

Another ontology is seen in the closed class of constituent categories that can comprise the nodes of a phrase structure. They are prototypically associated with certain categories of conceptual phenomena, as suggested next with some approximation.

Thus, a count noun is prototypically associated with the concept of a thing (or a phenomenon reified as a thing). A mass noun is associated with the concept of "stuff" (or other phenomenon reified as stuff). A verb is associated with an action or a state. A clause is associated with an event. A sentence is associated with a proposition. An adjective is associated with an attribute of a thing or of stuff. An adverb or adverbial marker is associated with an attribute of an action. A preposition is associated with a relationship of one thing to another. A subordinating conjunction is associated with a relationship of one event to another. A coordinating conjunction is associated with a relationship between equipollent events. And a trigger is associated with properties of a target.

In addition, a closed class of syntactic categories other than constituent types can augment the preceding ontology. Here, a word is associated with a concept and a morpheme with a basic concept. And closed-class morphemes are associated with conceptual structure while open-class morphemes are associated with conceptual content.

Further, there are closed-class operational (8.2) morphemes that shift a constituent's category and associated concept. Thus, the suffix *-ery* as in *bravery* changes an adjective expressing an attribute to a mass noun expressing stuff, while *-ous* as in *courageous* effects the reverse change.

7.1.9   D1i. Role Semantics

In the schematic system of role semantics, a closed-class morpheme represents the conceptual relation that one syntactic constituent has to another, each of the two belonging to a particular constituent category. The two constituents can occur within a phrase, a clause, a complex sentence, or a compound sentence, discussed next in order.

7.1.9.1   *Dii. In a Phrase*

To address one portion of its semantic range, the English possessive -*s*, as in *chef's hat*, can be cliticized to a noun representing an animate entity, the combination then in construction with a noun representing an inanimate entity. It then indicates that the second entity has the role of a possessum and the first entity the role of a possessor in a relationship of possession in which the second entity belongs to the first.

7.1.9.2   *Dii2. In a Clause*

Within a clause containing a verb and one or more major nominals, closed-class morphemes like constituent order, adpositions, and affixes can indicate that the nominals have such grammatical relations as subject, direct object, indirect object, and oblique object to the clause. The full set of such grammatical relations in a language is itself a closed class. For each of its polysemous senses, a verb has a certain "syntactic argument structure" that determines which nominals must or may appear with particular grammatical relations. In turn, the referent of each such nominal has a certain semantic role in relation to the event represented by the clause. Together, these referents in their particular semantic roles constitute the verb's "semantic argument structure."

Such roles can be conceived as coarser-grained and potentially universal, like the roles of Agent or Patient, Figure or Ground. Thus, the nominals in *The cyclist threw her helmet onto the bed* refer to objects with the respective semantic roles of Agent, Patient/Figure, and Ground in the event represented by the clause. The role of the Agent here includes acting on the Patient, while that of the (affected) Patient includes being acted on by the Agent. The Patient here also exhibits the role of Figure, which includes moving along a path, being located at a site, or having some orientation relative to the Ground, while the role of the Ground includes serving as a reference object with respect to which that path, site, or orientation is characterized.

Alternatively, the semantic roles can be finer-grained and specific to a small set of verbs. Thus, the nominals in *I bought a car from the dealer for $30,000* refer respectively to a person, an object, another person, and money with the relations of a buyer, goods, seller, and payment relative to the commercial frame represented by the verb (Fillmore, 1976).

7.1.9.3   *Dii3. In a Complex Sentence*

Within a complex sentence, subordinating conjunctions are closed-class forms that represent the semantic role of the main clause's event in relation to the subordinate clause's event (T1 c6). Some of these relations can be analyzed under other schematic systems above. Thus, the main-clause event's anteri-

ority, posteriority, and concurrence seen in *I shopped before the sun set/after
I jogged/while it snowed* can be treated as temporal schemas under configurational structure (7.1.1). And the causality and concession in *The bench is wet
because it rained/although I wiped it* can be treated under force dynamics (7.1.4).

But other relations would be treated here alone. These include conditional-
ity, as in *She'll move back here if she loses her job*; counterfactual exceptivity, as
in *I'd join you, only I'm feeling tired*; and negative additionality, as in *I can dance
no more than I can sing*.

Further relations are represented by constructions that are not technically
complex sentences but like them in representing two events separately and
hierarchically. These include additionality, as in *I was promoted besides (in addition to) getting a raise*; substitution (of a less for a more expected event), as in
The wind blew instead of the rain falling; and degree covariation, as in *The hotter
it is, the worse I feel*.

7.1.9.4   *D114. In a Compound Sentence*

Within a compound sentence, many of the same role relations just seen for
complex sentences—though now it is the role of the second clause to the
first—are represented by closed-class "adverbial pro-clauses" (T1 c6). They are
shown capitalized in the following counterparts to the earlier sentences: *The
sun set, but FIRST I shopped; I jogged and THEN I shopped; It was snowing, and
I shopped THE WHILE; It rained, and SO the bench is wet; I wiped the bench but
it was STILL wet; I'm feeling tired or ELSE I'd join you; I can't sing, and I can't
dance EITHER; I got a raise and I ALSO got promoted; The rain didn't fall but
the wind blew INSTEAD.*

7.1.10   Dıj. Quantity

Within the schematic system of quantity, closed-class morphemes represent
the number, amount, or degree of a referent. This system, potentially quite
extensive in a language, again structures conceptual content. Closed-class elements can represent either a single quantity or a comparison between quantities, as discussed next in order.

7.1.10.1   *Dıjı. Single Quantity*

A language can have distinct, though sometimes partially overlapping, sets of
closed-class forms that represent the number, amount, or degree of a phenomenon that is respectively individuated, continuous in substance, or continuous in quality.

Thus, for the individuated referents of a plural count noun in English, the
number of them from zero to the entirety can be represented by closed-class

forms like those in *No/few/some/many/most/all members were present*. Closed-class indication of two units is seen in English *both, either, neither,* and *between* as well as in some languages' noun affixation for dual, while the English plural noun suffix *-s* indicates two or more units.

For the continuous substance represented by a mass noun, the amount of it can be represented by closed-class forms like those in *No/little/some/much/ most/all water is polluted*. And for the continuously qualitative referent of an adjective, the degree of it can be represented by closed-class forms like those in *He is un-/somewhat/rather/quite/very friendly*.

7.1.10.2 *D1j2. Comparison of Quantities*

Other closed-class forms represent the comparison of one quantity with one or more others. This is seen for the individuated referents of a plural count noun in *As for books, he has more than you/fewer than you/as many as you/the most/least of anyone*. It is seen for the continuous referent of a mass noun in *As for money, he has more than you/less than you/as much as you/the most/least of anyone*. And it is seen for the continuous qualitative referent of an adjective in *He is friendlier than you/less friendly than you/as friendly as you/the friendliest/least friendly of all*.

Some closed-class forms represent a comparison with a set comparand. This comparand is semantically constrained and may refer to little more than necessity, desire, and expectation. Thus, *enough*, as in *I have enough food*, can be glossed as 'at least as much as needed'. *Too*, as in *I have too much food*, can be glossed as 'more than desired'. And, as seen (7.1.5), *only* as in *Only a hundred people came* can be glossed as 'less than expected'.

And closed-class prefixes can be added to verb roots to represent an increase or decrease in amount, as in *up/downsize*, or to indicate too much or not enough in degree, as in *over/underestimate*.

7.2 *D2. Content Patterning*

Another major mechanism by which language structures conceptual content might be called "content patterning." This consists of the patterns in which a language partitions and arranges what might otherwise be considered a conceptual continuum. Such patterns occur in the morpheme and the two arenas of its assembly, the lexicon (inventory) and the expression, discussed next in order.

7.2.1 D2a. In the Morpheme

The mechanism of content arrangement is first in effect in that every language bounds off portions of the conceptual continuum to form the individual meanings associated with its morphemes. This is the process of "lexicalizing" or "packaging." The mechanism is further in effect in that the content within those portions is structured. the patterns of such structuring constitute "frame semantics" (Fillmore, 1976).

With respect to such frame semantics, the content of a morpheme can in the first instance be divided into a core meaning and an associated meaning. In turn, its associated meaning can be subdivided into at least five sectors (T14). This patterning holds for both open-class morphemes and closed-class morphemes, but only the former are illustrated here.

The "holistic sector" within a morpheme's associated meaning represents the conceptual whole that the morpheme's core meaning is necessarily a part of. Thus, the core meaning of the verb *buy* most directly represents a buyer's acquisition of certain goods. But the verb's holistic sector represents the whole commercial transaction—including the transfer of goods from the seller to the buyer and of money from the buyer to the seller—of which that acquisition is only a part.

The "infrastructure sector" is a conceptual underpinning that the core meaning presupposes but is not wholly determined by. Thus, the core meaning of the noun *heaven* most directly represents a luminous space in the sky near God. But it rests on an infrastructure of particular beliefs about divinity, soul, afterlife, goodness, and reward vs. punishment.

The "collateral sector" adds concepts commonly associated with the core meaning but incidental to it. Thus, the core meaning of the noun *bucket* represents a roughly cylindrical tapered foot-high and wide object with an open top spanned by a handle. And its collateral sector represents the commonly associated function of using the object to convey material placed in it. But that association is only ancillary, suspended when referring, say, to a gold bucket sitting on a pedestal as an art exhibit.

The "disposition sector" comprises the aspects of a morpheme's meaning that arise from its grammatical properties. Thus, the core meaning of the Spanish noun *puente* is the concept of an inanimate bridge. But its grammatical masculine gender can induce a penumbra of concepts of maleness in its disposition sector.

And the "attitude sector" mainly consists of speaker attitudes pertaining to the morpheme or its use. Thus, the core meaning of the adjective *paltry* is the concept 'small in amount'. But its attitude sector represents a disparaging attitude by the speaker toward that smallness.

For its part, a morpheme's core meaning can—through procedures often called componential analysis or unpacking—be taken to include or consist of certain semantic components. These components can be either idiosyncratic or structured and, when structured, either outside or part of a closed class.

Idiosyncratic semantic components are seen in the core meaning of the verb *pry*, as in *I pried the board off the wall* (T6). The main components are 1) the force comes from an object inserted and pivoted between the Figure and Ground; 2) The Figure resists; 3) The Figure moves away gradually; 4) the Figure is relatively rigid.

Or a component within a core meaning can belong to a structural set unrelated to a closed-class category but recur across a family of open-class morphemes. Thus, English nouns referring to animate entities that include a semantic component for the species often differ by whether they also include a semantic component for the young or for a castrated male (as well as for an adult male or female), as seen in *cow/calf/ox; horse/foal/gelding; sheep/lamb/ wether; pig/piglet/barrow; chicken/chick/capon; person/child/eunuch.*

A component anywhere in the meaning of an open-class morpheme may also belong to a closed-class semantic category, as does the singular or plural component respectively in the nouns *cow* and *cattle*, or the negative component in the verb *fail*.

7.2.2 D2b. In the Lexicon
The mechanism of content arrangement when at work in the lexicon is seen in the size of different morpheme classes, in the balance between closed-and open-class forms, and in the semantic relations among the extant morphemes, discussed next in order.

7.2.2.1 *D2b1. Morpheme Class Size*
Across the lexicons of different languages, particular classes of morphemes, as defined by certain criteria, can vary greatly in size from prodigious to minimal. The pattern of certain large and small classes in a language often correlates with the presence of a particular productive closed-class construction—also in the lexicon—that assembles the larger classes in an expression. This design can be seen, for example, by comparing a satellite-framed with a verb-framed language, here, respectively English and Spanish (T2 c3).

The English lexicon includes a prodigious number of colloquial Manner verbs, few colloquial Path verbs, and very many Path satellites and prepositions. It also includes a colloquial construction in which all the sizable ones of these categories of elements readily fit together. The main portion of this construction—Manner verb-Path satellite-Path preposition—can be seen in *I ran out of the house*. The lexicon, however, lacks a colloquial construction that would string together a Path verb, a Manner-verb gerund, and a Path preposition, as in *I exited running from the house*, awkward at best.

By contrast, the Spanish lexicon includes comparatively fewer Manner verbs , a sizable number of colloquial Path verbs, almost no Path satellites, and a small number of Path prepositions. It also includes a colloquial construction—the one uncolloquial in English—that compatibly combines the more sizable ones of these categories, as seen in *Salí corriendo de la casa* which can be glossed much like the awkward English sentence above. Correlatively, it lacks the full colloquial English construction.[5]

7.2.2.2   *D2b2. Closed- and Open-Class Balance*
The presence in a lexicon of a closed class expressing a certain concept tends to correlate with the absence of that concept in the open class associated with it, and vice versa. This is the pattern of "semantic unilocality" (T13). Thus, the presence in English of an extensive system of satellites and prepositions expressing Path seems to correlate with the fact that the verbs associated with it express little Path. Complementarily, French has only a small closed-class system expressing Path while its verbs express it extensively, whether by itself or together with manner. Of the latter Path+Manner type, French for example has *grimper* 'climb up', *débouler* 'roll down a slope', *dériver* 'drift off from an expected course', and *arpenter* 'pace back and forth along the same straight bounded line'—a type of verb much rarer in English.

Semantic unilocality can also be in effect where the closed class at issue consists of just one or a few members. For example, the productive availability in English of the prefixes *un-/dis-/de-*expressing "reverse versality" (T13 s3.5)— as in *untie/disassemble/defund*—may correlate with a relative dearth of verb roots representing such reversal. But Mandarin, which lacks such a closed-class form, seemingly has more simplex verb roots expressing reversal, like *jiě* 'unknot' (e.g., a tied sack/braid), *chāi* 'disassemble' (e.g., a bookshelf) or 'unfasten' (e.g., a plaque on a wall), and *qù* 'remove' (e.g., a stain). And other actions that in English are conceptualized as reversals, like *unwind* (wire from a spool) and *unroll* (cloth from a bolt), are reconceptualized in Mandarin as "proverse" actions by constructions glossable respectively as "pull straight" and "pull flat" (Jian-Sheng Guo, p.c.).

7.2.2.3   *D2b3. Cross-Morpheme Relations*
The meanings represented by the morphemes present in a language's lexicon can in turn bear certain semantic relations to each other. Certain of these relations fall under the category of "hierarchy." Four specific hierarchies— indicated by the subordinate level first and the superordinate second (T14 s2)—

---

5   A simpler form of the English construction, however, is available for non-boundary-crossing paths.

are hyponym-hypernym (e.g., dog-mammal), part-whole (e.g., petal-flower), member-category (e.g., Chicago-city), and analytic-synthetic (e.g., two-pair).

Still further relations are synonymy—various forms with a roughly single meaning—and polysemy—a single form with various meanings. In the latter case, content patterning is again evident in the arrangement formed by the various meanings. By radial category theory (Brugmann and Lakoff, 1988), this arrangement is one in which one of the meanings is basic and the remaining meanings differ from it and from each other by conceptual increments that largely have a structuring function across languages.

7.2.3 D2c. In Expression

Where a larger conceptual whole is represented by a portion of discourse, the mechanism of content patterning is in play where the whole can be parceled out in different arrangements within that portion (T2 c4 s2). We can illustrate first with a crosslinguistic pattern difference over the scope of a sentence. Thus, where the conceptual whole is an agentive Motion situation, English characteristically expresses the Agent in the subject nominal, the coevent+Motion in the verb, the Figure in a direct object nominal, the Path in a satellite+preposition, and the Ground in an oblique nominal, as seen in *You tracked mud into my house.*

But Atsugewi places the Figure+Motion in the verb root, a causal coevent in a prefix, the path+ground in a suffix, and the pronominal Agent in inflections. This pattern occurs in the polysynthetic word /m-'-w-ma- sʈaq́ -ipsnᵘ-ik·-a/, which can function as a sentence referring to the same whole situation as the English example. In this word, an inflectional suffix (m-) expresses the Agent 'you'; a closed-class prefix (ma-) expresses the causal coevent 'by acting on the Figure with the feet'; a verb root (-sʈaq́-) expresses the Figure+Motion concept 'for runny icky material to move or be located'; a closed-class suffix (-ipsnᵘ) expresses the Path+Ground concept 'into a volumetric enclosure'; and a closed-class suffix (-ik·) expresses the deictic concept 'hither'. The English and Atsugewi representations of the same conceptual complex can thus be seen to arrange its content in quite different patterns.

Or, within a single language, elements of a larger conceptual complex can be arranged in different patterns over a discourse. For example, the events of an adventure can be recounted iconically in their original order or in a range of different sequences, each with its own semantic effect on the hearer (T2 c8).

7.3 *D3. Content Selection*

The remaining four major mechanisms for structuring conceptual content in language operate in concert to a great extent but, as feasible, are presented separately to highlight the characteristics of each. The present mechanism, then, "content selection," involves the speaker in the arena of expression. It is how the speaker "frames" her utterance(s). Specifically, given that she has a particular conceptual complex in mind to convey, it is largely her choice between whether to include or exclude the representation of certain content in that complex and, if included, the choice among alternative representations of it. We discuss these two types of choice next in order, and then constraints on choice.

7.3.1   D3a. Inclusion vs. Omission

In her production process, a speaker generally first has a conceptual complex that she wants the hearer to experience, and then selects enough of that complex for explicit representation so that he can infer the remainder. What the hearer infers thus complements the portion of the conceptual complex overtly included by the speaker and fully or approximately captures the omitted portion. The included concepts represented explicitly are generally more salient and belong to the area of semantics, while the omitted concepts to be inferred are less salient and belong to pragmatics (4.3).

Both the speaker and the hearer processes are presented here together due to their close correlation—though, in this taxonomy, the hearer's inference is also listed without further discussion as D4 in (7.4). The role of context in the speaker's selections and the hearer's interpretation of an utterance is discussed separately in (7.5).

Speaker omissions of different scopes can be considered and they are presented next roughly from smaller to larger. Correlatively, the hearer's process of inference generally proceeds from more to less constrained.

7.3.1.1   *D3a1. Ellipsis*

In ellipsis, the speaker omits the smallest amount of explicit content within a sentence under strict syntactic conditions and the hearer is under strong constraint in restoring it. The constraint is greatest where the hearer is to copy concepts already expressed overtly elsewhere in the current or preceding sentence. This covers most of the types of ellipsis addressed in the literature, such as gapping, stripping, sluicing, comparative deletion, and answer fragments. For example, gapping is seen in *Wes likes wine with dinner and his wife (likes) beer (with dinner)*.

In other types of ellipsis, the concept supplied by the hearer is not represented in the surrounding material but is one of a small set of alternatives, determined by the context—hence, still under much constraint but less than above (T11 s3.4). This circumstance is seen in *Rice is easy (for one/me/us/you/*

him/her/them) to digest. It is in *Can I have some (of this/that)?*, as said to someone standing nearby holding a pitcher of lemonade. And it is in *The bus stop
you want is across the street (from here/there).*

7.3.1.2   *D3a2. Other Intrasentential Omission*

A sometimes larger and less constrained type of content omission within a
sentence occurs in a form of coercion (8.4.1) where one element of a construction is altered. Thus, the modal-request construction (8.3) basically requires
the second person as subject. But in a certain circumstance, the third person
can appear instead, as in *Could your kids please turn their music down?* The
circumstance is that the second-person hearer has sway over the actions of
the third-person actors, a concept that the hearer can insert mentally, as if the
speaker had represented it explicitly with an expression like *Could you please
ask/tell your kids to turn their music down?*

In addition, a generally larger portion of conceptual content can be omitted
from explicit representation in a sentence in the process of "windowing" (T1
c4). The full content represented by the sentence is a conceptually bounded
"event frame" such as a bounded path, causal sequence, or turn of a cycle. To
illustrate for a bounded path, a speaker might express the whole of it, as in *The
crate fell out of the plane through the air into the ocean.* Or she could omit one
or two of the path's beginning, middle, or terminal portions. Thus, she could
omit the middle, as in *The crate fell out of the plane into the ocean* or the middle and end as in *The crate fell out of the plane.* Here, the hearer's conceptual
restoration would be respectively more and less constrained.

7.3.1.3   *D3a3. Intersentential Omission*

A speaker often omits a substantial amount of conceptual content between
neighboring sentences, and the hearer, generally under less constraint than
before, can infer it largely through general knowledge. For example, a host
might say to a guest *Would you like some music on? I have to go put my daughter
to sleep.* The hearer here is constrained by the conceptions expressed by the
two sentences, but might infer that the conceptual content connecting them
resembles what would be expressed if the speaker had inserted something like
*I ask because you might like the entertainment that music can provide to com-
pensate for your remaining alone without my company, since I will be gone for a
while due to the unavoidable fact that ....*

7.3.1.4   *D3a4. Extrasentential Omission*

The greatest amount of conceptual content generally unspecified in an utterance consists of what is taken for granted in our physical, psychological, and

societal knowledge of the world—that is, notions at large in the culture whose validity generally does not come under our conscious consideration. It would in fact be all but impossible to specify the entirety of such knowledge. Every utterance is thus conceptually abstractive (T6).

We can illustrate such omission first just for physical knowledge close to the conceptual scope of a sentence. Thus, a speaker saying *I put the glass of water down* would generally not specify the concepts that the glass was upright, not upside down; a few inches across, not three feet wide; gripped by my hand during its descent, not by a mechanical device; and at the end supported on a clear horizontal surface, not balanced on a wire. The hearer will supply all these unspecified concepts in his conceptualization of the utterance's total meaning.

And we can illustrate a broader scope of omission with the classic example of a guest saying to a host: *It's a bit chilly in here.* Within the content omitted by the speaker, the more immediately pertinent aspects of general knowledge include such physical concepts as that, in cold weather, cold air can enter an enclosure through an aperture; such psychological concepts as that a person can feel uncomfortable from contact with cold air; and such socio-cultural concepts as that, typically, a guest does not act directly on the host's property and a host aims for the guest's comfort. The hearer infers all this from the utterance and, from its context, infers that it is not a simple assertion of opinion but an indirect request for him to close the window.

7.3.2   D3b. Alternatives of Inclusion

Where a speaker has selected a certain portion of a conceptual complex for explicit representation in an utterance, she can further select among alternatives for such representation. This is her cognitive capacity for "conceptual alternativity" (T1 c3). The speaker selects among different construals (Langacker, 1993), "perspectives" (Clark, 1997), or conceptualizations (T1 c1) of that portion of content. Such alternatives can occur on a smaller or larger scale.

Within the scope of a single sentence, there are innumerably different categories of alternative choice, several of which are selected here to illustrate the range. In the category of spatial frames, a speaker opting to include reference to the spatial relation between a particular Figure and Ground—say, a bike and church—can select any of the alternatives in *The bike was behind/west of/left of the church* to represent respectively a Ground-based, field-based, and observer-based frame (T1 c3). Or for the category of reality status (7.1.6), a speaker might say either *I regret that I didn't see the film* or *I wish I had seen the film* to foreground either a factual or a counterfactual stance on the same situation (T1 c4 s7.2).

Or again, a speaker choosing to represent a subject's affect can select between representing inner state or outer behavior, as in saying either *He was happy/afraid/cold* or *He was smiling/trembling/shivering*. And a speaker choosing to express the concept 'very small' can lexically represent it together with any of a range of attitudes, such as that of amazement over the degree in *tiny*, scorn in *puny*, endearedness toward a child in *itsy-bitsy*, sarcasm in *teensy-weensy*, and seriousness in *minuscule* (T14 s6.5.2).

The alternatives available within a sentence can also range along innumerable parameters. Thus, a speaker choosing to represent a subject's Manner of motion can select its degree of specificity by saying *She went/walked/limped to the party*. Or where a hearer had heard the name "Chris" and mistakenly asked "Who is he?," a speaker might correct his gender choice with different degrees of elaboration from slight to great, as by saying *She's my boss* or *!-SHE's my boss*, or *It's a "she," not a "he": she's my boss*.

On a larger scale, a speaker can for example choose different styles in which to present the same conceptual content over a discourse. She might present it, say, earnestly, humorously, or melodramatically.

7.3.3   D3c. Constraints on Selection

The mechanism of content selection includes not only affordances, the focus so far, but also constraints. The speaker is constrained first regarding what to include—both obligatory inclusions and omissions. An example of obligatory inclusion is the requirement in English that a count noun indicate whether its referent is singular or plural—a speaker wanting to use the noun cannot choose to omit the conceptual category of number. And an example of obligatory omission is a "blocked argument" (T14). Thus, though the argument structure of the verb *buy* readily permits mention of the seller, as in *I bought a book for $50 from a clerk today*, the verb *spend* blocks explicit reference to the seller, though one is implicitly present, as seen in *I spent $50 for a book *from/by/with/to/at a clerk today*. A speaker wanting to include reference to the seller must use means other than a simple preposition.

A speaker is also constrained regarding the alternatives to select among. For example, she is limited to the constructions available in her language relevant to a given semantic domain. Thus, in the domain of argument prominence, a speaker of English, with its stronger constraints on constituent order, cannot select among the extensive constituent-order possibilities available to a Yiddish speaker to express subtly different patterns of emphasis. If comparable effects are to be achieved, she must draw on means other than constituent order (T2 c6).

7.4   *D4. Content Inference*

This fourth major mechanism for structuring content in language, "content inference," involves the hearer in the arena of expression. By it, a hearer infers the portion of the conceptual content that the speaker had intended him to become aware of but had omitted from explicit representation. This speaker process of omission was discussed in (7.3.1) and the hearer process, which complements it, was treated there as well and so is not further discussed here.

7.5   *D5. Context*

A fifth major mechanism by which language structures conceptual content is the use of context. This mechanism specifically pertains to language's built-in *reliance* on context for certain structuring functions that it accordingly need not mark explicitly.

For one characterization of it, context includes everything that can affect an utterance's framing by a speaker or interpretation by a hearer. Context outside an utterance proper can include personal or cognitive dimensions of its speaker and hearer, including status, common ground, and general knowledge; its spatial and temporal location; its physical surrounding; the societally defined category of its circumstances; and the thematic character of the discourse it is embedded in. Two further forms of context lie within the scope of an utterance. For any morpheme within an utterance, the remaining morphemes are context for it. And an utterance's modality—whether it is, say, spoken, signed, or written—can be considered part of its context. We next discuss context under three headers based on speaker and/or hearer use of it.

7.5.1   D5a. Context for Speaker Omission and Hearer Inference

In each example of (7.3.1), the use of context enabled the omission of content by the speaker and the inference of it by the hearer. Several of these are discussed next, organized by the type of context used.

The type of utterance-internal context consisting of the morphemes present there enabled the speaker to omit and the hearer to infer the gapped content in *Wes likes wine with dinner and his wife beer.* Specifically here, the constituents *likes* and *with dinner* already occurring in the earlier clause were tapped for a second application in the later clause.

The type of context consisting of the thematic character of the discourse containing an utterance was in play in the sentence *Rice is easy to digest.* If the theme had been the speaker's health, the likelihood was that she had omitted and the hearer had inferred the concept 'for me', referring back to herself. If the theme was about different kinds of foods, the likely concept was 'for one', referring to a generic eater.

But if the theme was the speaker's health, the likelihood was that she had omitted and the hearer had inferred the concept 'for me', referring back to herself.

Or again, the type of context consisting of the utterance's spatial location would have been in play in the lemonade requester's saying *Can I have some?*, where the speaker was able to omit and the hearer to infer the concept 'of this' or 'of that' in accord with the pitcher's distance from the speaker.

And another type of context consists of the speaker's and hearer's general knowledge. Knowledge about the physical world enabled the speaker to omit and the hearer to infer the middle portion—the concept 'through the air'—of the bounded path depicted in *The crate fell out of the plane into the ocean.*

And knowledge about the social world was in play in the two-sentence "music-daughter" example. It enabled the speaker to omit spelling out the connection between her offer of music and her need to attend to her daughter—and for the hearer to infer the connection.

A further type of context not illustrated above is the interlocutors' "common ground" (Clark and Brennan, 1991), which includes the concepts that the speaker and hearer know they hold jointly largely due to their history together. Thus, a speaker who shares the knowledge with a friend that the friend had planned to go to a movie earlier that day can begin a discourse by saying simply *What did you see?*, without further specifying time or category, and the friend will infer the event intended.

7.5.2 D5b Context for Speaker Selection among Alternatives

The speaker's use of context was just addressed for her selection of what to omit and is now addressed for her selection among alternatives for inclusion. The new examples here also illustrate still further types of context.

Thus, a speaker can select among different registers for expressing the same conceptual content based on certain personal dimensions of the hearer, as where she addresses either a toddler by saying *Gramma's going bye-bye* or an adult by saying *Your grandmother's leaving now.*

And the same conceptual content can be represented differently in accord with the societally defined circumstance of its expression. Thus, the sentence *Would you like to sit down?* might be produced in a coffee house; *Please take a seat* in a lawyer's office; and *I pray you be seated* in a medievally set fantasy novel.

7.5.3 D5c Context for Other Hearer Interpretation

In the preceding two subsections, context was discussed for its use in both kinds of speaker framing—inclusion/omission and alternative choice—as well as in one kind of hearer interpretation, his inference of omitted content. We here address its use in other kinds of hearer interpretation, namely, picking the relevant sense from a polysemous range, determining the target of a trigger (i.e., a deictic or anaphor), and resolving an ambiguity. Again, a range of context types helps these processes.

One major task for a hearer is to select the relevant sense from a morpheme's polysemous or homophonous range, and one kind of context abetting this task is utterance-internal—the morpheme's neighbors. Thus, if a speaker says *I checked the market figures—my stock is down*, the morphemes in the expression form each other's context. They lead the hearer to select the 'ascertain' sense of *check*, the 'financial exchange' sense of *market*, the 'number' sense of *figure*, the 'financial instrument' sense of *stock*, and the 'reduced' sense of *down* (T6 s2.3.2).

Another type of context abetting this task of polysemy selection is a discourse's overall theme. Thus, a discussion of cooking will lead a hearer to select the 'soup base' sense of *stock* instead of, say, its 'financial instrument' sense of the preceding example.

Or again, the type of context consisting of the perceivable physical surroundings can help a hearer determine the target of a deictic. Thus, if a speaker atop a hill points down toward a lagoon and says *Mist forms there in the morning*, the lagoon's having an outer perimeter as a perceivable element of environmental structure helps the hearer settle on the whole surface of the water as the target rather than the single point that the speaker gestures at (T11 s9.2.1).

And several types of context in concert can help a hearer resolve ambiguities. For example, consider a speaker saying *I got snowed under in my work and had to come up for air*. The hearer will decide against the more basic meaning of *snowed under* as 'buried under snow' and of *come up for air* as 'swim to the surface of a body of water'. He will instead opt for their more idiomatic senses respectively of 'overwhelmed' and of 'take some respite'. This choice may be based on the following forms of context. The utterance-internal type of context from the presence of the phrase *in my work* militates against the concepts of snow or water. A type of context consisting of conceptual coherence makes it implausible to combine being buried under snow and swimming through water. The thematic topic type of context may inform the hearer that the discussion had been about projects, not about last winter's weather or diving. And the common ground type of context may inform the hearer that the speaker's life circumstances exclude any likelihood of snow burial or underwater activity.

7.6   *D6. Interaction*

A sixth mechanism by which language structures conceptual content is interaction among the interlocutors of a speech event. Such interaction can consist of their taking each other's needs and actions into consideration, or the alternation of their roles as speaker and hearer—two possibilities addressed next in order.

7.6.1   D6a. Cross-Consideration

A speaker and hearer cannot simply undertake their respective processes of production and interpretation independently, heedless of each other's constraints and requirements, but rather must take these into consideration for a speech event to succeed as a communication. In particular, the speaker must function as a proactive agent ensuring that her framing (i.e., what she includes explicitly and how she phrases that) and the available forms of context are adequate for the hearer to reconstruct the conceptual complex she wanted him to experience. In turn, the hearer must maintain a model of such endeavors by the speaker to guide him in determining the relevant context and concepts.

This mechanism of cooperation was not foregrounded during the discussion of speaker-hearer complementation above (7.3.1 and 7.5.1) but can be retroactively considered as an addition to it. For a fresh example here, a speaker needs to ensure cue adequacy in an act of targeting (T11 S1.5.1). Thus, a birder in thick woods who points and says *That's a whippoorwill* to a novice some meters away must ensure that he is at or can move to a location from which he can see her finger (gestural cue) and the bird (targetive cue); that he can act fast enough so that the bird is still there when he looks (chronal cue); and that he knows to peer up deep into the branches that he will spot (epistemic and environmental cues). The hearer in turn must recognize these speaker's aims for cue adequacy in order to act quickly in spotting her gesture and following it to search visually through the branches for the target.

Such cooperation is also seen in Gricean maxims (Grice, 1975). Though these maxims are largely cast in terms of how the speaker should frame her utterance, their characterization as cooperative conversational principles also indicates that much of what guides the speaker is her understanding of the hearer's cognition. Thus, the maxim of quantity—basically, that a speaker's utterance should provide neither too little nor too much information—mainly depends on the needs of the hearer, not of the speaker. And the maxim of relevance can as readily concern what is relevant to the hearer as to the speaker.

7.6.2   D6b. Turn Taking

Another type of interaction is turn taking, where an utterance by one interlocutor can provide the basis for a response from a second interlocutor, which can in turn occasion a further response from the first, and so on. There are specific sequences of such alternations in which each turn consists of a particular type of utterance (T11 s13.1). Sequences from two to five steps in length are discussed next in order.

There is a partial overlap between the phenomena covered here and earlier under "communicative purpose" (7.1.7). The differences, though, are that earlier the communicative purpose had to be marked grammatically, which is not necessary here, and that a response was not in every case forthcoming from the initial addressee, which it is here.

7.6.2.1   D6b1. Two-Step Sequence

Frequent two-step turn-taking sequences—the "adjacency pairs" of conversation analysis (Schegloff and Sacks, 1973)—include a question and an answer (X: *Where are you?* Y: *In the kitchen*); a statement and a same-theme augment (X: *I didn't sleep much last night.* Y: *Yeah, I got up early myself*); a misstatement and a correction (X: *She is green-eyed.* Y: *No, she has !-blue eyes*); an offer and an acceptance or refusal (X: *Have some chocolate.* Y: *Okay, I will*); a degreeting and its reciprocation (X: *Bye now.* Y: *See you later*); and an order and a nonverbal action (X: *Pass the salt.* Y: ⟨passes it⟩). Content is structured here in that the initial speaker's utterance provides a conceptual template with certain conditions for a complementary response, which the addressee then fulfills.

7.6.2.2   D6b2. Three-Step Sequence

An interaction sequence can also consist of three alternating turns. Thus, the "follow-up question sequence" consists of a statement, a question about some of its particulars, and an answer, as in: X: *The game is over.* Y: *Who won?* X: *The Warriors.*

Another three-turn sequence is a "Wh-echo-question" repair. Here, X makes a statement; Y did not clearly hear one constituent there and, to request its reutterance, uses a heightened-stressed Wh-word in its place along with sustained high pitch over the whole expression; and X repeats the unclear constituent with heightened stress—as in: X: *My son totaled his car.* Y: *!-Who totaled his car?* X: *My !-son did.*

7.6.2.3   D6b3. Four-Step Sequence

Four-turn sequences occur as well, for example the sequence whose steps in succession represent the illocutionary effects of assertion, opposition, insistence, and concession. It is seen in: X: *I'm going to the store for cigarettes.* Y: *Please don't go—I need you here to get ready for the guests.* X: *Well, I'm going anyway.* Y: *So !-go then.* Here, each turn could end the sequence, but it is in effect lexicalized to occur at its particular step. Thus, the second utterance could end a two-turn "opposition sequence," the third utterance could end a three-turn "insistence sequence," and the fourth utterance could end a four-turn "concession sequence." It is this last case that exemplifies the four-turn sequence.

7.6.2.4   *D6b4. Five-Step Sequence*

The possibly longest sequence might be called the five-turn "exasperation sequence." It begins with the same three turns as in the Wh-echo-question sequence seen above. The fourth turn is then the "redoubled Wh-echo question construction" in which Y asks again about the still unclear constituent, now using doubly heightened stress on the Wh-word, as in: Y: *!!-Who totaled his car?* And in the fifth turn, the original speaker repeats the unclear word now with doubly heightened stress on it and at times also with an intonation pattern suggesting exasperation in what could be called the "redoubled Wh-echo answer construction," as in X: *My !!-son totaled his car.* This last construction is thus lexicalized to appear as the fifth turn in the five-turn exasperation sequence.

8   E. Combination

A foundational design feature of language is that it is richly "combinant"—in every system at every level, smaller units combine to form larger units (T12). Where the units are semantic, such combination is ipso facto a means by which language structures conceptual content (and might have been included as a further mechanism under (7) but is presented here as a separate category in part due to its extensiveness).

Perhaps the main parameter along which the combination of semantic units varies is their type of relationship—additive, operational, idiomatic, or constructively discrepant—subtypes treated next in order. Additional parameters involve whether the units combine cooccurrently or sequentially; whether they combine as a simple aggregate or in a structured pattern; and whether their combinations are pre-established in the language in a closed inventory or can be generated open-endedly by the speaker in an expression.

8.1   *E1. Additive*

In the first type of combination, the values of the combining units add together without interfering with each other. This relationship can be seen within a hierarchy, across language divisions, in contraction and suppletion, in conflation, and in nesting addressed next in order.

8.1.1   E1a. Within a Hierarchy

The combination of units can form a hierarchy in which—moving upwards, as it were—smaller units combine to form larger units at a lower level, and these in turn can function as the smaller units that combine to form still larger units at the next higher level. At each such level, the combination is not fully free but accords with certain "rules," that is, with a particular set of affordances and constraints. The units relate to each other in terms of their places within the hierarchical structure. But they are additive in that the total effect consists of the accumulation of their values within those relationships, and in that the units do not interfere with each other, each manifesting its value independently of the others.

Units of form can comprise this type of hierarchy as readily as those of meaning, and their hierarchy is addressed first because the addition of meaning units largely conforms to it.

8.1.1.1   *E1a1. The Form Hierarchy*

What might be called the "main sequence" for form begins in any language with a closed inventory of phonetic distinctive features. These features can combine cooccurrently into phonemes in accord with rules of feature cooccurrence restrictions. Those phonemes that are licensed by the language then themselves form a second closed inventory, the phonemic inventory. In turn, these phonemes can combine sequentially into full segmental morphemic shapes (with the potential of cooccurrent stress or tone) in accord with rules of phonotactics. Those morphemic shapes that the language licenses then themselves form a third closed inventory, the lexicon of morphemic shapes. These morphemic shapes provide the form component of full segmental morphemes, as addressed in (8.1.2). To this point in the main sequence, all the elements of form belong to closed inventories and are pre-established in the language. Forms at higher levels are generated by the speaker in expression.

Continuing the main sequence, in some languages, certain segmental morphemes in the inventory can next combine sequentially into multimorphemic words in accord with rules of morphology. In turn, segmental morphemes and multimorphemic words (if present) can combine sequentially and open-endedly into sentences in accord with rules of syntax. Such sentences can in turn be combined sequentially and open-endedly into a single-speaker discourse partly in accord with rules of information structure, and then such discourses into a dialog in accord with rules of turn taking.

8.1.1.2   *E1a2. The Meaning Hierarchy*

Semantic combination largely tracks this formal main sequence, beginning at the level of the segmental morphemic shape where meaning first enters.

For each such morphemic shape, semantic components can combine cooccurrently as a simple aggregate to yield a morphemic meaning in accord with rules of conceptual compatibility. Such components can be unrelated to closed-class semantic categories, like the 'nuclear family' and 'preceding / current / next generation' that cooccur to form the meanings respectively of *parent / sibling/ child*. Or they can all represent closed-semantic categories, as for the deictic in *My wife likes these* (said while gesturing). The semantic components of the morpheme *these* indicate that the target is entity-like (not, say, a location), multiplex, proximal, inanimate, and third-person, and that the ensemble is a "trigger" for the hearer's targeting process (T11 c2). All such semantic combinations form a closed inventory—the lexicon of morphemic meanings—larger than that for morphemic shapes due to polysemy.

The remaining types of additive semantic combination are all sequential, all generated by the speaker in the arena of expression and, beyond the multimorphemic word in some languages, all open-ended. To begin with the multimorphemic word, the combination can be a simple aggregation, as in *walked*, where the gait and tense concepts simply compound. Or it can exhibit a structured pattern, as in *juggler*, where the meaning of the suffix *-er* might be represented as 'person who __s', requiring that the meaning of the verb occur at the locus of the blank. In neither case do the combining concepts interfere with each other.

At the next level, that of the sentence, as in *The young woman walked slowly up to the juggler in the plaza to ask for lessons*, the meanings of the mono- and multimorphemic words that compose it do not simply aggregate but combine in accord with the rules of compositionality, which follow the branched hierarchical patterns of the sentence's phrase structure (with special provision for discontinuous constituents). Here, for example, the concept associated with the morpheme *young* combines in the first instance with that associated with *woman* in an attribute-substrate relation—rather than with the concept associated with, say, *plaza*. And this higher-level combination, together with the contribution from *the*, combines in the next instance with the concept associated with the verb *walk* in an Agent-action relation—and not, say, with the concept associated with the verb *juggle*.

The meanings of such sentences can in turn combine to form the meaning of a single speaker's discourse in accord with rules of coherence/cohesion. And the meanings of such discourses can in turn combine into the meaning of an interlocutor dialog in accord with, among other rules, Gricean maxims.

8.1.2   E1b. Across Language Divisions

For many of its types, a morpheme—that is, a minimal concept-associated linguistic construct (4.2)—constitutes a combination of elements from all three major divisions of language: form, grammar, and meaning (4). In any given language, all such cross-division combinations together constitute its lexicon of (full) morphemes. This three-part association thus amplifies Saussure's (1959) two-part association between form and meaning.[6]

To illustrate with a segmental type of morpheme, the morphemic shape consisting of the phonemic sequence /mʌðəɹ/ is combined with the semantic components 'woman who has borne a child', 'uniplex', 'entity', 'animate', and 'female'. It is further combined with the grammatical complex consisting of the lexical category "noun" and its subcategories "count," "common," and "relational"—the last of which generally requires it to be the head of a possessive construction. Further, it requires singular agreement, the anaphor *she*, and the relative *who* rather than *which*.

The reason for assigning the components of such a triune morpheme to the additive type of combination is that they are largely independent of each other. This independence is the basis for the principle of arbitrariness commonly associated with symbols.

However, this principle needs some hedges. One is that morphemic shapes associated with closed-class semantic categories tend to be shorter than those for open-class ones. Another is that some morphemic shapes are semantically constrained—for example, heightened stress readily combines with a concept of 'correction' but would be less likely to combine with one of, say, 'dog'. And a third is onomatopoeia or sound symbolism—a type of iconicity—where a morpheme's sound is taken to resemble its meaning, as in the reference of *bong* to a resonant large-bell sound.

8.1.3   E1c. In Contraction/Suppletion

A contraction and a suppletive form (of one type) are alike in that both consist of a single segmental form that represents the combined meanings of what would otherwise be two or more adjacent morphemes. They occur in a paradigm, some of whose other entries still consist of separate forms. In both cases, the single form adds together the meanings of the represented forms and their grammatical relationship. One difference is that, in a contraction, some phonemes of the represented morphemes are still present, whereas, in suppletion, the form is phonologically unrelated to them. Another difference is that the represented forms in general are free in contraction and bound in suppletion.

---

6   Some closed-class morphemes—for example, the one consisting of the association between the lexical category "adjective" and the concept 'attribute'—do combine only two language divisions, but these are those of grammar and of meaning without that of form.

In English, an example of contraction is *won't* representing *will not*—/wont/ for /wil nat/. An example of suppletion is *went* representing *go* plus the past-tense suffix *-ed*.

8.1.4   E1d. In Conflation

Seemingly every language can represent certain complex event structures either more analytically or more synthetically. In such a complex structure, one event is in a certain semantic relation with another event. The analytic representation consists of one clause in a corresponding syntactic relation with another clause. But the synthetic representation consists of a single clause, one in which the two analytic clauses and their relation are "conflated." Such a single clause thus represents all the components of a multi-event structure combined additively. It can be taken to represent the structure as if it were a new single complex event—what (T2 c3) calls a "macro-event."

Some complex event structures—for example, an if-then conditional—seem never to have single-clause representation. But others frequently do. One such is a "Manner" structure in which, to simplify, one component is a motion event consisting of a Figure moving with respect to a Ground, a second component is an activity event in which the Figure exhibits a certain action, and the third component is a relation in which the second event functions as the Manner in which the Figure moves in the first event. To illustrate, the first event could be that of a top moving into the kitchen and the second event that of the top spinning. English could represent this structure analytically with two clauses, as in *The top went into the kitchen, spinning the while,* or synthetically in the single clause: *The top spun into the kitchen.* This single clause represents all the components of the total Manner structure additively.

Another complex event structure often represented synthetically involves agentive causation. To specify one physical type, the first event is a Manner structure like that just described, the second consists of a volitional Agent acting physically on the Figure of the first event, and the relation of the second event to the first is that of causation—the first event takes place because of the second. English can again represent this structure more analytically as in *The top spun into the kitchen because I acted on the top* or more synthetically as in the single clause: *I spun the top into the kitchen.*

8.1.5   E1e. In Nesting

Multiple instances of the same conceptual category can be combined within a single sentence to represent a nesting pattern in which each level does not interfere conceptually with the others. Such a pattern can be represented by a mix of both closed- and open-class forms.

Thus, as (T1 c1) analyzes in detail for certain schematic systems, five levels of temporal configuration are nested in *The beacon flashed 5 times at a stretch for 3 hours*; five levels of spatial configuration in the exact same pattern are nested in *I saw 3 ponds full of groups of 5 ducks each*; and four levels of perspective are nested in *At the punchbowl, I was about to meet my first wife-to-be*. To these can be added the five levels from the schematic system of quantity seen nested in *I've gotten very much too many more summonses than him*.

8.2   *E2. Operational*

A second type of combination is in the arena of expression. In it, the meanings of two morphemes in a construction are not statically additive, but rather one of them dynamically operates on the other. Such an "operational" morpheme is lexicalized to alter a certain component of the other morpheme's meaning in a specific way. In particular, it initiates an operation which shifts that component from one specific value to another along a certain parameter.

A morpheme with this operational type of combination can be bound or free, closed- or open-class. A bound closed-class example is the English suffix *-s* that combines with a noun whose meaning includes a semantic component of 'uniplexity', such as *cow*. It performs an operation of "multiplexing" on it to yield the combination *cows* referring to a multiplexity—a different value along the parameter of plexity. The suffix requires a component of uniplexity to operate on and so cannot combine with a noun whose meaning includes multiplexity such as *cattle*—hence, the form **cattles* does not exist. Thus, *-s* does not independently represent a concept of multiplexity and show up additively in a noun whenever that concept occurs, but rather is dependently keyed to the uniplex semantics of the noun it combines with. Another example is the verb prefix *un-*, as in *untie*, which shifts 'proverse' to 'reverse' along a parameter of 'versality' (T13 s3.5).

A free closed-class example is *almost* which, when combining with an accomplishment verb as in *My leg almost healed*, operates on the aspectual component of the verb. When unaltered, the aspect of accomplishment indicates that some process affects progressively more of a finite phenomenon through some interval at whose endpoint the process stops and all of the phenomenon is affected. The operational morpheme shifts the time at which the process stops from that endpoint to a nearby earlier point, leaving a lesser portion of the phenomenon still unaffected.

And a free open-class example is *fake* as in *fake gun* (Lakoff, 1982). This operational morpheme is keyed to the semantic component of 'function' in the adjoining morpheme's meaning and shifts it from operable to inoperable along a parameter of operability, while leaving intact semantic components pertaining to appearance or feel.

8.3   *E3. Idiomatic*

A third type of combination constitutes an idiom. In it, two or more morphemes with their own meanings combine, largely in accord with rules of morphology or syntax, but this combination is associated with a novel meaning. That is, its overall meaning does not result additively (compositionally) or operationally from the input meanings, though some components of the latter may persist. Idioms are pre-established constructs in a language—not freely generated by a speaker—and so are part of a language's lexicon in the arena of the inventory. Idioms can occur within a multimorphemic word, across free words, and in a complex construction.

An example of an idiomatic multimorphemic word is *untold*—a morphological combination of three morphemes: *un-*'negative', *tell* 'recount', and the past participle indicating a passive-like focus shift to the Patient. The overall concept associated with this word is 'vast', which cannot be derived from its morphemic components.

An example of an idiom composed of free words is *have it out with*, whose overall meaning, again not derivable from its components, is '(for X to) finally air openly with (Y) an implicit dispute that had been growing between X and Y'. All the components conform with syntactic rules except that the expectedly anaphoric *it* has no target.

And an example of an idiom consisting of a complex construction is the "modal-request construction" seen in *Could you all please sign in?* and *Won't you take a seat, please?* Somewhat simplified, the general pattern of the construction can be represented as in (1), where at most one instance of *please* can occur. This construction is an idiom because the meanings of its components— which include ability, futurity, contingency, negation, and interrogation—do not combine into the concept of a request. However, some of the input meanings are consistent with that concept. Thus, the meaning of the interrogative intonation pattern is itself a request, though one for a verbal response; the futurity of *will* is consistent with the fact that the hearer's response follows the request; and the particle *please* expresses politeness in requesting.

(1)   *can/will* (CONDITIONAL) (NEGATIVE) YOU (*please*) VP (*please*) INTERROGATIVE

8.4   *E4 Constructively Discrepant*

A fourth type of combination again lies in the arena of expression. In it, the speaker intentionally combines linguistic elements that are conceptually incompatible with each other. The hearer can discern that a discrepancy is present. But the speaker intends that this discrepancy will initiate a process of resolution in the hearer that, through certain cognitive operations he performs, will yield the coherent conceptual complex that she had intended to convey. This type of combination can accordingly be characterized as "constructive discrepancy" (T11 c14).

Such constructive discrepancy is the basis for all tropes, as well as some linguistic phenomena not usually classed as tropes. Such tropes and other phenomena can be divided into two types based on whether the conceptual discrepancy is between morphemes within the utterance or between the utterance and general knowledge. These "inner-conflict" and "outer-conflict" types are discussed next in order.

8.4.1   E4a. Conflict between Morphemes

In the inner-conflict type of constructive discrepancy, the speaker intentionally combines morphemes whose standard meanings conflict with each other and so disaccord with rules of coherence. The hearer reconciles these conflicts, largely through general knowledge, using a certain range of semantic operations (T2 c5). The illustrations that follow are sequenced by the type of operation required.

8.4.1.1   *E4a1. Concept Insertion*

One operation a hearer can perform to reconcile discrepant meanings is "concept insertion". The tropes of the type under discussion here indicate their presence to a hearer through semantic conflict between morphemes, and a subset of these relies on this operation for resolution. Take the trope of metonymy (e.g., Radden and Kövecses, 2007), which largely rests on specifying an action together with an entity that cannot perform the action—hence the discrepancy—but that is related to the entity that can. The hearer can resolve the discrepancy by conceptually adding in the relation of the one entity to the other. Thus, in *The ham sandwich just left without paying*, the conflict lies in the hearer's knowledge that a sandwich cannot leave or pay. But he can resolve this conflict in his cognition by inserting the concept 'the person who had ordered' before the concept represented by *the ham sandwich*.

Another trope in the same subset is fictive motion, which predicates motion of a stationary object (T1 c2). An example is *The fence goes from the plateau down into the valley*. A hearer can reconcile this by inserting the concept 'one's focus of attention in scanning along' before the concept represented by *the fence*.

What might also be considered a trope in this subset is coercion (Pustejovsky, 1995), where the conflict generally involves a mismatch in grammatical agreement. Though underrecognized, coercion can also occur within a multimorphemic word, like the final one in *Our experiment uses several nitro-gens*. The suffix *-s* standardly combines with a count noun having a uniplex referent and multiplexes that referent (8.2), but here it is combined with a mass noun. The hearer may resolve this discrepancy through concept inser-tion, here adding the notion of different types (e.g., isotopes) or multiple units (e.g., molecules), as if the phrase were reworded as *several types/units of nitro-gen*.

8.4.1.2   *E4a2. Concept Adaptation*

An additional reconciling operation is "concept adaptation." It can be seen in metaphor—another trope that identifies itself through semantic conflict between its constituents—where the concepts of a source domain are struc-turally aligned with and adapted to the concepts of a target domain (e.g., Lakoff, 1993). An example is *I'm lurching through my term paper.* The conflict is between the verb *lurch*, which refers to a person in physical space stepping jerk-ily ahead in short irregular bursts punctuated by halts, and the nominal *term paper*, which refers to a written composition on an academic topic. But the hearer may resolve these by adapting the former concepts to the latter where they now consist of short irregular bursts of activity, punctuated by periods of inactivity, and without progression in a concerted thematic direction (T11 s14.4.1).

The operation of concept adaptation has a close variant in "cue adaptation," used where the combination of cues in a speaker's act of targeting are in con-flict. Consider, for example, a woman who sits across a restaurant table from a man and, while looking at his mouth, says *You've got something in your teeth right here* and gestures by touching her own teeth (T11 s14.1). The hearer/viewer recognizes the conflict between, on the one hand, the core cue from the deictic *here* and the gestural cue from her pointing finger, both indicating the speaker as the target, and, on the other hand, the co-form cue from the phrase *in your teeth* and the ocular cue from the speaker's line-of-sight, both indicating the hearer as the target. The hearer resolves this conflict by adapting the former set of cues to the latter, as if the woman instead had said *there* and had pointed toward his teeth.

8.4.1.3   *E4a3. Concept Blending*

Another operation that a hearer (or viewer) can perform on conflicting con-cepts associated with different morphemes in a sentence (or parts of an image) is to generate a conceptual blend that joins portions of each into a single conceptual structure (Fauconnier and Turner, 1996). This operation is gener-ally also at work in a metaphor in conjunction with the operation of concept adaptation, since the latter does not act thoroughly without a trace (if it did, a metaphor would be indistinguishable from its literal counterpart). Thus, in the "lurching" metaphor example above, the hearer probably does not convert the physical gait totally into a type of authorial progress but may also construct a blended image. The image here might consist of, say, the speaker corporeally lurching along on a field consisting of a giant physicalized term paper.

8.4.1.4   *E4a4. Concept Cancelation*
A further reconciling operation is "concept cancelation" (T4 s4.3). It is seen in an example like *The shopping cart rolled across the boulevard and was hit by an oncoming car*. The preposition *across* prototypically refers to a point-like Figure moving horizontally from one edge perpendicularly to the opposite edge of a planar Ground bounded by two parallel edges. But the second clause introduces a conflict: the cart did not reach the other side. The hearer resolves this conflict by canceling the concept 'to the opposite edge', otherwise part of the preposition's meaning.

8.4.1.5   *E4a5. Concept Stretching*
Yet another reconciling operation is "concept stretching." To illustrate it, we first note that the meaning of the preposition *across* includes an additional concept not cited in the characterization just above: the length of the Figure's perpendicular path is less than or equal to that of the edges. This concept is complied with in *I swam across the river/square pool from one side to the other*. But it is moderately conflicted with in *I swam across the oblong pool from one end to the other*. The hearer, however, can resolve this conflict by stretching the permitted ratios of the two axes just a bit. It cannot be stretched too much, though, as seen in **I swam across the river from one end to the other*.

Constructive discrepancy in language affords a number of advantages. Concept insertion permits a shortened utterance. Concept adaptation permits a quick setting up of an analogy. And concept cancelation and stretching permit a much smaller lexicon. Here, for example, English does not need multiple different prepositions for each slight geometric variation.

8.4.2   E4b. Conflict between Utterance and General Knowledge
In the outer-conflict type of constructive discrepancy, the speaker intentionally produces an utterance that is internally unconflicted—its literal compositional meaning affords no problem—but that conflicts with general knowledge. This discrepant combination again leads the hearer to undertake a reconciling operation.

Certain tropes rest on this type of discrepancy. Two such tropes are hyperbole and sarcasm, both of which in fact call on the hearer for a still further type of reconciling operation, "concept rescaling."

Hyperbole is illustrated by a speaker saying *I met the most interesting person on the planet last night.* The hearer's knowledge that the speaker does not know all the world's people and that encountering a pinnacle among them is improbable leads him to assess the utterance as a trope of hyperbole and hence to scale the superlative 'most (... on the planet)' down to just 'very'. That is, along a scale of interestingness which, from a neutral point, rises into a positive zone and descends into a negative zone, the virtually topmost point specified by the utterance is conceptually relocated downward to a much lower point, though one still in the positive zone and well above the neutral point.

Sarcasm is illustrated by a speaker who, on seeing a friend trip in climbing the stairs to her door, says *That was graceful.* Here, the hearer realizes that the conceptual content represented by her utterance conflicts with what he knows the actuality of his actions to have been and concludes that it was a trope of sarcasm. He reconciles the literal content of her utterance with the different conceptual complex she presumably had in mind through another operation of downscaling, here along a scale of gracefulness. But for this trope, unlike that of hyperbole, the shift takes the overtly indicated point in the positive zone down past the neutral point into the negative zone, here, that of clumsiness.

9   F. Diachronic Comparison

Another major means for investigating how language structures conceptual content is to compare its attributes across different instantiations of language. Such instantiations can consist of different stages in the temporal continuum of a single language under a diachronic comparison, as discussed here. Or it can consist of a single stage within different languages under a crosslinguistic comparison, as discussed under the next category. Where the next category will include a comparison of different dialects separated geographically, the present category compares different "chronolects" separated temporally.

Diachronic comparison is one branch of a larger category of "time scope" whose other branch is synchronic analysis. This covers any analysis of a language at a single stage of its existence. Most of the descriptions in our discussion are in fact cast in synchronic terms.

On the diachronic branch, comparison can show that some aspects of language—linguistic universals (10.1)—never change. But all other aspects of language can change. There are several major parameters of such change that could have formed the basis for organizing the present discussion, for example, the different causes of change such as analogy and borrowing. But the parameter selected here has received less attention—the time scale over which different types of change tend to occur, from long to short, discussed next in order. The investigation of what in language can change and what cannot and, in the case of change, the time scale over which it takes place, can reveal much about cognitive organization.

9.1   *F1. Long Time Scale*

One seemingly long-term aspect of language is its "body plan"—the patterns in which it characteristically arranges conceptual content (7.2) in certain classes of propositions. For one of the most enduring classes, from the earliest records of them to the present day, Indo-European languages seem to have maintained the same basic pattern for representing a proposition of "object maneuvering" (T2 c4 s2). In this pattern, a subject and direct-object noun phrase respectively represent the Agent and the Figure—the maneuvered object—while the verb represents the maneuvering.

This is seen in *I threw/kicked/carried/brought/took/pushed/pulled/held/had the ball* as well as in *I gave her the ball* and *I put the ball in the box*. The verb can represent such different aspects of maneuvering as phase and direction of placement: *hold, put, take (out)*; transport: *carry, bring, take (to)*; instrument: *throw, kick, bat*; of force: *push, pull*; deixis: *bring (to), take (to)*; and possession: *have, give, take (from)*.

Though this pattern may be continuous in Indo-European languages and seem inevitable to their speakers, Atsugewi presents quite a different body plan, possibly one of some time depth since forms of it appear in other Hokan languages. To begin with, Atsugewi simply lacks verb roots with meanings like those of *have, give, take, hold, put, carry, bring, throw, kick, push*, and *pull*.

Instead, the verb root characteristically represents a particular type of Figure object or material as moving or located, for example, *-qput-* 'for dirt to move/be located'. Different "instrumental" prefixes represent concepts like those of throwing, kicking, pushing, and pulling as prior events causal of the Figure's motion or location. Different directional suffixes represent concepts of placement and transport as paths or locations of the Figure relative to a Ground entity. This set of suffixes also includes three that represent the concepts of 'having', 'giving', and 'taking (from)' as directional concepts, respectively 'in (the subject's) possession', 'into (the object's) possession', and 'out of (the object's) possession'. And two deictic suffixes represent the direction of motion as toward or not toward the speaker.[7]

---

7 The Atsugewi pattern is so thoroughgoing that verb roots also represent body parts and gar-

Somewhat less abiding, though still on a longer time scale, is the class of propositions that represent a macro-event (8.1.4) and that are subject to the framing typology (T2 c3, T9). A proposition of this class places a "co-event" in a particular relation with a "framing event." The framing event can express Motion, temporal contouring, state change, action correlating, or realization. The typology is based on where the "core schema" of the framing event—for example, the Path of a Motion event—is represented. It is characteristically represented in the verb in a "verb-framed" language and in the satellite and/or adposition in a "satellite-framed" language. But a language can undergo a typological shift. Thus, while Indo-European has been satellite-framed from the earliest languages through to many present-day ones, the lineage descended from Latin shifted to being verb-framed in all the Romance languages. And the reverse typological shift has taken place in the continuum from Archaic Chinese to modern Mandarin (Li, 2018).

Comparably, some areal phenomena—linguistic patterns common across neighboring but unrelated languages and hence borrowed by some from others—seem to be realized over a longer time scale. For example, a wide swath of languages from different families, perhaps centered in northern California, have a set of "instrumental prefixes" that mainly represent the immediate cause of the event expressed by the verb root. Mithun (2007) proposes that what was borrowed was a pattern in which an open-class verb root is preceded by other open-class roots that modified it and that—over some time—codified into a closed set of prefixes.[8]

9.2   F2. Medium Time Scale

Certain types of semantic change seem to take place over a medium time scale. One type seems to be the loss of a sense from a morpheme's polysemous range (unlike the apparent swiftness of a sense gain (9.3)). A possible example is seen in the verb *mind*, whose strongest sense is 'object (to)', as in *Do you mind the smoke / if I smoke?* But another sense, 'be careful about', seems to be on the wane in the U.S. (though apparently still strong in the U.K.), so that *Mind the branches* would be likelier expressed as *Watch out for the branches*. Still, this sense remains available to U.S. hearers, who would probably settle on it in the relevant context.

---

ments as moving or located. They occur within multi-affixal verbs equivalent to such English object-maneuvering sentences as *I stuck my ear against the wall* or *I took my shoes off*.

8 An issue needing attention in such longer time scale shifts, as well as in medium scale ones, is whether the change takes place gradually over the interval or comparatively quickly at the end.

Another possible medium-scale type is a change in the particular preposition associated with an open-class word, often accompanied by a shift in conceptualization. Though needing confirmation, possible examples include a seeming shift from an older *immune to* to a newer *immune from*; from *ask X of Y* to *ask X to Y*; from *glad of* to *glad about*; and from (U.S.) *different from* to *different than*.

Another possible medium-scale type is grammaticalization (e.g., Bybee, 2014), in which a morpheme shifts in its categorization from open class to closed class and, through "semantic bleaching," loses some of its originally associated conceptual content. Whatever the semantic starting point, the final meaning must lie within the universally available repertory of closed-class concepts (10.3). An example is modern English *may*, which derives from an Old English fully inflected verb meaning 'have the power to' but is now a modal that, in its epistemic sense, expresses the possibility, outside the speaker's knowledge, of either the actuality or the non-actuality of a proposition, as seen in *I'll check—there may be some jam left*.

Language change can also arise through borrowing from an influencing language, and some such changes occur on a short time scale, for example the adoption of a foreign word with its original meaning. But other changes occur over a medium scale, as seen with regard to verb satellite meanings in Yiddish among Slavic languages (T2 c4). One such medium scale change is the borrowing of (most of) a polysemous range. Thus, the polysemous range of the Yiddish verb satellite *on-* came to resemble that of Slavic *na-* by losing some originally Germanic senses, gaining several Slavic senses, and retaining the senses already in common. Another such change is the adoption of a concept represented by a whole lexical category. Thus, while Yiddish verb satellites shared with their Slavic counterparts the representation of Path, Yiddish borrowed their systematic use as well for the indication of perfective aspect. And one more such change is the adoption of obligatoriness in the representation of a certain concept when present. Thus, Yiddish borrowed from its Slavic neighbors the requirement to use its satellites to mark perfectivity when present.

9.3   *F3. Short Time Scale*

The type of semantic change occurring over the shortest time scale may mostly consist of certain kinds of addition to a language's lexicon. One kind is the addition of a sense to the polysemous range of a morphemic shape. For example, the morphemic shape *bug*, after its 'insect' sense, added the sense 'defect' and later the sense 'concealed microphone'. A second kind is adding the use of another lexical category, as the verb *ask* has done with its recent use as a noun meaning '(a) request' (*My ask to you is to tell someone about this show*). And a third kind is a novel morphemic shape with a new sense, like *pizzazz* 'appealing dynamic flair (especially in a personality)'.

10.   G. Crosslinguistic Comparison

The present category continues the last category's comparison of conceptual structures across different instantiations of language. But here the instantiations consist of a single stage within different languages or varieties of a language under a crosslinguistic comparison, rather than of different stages within a single language under a diachronic comparison.

Crosslinguistic comparison is one branch of a larger category of "language span" whose other branch is single-language analysis, that is, an analysis of any single language or variety of a language. Much of the descriptions in our discussion are in fact cast in single-language terms.

Crosslinguistic comparison can be conducted over a range of scopes from smaller to larger. It might even be extended, at the smallest scope, to within a single individual. Thus, seemingly every individual is at least a "multi-code" speaker, able to use different contextually based variants of her language in accord with the situation—her capacity for "code switching" (Gumperz, 1976). An individual, further, can be multilingual, and a "crosslinguistic" comparison here can perform a cognitive analysis of her differing capabilities with each of her languages.

Several successive increases in scope involve comparisons across related varieties or languages. Thus, at the next larger scope, a comparison can be made across individuals who speak the same sociolect but do so with distinct idiolects—a study of individual differences. At a still larger scope is a comparison across groups of individuals that speak different sociolects of the same dialect within a single community—a study within sociolinguistics (e.g., Geeraerts, 2016). Larger yet is a comparison across different geographically separated dialects of the same language—a study within dialectology. Finally, comparisons can be made of related languages in the same language family, often involving diachrony since the differences largely result from changes in a common proto-language.

At a much larger scope are comparisons across the languages of the world regardless of their family membership. Such comparisons can uncover aspects of language that differ in their degree of commonality from total to lacking. Four such degrees are discussed next in order: absolutely universal, typological, repertorial, and indefinitely diverse (T7). All suggestions here about degree of commonality are heuristic pending extensive crosslinguistic investigation.

Each degree of crosslinguistic commonality calls for cognitive explanation. Though this is scarcely available at present, several bases can be proposed to account for those aspects of language that are universal. One basis might be that, in the lineage leading to humans, there evolved a cognitive system specifically organized for language that includes its ubiquitous properties. Another possible basis is that processes operating generally throughout cognition and the various systems in it also operate in our language capacity and alone determine universal properties there without need for specifically linguistic processes. A third basis is that those properties that are common across all languages fulfill functions that simply cannot be fulfilled any other way and so occur by necessity. Yet another possible basis is that the earliest language to appear happened to have certain characteristics, a number of which have simply remained in all its daughter languages.

And perhaps the complements of these bases can account for the non-universal aspects of language. That is, languages can and readily do diverge wherever no constraints arise from an evolved language system, from general cognitive processes, from the exigencies of internal or external circumstances, or from an original ur-language.

10.1   *G1. Absolutely Universal*

Absolute universals are linguistic phenomena present in all languages. Many of the linguistic phenomena already discussed in this taxonomy are in fact themselves absolute linguistic universals, and a number of these are identified next because of their significance to linguistic theory.

Thus, all languages have the three divisions of form, grammar, and meaning. All have morphemes—minimal meaning-associated constructs—that mostly associate all three divisions. All have both open-class and closed-class categories of morphemes. All have morpheme types consisting of segment combinations, intonation contours, idiomatic combinations, constituent categories, phrase structures, grammatical relations, and constructions. All have morphemes with a polysemous/homophonous set of senses. And all have both a lexicon and expression as arenas of morpheme assembly.

All languages have speech participation by speaker and hearer. All have a system of turn taking that alternates the speaker's and hearer's processes of production and interpretation. All have speaker selection of what to express explicitly and how to express it so as to represent a larger conceptual complex. All have hearer inference of the implicit remainder of such a complex as well as hearer resolution of polysemy. All have a distinction between explicit semantics and inferential pragmatics. And all use context of the same range of types in the preceding processes.

All languages use the meanings of closed-class morphemes to structure conceptual content in a particular range of schematic systems. These systems—themselves possibly absolute universals that always include or exclude certain concepts or conceptual categories—include the configurational structure of space and time, perspective point, the distribution of attention, force dynamics (including causation), cognitive state, reality status, communicative purpose, ontology, role semantics, and quantity. And all languages pattern conceptual content in their morphemes, lexicons, and expressions. The morphemes' overall meanings are partitioned into a core meaning consisting of semantic components and an associated meaning that can include a holistic, infrastructure, collateral, disposition, or attitude sector. The lexicons have particular morpheme class sizes and inter-morphemic relations. And the expressions have particular plans by which content is arranged.

All languages combine semantic units in accord with four different patterns, ones that are additive, operational, idiomatic, and constructively discrepant. In all languages, further, their additive pattern includes a hierarchy that, from lower to higher, consists of the meanings of semantic components, morphemes, phrases, clauses, sentences, one-speaker discourses, and interchanges. And their pattern of constructive discrepancy includes all tropes, both ones based on a semantic conflict between morphemes and ones based on a semantic conflict between literal meaning and general knowledge.

Finally, all languages change, and can do so with respect to any linguistic features except their universals, with some features changing more slowly and some more quickly. And across all languages, children tend to follow the same general temporal outline in the acquisition of their native language (11.1.2).

There are also absolute negative universals—phenomena excluded from the design of language that, significantly, can help bring that design into relief. We here present a representative sample out of a perhaps indefinitely large number.

Thus, 1) no language requires that an interchange, in addition to a speaker and hearer, must include a monitor directing their utterances. A language's lexicon, even with polysemous senses counted, has entries numbering in the multiple thousands but not in the millions. 3) Seemingly no language has a closed-class form used to mark a constituent as an antecedent about to be referred back to by an anaphor. 4) In no language can a particular concept, say, that of past tense, be represented by a speaker's on-the-spot choice of a morphemic shape not otherwise in the lexicon.

Further, 5) speaking the words of a sentence in reverse order to represent a concept, say, the negation of its proposition, is not a possible type of morpheme. 6) Verb roots in a language can be lexicalized to express aspect but apparently never tense. Thus, English cannot have a verb *to went* meaning 'to go in the past' so that *I am wenting* would mean 'I was going'. 7) Monomorphemic triggers (deictics or anaphors)—e.g., *there* 'at that location' *then* 'at that time'— can target phenomena over a wide ontological range (7.1.8). But they seemingly never target many other types of phenomena such as those in 'at that distance' or 'with that frequency' (T11 s3.2). And 8) no co-speech gesture system requires a fixed indicator, say, the left thumb, pointing at the intended gesture, say, the right hand extending forward, to inform the viewer which body part to focus on (T11 s5.1.2).

10.2   *G2. Typological*

Consider a class of linguistic phenomena with relatively few members. Such a class can itself be absolutely universal, having to be represented in every language. But classes of this kind can differ in the universality of their members. For some classes, all the members are themselves absolutely universal. For example, for the class whose members are the two arenas of morpheme assembly, both arenas are present in all languages—no language has just a lexicon and none just expression. And for the class consisting of the four types of combination, all languages exhibit all four types—additive, operational, idiomatic, and constructively discrepant (8)—no language has just a subset of these.

But the members of some classes are only "inventorially universal." That is, the identities of the members are fixed and form a closed set, but not all of them appear in all languages. In fact, for some of these classes, in general only one member appears in each language's most characteristic pattern, although other members may occur less characteristically. "Characteristic" here means that the pattern is colloquial, frequent, and, where applicable, pervasive, i.e., it occurs across a range of subtypes (T2 c1). A class of this kind constitutes a typology.

Two illustrations of a semantic typology both involve the relations between a semantic tier and a syntactic tier. Here, the semantic tier is a macro-event of the Motion-situation type. The framing typology, already discussed in (7.2.2) and (9.1), selects one component of the macro-event on the semantic tier to observe where it appears on the syntactic tier. This typology has basically two members. The Path component is characteristically expressed in a language either in its verb or in a satellite/adposition system.

Complementarily, the "actuating typology" (T2 c1, T10) selects one component on the syntactic tier—the verb—to observe which components from the semantic tier appear in it. This typology has mainly three members. Most languages characteristically use the verb to express the Path, the co-event, or the Figure—as seen respectively in Spanish, English, and Atsugewi.

The alternatives within a typology often exhibit a prevalence hierarchy across languages (11.2.1). Thus, within the actuating typology, the Path verb as the characteristic system seems the commonest, the co-event verb somewhat less so, and the Figure verb is rare. Further, a typology can be conceptually extended to allow consideration of potential alternatives that in fact do not occur. Such alternatives then fall at the zero level of the prevalence hierarchy and can be added to the inventory of negative universals. In the present case, no language characteristically uses its verb to express the Ground, nor a combination of two different Motion components, nor an absence of Motion components.

10.3 *G3. Repertorial*

Consider next a class of linguistic phenomena with relatively many members. As above, such a class can itself be absolutely universal, represented in every language. But the members of such a class are seemingly never all of them absolutely universal. Rather, they are more like a typology with inventorial universality. In particular, the identities of the members are largely fixed and form a relatively closed large set, but not all of them appear in all languages. Such a class is here called a "repertory." But certain differences exist between a typology and a repertory.

Each language typically selects just one member of a typological set for its characteristic use, and many languages are alike in selecting the same one. But each language selects a subset of the many members in a repertory, and each selects a different subset. This selection, further, must be representative across the repertory, at times guided by levels of organization above that of the repertory's most basic members.

In addition, much like a typology, a repertory can exhibit a prevalence hierarchy among its members down to potential members that never occur in any language. But it can also include members that occur in every language and that can accordingly be added to the set of absolute universals.

Finally, while the membership of a typology is wholly closed, that of a repertory is only preponderantly closed—the prevalence hierarchy can extend ever lower to rare members occurring in perhaps only one language.

A potential example of a repertory is the class of all possible tropes which, depending on the analysis, can number in the scores if not the hundreds (Baldrick, 2008). A coarse-grained glance that disregards any categories among them suggests that different subsets of these tropes, but never all of them, are found across different languages as spoken colloquially at any given time. Seemingly some tropes, perhaps metaphor and metonymy, occur universally. Others may be rare. An example might be that of "pretend addressee," as where, say, a mother standing alone with her son looks off to one side as if addressing someone there and says *Is he going to take out the garbage? Nooo.*

Another repertory is formed by the mechanism of closed-class semantics. As discussed (7.1), this mechanism consists of a certain number of large schematic systems that in turn are composed of conceptual categories, each of which contains a relatively small number of basic semantic components. The meanings of all the closed-class elements in the world's languages consist of particular selections from among those semantic components, arranged in particular patterns.

Actually, not only the whole mechanism but each level of it is a repertory exhibiting a prevalence hierarchy. Each level is next discussed in turn.

10.3.1   G3a. Schematic Systems within the Mechanism
At the level of schematic systems, all ten of the ones discussed in (7.1) may prove to be absolutely universal. However, if a schematic system of "status" can be posited, it may be common but it is not universal—English for one language lacks closed-class representation of it. And if "rate" can be regarded as a schematic system, it is a rare one, represented in only a few languages by verb affixes for 'fast' and 'slow'.

Further, indefinitely many candidates for schematic system status are excluded as absolute negative universals. Some candidates are excluded even though they occur in nonlinguistic cognitive systems. An example might be a seemingly absent schematic system of "sensory qualia" in that there is apparently no closed-class marking of visual phenomena like color or brightness, auditory phenomena like loudness or pitch, or haptic phenomena like soft/hard or smooth/rough. And certainly no schematic systems exist for such conceptual sets as types of work or of food.

10.3.2   G3b. Conceptual Categories within a Schematic System
At the next level down, within a schematic system, some conceptual categories may well be absolute universals. An example within the schematic system of communicative purpose may be the category of questioning if in fact every language has some closed-class interrogative marking. But it seems possible (since English has so little of it) that, within the schematic system of cognitive state, the conceptual category of affect may be common but not universal.

And at the negative end, the schematic system of configurational structure lacks a conceptual category of absolute magnitude beside its extant category of relative magnitude, at least with respect to the spatial domain. For example, while some languages like English have different deictics that distinguish proximal from distal with respect to relative distance from the speaker, apparently none have deictics that distinguish absolute distances of, say, inches vs. parsecs. This nondiscrimination is seen in *This speck is smaller than that speck* and *This planet is smaller than that planet*, where the same morpheme *that* serves for objects regardless of their absolute distance away.

10.3.3   G3c. Semantic Components within a Conceptual Category

Finally, within conceptual categories, some semantic components may be absolutely universal. For example, in the schematic system of reality status under the category "known as unrealized," the semantic component 'negative' may well have closed-class representation in every language. But in the schematic system of quantity under the conceptual category of number, the semantic component 'trial' is not universal but in fact rare. And at the negative end, the number concepts 'odd', 'even', and 'countable' are never represented by closed-class elements.

It can be difficult to distinguish between concepts wholly excluded from closed-class representation and ones able to occur sporadically in the trailing off portion of a repertory. But English does provide an example of the latter in the conceptual category of configurational structure, specifically in the spatial domain. The use of *in* vs. *on* for location within a vehicle—as in *in a car/on a bus, in a helicopter/on a plane, in a boat/on a ship, in a caboose/on a train*—distinguishes whether the vehicle respectively lacks or has a walkway. This is an unusual concept to be represented by a closed-class form, perhaps unique to English.

10.4   *G4. Indefinitely Diverse*

At the lowest degree of commonality, the linguistic phenomena in some classes are indefinitely diverse. Every language has a unique realization of such classes. Seemingly most if not all of such classes involve content patterning, though unstructured aspects of it, unlike the treatment of it as a content structuring mechanism in (7.2). The diversity is present in the meanings of morphemes, their ranges of applicability, their polysemies, and their partitioning of semantic areas, discussed next in order.

10.4.1   G4a. Morphemic Meaning

A comparison of different languages' lexicons can address the class consisting of open-class morphemes and focus on their meanings. Crosslinguistically, these meanings do not belong to an absolutely universal, a typological, or even a repertorial set but rather can differ enormously.

To illustrate with one pair of languages, a complete semantic correspondence between an Atsugewi and an English morpheme is relatively uncommon. For example, the verb root *-p̓-*, might be glossed as: 'for a planar fabric to move in a way that changes its pattern of bunching' and, when combined with different instrumental and directional affixes, can refer to straightening a dress bunched up under one while sitting, opening curtains, or putting on socks.

Or again, *-swal-*, which can be glossed as 'for a linear flexible object suspended at one end to move/be located', can occur with different affixes to refer to walking along while carrying dead rabbits strung down from one's belt, sliding a snake away by suspending it under the head with the end of a stick, pants blowing down from a clothesline, or having one's penis hang limp. These verb roots and many others clearly have little semantic correspondence to English morphemes of any lexical category.

It might be thought that certain substantive concepts would be represented by open-class morphemes across all languages on the grounds that human cognition or our encounter with the world is structured in a way that inevitably forms unitizing boundaries around particular portions of the phenomenal continuum. Still, many candidate concepts do not prove out. Thus, an action seemingly as basic as ingesting food, though represented by a single morpheme in both English *eat* and Atsugewi *am-*, has no single morpheme to represent it in Navajo, which instead divides the action into a number of types represented by distinct verb roots depending on characteristics of the food and how it is eaten (Young and Morgan, 1992).

10.4.2   G4b. Range of Applicability

Even where particular morphemes across two languages share certain aspects of their references, those references can differ in their "range of applicability." For example, the English words *friend* and *acquaintance* share much of their senses with Yiddish *fraynt* and *bakanter*. But if strength of comradeship can be conceptualized as diminishing radially outward from a center point, then the circle enclosing the meaning of English *friend* is wider than that for Yiddish *fraynt*—it has a greater range of applicability.

Range of applicability can also change from one stage of a language to another. Thus, several decades ago U.S. English *girl* could be used to refer to a female person from infancy to early middle age, but now only to the later teens.

10.4.3   G4c. Polysemous Range

Another class of linguistic phenomena is the set of polysemous/homonymous senses associated with a single morphemic shape. A crosslinguistic comparison suggests that even if all the senses of a particular morphemic shape are expressed as is in another language, they will likely fall in the polysemous ranges of different morphemic shapes there. Thus, consider the English noun *stock* whose polysemous range includes the senses 'financial instrument', 'soup base', 'certain rifle part', 'stored supplies', 'line of descendants', 'farm animals', and 'certain plant species'. It seems unlikely that all these senses would be expressed by the same morphemic shape in another language.

Another example that now combines polysemy with range of applicability demonstrates the sheer idiosyncrasy and unlikely recurrence of those linguistic classes. In the polysemous range of the English verb *arrest*, one sense can be glossed as 'legally detain to prevent freedom of movement', but it has application only to sufficiently adult live humans: *The police arrested the man/ *goat / *baby / *corpse / *getaway car.* Another sense is 'stop the body-intrinsic growth of' but applies only to unhealthy tissue: *The medical treatment arrested his tumor / *hair / *nails.* And a third sense is 'hold fixed through allure and thus prevent wandering' but applies only to a cognitive faculty prone to shifting its state: *The unusual painting arrested my attention/*interest/*observation.*

10.4.4   G4d. Partitioning of a Semantic Area
A consequence of crosslinguistic discorrespondence in the three preceding aspects of morphemic meaning is that any given semantic area is likely to be divided up in different patterns. Consider the semantic area of one person encountering and engaging another. For part of its system, English uses the verb *meet* either for 1) making someone's acquaintance for the first time (*I met the new principal*) or for 2) conducting a pre-arranged appointment (*I met my lawyer in her office*). It uses the expression *run into* for 3) a chance encounter (*I ran into an old friend downtown*). And it uses *see* either for 4) a get-together with someone already known (*I saw my uncle today—we had lunch together*) or for certain client-professional encounters (*I saw my doctor today.*).

Yiddish partitions this semantic area differently. For part of its system, it uses *bakenen zikh mit* for the first type of encounter, *trefn zikh mit* for the second and fourth type, *bagegenen* for the third, and *geyn tsu* or *zayn mit* for the fifth.

Differences between languages in their typological and repertorial selections as well as in their inventories of morpheme meanings and polysemous groupings make exact translation a near impossibility.

11.   H. Quantity of Manifestation

Linguistically represented conceptual content can have a greater or lesser quantity of manifestation either in elaboratedness or in prevalence, discussed next in order. In general, the greater the quantity, the more that it engages cognition and its processes. And certain manifestations of quantity can change through time.

11.1   *H1. Elaboratedness*

Linguistically represented conceptual content can be more or less elaborated, that is, more or less comprehensive and granular. This category can be seen at work in four venues—in a communication system, in a language user, in a lexicon, and in expression—discussed next in order. This parameter can pertain to the entirety of an expressive capacity (as in the first two subsections below) or to a particular conceptual category or idea (as in the second two subsections).

11.1.1   H1a. In a Communication System

The conceptual content that a communication system as a whole can represent can be more or less elaborated. Specifically, it can be more or less comprehensive in the total amount of ideation that it can represent and granular in the fineness and number of the conceptual distinctions that it can make.

A lesser degree of conceptual elaboration can be seen in a number of communication systems. In very roughly increasing order, these include a plant or nonhuman animal communication system; a smaller devised limited system such as emoji; body language, facial expression, and gesture; a larger devised limited system such as Basic English; home sign; a pidgin; a heritage language; and "restricted code" (Bernstein, 1964).

Toward the top of the scale, a great degree of conceptual elaboration is seen in every spoken or signed language with a sufficiently long history.

A communication system's degree of conceptual elaboratedness can increase, as when a pidgin develops into a creole, or when the signed language originally developed by the initial group of deaf students in Nicaragua turned into the full system of the later students (Kegl et al., 1999). And it can decrease, as in "language death"—that is, where a speech community's competence with an inherited language declines as that language is gradually replaced.

11.1.2   H1b. In a Language User

Individuals can also exhibit different degrees of conceptual elaboratedness in their language. A lesser degree is seen in a language learner at any stage in acquiring an L1 or L2. It is also present due to deficit, whether developmental, as through reduced exposure or deprivation during childhood, or biological, as with congenital language disorders. By contrast, great elaboration is seen in any fully fluent speaker.

Individual conceptual elaboration increases during language acquisition, as when the language of an L1 learner moves toward an adult level (e.g., Tomasello,

2010) or that of an L2 learner moves toward a native level (e.g., Robinson and Ellis, 2008). Such increase might also be invoked where the written language of an author evolves over her career. And it can decrease, as when a speaker becomes rusty in a language once known well, or in the case of a later-onset language disorder.

11.1.3   H1c. In a Lexicon

In the lexicon of a language, a particular conceptual category can be greatly elaborated, having many members making fine distinctions, or minimally represented. This issue was already discussed in (7.2.2) for the much greater elaboration of Manner verbs and Path prepositions in English than in Spanish.

For a fresh example, consider a lexicon's elaboration of the class of "expressives." These are morphemes in a sentence that in effect place a hearer vividly in the midst of a referent scene as if able to directly perceive a specific effect there. Japanese has a great elaboration of this class with its "mimetics," whereas English does so minimally with just a few instances like *lickety-split* (*The squirrel climbed lickety-split up the tree trunk*) and *kerplunk* (*A coconut from high in the tree landed kerplunk at his feet*).

11.1.4   H1d. In Expression

A speaker can represent roughly the same conceptual complex with greater or lesser elaboration, that is, she can render it more specific and precise or more general and approximate. The choice of degree is often keyed to the hearer's knowledge about the topic. For example, a speaker addressing a non-gardener might say *I used my trowel to dig a hole in the ground, place the bulb root-end down at the bottom, and filled the hole back up with soil*. But to a fellow gardener, she might instead say *I planted the bulb*.

11.2   *H2. Prevalence*

Various kinds of linguistically represented conceptual content can be more or less prevalent, that is, more or less frequent in occurrence. Differences in prevalence can occur across languages or within a single language, as discussed next in order.

11.2.1   H2a. Compared across Languages

A difference in prevalence across languages was already discussed for the members of a typology or repertory (10.2, 10.3). What can be added here is that some prevalence differences seem due to particular aspects of cognition—one's involving bias, efficiency, and load, addressed next in order.

Cognitive bias can be illustrated with a language's characteristic closed-class marking of number in count nominals. A language can grammatically treat number as consisting of one, two, three, or four sets. A two-set division is seemingly always between the singular and the "2-plural"—two or more units—never, say, between one or two units and a 3-plural. And the three-set division is between singular, dual, and a 3-plural, while a four-set division is between singular, dual, trial and a 4-plural.[9]

While it is not yet clear whether languages without number marking or one's with a two-set division are more prevalent, languages with successively more divisions are successively less prevalent. This pattern accords with its further status as an "implicational universal" (Greenberg 1963)—here holding, for example, that a language with trial marking must also have dual marking. This crosslinguistic prevalence pattern may reflect a particular cognitive bias—one toward locating any divisions within a scale near its low end and toward making fewer such divisions.

Another prevalence ranking across languages is seen in the actuating typology (10.2) where, it seems, the verb characteristically expresses the Path most often, the co-event next most often, the Figure rarely, and the Ground never. No cognitive basis for this ranking is yet obvious. But two excluded patterns may each have such a basis. Apparently no language characteristically uses the verb to express zero components of a Motion situation beyond 'move'—this would be a waste of an obligatory constituent perhaps reflecting a cognitive tendency against inefficiency. And seemingly no language characteristically uses the verb to express a combination of two components in addition to 'move'—this would require a prohibitive number of distinct lexical items, perhaps reflecting a tendency against an excessive cognitive load.

11.2.2 H2b. In a Single Language

Prevalence within a single language mainly pertains to the frequency with which various linguistic formations occur in expression or in the lexicon, addressed next in order.

11.2.2.1 *H2b1. In Expression*

In the arena of expression, the assessment of frequency is made not in the production of a single expression but across expressions produced in the aggregate. Prevalence of this kind is directly addressed by the usage-based approach (Langacker 1988) and is most readily studied through corpus research.

Where certain linguistic formations have comparable semantic effect, the relative frequency with which a speaker selects among them rests in part on a

---

9   It is not clear how some languages' "paucal" marking for several units fits this pattern.

certain property that the formations have in the lexicon: their different degrees of "privilege of occurrence" for a given syntactic or stylistic context. Thus in an informal context, a speaker choosing among lexical alternatives will say *start* more often than *commence* and will perhaps rank the likelihood of referring to great speed with a single morpheme in the following sequence: *fast, quick, rapid, swift, fleet.* And a speaker choosing among constructional alternatives will increase the ratio of main clauses to subordinate clauses. A language acquirer learns such formations' privilege of occurrence by noticing the different frequencies with which speakers use them across different contexts.

11.2.2.2   *H2b2. In the Lexicon*

In the arena of the lexicon, prevalence can be seen where closed-class forms with comparable semantic effect associate in different proportions with particular open-class forms. Thus, of the English alternatives for representing the plural of a uniplex count noun, the suffix *-s* is far more prevalent than the suffix *-en*, vowel alteration, or zero change. The degree of such a closed-class morpheme's "productivity," further, is the proportion with which a speaker chooses it for an open-class morpheme new to the lexicon, and generally accords with its prevalence in the established lexicon. Thus, *-s* is generally chosen as the pluralizer for novel nouns, as in *nerds.*

In addition, the prevalence with which a morpheme is used in a particular sense can determine whether that sense is a metaphoric extension of the morpheme's main sense or a member of its polysemous range. Thus, the use of *foot* to mean 'bottom', as in *foot of the mountain*, is sparse and thus seems metaphoric, but if it were to spread, 'bottom' would come to seem a literal sense.

Diachronic increases and decreases of prevalence in a language's lexicon are pervasive and can in fact occur hand-in-hand. Thus, consider the spread in English of the termination *-in-law*, which was suffixed to morphemes expressing a consanguineal kinship relation and represented a conceptual operation (8.2) of shift from such a relation to a corresponding affinal kinship relation. This spread correlated with the gradual loss from the lexicon of Old English monomorphemic words that directly represented the affinal relations, such as *sweor* 'father-in-law', *sweger* 'mother-in-law', and *snoru* 'daughter-in-law' (T13 s2.1). This example of frequency change has additional cognitive-semantic significance because it constitutes a switch from a direct to an operational type of conceptual representation.

12   I. Communication Systems

At its most general (T12 s1.1), communication is a process that has evolved or been devised in which one entity, the "sender," executes certain actions that have the function of inducing particular responses in a certain other entity, the "receiver." The sender's actions produce certain physical effects that the receiver can detect across the separation between them, the "medium." Where such communication has evolved, it can occur between components of a single cell, between single-celled organisms, between cells of a multicellular organism, or between multicellular organisms.

Cognitive semantics is mostly concerned with a particular configuration within this general phenomenon. In it, one sentient multicellular organism communicates volitionally with another, intending to induce a response consisting of experiencing certain conceptual content in consciousness.

For a further distinction, the "channel" or "modality" of a communication can be characterized in terms of the actions that the sender uses to produce a signal and the corresponding sensory modality that the receiver uses to perceive it, where the medium between the two participants can support the signal's transit. Different communication systems use different communication channels.

Thus, spoken language can be said to use the "vocal-auditory" channel, since the sender's actions are vocalizations and the receiver perceives through hearing—where the medium of air supports the passage of sound. Both co-speech gesture and signed language then use the "somatic-visual" channel, since the sender's actions are visible movements of particular body parts in certain configurations (other than for vocalization), and the receiver perceives through sight—where the medium of air supports the passage of light. The same channel is used by lip reading, which differs in that the actions of the sender that the receiver attends to are limited to those of the mouth. The communication system of the deaf-blind in turn uses the "somatic-haptic" channel, especially of a manual-manual kind, where the sender's actions consist of bodily movements that the receiver perceives through the haptic senses—and where the medium of direct contact supports the transmission of physical movement. To simplify its full trajectory, writing uses a visual-visual channel whose medium includes surfaces that support its display and viewing by readers.

In further forms of communication traditionally more the purview of semiotics, what is conveyed and appears in the receiver's consciousness is less precise and ideational and more vague and affective or mood-related. Such forms include music, dance, apparel, art, and architecture.

Since this taxonomy is mostly cast in terms of spoken language in the vocal-auditory channel, as a complement the next two subsections respectively address gesture and signed language in the somatic/visual channel. Each discussed aspect of these further communication systems engages cognitive phenomena absent or rare in spoken language.

12.1 *I₁. Co-speech Gesture*

Gestures that accompany speech can be divided into two classes, those produced in association with a deictic and those produced otherwise—respectively "targeting" and "non-targeting" gestures.

12.1.1 I₁a. Targeting Gestures

To begin with targeting gestures (T11 c5), the prototype of them is pointing, as when a speaker says *That's my horse* while aiming her straightened forefinger at the animal. This and all other types of targeting gestures share a property: the speaker's gesture is always at a different location than her target. The hearer/viewer accordingly must have a cognitive mechanism for spatially connecting the former with the latter.

One proposal for such a mechanism is that the hearer connects the gesture with the target by means of a cognitively generated "fictive chain." This is a succession of imaginal constructs—possibly from a relatively closed universal repertory—that are either schematic (largely geometric) structures or operations that affect such structures. Such a fictive chain may have three properties of a physical mechanical system: 1) It is fully connected without gaps. 2) It forms progressively from the gesture to the target, not in place all at once, nor from target to gesture. 3) It is causal: the gesture gives rise to the first fictive construct, the first construct to the second, and so on. To illustrate such a fictive chain with the present example, the pointing finger may be schematized as a straight line with a front point that coaxially emits a straight one-dimensional intangible projection that progresses quickly through space to intersect with and terminate at the horse to mark it as the intended target.

Numerous types of targeting gesture other than the prototype occur, and we select one to illustrate the fictive chain's range. Thus, in referring to two glasses standing respectively 10 and 11 feet in a straight line away from her, a speaker says *This glass is mine and that glass is yours*. She gestures by extending her arm toward the glasses with her flat hand held bent upward at the wrist, first orienting her palm and waving her fingers toward herself and then rotating her palm in the opposite direction and waving her fingers away from herself. The hearer may generate a fictive chain in which an imagined copy of the speaker's hand is first repositioned through space to a location between the two glasses. Then the first waving motion of this fictive hand constitutes a thrust that launches a fictive projection which in turn progresses through space to intersect with the closer glass to mark it as the initial target. The fictive hand then rotates in synchrony with the actual articulator to launch a fictive beam at the further glass to mark it as the second target.

12.1.2   I1b. Non-targeting Gestures

Co-speech gesturing not associated with a deictic includes body language, facial expressions, and different types of manual gestures (e.g., Kendon, 2004). Significantly, though, a semantic characteristic prevalent among the first two gestural categories as well as some manual types is that the meaning of the gestures—the conceptual content associated with them—is approximative, vague, or murky. For example, hunching may suggest only a rough sense of self-protection, and sweeping a hand with palm turned down away from oneself only a rough sense of not wanting.

By contrast, perhaps most spoken-language morphemes, especially those with segmental form, seem to be associated with concepts experienced as precise, crisp, and clear. This is the case even where the associated concept itself pertains to vagueness, like the word *amorphous*.

However, something of the approximative semantic character of much non-targeting gesturing does seem to occur in spoken language. Thus, among segmental morphemes, it may occur in some discourse-organizing forms like the *well* used to begin a sentence. It also seems to occur in English with certain bound Greco-Latin morphemes existing beside independent forms. For example, the termination -*cracy*—as in democracy, autocracy, plutocracy, theocracy, technocracy—seems to afford an approximate sense of 'rule of the government by', yet does not equal the clarity of this phrase. Even vaguer are the concepts associated with such non-segmental morphemes as grammatical relations, like that of direct-object status, or alternatives of constituent order expressing subtly different patterns of emphasis.

Still, non-targeting gesturing may be the best arena in which to examine the cognitive phenomenon of conceptual vagueness.

12.2   *I2. Signed Language*

Our focus in this section is on a major system seemingly present in all signed languages, the "classifier system," which is specialized for the representation of objects moving, located, or oriented with respect to each other in space and time (Emmorey, 2003). Considered in its own right, this is an extensive communication system with several substantial differences from spoken language (T3, T12).

To illustrate this system, it can within a single expression represent an event in which a car drives quickly along a bumpy road that curves uphill closely past a tree, starting further away from the tree than it ends up. The signer's dominant hand represents the Figure, here in the classifier shape for land vehicles, while her nondominant hand represents the Ground, here in the classifier shape for trees. The "vehicle" hand, "bumping" up and down, moves quickly across the chest and then along a curved path ascending closely around the "tree" hand, stopping shortly past it.

By comparison with spoken language, the signed classifier system has a far greater 1) number of different content-conveying parameters, 2) number of concurrent parameter appearances within a single expression, and 3) quantity of iconicity, addressed next in order.

First, regarding the number of content-conveying parameters, the term "parameter" here designates any substantive aspect of a communication system that can represent conceptual content independently of other such aspects. Then spoken language has basically three such parameters—phonetic quality, pitch, and loudness. But by one count, the signed classifier system has some thirty parameters (T12). In the example, for instance, these parameters include the shape of the Figure hand, the shape of the Ground hand, the Figure hands' speed, its oscillatory movement, the contour of its path (here, curved), the angle of its path (here, half upward), the distance of its path from the Ground (here, close), and the relative lengths of its path segments before and after encounter with the Ground. all these substantive aspects of the classifier system can vary independently of each other.

Second, the number of parameters that can be realized concurrently is far greater in the classifier system than in spoken language. True, all the parameters of spoken language can be concurrent, but that number is still only three. And while all thirty or so parameters of the classifier system cannot be realized at the same time, different subsets of up to some ten of them can be concurrent.

Third, the signed classifier system exhibits far more iconicity than spoken language. In iconicity, linguistic form represents conceptual content through similarity with it. An example of its limited spoken-language occurrence is seen in *The cell phone tower is waaay/waaaay/waaaaaay over there*. Here, the successive increases in the length of the vowel over the norm in *way* represent corresponding increases in the length of the tower's displacement from the speaker that simple *way* would have indicated. But of the 30 some parameters in the classifier system, all but the two for the Figure and Ground handshapes are iconic. For example, the contour of the Figure hand's path is iconic of the contour exhibited by the represented Figure's path. And the slant of the Figure hand's path, ranging from straight up to horizontal to straight down, is iconic of the same slant shown by the Figure's path. These parameters largely reflect the gradience of what they represent, unlike the pre-established discrete values of the structure-indicating elements of spoken language.

These substantial differences across two human communication systems require an analysis of linguistic cognition far more general than that provided by extant models of it based on spoken language alone, and suggest an advance in language theory (T3 s4).

13   J. Research Characteristics

Every study on conceptual structure in language is shaped by the methodologies and other aspects of approach used in the research—two features discussed next in order.

13.1   *J1. Methodology*

Linguistic meaning is amenable to study through a range of methodologies, that is, one or another system of procedures used to examine it (T5). Each methodology has a different profile of capacities and limitations that accords it a particular perspective on the nature of conceptual organization in language. Together, they thus afford an array of advantages and compensate for each other's deficits. Used in conjunction with all of these is one "meta-methodology," analytic thought, which includes abstraction, comparison, correlation, classification, pattern detection, inference, and in general the systematic manipulation of ideas.

Some of the main methodologies used to research linguistic conceptual structure can be enumerated. The traditional and still most prevalent methodology in cognitive semantics is metacognition. This is the use of directed conscious attention to introspectively accessed aspects of language in one's own cognition. Metacognition plays a role at three levels of remove. At the most immediate, a linguist examines her own native language. At the second, a linguist elicits and examines reports by others using introspection on their native language, as a descriptive linguist does with native speakers. At the third level, a linguist examines written descriptions by other linguists of their work with native speakers, as a typologist does with the grammars of different languages.

Another methodology is corpus research, the largely computer-aided examination of representative and often annotated collections of portions of writing or spontaneous speech. Another is the analysis of audio- and videographic recordings of naturally occurring communication. Still others are the experimental techniques of psycholinguistics; the instrumental probes of the brain's linguistic functioning in neuroscience; and the simulations of human linguistic functions in artificial intelligence.

Some comparison of the profiles of these methodologies can suggest where they excel and where they offset each other's limitations. What metacognition seems best at is determining certain types of meaning. These are mainly the concepts associated with individual open-class segmental morphemes, idioms, and tropes, as well as whole utterances and interchanges. As a consciousness phenomenon, metacognition may in fact be the only methodology able to access meaning, another consciousness phenomenon. Metacognition also excels at determining whether an utterance is well-formed semantically and syntactically, the latter being the basis of grammaticality judgments.

At a somewhat lower level, metacognition has partial but not thoroughgoing access to cross-morphemic relations in the lexicon (D2b3). Thus, regarding access to a morpheme's polysemous range, a speaker asked to identify the various senses of the noun *stock* might come up with several, but scarcely all, of those listed in (10.4.3). And regarding access to synonymy, if asked to think of other words with roughly the same meaning as, say, *tendency*, a respondent might come up with a couple, but probably not all, of the following: *inclination, leaning, disposition, proneness, propensity, proclivity*. Here, though, lexicography—a methodology akin to corpus research that collates dispersed occurrences of particular forms and meanings—compensates for this deficit in metacognition in the form of dictionaries and thesauruses, respectively.

Perhaps still less accessible through metacognition are the particular forms and conceptual import of certain concomitants of speech—auditory ones like vocal dynamics and intonation and visual ones like gesture, facial expression, and body language. But this introspective shortfall can be made up for through the methodology of audiovisual recording and its subsequent analysis.

And perhaps even more inaccessible to introspection are the bases, whether purely formal or also partly semantic, of certain syntactic effects. For example, if asked to consider the two sentences *Whose dog did our cat bite?* and *Whose dog bit our cat?*, an average speaker would have little direct sense for what it is about the first sentence that requires the inclusion of the word *did*, the basic form of the verb *bite*, and the positioning of this verb at the sentence's end, while the second sentence requires an absence of *did*, the past-tense form of the verb, and the positioning of the verb within the sentence. In compensation for this introspective deficiency, however, syntacticians combine their metacognitive access to whether a sentence is well- or ill-formed with the meta-methodology of analytic thought to uncover the underlying patterns.

And at the lowest level, some aspects of linguistically represented meaning are entirely inaccessible to metacognition and rely wholly on other methodologies for any understanding of them. Thus, there is no introspective access to cognitive processing of meaning that takes place in fractions of a second nor that occurs across different individuals. But the techniques of psycholinguistics, among their capabilities, can access that time scale and can compare the performances of different individuals on a particular semantic function. Metacognition can also not access which brain systems are involved in different types of semantic processing, but that lack is partly made up for by neuroscientific imaging techniques. And there can be no direct metacognitive access to methods for processing linguistically represented conceptual content other than those actually present in cognition, whereas artificial intelligence, aided by the meta-methodology of analytic thought, has developed just such methods.

13.2   *J2. Other Aspects of Approach*

In addition to the methodologies used, studies in cognitive semantics can differ with respect to certain structural research parameters. To briefly identify four of these, one parameter is scope, ranging from a larger swath to a more focused area under examination. Another parameter, that of granularity, tends to correlate inversely with that of scope, ranging from an analysis in broader strokes for a larger scope to one in finer detail for a smaller scope. Another parameter involves a study's balance between the theoretical and the descriptive. And yet another parameter involves a balance between the introduction of new ideas and the elaboration of familiar ideas.

14   Postscript

Together, the contributions to this Handbook are representative of the preceding four research parameters at both of their strong ends. Collectively, they present both big-picture perspectives and focus, both generalization and detail, both theory and description, and both new ideas and the development of familiar ones in the field of cognitive semantics.

Acknowledgments

I would like to thank Thomas Fuyin Li for his unparalleled work over the years in promoting and contributing to cognitive semantics, thus helping in the expansion of the field that this Foreword and Handbook report on. And as always, my great thanks to Stacy Krainz for her help with research and editing.

References

Baldrick, Chris. 2008. *Oxford Dictionary of Literary Terms*. New York: Oxford University Press.

Bernstein, Basil. 1964. Elaborated and restricted codes: Their social origins and some consequences. *American Anthropologist* 66(6): 55–69.

Brugmann, Claudia and George Lakoff. 1988. Cognitive topology and lexical networks. In S. Small, G. Cottrell, and M. Tanenhaus (eds.), *Lexical Ambiguity Resolution: Perspectives from Psycholinguistics, Neuropsychology, and Artificial Intelligence*, 477–508. Menlo Park: Morgan Kaufmann.

Bybee, Joan. 2014. Cognitive processes in grammaticalization. In M. Tomasello (ed.), *The New Psychology of Language: Cognitive and Functional Approaches to Language Structure*, Volume II, 145–167. Mahwah: Lawrence Erlbaum.

Clark, Herbert H., and Susan E. Brennan. 1991. Grounding in communication. In L.B. Resnick, J.M. Levine, and S.D. Teasley (eds.), *Perspectives on Socially Shared Cognition*, 127–149. Washington: APA Books.

Clark, Eve V. 1997. Conceptual perspective and lexical choice in acquisition. *Cognition* 64(1): 1–37.

Emmorey, Karen. 2003. *Language, Cognition, and the Brain: Insights from Sign Language Research*. Mahwah: Lawrence Erlbaum.

Fauconnier, Gilles and Mark B. Turner. 1996. Blending as a central process of grammar. In A. Goldberg (ed.), *Conceptual Structure, Discourse and Language*, 113–130. Stanford: Center for the Study of Language and Information.

Fillmore, Charles. 1976. Frame semantics and the nature of language. *Annals of the New York Academy of Sciences: Conference on the Origin and Development of Language and Speech* 280: 20–32.

Geeraerts, Dirk. 2016. The sociosemiotic commitment. *Cognitive Linguistics* 27: 527–542.

Greenberg, Joseph H. 1963. Some universals of grammar with particular reference to the order of meaningful elements. In J.H. Greenberg (ed.), *Universals of Human Language*, 73–113. Cambridge, MA: MIT Press.

Grice, Paul. 1975. Logic and conversation. In P. Cole and J. Morgan (eds.), *Syntax and Semantics*, volume III: *Speech Acts*, 41–58. New York: Academic Press.

Gumperz, John. 1976. The sociolinguistic significance of conversational code-switching. In J. Cook-Gumperz and J.J. Gumperz (eds.), *Papers on Language and Context, Working Paper 46*, 1–46. Berkeley: Language Behavior Research Laboratory, University of California.

Kegl, Judy, Ann Seghas, and Marie Coppola. 1999. Creation through contact: Sign language emergence and sign language change in Nicaragua. In M. DeGraff (ed.), *Language Creation and Language Change: Creolization, Diachrony, and Development*, 179–238. Cambridge, MA: MIT Press.

Kendon, Adam. 2004. *Gesture: Visible Action as Utterance.* Cambridge, UK: Cambridge University Press.

Lakoff, George. 1982. *Categories and Cognitive Models.* Berkeley: University of California, Institute of Cognitive Studies.

Lakoff, George. 1993. The contemporary theory of metaphor. In A. Ortony (ed.) *Metaphor and Thought*, 202–251. Cambridge, UK: Cambridge University Press.

Langacker, Ronald W. 1987. *Foundations of Cognitive Grammar, Volume I, Theoretical Prerequisites.* Stanford: Stanford University Press.

Langacker, Ronald W. 1988. A usage-based model. In B. Rudzka-Ostyn (ed.), *Topics in Cognitive Linguistics*, 127–161. Amsterdam: John Benjamins.

Langacker, Ronald W. 1993. Universals of construal. In J.S. Guenther, B.A. Kaiser, and C.S. Zoll (eds.), *Proceedings of the Nineteenth Annual Meeting of the Berkeley Linguistics Society: General Session and Parasession on Semantic Typology and Semantic Universals*, 447–463. Berkeley: Berkeley Linguistics Society.

Li, Thomas Fuyin. 2018. Extending the Talmyan typology: A case study of the macro-event as event integration and grammaticalization in Mandarin. *Cognitive Linguistics* 29(3): 585–621.

Mithun, Marianne. 2007. Grammar, contact, and time. *Journal of Language Contact* 6(1): 144–167.

Pustejovsky, James. 1995. *The Generative Lexicon.* Cambridge, MA: MIT Press.

Radden, Guenter and Zoltan Kövecses. 2007. Towards a theory of metonymy. In K. Panther and G. Radden (eds.), *Metonymy in Language and Thought*, 17–59. Amsterdam: John Benjamins.

Robinson, Peter and Nick C. Ellis (eds.). 2008. *Handbook of Cognitive Linguistics and Second Language Acquisition.* Mahwah: Lawrence Erlbaum.

Saussure, Ferdinand de. 1959. *Course in General Linguistics.* In E. Bally and A. Sechehaye (eds.) (Translated from the French by Wade Baskin). New York: The Philosophical Society.

Schegloff, Emanuel and Harvey Sacks. 1973. Opening up closings. *Semiotica* 8(4): 289–327. Available at doi:10.1515/se-mi.1973.8.4.289.

Talmy, Leonard. 2000a (T1). *Toward a Cognitive Semantics*, volume I: *Concept Structuring Systems*. i–viii, 1–565. Cambridge, MA: MIT Press.

Talmy, Leonard. 2000b (T2) *Toward a Cognitive Semantics*, volume II: *Typology and Process in Concept Structuring*. i–viii, 1–495. Cambridge, MA: MIT Press.

Talmy, Leonard. 2003. (T3). The representation of spatial structure in spoken and signed language. In B. Hampe (ed.), *Perspectives on Classifier Constructions in Sign Language*, 169–196. Mahwah: Lawrence Erlbaum.

Talmy, Leonard. 2005 (T4). The fundamental system of spatial schemas in language. In B. Hampe (ed.), *From Perception to Meaning: Image Schemas in Cognitive Linguistics*, 199–234. Berlin: Mouton de Gruyter.

Talmy, Leonard. 2007a (T5). Foreword (Comparing introspection with other methodologies). In M. Gonzalez-Marquez, I. Mittelberg, S. Coulson, and M. Spivey (eds.), *Methods in Cognitive Linguistics: Ithaca*. Amsterdam: John Benjamins.

Talmy, Leonard. 2007b (T6). Attention phenomena. In D. Geeraerts and H. Cuyckens (eds.), *Oxford Handbook of Cognitive Linguistics*, 264–293. Oxford: Oxford University Press.

Talmy, Leonard. 2011 (T7). Universals of semantics. In P. Hogan (ed.), *Cambridge Encyclopedia of the Language Sciences*, 754–757. Cambridge, UK: Cambridge University Press.

Talmy, Leonard. 2015 (T8). Relating language to other cognitive systems: An overview. *Cognitive Semantics* 1(1): 1–44.

Talmy, Leonard. 2016 (T9). Properties of main verbs. *Cognitive Semantics* 2(2): 133–163.

Talmy, Leonard. 2017 (T10). Foreword: Past, present, and future of motion research. In I. Ibarretxe-Antuqano (ed.), *Motion and Space across Languages: Theory and Applications*. HCP (Human Cognitive Processing) Series. Amsterdam: John Benjamins.

Talmy, Leonard. 2018a (T11). *The Targeting System of Language*. Cambridge, MA: MIT Press.

Talmy, Leonard. 2018b (T12). Combinance in the evolution of language: Overcoming limitations. *Cognitive Semantics* 4(2): 135–183.

Talmy, Leonard. 2020 (T13). Semantic unilocality. *Cognitive Semantics* 6(2): 131–169.

Talmy, Leonard. 2021 (T14). Structure within morphemic meaning. *Cognitive Semantics* 7(2): 155–231.

Tomasello, Michael. 2010. Cognitive linguistics and first language acquisition. In D. Geeraerts and H. Cuyckens (eds.), *Oxford Handbook of Cognitive Linguistics*, 1092–1112. Oxford: Oxford University Press.

Young, Robert and William Morgan, with Sally Midgette. 1992. *Analytical Lexicon of Navajo*. Albuquerque: University of New Mexico Press.

CHAPTER 2

Introducing Cognitive Semantics

Fuyin Thomas Li

1   Introduction

Cognitive semantics is an interdisciplinary approach to the study of meaning and mind. It is generally taken as a subfield of Cognitive Linguistics. In the most specific sense, it is the field that is defined by the research on conceptual structure conducted by Leonard Talmy. In a broader sense, the term also covers research in philosophy, psychology, neuroscience, artificial intelligence, and other subject fields in cognitive science that takes the relationship between meaning and mind as the main object of study. Cognitive Semantics views language as one of the major cognitive systems and is best characterized at different levels and perspectives. Evolutionarily, cognitive semantics considers language to be among the most recent cognitive systems to evolve in the human lineage. Paralleled with language are culture, story, music, and dance; later cognitive systems include affect, forward simulation, and inferencing; the earliest systems are perception in general and motor control. Cognitively, cognitive semantics studies the many and varied aspects of human cognition through conceptual organization by analyzing a crucial set of fundamental conceptual domains including space and time, motion and location, causation and force interaction, attention and viewpoint, action and events, etc. Cross-linguistically, cognitive semantics studies the conceptual patterns, conceptual schemas, linguistic typologies, motivating mechanisms etc. that are formed in conceptual structuring processes. More specifically, cognitive semantics studies the cognitive process that is involved in the grammatical manipulation. For instance, the process of adding a plural form 's' to 'apple' to form 'apples' involves the cognitive process of pluralizing. Process that proceeds from representing the same conceptual content in two clauses to a representation in a single clause involves the cognitive process of the integration of a macro-event. Diachronically, cognitive semantics studies the mechanisms that motivate a semantic change, especially, change from an open-class form to a closed-class form, and the mechanisms that motivate the shift of conceptual patterns and typologies. This is the intersection of work on semantic change and grammaticalization.

© KONINKLIJKE BRILL NV, LEIDEN, 2023 | DOI:10.1163/_003

This handbook aims to provide a practical guide for approaching cognitive semantics. It intends to expand the boundaries of cognitive semantics, even though the boundaries are in no sense clear-cut—they are blurred and fuzzy. The approach to natural language analysis, which is known as Cognitive Linguistics, can be roughly divided into two broad categories, cognitive grammar and cognitive semantics. This approach originated in the late seventies and early eighties in the work of George Lakoff, Ronald Langacker, and Leonard Talmy. These three scholars are known as founding fathers of Cognitive Linguistics. The founding of the present handbook is consistent with the claim made by the journal *Cognitive Semantics* that cognitive semantics "takes the relationship between meaning and mind as its central concern." In this way, Talmy's cognitive semantics lies in the center of cognitive semantics within Cognitive Linguistics. There are topics in Cognitive Linguistics which are not included in Talmy's cognitive semantics, but are obviously cognitive semantics, such as metaphor, metonymy, image schemas, Idealized Cognitive Models, etc. By the definition that *cognitive semantics is an interdisciplinary approach to the study of meaning and mind,* we intend to cover topics not traditionally covered in Cognitive Linguistics. Topics concerning meaning and mind within Generative Grammar are also cognitive semantics. The opposition between Cognitive Linguistics (led by Lakoff, Langacker, and Talmy) and cognitive linguistics (led by Chomsky) is diminished. The two approaches share the eternal goal, that is, to find the truth of meaning and mind. Both are complementary in methodology.

This chapter is organized as follows. Section 2 provides some foundational works in cognitive semantics. Section 3 introduces twelve traditional areas of cognitive semantics, and some core literature in each area. Section 2 and 3, together with a large part of section 1, are adapted from the article *Cognitive Semantics* (Li, 2021) appeared in *Oxford Bibliographies in Linguistics*. Section 4 is an overview of the handbook. Section 5 concludes this chapter by pointing to some future directions.

2   Foundational Works

Cognitive semantics was developed with Cognitive Linguistics. Lakoff contributed mostly to the philosophical foundation of the enterprise. Lakoff (1987), and Lakoff and Johnson (1980), are basically on cognitive semantics. The two-volume set Talmy (2000a) and Talmy (2000b) on conceptual structure lays the foundation of cognitive semantics. Langacker (1987) and Langacker (1991) develop the theory of cognitive grammar. Johnson (1987) develops the theory of image schemas based on embodied experiences. Rosch (1973) develops the theory of the prototype, which plays an important role at all linguistic levels as explained in Taylor (2003). Fauconnier and Turner (1998) contributes to online meaning construction in its theory of conceptual integration networks.

There are a few international journals devoted to cognitive semantics. *Cognitive Semantics* is explicitly dedicated to publishing research in cognitive semantics. *Cognitive Linguistics* is the most authoritative journal devoted to Cognitive Linguistics, including cognitive semantics. *Review of Cognitive Linguistics* and *Language and Cognition* publish research on cognitive semantics. *Cognitive Semiotics* is concerned with language and mind. *Metaphor and Symbol* is devoted to metaphor study, a major topic in cognitive semantics.

China International Forum on Cognitive Linguistics (CIFCL) is devoted to the promotion of the best scholarship in Cognitive Linguistics. It was founded by its first speaker, George Lakoff in 2004 at Beihang University, Beijing. CIFCL has continued to invite prominent scholars since then. Each invited speaker gives 10 lectures on a topic area and the transcripts are published in the Distinguished Lectures in Cognitive Linguistics (DLCL) in Brill, Leiden. 30 series of lectures were delivered by the end of 2021. One of the unique features of the series is the audio files of the lectures. Some of the lectures are essentially on cognitive semantics, including Fauconnier (2018), Geeraerts (2018), Goddard (2018), Lakoff (2018), Langacker (2017), Talmy (2018b), Taylor (2018), etc. This forum invites scholars from interdisciplinary background. It mainly focuses on the latest developments on meaning and mind in linguistics, psychology, and philosophy.

3 Classical Areas of Cognitive Semantics

Even though it is difficult to draw a distinct clear line between cognitive semantics and cognitive grammar, we can still enumerate some traditional topic areas that obviously fall into cognitive semantics.

3.1 *Form and Meaning*

The form-meaning relation is the central concern of different linguistic approaches. In cognitive semantics, it is assumed that it is possible to isolate semantic elements separately within the domain of meaning and linguistic forms within the domain of form, and to study the patterns of meaning-form mapping and the cognitive mechanisms motivating the mapping, thus linking the research to a number of related areas, including typology, iconicity, grammaticalization etc. As a basis of form-meaning study, a series of metalanguage terms for meaning are proposed. Chapter 2 in Talmy (2000b) examines the systematic relations between 35 semantic elements and the verb complex. Dowty (1991) proposes the concepts of PROTO-AGENT and PROTO-PATIENT. Langacker (1978) offers an integrated account of the meaning of the English auxiliary.

3.2   Motion Event Typology

The bifurcation of languages into verb-framed languages and satellite-framed languages is one of the most influential theories in Cognitive Linguistics. This theory, also known as the two-way typology, is developed on the basis of the detailed analysis of the meaning-form mapping in the representation of the motion event. It also represents a major contribution to the study of conceptual structuring and process in the semantic domain of motion and location. Chapter 1 and chapter 3 in Talmy (2000b) represent the most original and the most comprehensive literature on the two-way typology. Beavers et al. (2010) argues that most languages employ more than one strategy to encode motion, which is supported by Ji et al. (2011). Slobin (2004) emphasizes the manner element and extends the theory to equipotently-framed languages. Talmy (2016) specifically aims to refute Slobin's challenge based on equipollence. Croft et al. (2010) combines the two-way typology with grammaticalization. Bohnemeyer et al. (2007) proposes the term MACRO-EVENT PROPERTY (MEP), which refers to a property of constructions that assesses the event construal they convey—specifically, the 'tightness of packaging' of subevents in the construction, according to which languages are classified into three types. Li (2018) proposes a mechanism and motivation for typological shift in Mandarin.

3.3   Attention

Attention is a separate cognitive system proposed by Leonard Talmy. Two key terms related to attention are Figure and Ground. They are borrowed initially from cognitive psychology, now used in cognitive semantic analysis. Using the perspective of cognitive semantics, the windowing of attention is proposed to explain some event frames. Language can place a portion of a coherent referent situation into the foreground of attention by the explicit mention of that portion, while placing the remainder of that situation into the background of attention by omitting mention of it. A comprehensive version of Figure and Ground can be found in Talmy (2000d), which is substantially revised from the original first version of Talmy (1975). Talmy (2007) represents the most comprehensive and original contribution to the relationship between linguistic factors and the strength of attention. A systematic discussion on windowing of attention can be found in Talmy (2000c). De Vega et al. (2007) discusses how to locate Figure and Ground in the temporal domain. Khalil (2005) distinguishes Figure-

Ground and foregrounding-backgrounding on the textual level. Included in this larger framework of attention are Figure and Ground, windowing of attention, perspective, construal, etc. The cognitive system of attention is studied from different perspectives and levels.

3.4   *Force and Causation*

Following the philosophical foundation of Cognitive Linguistics holding that conceptual structure is intrinsically embodied, Talmy explores how the forces in the physical world are reflected in the conceptual structuring system and proposes the theory of *force dynamics*. Included in the theory is the exertion of force, resistance to such a force, the overcoming of such a resistance, blockage of the expression of force, removal of such blockage, and the like. Force dynamics is studied as a previously neglected semantic domain. It can be found in a range of linguistic domains, modal verbs, aspectual systems, sentence patterns. It is specifically related to causation and causative since it is a generalization over the traditional linguistic notion of causative. Talmy (1988) represents the very early seminal work on force dynamics. De Mulder (2007) provides a comprehensive review on this topic. Wolff (2017) extends force dynamics in explaining a series of causal phenomena. Wolff (2003) concerns direct causation and event individuation in a causal chain. Beebee et al. (2009) represents an important collection on causation. Shipley and Zacks (2008) represents an important handbook on understanding events from a psychological perspective. Koons (2000) is a philosophical work on causation, proposed from the teleological perspective. Copley and Martin (2014) intends to provide a unified account of causation from a psychological, philosophical and linguistic perspective.

3.5   *Macro-event*

The macro-event is a term proposed by Talmy in his two-way typology, that is, verb-framed languages and satellite-framed languages. It is an offspring of the motion typology, and has recently attracted much attention, establishing itself as a new area of research. Issues of interest concerned are semantic and syntactic features of macro-events, diachronic path of macro-events, and typology of macro-events. Li (2020) proposes the macro-event hypothesis, which claims that language can often represent a complex situation either more analytically in a set of simpler events, or more synthetically as a single integrated complex event, termed a "macro-event." Diachronically, a language might then progressively change its representation of a privileged relation from having solely a highly analytic one to also having a highly synthetic one. On this basis, languages may fall into two major categories: macro-event languages and non-macro-event languages, which then might be further divided into four distinctive types, respectively: steady state macro-event languages versus conflated macro-event languages, and steady state non-macro-event languages versus deconflated non-macro-event languages. Li (2019) studies the diachronic order of 5 types of macro-events, which paved the way for the proposal of the macro-event hypothesis in Li (2020). Goldberg and Jackendoff (2004) may be taken as research on the semantics of subevents as motivating the overall syntactic structure of macro-event. Rappaport Hovav and Levin (2001) offers an alternative approach to the event structure-to-syntax mapping. Aikhenvald (1999) studies the serial verb constructions (SVCs) and verb compounding in Tariana, a North Arawak language from northwest Amazonia. Altakhaineh and Zibin (2018) distinguishes serial verb constructions and V + V compounds.

3.6   *Space and Time*

Both space and time are basic domains in concept structuring. Cognitive semantics concerns the organizing functions in concept structuring using space and time, and the relationship between the two. In cognitive semantics, much attention has been given to image schemas, the recurring abstract patterns acquired from constant bodily interaction with the world. Image schemas are used to structure more abstract semantic domains. Chapter 3 in Talmy (2000a) analyzes the ways that language structures space. Mandler published a series of articles on image schemas, the most prominent being Mandler (2010) and Mandler and Canovas (2014). Evans (2013) argues about the ways in which how temporal reference is based on space. Levinson (2003) explores the relation between language and spatial cognition.

3.7   *Closed-Class Semantics*

Linguistic forms are traditionally classified into two classes, open-class and closed-class. A class of morphemes is considered open if it is quite large in number and readily augmentable. Open-class forms mainly include the roots of verbs, of nouns, and of adjectives. Otherwise, a class is considered closed if it is relatively small and fixed in membership. The inflections added to the roots of verbs, nouns and adjectives are closed-class forms, such as the plural form marker "s", past tense marker "-ed", and adverbial "-ly". Closed-class semantics (CCS) can also be called the semantics of grammar. In cognitive semantics, CCS concerns the cognitive basis of the general features of closed-class forms, that is, the overall shape and motivation of closed class. Chapter 1 in Talmy (2000a) discusses some important issues in CCS, including the constraint on grammatical meaning, some characteristics including neutralities, and the idea of a universally available inventory. Research in this area can also be related to some topics in grammaticalization, a path linking the open-class forms to the

closed-class ones. Bradley and Garrett (1983) explores the hemisphere difference in recognizing closed and open class, which might lend support to the idea
that open-class forms are responsible for conceptual contents, and closed-class
forms are responsible for conceptual structure. Haspelmath (1997) discusses
the conceptual transfer between space and time, and the universal differences
in expressing the basic domains of space and time. Biassou et al. (1997) conducted an experiment on the processing of open-class and closed-class words
in dual coding theory.

3.8   Cognitive Mechanisms

Broadly speaking, metaphor, metonymy, and analogy, are widely recognized as
cognitive mechanisms. The amount of literature on metaphor and metonymy
is large, but research on cognitive mechanism per se is rare. In Talmyan cognitive semantics, some cognitive mechanisms are mentioned, including conceptual splicing, cognitive operations, cognitive processing, etc., but not dealt
with in any depth. Grady (2000) discusses the cognitive mechanism that motivates conceptual integration. Ruiz de Mendoza and Galera (2014) extends the
idea that idealized cognitive models result from structuring principles working on conceptual material. Chen (2003) examines a cognitive mechanism of
incommensurability. Patel (2017) uses music to explore language relevant cognitive mechanism. Xu and Li (2011) explores the common cognitive mechanisms behind abduction and metaphor.

3.9   Diachronic Cognitive Semantics

Diachronic cognitive semantics (DCS) concerns patterns and regularities in
semantic change, and how they are motivated by cognitive mechanisms. Du
et al. (2020) explores the conceptual boundary shift among *break*, *cut*, and
open in Mandarin. Geeraerts (1997) studies the relation between prototype
and cognitive semantics from a diachronic perspective. Traugott and Dasher
(2001) reports recent developments in cross-linguistic research on historical
semantics and pragmatics, with special reference to the histories of English
and Japanese. Croft (2000) presents a framework for understanding language
change as a fundamentally evolutionary phenomenon.

3.10   Neurocognitive Semantics

Cognitive Linguistics has emphasized the study of the neural cognitive basis of
language from the very beginning of the enterprise. That is, what the "Cognitive" means in the name of "Cognitive Linguistics". Lakoff (1990) claims that
Cognitive Linguistics is defined by two primary commitments, the Generalization Commitment and the Cognitive Commitment. To study the mecha-

nisms, psychological realities, and most importantly, the neurocognitive basis of language has become a trend in Cognitive Linguistics. Conceptual metaphor theory has become very popular since early 1980s. Recently, this theory has been put under experimental test in psychology, such as Katz and Reid (2020). Gallese and Lakoff (2005) proposes a neural theory of concepts.

3.11   Cognitive Systems

In cognitive semantics, language itself is treated as a cognitive system which parallels other cognitive systems, including attention, perception, motor control, affect, forward simulation, inferencing, culture and so on. Talmy (2015) elucidates the organizing factors of these systems and proposes the overlapping systems model. The cognitive system of language itself consists of several sub-systems, termed schematic systems, including the following five: the schematic system of configurational structure, the schematic system of attention, the schematic system of force dynamics, the schematic system of perspective, and the schematic system of cognitive state. Chapter 1 in Talmy (2000a) has a detailed account of the first four types of schematic systems. Reboul (2015) argues from an evolutionary perspective that language is a cognitive system. Rupert (2019) presents a theory of individuation of cognitive systems.

3.12   Universals of Semantics

A semantic universal is any aspect of meaning that is represented in all languages. Talmy (2011) outlines three basic parameters of a universal, including the level of a universal, the weighting of a universal, and the subject of a universal. Semantic universality concerns basically the closed-class forms, that is, the grammatical forms. The natural semantic metalanguage (NSM), developed by Anna Wierzbicka and Cliff Goddard, represents another approach to universalist semantics. The NSM theory posits that a specific small set of fundamental concepts, terms semantic primes, exists in all languages. These semantic primes can represent the basic semantic content of that particular language. Wierzbicka (1996) represents the original and comprehensive account of the NSM theory, though not the earliest one. Goddard (2001) intends to justify the conclusions about some 100 semantic primes proposed by Wierzbicka (1996). The four-volume set by Greenberg (1978) represents the most comprehensive and possibly also the most authoritative work on language universals, even today.

The above are considered to be the core areas of cognitive semantics. Section 4 provides an overview of what is included in this handbook.

4   An Overview of the Handbook

The handbook contains 46 chapters. In Chapter 1, Talmy provides a taxonomy of cognitive semantics. In Chapter 2, the editor introduces cognitive semantics from a multi-level perspective. Besides the first two preliminary chapters, the contents are organized into 12 Parts containing the rest of the 44 chapters. Sections 4.1 to 4.12 below introduce these 12 Parts respectively, and describe how they are structured. Section 4.13 will show how these chapters can be fitted into the taxonomy described in chapter 1 by Talmy.

In terms of people, the 46 chapters are contributed by 49 contributors. The majority of the contributors are from the first-generation cognitive linguists and well-established second-generation cognitive linguists. In terms of countries, these contributors come from as many as 19 countries or districts, including Australia, Belgium, Canada, China, Czech Republic, Denmark, Germany, Hong Kong (SAR), Hungary, Iraq, Israel, Italy, Japan, Mexico, Poland, Spain, Sweden, UK, and USA.

Now I start with Part I.

4.1   *Part I: Conceptual Semantics*
The following fundamental cognitive semantic theories are characterized: NSM, Frame Semantics, Conceptual Semantics, and Simulation Semantics.

Chapter 3 (by Cliff Goddard, Anna Wierzbicka, and Zhengdao Ye) introduces the Natural Semantic Metalanguage (NSM) approach. NSM represents a widely accepted cognitive approach to meaning which uses a metalanguage of simple, cross-translatable words and grammar. This chapter illustrates the theory and practice, including concepts such as semantic primes, semantic molecules, and semantic templates.

As Goddard, Wierzbicka, and Ye described in this chapter:

> From a theory point of view, the most distinctive feature of the NSM approach is its insistence on the crucial importance of metalanguage, a consideration largely neglected by other approaches to cognitive semantics. From a practice point of view, its most distinctive features are its use of paraphrase as a technique for modelling meanings and concepts, and its "words-first" focus, including words-in-combination and words-in-construction.

Chapter 4 (by Esra' M. Abdelzaher) presents an overview of Frame Semantics, the most important theoretical contribution made by Charles Fillmore, one of the earliest founding figures in Cognitive Linguistics. Frame semantics represents a new stage that Fillmore achieved after years of working on Case Grammar, a much-elaborated version of Case Grammar. The basic claim that the existence of a lexical item entails its correspondence to a frame led to the emergence of many conceptions in cognitive semantics. It can also be taken as a prelude to construction grammar.

Chapter 5 (by Ronald W. Langacker) describes a conceptual semantic model on which Langacker based his cognitive grammar. In this model, construal is given an essentially important position. Construal is our ability to conceive and portray the same situation in different ways, including three broad classes: specificity, prominence, and perspective.

Chapter 6 (by Daniel Casasanto) presents a model of Embodied Semantics. This model's basic claims are that part of a word's meaning is a simulation of its referent, implemented in neural and cognitive systems that support perception, action, and emotion. The basic concepts of embodied meaning and simulation are characterized. Some empirical tests are introduced.

Chapter 7 (by Nian Liu) discusses more details of the Simulation Semantics hypothesis and highlights results from behavioral and neuroimaging studies to show that people create mental simulations in response to language.

Simulation Semantics is another term for Embodied Semantics. Chapter 6 and Chapter 7 are complementary to each other.

4.2   *Part II: Basic Issues*

Some basic issues are characterized, including the demarcation between semantics and pragmatics, the continuum of encyclopedic knowledge and linguistic meaning, meaning and intersubjectivity.

Chapter 8 (by Mira Ariel) compares the Gricean proposal for a semantics/pragmatics division of labor and for a Usage-Based approach. It applies the two approaches in analyzing the scalar *and*, and *or*, and has demonstrated the advantages of the Usage-Based approach.

Chapter 9 (by Patrick Duffley) surveys various issues pertaining to the cognitive linguistic view that there is no distinction between linguistic and extralinguistic knowledge, that is, there is no distinct boundary between a word's meaning and world knowledge.

Chapter 10 (by Magdalena Rybarczyk and Michael Stevens Pérez) attempts to incorporate intersubjectivity with meaning, aiming to bring recognition to the broader implications of the findings toward an account of embodied intersubjectivity and a methodology for studying it.

Chapter 11 (by Peter Harder) explicates how cognitive semantics has made important contributions to the understanding of political communication. It explains the role of so-called 'identity politics'. It is argued that identity politics calls for an analysis that takes into account not only the conceptual (or ideological) models that people identify with, but also addresses the relationship between those models and their grounding in social reality.

4.3   *Part III: Essential Concepts*

This part contains four chapters on some essentially important concepts in cognitive semantics, including Figure-Ground, Figure-Ground in temporal reference, the closed class and the open class, and conceptualization.

Chapter 12 (by Rong Chen) discusses Figure-Ground, one of the most important theoretical constructs in the study of cognitive semantics.

Chapter 13 (by Kevin Ezra Moore) is devoted to temporal Figure-Ground relationships, an extension of chapter 12.

Chapter 14 (by Ye Yuan) characterizes a universal bifurcation across natural languages, the open class and the closed class.

Chapter 15 (by Baoyi Niu) surveys varied aspects of conceptualization, which is equated with meaning in cognitive semantics.

4.4   *Part IV: Semantic Categories*

In part IV, we include three chapters on ideophones, degree modifiers, and possession.

Chapter 16 (by Thomas Van Hoey) studies the semantics of ideophones, also known as mimetics or expressives. Ideophones are defined as marked words that depict sensory imagery and belong to an open lexical class.

Chapter 17 (by Tuomas Huumo) surveys research on degree modifiers—words that modify other words, such as adjectives or adverbs, by specifying their scalar meanings—in relation with Figure and Ground, with specific examples from English and Finnish.

Chapter 18 (by Ricardo Maldonado) is on possession, a complex category involving an ample set of meanings and syntactic constructions.

4.5   *Part V: Methodology*

Part V contains four chapters on methodology, including data collection methods, quantitative methods, and person-oriented methods.

Chapter 19 (by Jürgen Bohnemeyer) surveys data collection methods for the study of linguistic meaning, that is, empirical approaches to semantic research, i.e., approaches that do not rely on the researcher's first (or "native") language speaker intuitions.

Chapter 20 (by Sally Rice) "addresses the application of cognitive semantic insights that put meaning and use front and center for linguists aiming for more veridical, situated, and intuitively comprehensible samples and analyses of language patterning in service of those on the front lines in endangered language communities working to support speakers and learners".

Chapter 21 (by Stefan Th. Gries) is on a range of quantitative methods, including frequencies/probabilities, association measures, hypothesis-testing methods, hypothesis-generating methods, and recent developments involving distributional semantics and deep learning.

Chapter 22 (by John Newman) introduces a 'person-oriented' approach to the study of language that focuses attention on the language use of the individual and the role that an individual's personal experience plays in influencing their language use.

4.6   *Part VI: Models and Schemas*

Part VI contains three chapters on the most important theoretical models: image schema, theory of prototype, and theory of cognitive domain.

Chapter 23 (by Aleksander Szwedek) defines image schema as "a mental structure with at least one OBJECT image schema conceptually independent and grounded in physical experience". This definition reveals a cognitive chain from perception through image schemas and their thematic roles to syntactic structures.

Chapter 24 (by Dirk Geeraerts) describes the psycholinguistic origins of prototype theory and illustrates prototype effects.

Chapter 25 (by Zeki Hamawand) reviews the theory of cognitive domains, which structure conceptually related items in the mind.

4.7   *Part VII: Space and Time*

Space and time are inseparable. Each exists as a pre-condition of the other.

> What, then, is time? If no one asks me, I know; but, if I want to explain it to a questioner, I do not know. Yet, I say with confidence that I know that, if nothing passed away, there would be no past time; if nothing were coming, there would be no future time; and if nothing were existing, there would be no present time (Augustine, 1953).

Chapter 26 (by Thora Tenbrink) addresses the conceptual frames of reference that are used to locate objects in space or events in time.

Chapter 27 (by Barbara Tversky) reviews literature of gesture and graphics in representing meaning.

Chapter 28 (by Yiting Chen) surveys the motivations behind various linguistic properties in complex words, based on the quasi-spatiotemporal relationship in baseline/elaboration (B/E) organization. According to this theory, word formation can be viewed as an elaboration that operates on a baseline.

Chapter 29 (by Wei-lun Lu) explores the issue of vertical viewpointing constructions in language, and presents an innovative method that helps identify
the correspondence and stability of viewpoint representation across languages.

4.8   Part VIII: Event Typology

Event typology represents one of the hot areas in cognitive semantics.

Chapter 30 (by Fuyin Thomas Li) enumerates some major criticisms of the
two-way typology, and provides some justifications and rebuttals, at the same
time proposing the macro-event hypothesis that language can often represent a complex situation either more analytically in a set of simpler events,
or more synthetically as a single integrated complex event, termed a "macro-
event".

Chapter 31 (by Liulin Zhang) analyzes the nature of verbal transitivity, which
is posited as residing solely in the likelihood of verbal semantics to relate two
or more distinct thematic roles. Semantically complex verbs, involving multiple event structures that can be profiled in diverse ways, tend to be somewhere
between prototypical transitive and prototypical intransitive verbs.

4.9   Part IX: Meaning Construction

Part IX contains eight chapters on various aspects of meaning construction,
including human scale meaning, metaphor and metonymy in speech acts, fictive motion and cognitive models, conceptual metaphor, lexico-encyclopedic
conceptual metaphor, analogy, meaning construction across languages, and
metaphoric gesture.

Chapter 32 (by Mark Turner) reviews "the ways in which both meaning and
communication systems that would otherwise be intractable become tractable
through varieties of compression in conceptual integration networks that
achieve human-scale blends."

Chapter 33 (by Klaus-Uwe Panther) "presents evidence for the thesis that
figures of thought and language play an important role in the interpretation of
speech acts."

Chapter 34 (by Francisco José Ruiz de Mendoza Ibáñez) "first provides an
overview of traditional work on the Talmyan notion of fictive motion, including experimental research by Matlock and her associates, which it then places
within the purview of a broader theory of cognition grounded in recent developments of the Lakoffian notion of the cognitive model."

Chapter 35 (by Javier Valenzuela and Iraide Ibarretxe-Antuñano) reviews
conceptual metaphor theory, a theory which has a profound influence in Cognitive Linguistics. "The postulates of CMT have had an enormous repercussion
and have been examined from very diverse disciplines within cognitive sci-

ence, including linguistics, philosophy, anthropology, psycholinguistics, neuroscience and artificial intelligence, among others."

Chapter 36 (by Marlene Johansson Falck) presents lexico-encyclopedic conceptual metaphors, which can be taken as the latest extension of Conceptual Metaphor Theory.

Chapter 37 (by Aleksander Gomola) demonstrates the significance of analogy in cognitive semantics and shows how it manifests itself in many linguistic phenomena.

Chapter 38 (by Mikołaj Deckert) aims "to show how cognitive constructs have been employed to talk about translation choices, with the underlying argument that the toolkit of Cognitive Linguistics offers much potential to scholars who wish to systematically and precisely examine translation phenomena in a range of language use contexts including literature and film."

Chapter 39 (by Yuan Gao and Juan Wang) "probes into the fundamental issues of metaphoric gestures from diverse perspectives."

4.10   Part X: Force and Causation

Part X contains two chapters on force and causation.

Chapter 40 (by Zoltán Kövecses) outlines an account of the relationship between Talmy's force dynamics and conceptual metaphor theory and puts together Talmy's force dynamics with conceptual metaphor theory in a coherent framework of ideas.

Chapter 41 (by Corrine Occhino) discusses the history of research on iconicity and force in signed language linguistics. It explains the importance of image schematic and force dynamic structures in the grammar of American Sign Language (ASL). It shows how force is systematically encoded in motivated meaning-form mappings in ASL.

4.11   Part XI: Attention

Chapter 42 (by Konrad Szczesniak) "looks at the role of attention in memorizing new sensory information, especially in what pertains to language learning. In keeping with cognitive linguistic usage-based models of language learning, it is assumed that the acquisition of language relies heavily on input, whose elements must be memorized."

Chapter 43 (by Giorgio Marchetti) presents a model of the cognitive architecture necessary to produce conscious experience (CE). The main cognitive systems of the model are attention and the self, which feeds, guides and modulates attention.

4.12   *Part XII: The Targeting System of Language*

The last three chapters contained in Part XII do not conform to the format of standard handbook chapters, typically review articles. The book *The Targeting System of Language* (Talmy, 2018a) was only recently published. In this part, we present only Talmy's theory and two applications.

Chapter 44 (by Leonard Talmy) proposes that a single cognitive system underlies the two domains of linguistic reference traditionally termed anaphora and deixis.

Chapter 45 (by Martina Lampert) probes into an extension of Talmy's Targeting System to quoting, and scrutinizes the model's two routes of targeting: algorithmic parsing versus trigger-to-cue-to-target processing.

Chapter 46 (by Günther Lampert) extends the range of targeting to explain evidentiality, sense activation, and discourse deixis.

5   Future Directions

The handbook aims to delineate the boundary of cognitive semantics, and intends to expand the boundary, even though such a boundary itself is blurred. The handbook holds fast to the definition that *cognitive semantics is an interdisciplinary approach to the study of meaning and mind*. This definition is consistent with the editorial claim made by the journal *Cognitive Semantics*. In section 5.1, we will describe the taxonomy of cognitive semantics (Chapter 1 in this volume) and how all other chapters fit in this taxonomy. Section 5.2 lists some other topic areas in cognitive semantics.

5.1   *Talmy's Taxonomy of Cognitive Semantics*

In chapter 1 of this handbook, Talmy provides a comprehensive and all-inclusive taxonomy of cognitive semantics in ten major categories. Here in this section, I intend to show how these 44 chapters (except chapter 1 and 2) are situated in the taxonomy. Some research gaps are revealed.

TABLE 2.1   Chapters in the taxonomy

Categories	Subcategories		Chapters
A. Major language divisions—The three main compartments of language	1. Form		
	2. Grammar		
	3. Meaning (semantics / pragmatics)		8, 30–39
B. Participant structure—the sending vs. receiving of a communication	1. Participant types		
	2. Participant numbers		
	3. Participant directionality		22
C. Arenas of assembly—the venues in which meaning-associated units come together	1. Inventory		9
	2. Expression		10, 16–18
	3. Part inventory part expression		
D. Content structuring mechanisms—the major systems by which language structures conceptual content	1. Closed-class semantics—the conceptual "schematic systems" represented by explicit or implicit elements of grammar	a. Configurational structure	14
		b. Perspective	26–29
		c. Attention	12, 13, 15, 42–46
		d. Force dynamics	40
		e. Cognitive state	11
		f. Reality status	
		g. Communicative purpose	
		h. Ontology	23–25
		i. Role semantics	
		j. Quantity	

TABLE 2.1   Chapters in the taxonomy (*cont.*)

Categories	Subcategories		Chapters
	2. Content patterning—the patterns in which the conceptual continuum is partitioned and arranged	a. In the morpheme	
		b. In the lexicon	
		c. In expression	
	3. Content selection—whether/which content is expressed by a speaker	a. Inclusion vs. omission	
		b. Alternatives for inclusion	
	4. Content inference—The hearer infers conceptual content additional to what is explicit		
	5. Context—constraints from, e.g., linguistic/thematic/physical/interlocutory/epistemic/social circumstances		
	6. Interaction—the structuring of content through cross-participant accommodation	a. Cross-consideration	
		b. Turn taking	
E. Combination—the patterns in which linguistic elements can combine	1. Additive		
	2. Operational		
	3. Idiomatic		
	4. Constructively discrepant		33, 35–36

TABLE 2.1   Chapters in the taxonomy (*cont.*)

Categories	Subcategories		Chapters
F. Diachronic comparison—comparing conceptual structures in a single language across different points of its temporal continuum	1. Long time scale		
	2. Medium time scale		
	3. Short time scale		
G. Crosslinguistic comparison—comparing conceptual structures across different (varieties of) languages	1. Absolutely universal		3–7
	2. Typological		28–29
	3. Repertorial		
	4. Indefinitely diverse		
H. Quantity of manifestation—(changes in) the amount of conceptual content that is represented or occurs	1. Elaboratedness—the comprehensiveness and granularity of conceptual content	a. In a communication system	
		b. In a language user	
		c. In a lexicon	
		d. In expression	
	2. Prevalence—the frequency of occurrence of conceptual content	a. Compared across languages	
		b. Usage in a single language	
I. Communication systems—the use of different channels based on the mode of the sender's production and the receiver's perception	1. Co-speech gesture		44–46
	2. Signed language		41

TABLE 2.1   Chapters in the taxonomy (*cont.*)

Categories	Subcategories		Chapters
J. Research characteristics—the methodologies and other aspects of approach that shape a language study			19–21

5.2   *Other Topics in Cognitive Semantics*

The central concern in cognitive semantics will be characterized through the chapters in the handbook. Meanwhile we stick to the definition that *cognitive semantics is an interdisciplinary approach to the study of meaning and mind*. This definition is consistent with the editorial claim made in the inner cover page of *Cognitive Semantics*, a journal devoted to the enterprise. We hold the position that the Cognitive Linguistics approach to meaning is complementary with the approach taken by Generative Grammar (GG). The two approaches are not opposed to each other.

References

Aikhenbald, Alexandra Y. 1999. Serial constructions and verb compounding: Evidence from Tariana (North Arawak). *Studies in Language* 23(3): 469–497.

Altakhaineh, Abdel R.M., and Aseel Zibin. 2018. Verb + verb compound and serial verb construction in Jordanian Arabic (JA) and English. *Lingua* 201: 45–56.

Augustine, A. 1953. *Confessions*. Vernon J. Bourke (transl.). Washington: The Catholic University of America Press.

Beavers, John, Beth Levin, and Shiao Wei Tham. 2010. The typology of motion expressions revisited. *Journal of Linguistics* 46(2): 331–377.

Beebee, Helen, Christopher Hitchcock, and Peter Menzies. 2009. *The Oxford Handbook of Causation*. Oxford: Oxford University Press.

Biassou, Nadia, Loraine K. Obler, Jean-Luc Nespoulous, Monique Dordain, and Katherine S. Harris. 1997. Dual processing of open- and closed-class words. *Brain and Language* 57(3): 360–373.

Bohnemeyer, Juergen, Nicholas J. Enfield, James Essegbey, Iraide Ibarretxe-Antunano, Sotari Kita, Frederika Lupke, and Felix K. Ameka. 2007. Principles of event segmentation in language: The case of motion events. *Language* 83(3): 495–532.

Bradley, Dianne C., and Merrill F. Garrett. 1983. Hemisphere differences in the recognition of closed and open class words. *Neuropsychologia* 21(2): 155–159.

Chen, Xiang. 2003. Object and event concepts: A cognitive mechanism of incommensurability. *Philosophy of Science* 70(5): 962–974.

Copley, Bridget and Fabienne Martin. 2014. *Causation in Grammatical Structures*. Oxford: Oxford University Press.

Croft, William. 2000. *Explaining Language Change*. England: Pearson Education Limited.

Croft, William, Jóhanna Barðdal, Willem Hollmann, Violeta Sotirova and Chiaki Taoka. 2010. Revising Talmy's typological classification of complex event constructions. In H.C. Boas (ed.), *Contrastive Studies in Construction Grammar* 201–236. Amsterdam: John Benjamins.

De Mulder, Walter. 2007. Force dynamics. In D. Geeraerts and H. Cuyckens (eds.). *The Oxford Handbook of Cognitive Linguistics*, 294–317. Oxford: Oxford University Press.

De Vega, Manuel, Mike Rinck, Jose M. Díaz and Inmaculada León. 2007. Figure and ground in temporal sentences: The role of the adverbs when and while. *Discourse Processes* 43(1): 1–23.

Dowty, David. 1991. Thematic proto-roles and argument selection. *Language* 67(3): 547–619.

Du, Jing, Fuyin Thomas Li, and Mengmin Xu. 2020. Pò (BREAK), qiē (CUT) and kāi (OPEN) in Chinese: A diachronic conceptual variational approach. *Review of Cognitive Linguistics* 18(1): 213–243.

Evans, Vyvyan. 2013. Temporal frames of reference. *Cognitive Linguistics* 24(3): 393–435.

Fauconnier, Gilles. 2018. *Ten Lectures on Cognitive Construction of Meaning*. Leiden: Brill.

Fauconnier, Gilles, and Mark Turner. 1998. Conceptual integration networks. *Cognitive Science* 22(2): 133–187.

Gallese, Vittorio and George Lakoff. 2005. The brain's concepts: The role of the sensory-motor system in conceptual knowledge. *Cognitive Neuropsychology* 22(3): 455–479.

Geeraerts, Dirk. 1997. *Diachronic Prototype Semantics*. Oxford: Oxford University Press.

Geeraerts, Dirk. 2018. *Ten Lectures on Cognitive Sociolinguistics*. Leiden: Brill.

Goddard, Cliff. 2001. Lexico-semantic universals: A critical overview. *Linguistic Typology* 5(1): 1–65.

Goddard, Cliff. 2018. *Ten Lectures on Natural Semantic Metalanguage*. Leiden: Brill.

Goldberg, Adele E. and Ray Jackendoff. 2004. The English resultative as a family of constructions. *Language* 80(3): 532–568.

Grady, Joseph. 2000. Cognitive mechanisms of conceptual integration. *Cognitive Linguistics* 11(3): 335–345.

Greenberg, Joseph H. (ed.). 1978. *Universals of Human Language*, volumes I–IV. Stanford: Stanford University Press.

Gries, Stefan Th. 2017. *Ten Lectures on Quantitative Approaches in Cognitive Linguistics: Corpus-linguistic, Experimental, and Statistical Applications*. Leiden: Brill.

Gries, Stefan Th. 2019. *Ten Lectures on Corpus Linguistics with R: Applications for Usage-Based and Psycholinguistic Research*. Leiden: Brill.

Haspelmath, Martin. 1997. *From Space to Time Temporal Adverbials in the World's Languages*. München: Lincom Europa.

Ji, Yinglin, Henriette Hendriks and Maya Hickmann. 2011. The expression of caused motion events in Chinese and in English: Some typological issues. *Linguistics* 49(5): 1041–1077.

Johnson, Mark. 1987. *The Body in the Mind: The Bodily Basis of Meaning, Imagination, and Reason*. Chicago: University of Chicago Press.

Katz, Albert N. and J. Nick Reid. 2020. Tests of conceptual metaphor theory with episodic memory tests. *Cognitive Semantics* 6(1): 56–82.

Khalil, Esam N. 2005. Grounding between figure-ground and foregrounding-backgrounding. *Annual Review of Cognitive Linguistics* 3: 1–21.

Koons, R.C. 2000. *Realism Regained: An Exact Theory of Causation, Teleology, and the Mind*. New York: Oxford University Press.

Lakoff, George. 1987. *Women, Fire, and Dangerous Things: What Categories Reveal about the Mind*. Chicago: The University of Chicago Press.

Lakoff, George. 1990. The invariance hypothesis: Is abstract reason based on image-schemas? *Cognitive Linguistics* 1(1): 39–74.

Lakoff, George. 2018. *Ten Lectures on Cognitive Linguistics*. Leiden: Brill.

Lakoff, George, and Mark Johnson. 1980/2003. *Metaphors We Live By* (2nd ed.). Chicago: University of Chicago Press.

Langacker, Ronald W. 1978. The form and meaning of the English auxiliary. *Language* 54(4): 853–882.

Langacker, Ronald. 1987. *Foundations of Cognitive Grammar*, volume I. Stanford: Stanford University Press.

Langacker, Ronald. 1991. *Foundations of Cognitive Grammar*, volume II. Stanford: Stanford University Press.

Langacker, Ronald. 2017. *Ten Lectures on the Elaboration of Cognitive Grammar*. Leiden: Brill.

Levinson, Stephen C. 2003. *Space in Language and Cognition: Explorations in Cognitive Diversity*. Cambridge, UK: Cambridge University Press.

Li, Thomas Fuyin. 2018. Extending the Talmyan typology: A case study of the macro-event as event integration and grammaticalization in Mandarin. *Cognitive Linguistics* 29(3): 585–621.

Li, Thomas Fuyin. 2019. Evolutionary order of macro-events in Mandarin. *Review of Cognitive Linguistics* 17(1): 155–186.

Li, Thomas Fuyin. 2020. Macro-event hypothesis and its empirical studies in Mandarin. *Foreign Language Teaching and Research* 52(3): 349–360.

Li, Thomas Fuyin. 2021. Cognitive semantics. In M. Aronoff (ed.), *Oxford Bibliographies in Linguistics*. New York: Oxford University Press.

Mandler, Jean M. 2010. The spatial foundations of the conceptual system. *Language and Cognition* 2(1): 21–44.

Mandler, Jean M. and Cristobal Pagan Canovas. 2014. On defining image schemas. *Language and Cognition* 6(4): 510–532.

Patel, Aniruddh D. 2017. Using music to study the evolution of cognitive mechanisms relevant to language. *Psychonomic Bulletin and Review* 24: 177–180.

Rappaport Hovav, Malka and Beth Levin. 2001. An event structure account of English resultatives. *Language* 77(4): 766–797.

Reboul, Anne C. 2015. Why language really is not a communication system: A cognitive view of language evolution. *Frontiers in Psychology* 6(1434): 1–12.

Rosch, Eleanor. 1973. Natural categories. *Cognitive Psychology* 4(3): 328–350.

Ruiz de Mendoza, F.J. and Galera, A. 2014. Cognitive modeling: A linguistic perspective. Amsterdam: John Benjamins.

Rupert, Robert D. 2019. What is a cognitive system? In defense of the conditional probability of co-contribution account. *Cognitive Semantics* 5(2): 175–200.

Rupert, Robert D. 2022. *Ten Lectures on Cognition, Mental Representation, and the Self.* Leiden: Brill.

Shipley, Thomas and Jeffrey M. Zacks. 2008. *Understanding Events.* Oxford: Oxford University Press.

Slobin, Dan I. 2004. The many ways to search for a frog: Linguistic typology and the expression of motion events. In S. Strömqvist and L. Verhoeven (eds.), *Relating Events in Narrative: Typological and Contextual Perspectives*, 219–257. Mahwah: Lawrence Erlbaum Associates.

Talmy, Leonard. 1975. Figure and ground in complex sentences. *Proceedings of the First Annual Meeting of the Berkeley Linguistics Society*, 419–430. Available at https://journals.linguisticsociety.org/proceedings/index.php/BLS/article/view/2322/2092.

Talmy, Leonard. 1988. Force dynamics in language and cognition. *Cognitive Science* 12(1): 49–100.

Talmy, Leonard. 2000a. *Toward a Cognitive Semantics*, volume I: *Concept Structuring Systems*. Cambridge, MA: MIT Press.

Talmy, Leonard. 2000b. *Toward a Cognitive Semantics*, volume II: *Typology and Process in Concept Structuring*. Cambridge, MA: MIT Press.

Talmy, Leonard. 2000c. The windowing of attention in languages. In L. Talmy (2000a), *Toward a Cognitive Semantics*, volume I: *Concept Structuring Systems*, 257–309. Cambridge, MA: MIT Press.

Talmy, Leonard. 2000d. Figure and ground in languages. In L. Talmy (2000a) *Toward a Cognitive Semantics*, volume I: *Concept Structuring Systems*, 311–344. Cambridge, MA: MIT Press.

Talmy, Leonard. 2007. Attention phenomena. In D. Geeraerts and H. Cuyckens (eds.), *The Oxford Handbook of Cognitive Linguistics*, 264–293. Oxford: Oxford University Press.

Talmy, Leonard. 2011. Universals of semantics. In P. Hogan (ed.), *Cambridge Encyclopedia of the Language Sciences*, 754–757. Cambridge, UK: Cambridge University Press.

Talmy, Leonard. 2015. Relating language to other cognitive systems: An overview. *Cognitive Semantics*. 1(1): 1–44.

Talmy, Leonard. 2016. Properties of main verbs. *Cognitive Semantics* 2(2): 133–163.

Talmy, Leonard. 2018a. *The Targeting System of Language*. Cambridge, MA: MIT Press

Talmy, Leonard. 2018b. *Ten Lectures on Cognitive Semantics*. Leiden: Brill.

Taylor, John. 2003. *Linguistic Categorization: Prototype in Linguistic Theory*. Oxford: Clarendon Press.

Taylor, John. 2018. *Ten Lectures on Applied Cognitive Linguistics*. Leiden: Brill.

Traugott, Elizabeth Closs and Richard B. Dasher. 2001. *Regularity in Semantic Change*. Cambridge, UK: Cambridge University Press.

Wierzbicka, Anna. 1996. *Semantics: Primes and Universals*. Oxford: Oxford University Press.

Wolff, Phillip. 2003. Direct causation in the linguistic coding and individuation of causal events. *Cognition* 88(1): 1–48.

Wolff, Phillip. 2017. Force dynamics. In M.R. Waldmann (ed.), *The Oxford Handbook of Causal Reasoning*, 1–37. Oxford: Oxford University Press.

Xu, Cihua and Li Hengwei. 2011. Abduction and metaphor: An inquiry into common cognitive mechanism. *Frontiers of Philosophy in China* 6(3): 480–491.

Zacks, Jeffrey M. 2019. *Ten Lectures on the Representation of Events in Language, Perception, Memory, and Action Control*. Leiden: Brill.

PART 1

Conceptual Semantics

∵

CHAPTER 3

The Natural Semantic Metalanguage (NSM) Approach

Cliff Goddard, Anna Wierzbicka, and Zhengdao Ye

1 Critical Issues for Cognitive Semantics

1.1 *Opening Remarks*

The NSM approach is a cognitive approach to meaning which uses a metalanguage of simple, cross-translatable words and grammar. At base, this metalanguage relies on 65 semantic/conceptual primes (often termed simply, semantic primes), for example: I and YOU, SOMEONE and SOMETHING, HAPPEN and DO, WANT and KNOW, GOOD and BAD, IF and BECAUSE. Semantic/conceptual primes are posited to be shared human concepts. Evidence accumulated over 30+ years suggests that they manifest themselves as words or word-like expressions in all human languages (Goddard and Wierzbicka, 2014a; Goddard, 2011; 2018a).

From a theoretical point of view, the most distinctive feature of the NSM approach is its insistence on the crucial importance of metalanguage, a consideration largely neglected by other approaches to cognitive semantics. From a practice point of view, its most distinctive features are its use of paraphrase as a technique for modelling meanings and concepts, and its "words-first" focus, including words-in-combination and words-in-construction.

The only other major school of semantics which acknowledges the fundamental importance of metalanguage is the Moscow Semantic School, whose leading figures are Jurij Apresjan and Igor Mel'čuk. Within cognitive linguistics, NSM's closest affiliations are with Frame Semantics and with Cultural Linguistics, as conceived by Farzad Sharifian (2011).

1.2 *Why Semantic Metalanguage Must Be Based On Natural Language*

The logic behind the NSM approach can be summarized as follows. In order to describe the meanings of words or concepts, there is simply no choice but to use words themselves, or other derivative or language-dependent devices, such as logical symbols or diagrams (see below). One therefore needs to choose one's words—one's theoretical vocabulary—very carefully. In order to avoid getting tangled up in conceptual circularity and confusion, the safest strategy is to rely on words (more precisely, word-meanings) which are as clear and simple as possible. In addition, in order to avoid any hidden Anglo/Euro bias, it is preferable to rely on words and meanings which have equivalents in all or most languages.

The ideal semantic metalanguage, i.e. a language for describing meanings and concepts, therefore consists of words which are maximally clear and simple in meaning and maximally cross-translatable between languages. NSM linguists have been working for nearly four decades to construct and refine such a metalanguage, on the basis of empirical cross-linguistic evidence. The NSM metalanguage, which is now regarded as substantially complete, is described in Section 2.

Most cognitive linguists prefer to use technical or semi-technical terms instead of "ordinary" words from natural language. Expanding briefly, one can list five reasons for favouring a semantic metalanguage based on the words and meanings of natural language:

(i)   To be cognitively authentic. If we want to understand the content of people's everyday thinking, as expressed in language, it seems self-defeating to represent that thinking in terms which are obscure or even unrecognizable to the people concerned.

(ii)   For clarity. The technical terminology of cognitive linguistics is plagued by "problems of definition." Scholars often disagree about the correct or preferred meanings of their own technical terms, and different scholars often use the same terms with somewhat different meanings. This problem can be reduced if explanations and definitions can be grounded in simple everyday words.

(iii)   To avoid circularity. Even in ordinary language, a definition or explanation which is circular, i.e. self-referential, explains nothing; as for example, when 'light' is explained as 'illumination,' and 'illumination' as 'light.' Technical terms and other neologisms are particularly prone to circularity.

(iv)   For a high standard of verifiability. Unlike technical terms, paraphrases in ordinary language can be substituted into contexts of use and checked against the intuitions of ordinary speakers.

(v)   To be practical. Many cognitive linguists want to see their research findings applied to real-world problems, e.g. in language teaching, intercultural education, combatting misinformation. If the basic research is carried out in terms which are close to natural language, it becomes easier to communicate the findings to non-specialists.

1.3   *A Note on Diagrams*

Many varieties of cognitive semantics make extensive use of diagrams of various kinds, such as image schemas, integration networks, semantic maps, Cognitive Grammar schemas. There is no doubt that diagrams can be very helpful but NSM linguists point out that no diagram can be semiotically self-contained. Any diagram stands in need of verbal support. To take a simple example, even a circle with an "X" inside it does not, in and of itself, stand for the concept INSIDE, although it may serve to represent that concept once it has been linked with words like "Inside" or "Container Schema."

Many cognitive semantic diagrams are very complex, relying on culture-specific iconography, such as the arrow symbol → to indicate movement or connection; or purpose-built icons, such as • to represent "tendency to rest" in Force Dynamic diagrams; or technical captions, such as "TR" for "Trajector" in Cognitive Grammar diagrams. Expert practitioners, who can read these diagrams fluently, are prone to forget how opaque they are for the uninitiated. The point is that when one looks at a diagram and "sees" meaning in it, one is depending on certain interpretive conventions which can only be stated explicitly in words.

The same applies to the data visualizations used in "distributive semantics" to summarize the associations between words in massive collections of texts. Until and unless they are interpreted into words, visualizations are merely summaries of raw quantitative data. This is not an issue which is specific to linguistics but a general semiotic problem turning on the relationship between quantitative (i.e., number-based) data and qualitative (i.e., concept-based) interpretation.

One cannot assign meanings, describe concepts, or identify categories—let alone discuss them—except in some language. Some fundamental questions then arise: In what language or metalanguage? In whose language or metalanguage?

1.4   *Meanings vs. Functions*

In many areas of linguistics, including in cognitive semantics, the terms "meaning" and "function" are not clearly distinguished, and, indeed, even in ordinary language, the word *meaning* has (ironically) many meanings. In NSM semantics, the "meaning" of a word, expression, or construction is a paraphrase substitutable into the same contexts of use as the original word, expression, or construction. This is similar to the traditional concept of meaning as reflected in ordinary dictionaries. Given this understanding, it should be obvious that the same meaning can serve many functions; or, to put it another way, the same meaning can have many uses.

In principle NSM linguists have no problem with language analysis or discourse analysis carried out in terms of "functions," although in our view understanding a word's meaning helps a great deal in understanding its range of functions.

2 Theory and Practice of NSM Approach

2.1 *Universal Semantic Primes and Conceptual Grammar*
2.1.1 The Mini-lexicon of Semantic/Conceptual Primes
The NSM approach depends on empirical findings from a long program of cross-linguistic research which indicate the existence of a small set of elementary concepts, i.e. semantic/conceptual primes, that are expressible by means of words or word-like expressions in all languages. Words which stand for semantic/conceptual primes in a given language are known as exponents of primes. Table 3.1 lists the full inventory of primes, using English exponents. Comparable tables have been drawn up for about 30 languages. The Notes at the bottom of Table 3.1 summarize a number of important points which will be discussed in some detail in section 2.2.

Primes can be combined into phrases, sentences and texts in ways which also appear to be essentially language-independent, in the sense that the same combinations can be realized in all languages, despite formal differences in word order, case marking, etc. In short, the NSM claim is that every language has an irreducible conceptual core: a mini-lexicon of semantic/conceptual primes and a mini-syntax whereby they can be combined.

The proposition that semantic/conceptual primes and their grammar are fundamentally the same in all languages has two profound implications: first, that the bedrock of human thinking is the same for all humans, i.e. that there truly is some "psychic unity" among all the people of the world; second, that all natural languages are equally adequate to represent their own semantics via language-internal paraphrase; i.e., belief in the "metasemantic adequacy" of all natural languages.

TABLE 3.1   Semantic/conceptual primes, English exponents (after Goddard & Wierzbicka 2014a)

I, YOU, SOMEONE, SOMETHING~THING, PEOPLE, BODY	substantives
KINDS, (HAVE) PARTS	relational substantives

TABLE 3.1   Semantic/conceptual primes, English exponents (*cont.*)

THIS, THE SAME, OTHER~ELSE	determiners
ONE, TWO, SOME, ALL, MUCH~MANY, LITTLE~FEW	quantifiers
GOOD, BAD	evaluators
BIG, SMALL	descriptors
KNOW, THINK, WANT, DON'T WANT, FEEL, SEE, HEAR	mental predicates
SAY, WORDS, TRUE	speech
DO, HAPPEN, MOVE	actions, events, movement
BE (SOMEWHERE), THERE IS, BE (SOME- ONE/SOMETHING)	location, existence, specification
(IS) MINE	possession
LIVE, DIE	life and death
TIME~WHEN, NOW, BEFORE, AFTER, A LONG TIME, A SHORT TIME, FOR SOME TIME, MOMENT	time
PLACE~WHERE, HERE, ABOVE, BELOW, FAR, NEAR, SIDE, INSIDE, TOUCH	place
NOT, MAYBE, CAN, BECAUSE, IF	logical concepts
VERY, MORE	augmentor, intensifier
LIKE	similarity

Notes: – Exponents of primes can be polysemous, i.e., they can have other, additional meanings – Exponents of primes may be words, bound morphemes, or phrasemes – They can be formally complex – They can have language-specific combinatorial variants (allolexes, indicated with ~) – Each prime has well-specified syntactic (combinatorial) properties.

2.1.2   Semantic Explications

What is a semantic explication? It is a paraphrase in simpler words, i.e. a way of saying the thing as another word or expression, using simpler words. The accuracy of a semantic explication is to be gauged by the extent to which it "mimics" and accounts for the semantic properties of the original word or expression (how well it substitutes into natural contexts of use, its relations with other words, its entailments, implications, and so on), and the extent to which it satisfies the intuitions of native speakers.

When devising explications, NSM researchers undertake a process of conceptual analysis but at the same time they typically take account of a wide range of linguistic evidence, such as usage patterns accessible from linguistic corpora, collocational data, and syntactic properties, including micro-syntactic constructional patterns. A good explication ought to allow an integrated account of a wide range of formal and distributional properties of a word.

Over four decades NSM researchers have proposed literally thousands of semantic explications, each one embodying a highly concrete hypothesis about the meaning of a word, phrase or construction. A comprehensive bibliography is available at the website (nsm-approach.net), which also has a search function for locating published explications. A useful starter-list of references is as follows: Amberber (2007), Bromhead (2018), Bromhead and Ye (2020), Farese (2018a), Goddard (2013, 2018a, 2021b), Goddard and Wierzbicka (2014a), Goddard and Ye (2016), Levisen and Waters (2017), Peeters, Mullan and Sadow (2020), Tien (2015), Wierzbicka (1997; 1999; 2014), Ye (2017).

NSM explications are not external descriptions but ways of capturing human understandings. It therefore makes sense that they often contain components such as the following:

> people can think about it like this: ...
> often when someone does this, it is like this: ....
> people often do this because they think like this: ...

Explications typically range from 5–25 lines of semantic text. The repeated use of simple words and grammar gives them an unusual stylistic quality which can be disconcerting at first. Despite the simple phrasing of individual components, explications often display great complexity when considered as a whole. Writing explications typically takes weeks or months, often passing through many iterations.

To see what explications look like, consider (A)–(C) below. Here we are not concerned with justifying the details of content or phrasing, but rather with drawing out some general points about explications. First, an explication taken as a whole is a rather complex structure. It appears to be an empirical fact that many human concepts have this kind of intricate structure.

Second, one can note the range and diversity of semantic primes that typically occur in explications. Between them, explications (A)–(C) use more than half the prime inventory. This underlines the point that to have a solid foundation for cognitive semantics one ideally needs a fully-fledged metalanguage.

Third, explications are essentially texts, and as such they have discursive and aesthetic properties. Explications (A)–(C) exhibit a hard-to-capture property that one might call "flow": the order of components makes sense, there is good cohesion between the individual lines, and the explication as a whole feels balanced and complete.

(A) *sky*

    a very big place, it is above all the places where people live
    in all places where people live, people can see this very big place
    they can see it far above the places where they live

(B) *hands*

    people's bodies have many parts, these are two of them, one is like the other
    when people think about their bodies, they can think about these two parts
      like this:
        "they are on two sides of the body
        one of them is on one side of the body, one is on the other side of the
          body
        these two parts have many parts
        people can move these two parts of the body as they want"
    because people's bodies have these two parts, people can do many things
      with many things as they want

(C) *children*

    people of one kind
    all people are people of this kind for some time
    when someone is someone of this kind, it is like this:
      this someone's body is small
      this someone can do some things, this someone can't do many other things
      because of this, if other people don't often do good things for this someone,
        bad things can happen to this someone

Explications (A)–(C) are all composed exclusively in semantic primes. NSM research indicates that meanings from many domains, such emotion terms, speech-acts, value terms, and discourse particles, can be successfully explicated directly into semantic primes. Equally however, it is true that explications for innumerable words and concepts cannot be composed in terms of semantic primes alone. They require not only semantic primes but also certain more complex words (termed, semantic molecules), which are themselves decomposable into primes but which function alongside primes as "chunks" of meaning.

(D) below shows an explication of moderate complexity that employs semantic molecules in addition to primes. By convention, molecules are marked in explications with the notation [m]. In this chapter, molecules are marked only once in each explication, at first use.

(D)   (the) sun
        something
        people in many places can often see this something in the sky [m] during the
            day [m]
        they can't see it at night [m]
        when people see it, they can think like this: "it is big, it is round [m]"
        sometimes people in a place can see it above this place for some time,
            sometimes they can feel something in their bodies because of it
        for some time during the day, people can see this something on one side of the
            sky, after this for some time, they can see it on the other side of the sky

Explication (D) uses four semantic molecules: 'sky' (whose explication is given above), 'during the day,' 'at night,' and 'round.' Very complex explications may include a dozen or more semantic molecules. For more detail on semantic molecules, cf. 2.3.1.

2.1.3   A Note on Polysemy

One of the advantages of the NSM system is that it provides a procedure for operationalizing the traditional distinction between semantic generality, on the one hand, and polysemy, on the other. A word can be said to have a single general meaning if its range of use can be covered by a single explication, i.e., by a single non-circular paraphrase. Conversely, a word is polysemous if two (or more) related explications are necessary. Paraphrase into semantic primes thus provides a litmus test, sometimes termed the "language-internal paraphrase test," for distinguishing between semantic generality and polysemy (Wierzbicka, 1996: Ch 8–9; Goddard, 2000; Goddard and Wierzbicka, 2014a: 28–29).

2.2   *Identifying Exponents of Semantic Primes*

Readers are advised that a document titled "150 Sentences for identifying NSM semantic primes in different languages" is available on the internet (nsm-approach.net).

2.2.1   The "Strong Lexicalization Hypothesis"

One of the foundational publications in NSM research was the collective volume *Semantic and Lexical Universals* (Goddard and Wierzbicka, 1994). In that volume one of the present authors formulated the "Strong Lexicalisation Hypothesis" as follows: "Every semantically primitive meaning can be expressed through a distinct word, morpheme or fixed phrase in every language."

Having said this, he immediately went on as follows:

> This does not entail that there should be a single unique form for each primitive. Some languages have several forms (allolexes or allomorphs of the same item) functioning as contextual variants expressing the same primitive meaning. Conversely, it sometimes happens that the same form serves as an exponent of different primitives, although their distinct syntactic frames make it appropriate to recognise polysemy
>
> GODDARD, 1994: 13

Unfortunately, this explanation has often been overlooked, leading to the common misconception that NSM theory expects every language to have a single, unique word for each prime. When identifying words for semantic primes, one has to be aware of several potential complications: allolexy and polysemy, as mentioned in the quote above, and also portmanteau expressions.

2.2.2   Allolexy and Portmanteau Expressions

Allolexy is when two or more words in the semantic metalanguage can each serve as exponents of a single semantic prime. A simple example is *other* and *else* in English. The words are termed allolexes. Allolexes are typically used in different contexts. Often one of them can be designated as the primary allolex and used as a citation form for the prime. One can say, for example, that English *else* is an allolex of the prime OTHER. To take another example, in some languages GOOD and BAD have adverbial allolexes. One can say that English *well* is an allolex of GOOD in contexts such as: *I know this man/woman well* and *Few people can do this well*. In inflectional languages, many words display complex patterns of allolexy.

Essential to the concept of allolexy is that there is no viable, non-circular way to capture any semantic difference between the items in question in the form of a substitutable paraphrase. It is also important to note that allolexy is a relationship that only applies within the confines of the NSM metalanguage. This means that words can be allolexes in the NSM based on a particular language without necessarily being synonyms in the 'full' language.[1]

---

1   In full English, for example, *good* and *well* are not always synonymous because there are contrasts between sentences like *You look good* vs. *You look well*. Sentences like these are not possible, however, within the restricted lexicon and grammar of the NSM metalanguage. Moreover, in English *You look well, I feel well*, etc. the word *well* is used in a distinct health-related sense (cf. the form *unwell*), which is different from its meaning in *I know him well* and *Few people can do this well*.

As for portmanteau expressions, this refers to the situation in which a combination of primes is expressed as a single word, e.g. English *often* for 'at many times,' Polish *tak* for 'like this.' In some languages, certain combinations of primes can only be realised via portmanteaus. For more on allolexy and portmanteaus, see Goddard (2002: 20–23).

2.2.3   Polysemy of Exponents of Semantic Primes

As mentioned, exponents of semantic primes are often polysemous and this is only to be expected given that they are usually high-frequency words. After 30 years research, much is known about recurrent patterns of polysemy involving exponents of semantic primes. See Table 3.2.

TABLE 3.2   Selected common polysemies of exponents of semantic primes

Semantic prime	Additional meaning(s)	Language and relevant lexical item
DO	make	Amharic (*adərrəgə*), Ewe (*wɔ*), Italian (*fare*), Kalam (*g-*), Malay (*buat*), Mbula (*-kam*), Russian (*delat'*), Spanish (*hacer*), Swedish (*göra*), Yankunytjatjara (*paḻyani*)
FEEL	taste and/or smell	Ewe (*se le lãme*), Italian (*sentire*), Kalam (*ŋŋ*), Malay (*rasa*), Russian (*čuvstvovat'*), Spanish (*sentir*)
	hear	Amharic (*tə-səmma-*), Italian (*sentire*), Kalam (*ŋŋ*), Spanish (*sentir*)
	feel by touch	Acehnese (*rasa*), English (*feel*), Italian (*sentire*), Spanish (*sentir*)
BEFORE	first	Kalam (*nd*), Kayardild (*ngariija*), Lao (*kòòn¹*), Mbula (*muŋgu*), Samoan (*muamua*)
	ahead of and/or in front of	Kalam (*nd*), Kayardild (*ngariija*), Russian (*do*), Samoan (*muamua*)
WORDS	what is said and/or message	Amharic (*k'al*), English (*words*), Malay (*perkataan*), Mbula (*sua*), Russian (*slova*)
	talk and/or language	Amharic (*k'al*), Kayardild (*kangka*), Korean (*mal*), Mandarin (*huà*), Mbula (*sua*)

DATA FROM STUDIES IN GODDARD AND WIERZBICKA, 1994; 2002; PEETERS, 2006; GODDARD, 2008; GLADKOVA, 2010

As mentioned in 2.1.3, normal cases of lexical polysemy can be resolved using paraphrase analysis. A more puzzling situation, which can pose serious problems of interpretation, is when two (or more) semantic primes are expressed by the same word form. This is not ordinary polysemy since two primitive meanings cannot have any semantic components in common. To suggest a kind of affiliation between meanings which is not based on shared components, NSM researchers have long used the term 'non-compositional polysemy,' though perhaps a more recent term 'co-lexicalization' (borrowed from lexical typology) would be more suitable.

To give three simple examples, it is known that in some languages, such as Samoan, the exponents of DO and SAY share the same form; in others, such as Polish, CAN and MAYBE share the same form; in still others, VERY and BIG share the same form. These are obviously not accidental coincidences. The meanings are similar to one another, even though neither of them can be paraphrased into simpler terms.

Non-compositional polysemy (co-lexicalization) of primes can make it look as if a semantic prime is missing from a language, so it is essential to note that each of the distinct meanings appears unambiguously in certain lexicogrammatical contexts. As well, in many languages the different meanings are associated with different morphosyntactic properties. For example, in Samoan the two meanings of the verb *fai*, DO and SAY, appear unambiguously the contexts shown in (1) and (2), respectively. As well, *fai* as DO takes an ergative-marked subject, while *fai* as SAY takes an absolutive subject (Goddard 2002: 17–18).[2]

(1) *'ua   fa'apênâ lava   ona fai e   le   tama.*
     PERF like.this EMPH   that do ERG the youth
     "The youth did it like this."

(2) *Ona   toe   fai atu lea   'o   le   fafine,   "Se, ...*
     Then again   say DIR then   ABS the woman friend
     "Then the woman said again, 'Friend, ...'"

From the point of view of its lexical status, the most controversial semantic prime is PARTS, or, as we now prefer to cite it: HAVE PARTS.[3] Goddard and

---

2 Interlinear glosses for Samoan sentences (1) and (2) (from Mosel, 1994) are: ABS absolutive, DIR directional, ERG ergative, EMPH emphatic particle, PERF perfect.

3 Goddard and Wierzbicka (1994: 46) stated that "Rather than ... taking a form analogous to English *part of*, recent research suggests an exponent with the converse orientation is more widely attested, that is, an element like HAVE PARTS." Despite this, for many years the prime was listed in NSM tables as PART.

Wierzbicka (1994) already acknowledged that there are languages which lack a distinct word like English *part*, but argued that in many such languages the same meaning can be expressed by the word for 'something,' 'thing,' or 'what,' used in a specific lexicogrammatical frame. They adduced supporting examples about parts of the body from several languages (Yankunytjatjara, Acehnese, Mangaaba-Mbula). Their argumentation has sometimes been challenged or rejected, however, even by linguists with some sympathy for the NSM approach.

Seeking to refine the NSM position, Wierzbicka (2021) focuses on one specific lexicogrammatical context in which, she argues, the "parts" concept ought to be clearly expressible in all languages, namely, in a sentence like: "people's bodies have many parts (one of them is the liver)." If in a language without a word like English *part*, such a sentence appears as "people's bodies have many things," this clearly shows that in this context the expression 'has many things' expresses the same meaning as "has many parts."

A further complication is that in some languages the equivalent expression does not, or at least need not, include a word corresponding to 'thing' or 'things' at all. A much discussed example is the following, from the Australian language Warlpiri. It comes from a translation of a passage in the Bible (1 Cor 12:12).

(3)   *Yapa-kurlangurlu palkangku-ka mardarni jurru, rdaka-jarra, wirliya-jarra manu panu-kari.* (Warlpiri)

      "A person's body (*palka*) has (*mardarni*) a head, two arms, two legs and many others (*panu-kari*)."

Notice that there is no word in the Warlpiri sentence corresponding to 'things.' Even so, for NSM linguists it is clear that when a Warlpiri translator writes that a person's body (*palka*) "has" (*mardarni*) a head (*jurru*), arms (*rdaka-jarra*), and "and many others" (*munu panu-kari*), the same generalization is being expressed as would be expressed in English by saying "has many other parts."[4] We may perhaps term this a "portmanteau strategy."

Leaving Warlpiri at this juncture, there are three further points to be made about the expression of HAVE PARTS. First, it appears that the portmanteau

---

4   For critics Nash and Wilkins (2020), the meaning expressed by Warlpiri *mardarni*, even in this context, is not HAVE PARTS but "possession" or a "possessive relationship." For a cognitive semantic critique of this technical usage of "possession" in linguistic jargon, see Goddard and Wierzbicka (2019).

strategy is the favored way of expressing it in other languages as well. For example, the Algonquian languages East Cree, Atikamekw and Innu have verbs that when used about a group of people or things, mean 'there.are.two (of them)' and 'there.are.many (of them).' However, when used about a singular-marked subject, and about an object or the body (not about a person), they express the meanings "have two parts" and "have many parts," respectively. One can say about a knife, for example, that 'there.are.two (of it),' meaning "it has two parts" (Marie-Odile Junker personal email, September 30, 2020).

The second point to be mentioned is that in English and other European languages the word 'part' is polysemous in ways which have led NSM linguists to overuse it in explications. In particular, English *part* can sometimes be an exponent of SOME, as in a sentence like *Part of the meat was burnt*. Wierzbicka and Goddard (2017: 52) admit that "(A) lack of clarity and a measure of confusion between PART and SOME ... may have contributed to the misunderstandings surrounding the universal status of PARTS."

For more on the polysemy of semantic primes and allegedly missing exponents, see Goddard (2002: 24–30; 2008: 8–11), Goddard and Wierzbicka (2014b), Farese (2018b).

2.3   *More Detail on Key NSM Concepts*

2.3.1   Semantic Molecules

As mentioned in 2.1.2, semantic molecules are packages of meaning, encapsulated in words, that function alongside semantic primes as building blocks of meaning. This section expands on this uniquely NSM concept and backgrounds current research, under four points.

First, whether a word is or isn't a semantic molecule can only be determined by careful analysis of a large number of interrelated words. Semantic molecules should not be posited merely for convenience, i.e., to save the analyst time and effort. This would open the floodgates to arbitrariness. As well, first impressions can be misleading. For example, linguists often refer to English *punch*, *slap*, and *kick* as "verbs of hitting"; yet it can be shown that 'hit' is not needed as a molecule in explications for these verbs and that English *hit* actually contains some semantic components that make it unsuitable for this purpose. It is also known that words for 'hit' vary greatly across languages.

Second, there can be molecules within molecules, reflecting semantic dependencies between concepts of differing levels of complexity (see Figure 3.1). This architecture enables the mind to hold and manipulate huge amounts of conceptual content.

Third, research suggests that certain semantic molecules are likely to be found with precisely the same conceptual makeup in all or most languages,

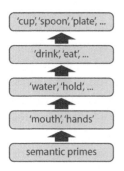

FIGURE 3.1
How complex concepts are successively built up from simpler ones.
GODDARD 2018A

betokening shared human experience. Equally, however, there are aspects of shared human experience that are not associated with any strictly universal words. 'Eat' and 'drink,' for example, are not strictly universal because some languages use one verb to cover both activities, and in others the semantic boundary between them is drawn differently to English (Newman, 2009; Ye, 2010). Even so, it can hardly be doubted that the nearest equivalents to 'eat' and 'drink' are semantic molecules in any language.[5] Such examples are termed "approximate" universal molecules. Equally, it is clear that there are language/culture-specific semantic molecules, which are tied to local geography, history and culture. These can be extremely important to the conceptual structure of their respective languages and to habitual ways of thinking in their respective cultures. The "literacy-related" molecules 'read,' 'write,' and 'book,' for example, are important in many concepts related to modern life, as are the molecules 'number,' 'money,' and 'God.' Many culture-specific molecules are not confined to a single language or culture, but are found across a broad cultural area. A sample of proposed semantic molecules of different kinds is given in Figure 3.2.

Fourth, findings about semantic molecules can have far-reaching implications for our understanding not only of lexical semantics, but for human cognition in general (cf. Goddard, Wierzbicka, and Fábrega, 2014; Goddard and Wierzbicka, 2021a).

2.3.2   Semantic Templates

A key concept of NSM semantics is the idea of semantic templates (Goddard, 2012). This means an arrangement of component types which is shared by

---

5   It would violate NSM assumptions to posit 'ingest food' as a universal semantic molecule (as suggested by one reviewer) because complex words like 'ingest' and 'food' lack equivalents in many languages.

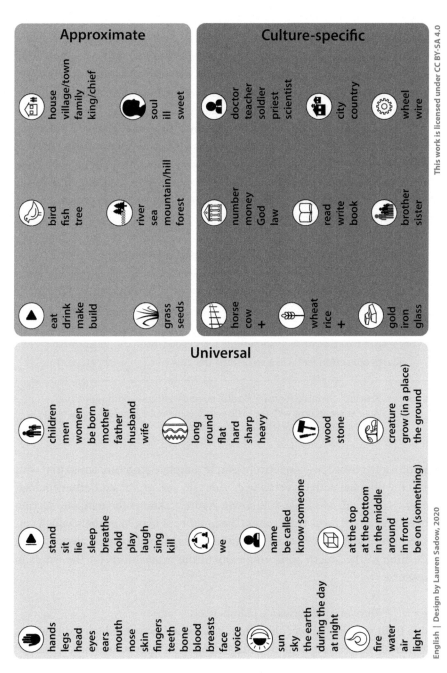

FIGURE 3.2 Selection of proposed semantic molecules of different kinds: universal, approximate, culture-specific.

English | Design by Lauren Sadow, 2020

words of a particular semantic class or subclass. In any language, one may expect dozens of templates for various subclasses of verbs, nouns, adjectives, and so on. From a cognitive point of view, templates assist with managing large volumes of conceptual content. Presumably semantic templates arise as generalizations over high-frequency exemplar words, whose conceptual structures are acquired and elaborated in early childhood.

Semantic templates differ considerably in complexity. Figure 3.3 shows a simple template structure, applicable to many English emotion adjectives. It has three main sections, which can be labelled Prototypical Thought, Feeling, and Typicality. This explication structure enables subtle meaning differences to be modeled, largely on account of the great variety which is possible in the Prototypical Thought section.

Someone X is afraid, angry, ashamed, etc. ... (*at this time*)

---

a.	this someone X thinks like this (at this time):	PROTOTYPICAL
	"----	THOUGHT
	----"	
b.	because of this, he/she feels something (very) good/bad	FEELING
c.	like people often feel when they think like this	TYPICALITY

FIGURE 3.3   Semantic template for many English emotion adjectives with verb 'to be'.
           Note: For sentences with the main verb 'feel,' a similar-but-different template is
           needed, with a different order of components.

Emotion adjectives have a relatively simple template structure compared with those for physical activity verbs (e.g., *run, eat, cut, grind*) and ethnozoological terms (e.g., *cat, horse, fox, kangaroo*). Figure 3.4 shows the template section labels for words of these two classes. The number of template labels, which corresponds to the number of sections needed in the explications, gives a rough indication of the length and complexity of the explications for the words in question.

2.3.3   Derivational Bases ((d) Elements)

Aside from semantic molecules, there is a second way in which explications can include complex lexical meanings: namely, as derivational bases, marked in explications as (d). Whereas semantic molecules appear in many concepts and domains, derivational bases enter into explications in a much more localized fashion.

LEXICOSYNTACTIC FRAME	CATEGORY
PROTOTYPICAL SCENARIO	MAIN FEATURES
HOW IT HAPPENS (MANNER)	WHERE THEY LIVE
POTENTIAL OUTCOME	SIZE
	BODY
	SOUNDS
	BEHAVIOR
	RELATION TO PEOPLE
	HOW PEOPLE THINK ABOUT THEM

FIGURE 3.4 Template section labels for physical activity verbs (left) and ethnozoological terms (right).

The concept of (d) elements was first developed to deal with derivational relationships, e.g., between the words *ill* and *illness*, or between the noun *knife* and the verb *to knife* (*someone*). The idea is that the simpler of the two meanings appears inside the explication of the more complex one, i.e., the explication of *illness* includes 'ill (d)'; the explication of *to knife* includes 'knife (d).' The notion of (d) elements has since turned out to have far broader applications; e.g., in NSM accounts of valency alternations and semantically specialized grammatical constructions (Goddard, 2018a: Ch 8; Goddard 2020a).

2.3.4   Lexicosyntactic Molecules

The notion of lexicosyntactic molecules is a recent development in NSM theory. The basic idea is that some semantic primes can appear in grammatical constructions which are decomposable but which nonetheless function as chunks in the explications of other concepts. Essentially, the prime-in-construction functions like a semantic molecule. To date, this idea has been worked through chiefly in relation to the so-called *that*-complement of KNOW (see below) and in relation to "possessive" constructions (Goddard and Wierzbicka, 2016; 2019). We will look briefly at the first of these.

KNOW is one of the oldest semantic primes. For decades it was believed that one of its inherent syntactic properties was its capacity to take a propositional complement, often described, using English-based terminology, as a *that*-complement. Accordingly, accounts of NSM syntax included this construction as part of the grammar of the natural semantic metalanguage. In recent years, however, a pathway has opened up whereby the propositional complement construction with KNOW can be decomposed (Wierzbicka, 2018a; Goddard, 2020b).

It is now proposed that 'know that' sentences can be decomposed as shown below in (E) and (F) below. They represent a kind of grammatical packaging whereby several meaning components are expressed in a single complex sentence. These explications also show how the phenomenon of referential opacity can be modeled in paraphrases, but this is not an angle we can pursue here.

(E) *I know that he did it.*
     it is like this: he (= this someone) did it
     I know it

(F) *He knows that I did it.*
     it is like this: I did it
     he (= this someone) knows it

Despite their non-primitive status, it appears that 'know that ...' sentences, especially in the first-person, are needed in explications for many words where it is necessary to spell out speaker assumptions (e.g. speech act verbs; cf. Goddard and Wierzbicka, 2014a: Ch 7).

Though much work remains to be done in this area, it seems clear that lexicosyntactic molecules are cognitively real, just as (lexical) semantic molecules are cognitively real. It is possible that some grammatical frames in the metalanguage which are presently regarded as basic and irreducible will also turn out be "molecular."

2.4   Revising Explications

NSM researchers often revisit and revise earlier explications, sometimes in response to new evidence and argumentation, sometimes in response to changes in the NSM metalanguage itself. This section presents two examples based on recent work. Both revisions were prompted by our improved understanding of the semantic prime (HAVE) PARTS, mentioned in 2.2.3; but while implementing the necessary changes, it turned out that other improvements could be made at the same time.

Below are two explications for "head": one from 2012, one from 2021. Broadly speaking, one could say that both are referentially adequate, in the sense that they would be sufficient to pick out the intended class of referents. The reader is invited to read and reflect on both of them, before considering the commentary below.

(G) *head (someone's head)* (Goddard, 2012)
     one part of someone's body
     this part is like something round [m]

this part is above all the other parts of the body
when someone thinks about something, something happens in this part
   of this someone's body

(H)   *head (someone's head)* (Goddard and Wierzbicka 2021b)
people's bodies have many parts, this is one of them
when people think about people's bodies, they can think about this part
   like this:
      "it is above everything else
      it is big, it is round [m]
      people can move it when they want"
at the same time they can think about this part like this:
      "it has some parts not like anything else in the body
      because it has these parts, people can know many things about the
         places where they are"
because people's bodies have such a part, people can know many things
   about many things

Comparing the two explications, one can see that the recent version (H) is more explicit, has additional content, and relies more on the HAVE PARTS frame. It begins with an explicit overall statement about human bodies ("people's bodies have many parts") and then identifies the head as one of them. It also has a clear template structure, falling into several sections.

The second section of explication (H) is introduced by a line with no counterpart in the earlier version. This line ("when people think about people's bodies, they can think about this part like this: ...") makes it clear that what follows are conventional ways of thinking, rather than "objective" statements. In response to the earlier version (G) it might be questioned whether someone's head can be validly described as 'above all other parts of the body.' What about when the person is lying down, for example? In (H), however, the claim is only that people **can think** of their heads as above the rest of their bodies. The third section of (H) says that people are aware that the head has "some parts not like anything else in the body" (alluding to eyes, ears, and nose), which enable people to know "about the places where they are."

The final section of (H) spells out the affordances of the head: "because people's bodies have such a part, people can know many things about many things." For more discussion, see Goddard and Wierzbicka (2021b).[6]

---

6 'Eyes' and 'ears' are not mentioned by name in explication (H) because to do so would incur

'Sharp [m]' is needed as a semantic molecule for verbs of "cutting" and for nouns like 'knife,' 'axe,' 'sword,' 'saw,' etc. The two explications below are both based on the same idea, i.e. that when something comes into contact with 'something sharp' there can be a localized "penetrating effect." To save space, only the relevant parts of the two explications are given here.[7]

(I)   *sharp*, e.g. *This thing is sharp* (Goddard and Wierzbicka, 2014a: 74) (partial)
        (…)

> "if this thing moves when some parts of it are touching something else,
>   something can happen to this other thing because of it
> it can happen in one moment
> when it happens, some parts of this thing can be inside this other thing
>   because of it

(J)   *sharp*, e.g. *This is something sharp* (December 2021, unpublished) (partial)
        (…)

> "if this thing moves when it is touching something else in some places,
>   it can be like this:
>   some of it is inside this something else for some time
>   something happens to this something else because of this

The idea of selective contact and a localized effect "penetrating effect" is implemented differently in the two explications. In the earlier version (I) it was done using expressions involving 'parts' in a context not referring to discrete parts. Such uses are not cross-translatable and are therefore no longer allowed in the NSM metalanguage, cf. 2.2.3. In the recent version (J), these components have been re-worded in two ways. First, there is greater use of the prime PLACE (e.g. "touching … in some places"). Second, when it is necessary to refer to a non-discrete "part" of the sharp thing (essentially, a portion of the blade or sharp edge), a newly proposed combination for SOME, i.e. SOME (OF) SOMETHING, is used. Admittedly, further research is needed before this strategy can be regarded as secure.[8]

---

circularity. Explications for these words both include 'head' by way of indicating their location; for example, the explication for 'eyes' includes the components: 'they are on one side of the head [m], they are small, one is near the other.'

7   As well, both explications include a final "anthropocentric" component, not shown here, saying, roughly speaking, that sharp things have the potential to cause harm to the body.

8   The phrasing of (J) implies that when a pin or thorn is described as 'sharp,' a slightly different

3   Examples of NSM Studies

3.1   *Major NSM Research Themes*
Major research themes in the NSM approach can be roughly grouped as follows.
– Cross-linguistic lexical semantics
– Cultural key words
– Lexicogrammar
– Discourse particles, interjections and terms of address
– NSM metalanguage studies
– Cultural and historical semantics of English
– Ethnopragmatics (not covered in this chapter)
The remainder of this section presents sketches of NSM research in three areas: kinship semantics, lexicogrammar, and cultural keywords. In each case the coverage is condensed and partial for reasons of space.

3.2   *Kinship Semantics*
Kinship plays an indispensable role in all human societies. Arguably, the lexical semantics of kin terms is the most reliable window on how speakers of a language conceptualize their kin (family) relationships. NSM studies in kin semantics have been largely driven by Anna Wierzbicka (1992: Ch 9; 2013; 2016; 2017). Among the challenges facing kinship semantics are its inherent complexity and the quest to achieve psychological reality (aka cognitive authenticity).

3.2.1   Background
Perhaps the greatest barrier to achieving cognitive authenticity is the inappropriate use of culture-bound descriptive terminologies from English when these do not correspond to indigenous or local categories. For example, many languages outside Europe do not have words corresponding to 'brother' and 'sister,' because they have distinct words for older brother and for older sister, as opposed to younger brothers and sisters. Of course, describing the situation in such a fashion, i.e. using culture-bound terms like English 'brother' and 'sister,' precisely illustrates the problem of terminological ethnocentrism.

(polysemic) meaning is invoked, if only because the "sharp point" of a pin, thorn, etc., normally touches and penetrates in one place, not 'in some places.' This analysis concurs with languages like Korean, which have different words for "sharp like a knife" and "sharp like a pin."

Wierzbicka (2013; 2016; 2017) argues that kin semantics can be placed on a non-ethnocentric footing if anchored in meanings which are universal: specifically, *men, women, children, mother, father, wife, husband,* and *be born.*

A useful semantic template for kin terms is shown in a schematic fashion in Figure 3.5. Section (a) of the template links two people by stating that one can describe the other by using a kinship "label" in a first-person frame, i.e. by saying "this is my so-and-so." Section (b) states that this possibility is conditional upon a speaker being able to think about the other person in a certain way. Included in this way of thinking are various configurations of the basic kinship molecules. Section (c) allows explications to be adapted to persons of different biological genders and stages of life.

person-X's "so-and-so" (e.g. *brother, daughter, uncle, cousin, ...*)

---

a.   someone, person-X can say about this someone: this is my 'so-and-so'
b.   someone can say this about someone else if they can think about this
     someone else like this:
        " .... "
        " .... "
c.   someone can say this about a man [m]/woman [m], someone can
     say this about a child [m] if after some time this child can be a
     man/woman

FIGURE 3.5 A partial and schematic semantic template for kin terms

To see how this works in practice, consider explications (K) and (L) below. Explication (K) is for the core or central meaning of the English word *brother*, which according to Wierzbicka (2016; 2017), has equivalents in all European languages. Explication (L) is for the core or central meaning of the Pitjantjatjara word *maḻanypa*. Pitjantjatjara is an indigenous language from Central Australia (Goddard and Defina, 2020). Like other Australian languages, it has no general term corresponding to English 'brother.' Using English-based terminology, one can say that older brothers are termed *kuṯa*, older sisters are termed *kangkuṟu*, and younger siblings of both genders are termed *maḻanypa*.[9]

---

9 Explications (K) and (L) employ English 'singular *they*' as a convenient portmanteau expression for "this someone."

(K)   *person-X's brother* (English)

    someone, person-X can say about this someone: this is my 'brother'
    someone can say this about someone else if they can think about this some-
        one else like this:
        "their mother [m] is my mother, their father [m] is my father"
    someone can say this about a man [m], someone can say this about a child [m]
        if after some time this child can be a man

(L)   *person-X's malanypa* (Pitjantjatjara)

    someone, person-X can say about this someone: this is my 'malanypa'
    someone can say this about someone else if they can think about this some-
        one else like this:
        "their mother [m] is my mother, their father [m] is my father
        they were born [m] after me"

Comparing the explications, it can be seen that *brother* and *malanypa* have something in common, i.e. both designate someone who shares the same mother and father as oneself. *Brother*, however, can only be used about a man or about a male child, i.e. a child who is a "potential man." Birth-order is irrelevant. In contrast, *malanypa* can only be used about those born after oneself. Biological gender is irrelevant.[10]

In cross-linguistic perspective, then, it is clear that 'brother' is not a lexical universal. It is a culture-bound term. Even so, this does not mean that it cannot play a role as a semantic molecule in languages which do have such a word, such as the languages of Europe. Indeed, it can well be argued that 'brother' is needed—in the interests of conceptual authenticity—as a culture-specific semantic molecule (cf. 2.3.1) in explications of various kin terms in European languages, including English *uncle*. Native speakers do not hesitate to explain the core meaning of *uncle* as 'the brother of someone's mother or father.'

Re-framing this idea into a semantic explication leads to explication (M).[11]

---

10   Pitjantjatjara has a classificatory kin system, meaning that kinterms are used far beyond one's immediate and extended family: potentially, everyone one knows can be regarded as falling into a kinship relationship with oneself. Explication (L) is therefore only one part of the picture. For discussion of the polysemy and extended uses of Pitjantjatjara kinterms, see Wierzbicka (2013).

11   Two notes on explication (M): (i) The explication assumes that "uncle words" are focussed on adult referents, i.e. on men. Limitations of space preclude discussion of this point. (ii) To say that European uncle-words depend on the semantic molecule 'brother' does not

(M) *person-X's uncle* (English)
      a man [m], person-X can say about this man: this is my 'uncle'
      someone can say this about a man if they can think about this man like this:
          "he is my mother's [m] brother [m]"
      someone can say this about a man if they can think about this man like this:
          "he is my father's [m] brother"

For speakers of many languages outside Europe, the meaning expressed in (M) seems strange, if not bizarre, in that it lumps together relationships which are seen as very different from one another. Sinitic languages are a case in point.

3.2.2   "Uncle-Terms" in Sinitic Languages

Compared with European languages, the kinship lexicons of Sinitic languages draw a great number of fine-grained semantic distinctions. Among these are multiple terms which are semantically related to English *uncle*. This section, based on Xue (2016), deals with uncle-terms in Sinitic languages. It focuses on Cantonese (specifically Guangzhou Cantonese: henceforth, GZ Cantonese), but the situation in relation to uncle-terms is essentially identical in Mandarin and other Sinitic languages.[12] Only referential or designative uses are considered here.

Xue (2016) argues that in order to achieve cognitive authenticity, explications for Sinitic uncle-terms must include four Chinese-specific semantic molecules, whose closest English translations are 'older brother,' 'younger brother,' 'older sister,' and 'younger sister.' From a Chinese point of view, the distinctiveness of each of these kin relations is self-evident. It is reinforced from childhood in address practices and in kinship-related songs and stories for children. Predictably, nearly all the many Chinese apps for calculating kin terms, such as 'Chēnghū' (称呼 'Terms of Address') and 'Qīnqi Láile' (亲戚来了 'Here Come the Relatives'), treat the four proposed Chinese-specific molecules as "kin digits" for the purpose of kin calculation.

Explications (N) and (O) show how the two Chinese-specific "brother molecules" can be explicated, using the GZ Cantonese forms *agō* (阿哥) and

---

imply that their meanings are identical in every respect. Wierzbicka (2017) argues that Russian and Polish uncle-words (*djadja* and *wujek*, respectively) have additional components reflecting the viewpoint of a child.

12   The romanization for GZ Cantonese is a modified Yale system. Xue's (2016) study also describes the similar but not identical kin system of Teochow (Min), considering additional terms, such as those for affinal uncles, and many points of detail not covered here. Overall, her findings show a greater-than-expected diversity in Han Chinese kin semantics.

sailóu (细佬). Parallel explications can be posited for *jèhjē* (姐姐) and *mùih-múi* (妹妹) which designate older and younger sisters, respectively, with the semantic molecule 'woman' substituted for 'man.'

(N)   person-X's *agō* (阿哥) "older brother" (GZ Cantonese)
       someone, person-X can say about this someone: this is my 'agō'
       someone can say this about someone else if they can think about this some-
            one else like this:
            "his mother [m] is my mother, his father [m] is my father
            he was born [m] before me"
       someone can say this about a man [m], someone can say this about a child [m]
            if after some time this child can be a man

(O)   person-X's *sailóu* (细佬) "younger brother" (GZ Cantonese)
       someone, person-X can say about this someone: this is my 'sailóu'
       someone can say this about someone else if they can think about this some-
            one else like this:
            "his mother [m] is my mother, his father [m] is my father
            he was born [m] after me"
       someone can say this about a man [m], someone can say this about a child [m]
            if after some time this child can be a man

The two Chinese-specific "brother terms" (*agō* and *sailóu* in GZ Cantonese) are needed in the explications of Chinese uncle-terms, both on the father's side and on the mother's side. In GZ Cantonese the situation is clearest on the father's side. There are two interchangeable terms for father's older brothers: *baakfuh* (伯父) and *a-baak* (阿伯). They are explicated in (P). Likewise, there are two interchangeable terms for father's younger brothers: *sūksūk* (叔叔) and *a-sūk* (阿叔). They can be explicated in similar fashion, as shown in (Q).[13]

(P)   *person-X's baakfuh* (伯父)/*a-baak* (阿伯) (GZ Cantonese)
       a man [m], person-X can say about this man: this is my 'baakfuh/a-baak'
       someone can say this about a man if this someone can think about this man
            like this:
            "he is my father's [m] agō [m]"

---

13   There are also terms for the first-born of one's father's older brothers (*daaihbaak* [大伯], *daaihbaakfuh* [大伯父], where *daaih* 大 means 'big') and for the last-born of his younger brothers (*lāaisūk* [孻叔], *saisūk* [细叔]). Affinal uncles, another essential category in Sinitic languages, involve further complexities.

(Q)   *person-X's sūksūk* (叔叔)/*a-sūk* (阿叔). (GZ Cantonese)
      a man [m], person-X can say about this man: this is my 'sūksūk/a-sūk'
      someone can say this about a man if this someone can think about this man
        like this:
            "he is my father's [m] sailóu [m]"

The situation on the mother's side is a little different and cannot be dealt with
here in any detail. In brief, GZ Cantonese has a general word *kauhfú* (舅父) for
mother's brothers, both older and younger; but birth-order is still important
on account of the existence of specialised terms for first-born mother's brother
daaihkauhfú (大舅父) and last-born mother's brother *saikauhfú* (细舅父); cf.
Note 13.

   It should be clear that using *agō* [m] and *sailóu* [m] as semantic molecules
creates a simpler and more coherent set of explications, as well as satisfying
native speaker intuitions.

3.3   *Syntax and Semantics of Verbs of Cognition*
3.3.1   Background
Verbs of cognition are, or ought to be, a topic of great interest for cognitive
semanticists of all persuasions. For reasons of space, we can make only two
points here, from the standpoint of the NSM approach. First, the inventory of
semantic primes provides a rich palette of cognitive and experiential primes:
WANT, DON'T WANT, THINK, KNOW, SEE, HEAR, and FEEL. These have important implications for modeling human subjectivity and intersubjectivity.

   Second, in this domain, as in all others, it is important not to unthinkingly
adopt English-specific terms as an informal metalanguage, a practice which
is unfortunately rife not only in linguistics but also in cognitive psychology.
We refer to English-specific terms such as *mind, memory, believe* and *trust*. For
critiques and alternative ways forward, see Amberber (2007), Goddard (2010;
2013), and Levisen (2017).

   In the case study reported below, we address another aspect of cognitive
verbs, namely, their propensity to exhibit complex complementation syntax,
by which we mean their capacity to appear with embedded clauses that, so to
speak, depict the "content" of mental states, i.e. to say what we know, what we
want, what we think, and so on.

   In many languages a given cognitive verb may appear with several different
complement formations, and so it is with the English verb *forget*. Section 3.3.2
seeks to show that each of the major complement types with *forget* expresses a
different-but-related meaning. In so doing, it provides a case study in the NSM
approach to constructional semantics.

3.3.2   Three Lexicogrammatical Constructions with English *forget*
This section is based on Goddard (2007). That study was corpus-assisted. It set out to cover a wide range of uses and constructions of the English verb *forget*, including in fixed expressions. This section reports selectively on a single aspect, namely, the semantics of three different complement constructions, normally designated as *to*-complement, *that*-complement and *wh*-complement. See examples below.

(4)   I forgot to lock the door this morning.

(5)   I'm sorry, I forgot that you've never done this before.

(6)   I forgot where I put my keys.

Forget *with to*-complement. One notable property of *forget* with a *to*-complement is sometimes termed factivity, or more precisely, in the case of *forget*, "counter-factivity." Sentence (4), for example, conveys the message that I did not lock the door. Similarly, a sentence like *I forgot to mention one important thing* conveys the message that I did not mention that one important thing. Indeed, the assertion that someone didn't do something seems quite central to the meaning of *forget*, in conjunction, of course, with a certain explanation of that fact, i.e. that although the person intended to do it, they didn't think about it at the relevant time.

   Explication (R) attempts to accommodate these observations in an explication. Section (a) identifies the assertion part of the utterance, as indicated by the illocutionary expression 'I say.' The components in (b) and (c) set out what could be termed the presuppositions: namely, that I had thought about the situation before and that I wanted to perform the action in question.'

(R)   *I forgot to lock the door (at that time)*, i.e. forget to VP (do something)
          a. (I say:) I didn't do something (lock the door) at that time
                 because I didn't think about it at that time
          b. I thought about it before
          c. I wanted to do it

Forget *with that-complement.* While the *to*-complement construction involves DO and WANT, the *that*-complement construction involves KNOW. Roughly speaking, 'to forget that Z' means to know that Z, but not to think about it at the designated time. It does not mean that the knowledge has gone out of your head forever; one can, after all, forget something for a while or for a moment.

(S)   (*at that time*) *I forgot that you've never done this before*, i.e. forget that (--)s
      a. I knew that (--)s (e.g. you've never done this before)
      b. (I say:) I didn't think about it at that time
      c. I thought about it before

Forget *with* wh-*complement* (*forget where, what, why, etc.*). *Wh*-complements
are also concerned with "knowing," as indicated (among other ways) by the
high frequency of examples like *I know I put it around here somewhere, but I
forget where*. Such an utterance is focused very much on the present moment:
I am trying to think of it now, but I can't. It is not implied that the knowledge has gone forever (although it may have), but I was able to think of it at
some earlier time and the implication is that I ought to be able to think of it
now.

   Wh-complements with *forget* can be explicated as shown below in (T).
Notice the wording of section (a), which includes an unspecified "topic of
cognition" argument in the first line ('I can think like this about a place'),
followed by a corresponding specified argument in the second line ('I put
it in this place'). The first mention allows the semantic type of the information to be characterized (a person, thing, place, time, etc.) which correlates with the identity of the *wh*-item (who, what, where, when, etc.), while
the second mention sees the implied referent embedded into the complement.

(T)   *I forget where I put it*, i.e. forget wh- ...
      a. I know that I can think like this about a place:
              "I put it in this place"
      b. (I say:) I can't think like this now
      c. I could think like this before

Aside from the inherent interest of cognitive verbs, the study provides an example of a set of interrelated lexicogrammatical constructions, each with a specific meaning.

3.4   *Cultural Key Words*
3.4.1   Background
The idea of cultural "key words," i.e. the notion that certain important words
function as focal points in culturally shaped ways of thinking, acting, feeling,
and speaking, is not confined to NSM semantics. It is a leading idea in cognitive linguistics generally, in cultural anthropology and in communication studies. In some cases, key words rise to public attention and may become iconic

of whole cultures, but they often remain below conscious awareness, even as entire cultural discourses are built around them (Wierzbicka, 1997; Levisen and Waters, 2017).

Emotions have been a rich vein for studies of cultural key words. One major finding is that although some universal themes can be identified, there are no words for "universal emotions," i.e. emotion words which are present in all languages with exactly the same meanings. Classic NSM studies have examined English *happiness*, German *Angst* 'fear, anxiety,' and Chinese *xìngfú* 'belief that one is cared for and loved.' Cultural values and ideals have also proven to be fertile hunting ground for cultural key words, especially words which implicate sociality and relationship thinking, as with Chinese *xiào* 'filial piety,' Japanese *wa* 'harmony, unity,' Danish *hygge* 'cosy sociality.' Somewhat related are models of the makeup of the human person, especially concerning the non-bodily aspects of a person, i.e. concepts comparable to 'mind,' 'spirit,' and 'soul'; e.g. English *heart*, Russian *duša*, Persian *del* 'stomach/heart.' For references, see (nsm-approach.net).

In the next two subsections, we explore similar-yet-different cultural key words in English and in Chinese, based on Goddard, Ye, and Junker (forthcoming). This is a corpus-assisted study making frequent reference to collocations and phraseology, but for reasons of space, we will be able to adduce only a few selective examples of this evidence.

3.4.2   English *security*

One of the striking things about English is the lexical distinction it draws between *security* and *safety*. Roughly speaking, *security* is linked with "threats" (from other people), while *safety* is linked with "danger" (not necessarily from other people). We begin by looking briefly at *safety*, partly because it provides a useful counterpoint to English *security*, but also because Chinese *ānquán* is often translated into English as 'safe/safety,' as well as 'secure/security.'

Many common expressions using *safety* are place-based, in that the modifier indicates a location, e.g. *Road Safety, mine safety, airline safety*. Often common expressions connected with *safety* designate equipment, personnel, and procedures, e.g. *safety railing, safety inspection, safety measures*.

Goddard, Ye, and Junker (forthcoming) propose a two-part structure for what they term the "*safety* scenario." It starts: "someone is in a place (of one kind) for some time." It then envisages potential bodily harm befalling this someone as a result of a localized event which is not due to deliberate human action ("something bad happens to this someone's body because something happens in this place, not because someone wanted it"). This, furthermore, is seen as unpredictable ("people don't know when something like this can happen"). The rest of the scenario says that such a potential event is avoidable if the individuals concerned take some specific actions while they are in the place concerned or if 'some people' take some specific actions in the place before-hand (precautions).

Security is clearly an English cultural key word and, indeed, a dominant word in international discourse (Levisen and Waters, 2017). Disregarding proper nouns such as *Social Security* and the *Security Council,* many high-frequency uses can be exemplified by expressions such as those shown below. Broadly speaking, the examples in (7) envisage the possibility of dangerous events hap-pening in a place due to deliberate human action and imply a pressing need to prevent this. The examples in (8) designate items of equipment, personnel and procedures that exist for the purpose of preventing or controlling such poten-tial 'threats.'[14]

(7)   a. New security concerns, ranging from identity theft to terrorism, have surfaced since the start of the past decade.
      b. security before politics; security vs. civil liberties; in the interests of security
      c. airport security, office security, home security, border security

(8)   a. security screen, security camera, security alarms, security fence
      b. security measures, security guard(s), security standards
      c. security breach, security check, security office

Goddard, Ye, and Junker (forthcoming) propose the following for what they term the "*security* scenario."

(U)   *security* (the "security scenario")
      a. it can be like this:
              something bad happens in a place (of one kind)
                  because someone does some bad things in this place
              people don't know when something like this can happen
              at the same time they know that if something like this happens,
                  it can be very bad for many people

---

14   The English word *security* has other, polysemic meanings, including the psychological meaning that appears in phrases like *a sense of security, comfort and security,* and *secu-rity blanket,* and in grammatical contexts such as: *the security of knowing that* ...

    b. it can be not like this if some other people do some things
      it is good for many people if these people do these things

Section (a) envisages a bad event taking place on account of reprehensible human action. The wording ("because someone does some bad things in this place") allows for the bad actions to have been carried out beforehand, e.g. planting a bomb in a public place. People don't know when such a thing can happen, but any such event would be very serious and far-reaching ("if something like this happens, it can be very bad for many people"). Section (b) says that this possibility can be avoided "if some other people do some things" (e.g. to prevent it, to reduce its severity), followed by a component saying that this would be "good for many people." The final components invite us, so to speak, to put our trust in "some other people" (whose identity is out of focus) who can help prevent this.

There are many fixed expressions involving the noun *security*, such as *national security, financial security, job security, computer security*. In general, the modifying word supplies a frame of background assumptions that amplifies and modulates the scenario. For example, *national security* focusses on serious threats to people in a country, so its explication requires use of 'country' as a semantic molecule; similarly, *financial security* requires use of 'money' as a semantic molecule.

3.4.3   Chinese *ānquán* 安全

Mandarin *ānquán* is often translated into English either as 'safe/safety' or as 'secure/security.' Beyond some surface correspondence between the use of *ānquán* and that of the two English words, such as *ānquán dài* ('safety belt') and *ānquán lǐshìhuì* ('Security Council'), Chinese *ānquán* presents a significantly different picture. On Goddard, Ye, and Junker's (forthcoming) analysis, the Chinese word is two-ways polysemous, i.e. it has two meanings *ānquán₁* and *ānquán₂*, but we will deal only with the first one.

Common collocations in the Centre for Chinese Linguistics (CCL) corpus include: *zhùyì ānquán* 'pay attention to safety,' *rénshēng ānquán* 'personal safety,' *shípǐn ānquán* 'food safety,'[15] *shēngmìng ānquán* 'life safety.' The meaning focuses on the risks and dangers people may encounter when they are engaged in certain activities. Every day, parents remind their children 'pay

---

15   The high frequency of *shípǐn ānquán* 'food safety' is due to tragic incidents such as when fake milk formula led to the death of several infants.

attention to *ānquán* when you go out,' 'pay attention to *ānquán* when you drive,' and so on.

Corpus data with the expression *zhùyì ānquán* 'pay attention to *ānquán*' illustrate a very wide range of activities and contexts, including everyday routines: going up or down stairs, crossing the road, going to school, driving a car, going on excursions, traveling, handling sharp objects at home, firing fire crackers, working with machines, doing experiments in labs with inflammable materials. Evidently from a Chinese point of view, most activities involve certain risks and dangers, especially for children. The purpose of the formula *zhùyì ānquán* is to caution people to take appropriate care.

CCL gives an example taken from some official regulations to the effect that: "All people should establish awareness of *ānquán*, paying attention to *ānquán* in production, work, study and everyday life in order to prevent unexpected casualty and loss of life." Another piece of evidence indicating the link between *ānquán* and "life and death" is the frequent use of the expression *shēngmìng (de) ānquán*, in which *shēngmìng* means life, as opposed to death.

Explication (V) presents an analysis of *ānquán₁*. Section (a) gives the background assumptions. Section (b) presents the potential scenario. Section (c) advises that people keep this scenario in mind and spells out the recommended mindset for someone going about their activities; namely, to take steps to reduce the risk (e.g. when driving, to check the rear-view mirror regularly, not to have music playing in the car).

(V)   *ānquán₁* (the "*ānquán*" scenario") (Chinese)
    a. people can do things of many kinds, they do some things often,
         they do some things every day [m]
    b. it is like this:
        often when someone does something of one kind for some time,
           something bad can happen to this someone's body during this time
        sometimes when something like this happens, this someone
           can die because of it
    c. it is good if people often think about this
        when someone does something for some time, it is good if they think like this:
           "I don't want something bad to happen to me during this time
           because of this, when I am doing this it is good if I do some things
           at the same time, it is good if I don't do some other things"

The key points are as follows. First, *ānquán₁* is linked to activity 'doing something (of one kind)' and concerns general hazards and risks inherent in such activities. Second, the body is involved evoking the notion of harm; indeed, potentially serious harm. Third, there is no implication of there being an identifiable agent of "bad doing." Fourth, the call to action is a call for people to be careful (mindful of danger) when they are doing the activity in question. Fifth, the onus is on the individuals concerned.

As mentioned, *ānquán* also has second meaning (*ānquán₂*). It concerns people's belongings. It is commonly found in the expressions advising people to pay attention to *cáichǎn (de) ānquán* (roughly, security of one's property) and to safeguard their belongings by taking timely actions, such as watching carefully, locking doors and windows.

Ānquán, in both senses, is central to Chinese public discourse, both domestic and international. Example (9) gives a sense of its wide range of use. Note that in the English translation, many instances of 'security' could be re-phrased in terms of 'safety.'

(7) … 今后中国将大力发展 "安全气象," 为公共安全、社会安全、军事安全、国土安全、环境安全、生态安全、能源安全、粮食安全、水资源安全、人民生命财产安全等提供，。

… in the future, China will strongly develop a 'secure meteorology' service. It will provide for public security, social safety, military security, land resource security, environmental security, ecological security, resource security, food security, water security, and people's livelihood and property security ….

Clearly *ānquán* and *security* have much in common. They overlap semantically and both are major cultural key words in their respective spheres of discourse. Yet when viewed through the NSM microscope, semantic differences can also be seen. *Ānquán* is at least as close to English *safety* as it is to *security*.

4   Looking Forward

4.1   *Discourse Scripts and Discourse Semantics*
One future horizon for NSM research is discourse semantics. Four examples will have to suffice. One is Wierzbicka's (2020) use of what may be termed "belief scripts" for unpacking the content of key Christian texts. Forbes (2020) proposes a set of semantic texts to capture shared beliefs and attitudes underpinning the discourse community of parents of autistic children. Hein (2020)

combines NSM analysis with conceptual blending theory to give an account of the discursive construction of Argentina as a "European" nation in South America. Bromhead (2021) explores ways to use NSM techniques for what she terms "semantically-enhanced discourse analysis."

In all these cases the NSM metalanguage and/or Minimal English (see below) is being used not for explicating words or constructions, but for modelling the contours and "grooves" of discourse.

4.2   *Applied Semantics and Minimal Languages*

Because NSM research is conducted using words of ordinary language, it lends itself to real-world applications. In past years these applications were mainly in language teaching and intercultural education. Recent times have seen the development of Minimal English and other minimal languages (Goddard, 2018b; 2021a; Sadow, Peeters, and Mullan, 2020). A minimal language is a radically simplified version of a language designed, usually in collaboration with non-linguists, to be clear, explicit and cross-translatable, but at the same time adapted or tailored to the needs of particular user groups. In developing and popularizing minimal languages, NSM researchers are taking their work "out of the lab" and into the public space.

Minimal languages have applications in language teaching, language revival, science communication, health care, development training, use with people with autism or cognitive impairments, and in other spaces where clear, explicit and accessible communication is essential (cf. Bullock, 2012–2020; Wierzbicka, 2018b; 2018c; Jordan, 2017; and chapters in Goddard, 2018b; 2021a).

Minimal languages also have a role in a new kind of communication that one may term global communication, meaning the circulation of messages and ideas of global significance across all parts of planet earth. Before the 21st century, communication with such scope could hardly be imagined. Today, with the internet, English as a global lingua franca, and common global challenges such as the coronavirus pandemic and climate change, both the means and the motivation for genuinely global communication—in the interest of human unity and human solidarity—may have arrived.

Despite the convenience of English as a lingua franca, English in the normal sense cannot be the working language of successful global communication; not unless, that is, people confine themselves to English words which are cross-translatable into other languages. Hopefully, in the coming years and decades minimal languages will make a helpful contribution to improved global communication about questions that concern us all, such as ethics, the earth and its future, and the health and well-being of all people on earth.

References

Amberber, Mengistu (ed.). 2007. *The Language of Memory in a Cross-Linguistic Perspective*. Amsterdam: John Benjamins.

Bromhead, Helen. 2018. *Landscape and Culture—Cross-linguistic Perspectives*. Amsterdam: John Benjamins.

Bromhead, Helen. 2021. Disaster linguistics, climate change semantics and public discourse studies: A semantically-enhanced discourse study of 2011 Queensland floods. *Language Sciences* 85: 101381 (e-pub).

Bromhead, Helen and Zhengdao Ye (eds.). 2020. *Meaning, Life and Culture: In Conversation with Anna Wierzbicka*. Canberra: ANU Press. Available at http://doi.org/10.22459/MLC.2020.

Bullock, David. 2012–2020. *Learn These Words First. Multi-layer Dictionary for Second-language Learners of English*. Available at https://learnthesewordsfirst.com.

Farese, Gian Marco. 2018a. *The Cultural Semantics of Address Practices: A Contrastive Study between English and Italian*. London: Lexington Books.

Farese, Gian Marco. 2018b. Is KNOW a semantic universal? *Shiru, wakaru* and Japanese ethno-epistemology. *Language Sciences* 66: 135–150.

Forbes, Alex. 2020. Using Minimal English to model a parental understanding of Autism. In L. Sadow et al. (eds.), *Studies in Ethnopragmatics, Cultural Semantics, and Intercultural Communication*, 143–163. Singapore: Springer.

Gladkova, Anna. 2010. *Russkaja kul'turnaja semantika: Emocii, cennosti, žiznennyeustanovki* (Russian Cultural Semantics: Emotions, Values, Attitudes). Moscow: Languages of Slavic Cultures.

Goddard, Cliff. 1994. Semantic theory and semantic universals. In C. Goddard and A. Wierzbicka (eds.), *Semantic and Lexical Universals—Theory and Empirical Findings*, 7–30. Amsterdam: John Benjamins.

Goddard, Cliff. 2000. Polysemy: A problem of definition. In Y. Ravin and C. Leacock (eds.), *Polysemy: Theoretical and computational approaches*, 129–151. Oxford: Oxford University Press.

Goddard, Cliff. 2002. The search for the shared semantic core of all languages. In C. Goddard and A. Wierzbicka (eds.), *Meaning and Universal Grammar—Theory and Empirical Findings*, volume 1, 5–41. Amsterdam: John Benjamins.

Goddard, Cliff. 2007. A "lexicographic portrait" of *forgetting*. In M. Amberber (ed.), *The Language of Memory in a Cross-Linguistic Perspective*, 119–137. Amsterdam: John Benjamins.

Goddard, Cliff. 2008. NSM: The state of the art. In C. Goddard (ed.), *Cross-Linguistic Semantics*, 1–34. Amsterdam: John Benjamins.

Goddard, Cliff. (ed.). 2008. *Cross-Linguistic Semantics*. Amsterdam: John Benjamins.

Goddard, Cliff. 2010. Universals and variation in the lexicon of mental state concepts.

In B.C. Malt and P. Wolff (eds.), *Words and the Mind: How words capture human experience*, 72–92. New York: Oxford University Press.

Goddard, Cliff. 2011. *Semantic Analysis: A Practical Introduction* (2nd ed.). Oxford: Oxford University Press.

Goddard, Cliff. 2012. Semantic primes, semantic molecules, semantic templates: Key concepts in the NSM approach to lexical typology. *Linguistics* 50(3): 711–743.

Goddard, Cliff (ed.). 2013. Semantics and/in social cognition. Special Issue of *Australian Journal of Linguistics* 33(3).

Goddard, Cliff. 2018a. *Ten Lectures on Natural Semantic Metalanguage: Exploring Language, Thought and Culture Using Simple, Translatable Words*. Leiden: Brill.

Goddard, Cliff (ed.). 2018b. *Minimal English for a Global World: Improved Communication Using Fewer Words*. Cham: Palgrave Macmillan.

Goddard, Cliff. 2020a. Prototypes, polysemy, and constructional semantics: The lexicogrammar of the English verb climb. In H. Bromhead and Z. Ye (eds.), *Meaning, Life and Culture: In Conversation with Anna Wierzbicka*, 13–32. Canberra: ANU Press. (open access http://press-files.anu.edu.au/downloads/press/n7194/pdf/ch01.pdf)

Goddard, Cliff. 2020b. Overcoming the linguistic challenges for ethno-epistemology: NSM perspectives. In M. Mizumoto, J. Ganeri and C. Goddard (eds.), *Ethno-Epistemology: New Directions for Global Epistemology*. London: Routledge.

Goddard, Cliff (ed.). 2021a. *Minimal Languages in Action*. Cham: Palgrave Macmillan.

Goddard, Cliff. 2021b. Natural Semantic Metalanguage. In X. Wen and J.R. Taylor (eds.), *The Routledge Handbook of Cognitive Linguistics*, 93–110. London: Routledge.

Goddard, Cliff and Rebecca Defina. 2020. *Pitjantjatjara/Yankunytjatjara to English Dictionary* (Revised 2nd ed.). Alice Springs: IAD Press.

Goddard, Cliff and Anna Wierzbicka (eds.). 1994. *Semantic and Lexical Universals— Theory and Empirical Findings*. Amsterdam: John Benjamins.

Goddard, Cliff and Anna Wierzbicka (eds.). 2002. *Meaning and Universal Grammar— Theory and Empirical Findings*, volumes I and II. Amsterdam: John Benjamins.

Goddard, Cliff and Anna Wierzbicka. 2014a. *Words and Meanings: Lexical Semantics Across Domains, Languages and Cultures*. Oxford: Oxford University Press.

Goddard, Cliff and Anna Wierzbicka. 2014b. Semantic fieldwork and lexical universals. *Studies in Language* 38(1): 80–127.

Goddard, Cliff and Anna Wierzbicka. 2016. "It's mine!". Re-thinking the conceptual semantics of "possession" through NSM. *Language Sciences* 56: 93–104.

Goddard, Cliff and Anna Wierzbicka. 2019. Cognitive semantics, linguistic typology and grammatical polysemy: "Possession" and the English genitive. *Cognitive Semantics* 5: 224–247.

Goddard, Cliff and Anna Wierzbicka. 2022. Chart of NSM Semantic Primes. May 2022 (v20). Available at nsm-approach.net.

Goddard, Cliff and Anna Wierzbicka. 2022. 150 Sentences for Identifying NSM Semantic Primes in Different Languages. April 2022 (v7). Available at nsm-approach.net.

Goddard, Cliff and Anna Wierzbicka. 2021a. "We": Conceptual semantics, linguistic typology and social cognition. *Language Sciences* 83: 101327 (online publication October 2020)

Goddard, Cliff and Anna Wierzbicka. 2021b. "Head," "eyes," "ears": Words and meanings as clues to common human thinking. *Cahiers de lexicologie* 119: 125–150.

Goddard, Cliff, Anna Wierzbicka and Horacio Fábrega, Jr. 2014. Evolutionary semantics: Using NSM to model stages in human cognitive evolution. *Language Sciences* 42: 60–79.

Goddard, Cliff and Zhengdao Ye (eds.). 2016. *"Happiness" and "Pain" Across Languages and Cultures*. Amsterdam: John Benjamins.

Goddard, Cliff, Zhengdao Ye and Tine Junker. Forthcoming. *Security, Ānquán, Sicherheit*: Similar-but-different key concepts in English, Chinese, and German. In C. Levisen, and Z. Ye (eds.) *The Cultural Pragmatics of "Danger"*.

Hein, Jan. 2020. Europeanized places, Europeanized people: The discursive construction of Argentina. *Journal of Postcolonial Linguistics* 2: 28–45.

Jordan, Paul. 2017. *How to Start, Carry on, and End Conversations. Scripts for Social Interaction for People on the Autism Spectrum*. London: Jessica Kingsley Publications.

Levisen, Carsten. 2017. Personhood constructs in language and thought: New evidence from Danish. In Z. Ye (ed.), *The Semantics of Nouns*, 120–144. Oxford: Oxford University Press.

Levisen, Carsten and Sophia Waters (eds.). 2017. *Cultural Keywords in Discourse*. Amsterdam: John Benjamins.

Mosel, Ulrike. 1994. Samoan. In C. Goddard and A. Wierzbicka (eds.), *Semantic and Lexical Universals—Theory and Empirical Evidence*, 331–360. Amsterdam: John Benjamins.

Nash, David and David Wilkins. 2020. Where we part from NSM: Understanding Warlpiri *yangka* and the Warlpiri expression of part-hood. In H. Bromhead and Z. Ye (eds.), *Meaning, Life and Culture: In Conversation with Anna Wierzbicka*. Canberra: ANU Press. Available at http://doi.org/10.22459/MLC.2020.

Newman, John (ed.). 2009. *The Linguistics of Eating and Drinking*. Amsterdam: John Benjamins.

Peeters, Bert (ed.). 2006. *Semantic Primes and Universal Grammar: Empirical Findings from the Romance Languages*. Amsterdam: John Benjamins.

Peeters, Bert, Kerry Mullan and Lauren Sadow (eds.). 2020. *Studies in Ethnopragmatics, Cultural Semantics, and Intercultural Communication: Meaning and Culture*. Singapore: Springer.

Sadow, Lauren, Bert Peeters and Kerry Mullan (eds.). 2020. *Studies in Ethnopragmatics, Cultural Semantics, and Intercultural Communication: Minimal English (and Beyond)*. Singapore: Springer.

Sharifian, Farzad. 2011. *Cultural Conceptualisations and Language*. Amsterdam: John Benjamins.

Tien, Adrian. 2015. *The Semantics of Chinese Music*. Amsterdam: John Benjamins.

Wierzbicka, Anna. 1992. *Semantics: Culture and Cognition*. New York: Oxford University Press.

Wierzbicka, Anna. 1996. *Semantics: Primes and Universals*. New York: Oxford University Press.

Wierzbicka, Anna. 1997. *Understanding Cultures Through Their Key Words*. New York: Oxford University Press.

Wierzbicka, Anna. 1999. *Emotions Across Languages and Cultures*. Cambridge, UK: Cambridge University Press.

Wierzbicka, Anna. 2013. Kinship and social cognition in Australian languages: Kayardild and Pitjantjatjara. *Australian Journal of Linguistics* 33(3): 302–321.

Wierzbicka, Anna. 2014. *Imprisoned in English: The Hazards of English as a Default Language*. New York: Oxford University Press.

Wierzbicka, Anna. 2016. Back to "mother" and "father": Overcoming the eurocentrism of kinship studies through eight lexical universals. *Current Anthropology* 57(4): 408–427.

Wierzbicka, Anna. 2017. The meaning of kinship terms: A developmental and cross-linguistic perspective. In Z. Ye (ed.), *The Semantics of Nouns*, 19–62. Oxford: Oxford University Press.

Wierzbicka, Anna. 2018a. I KNOW: A human universal. In M. Mizumoto, S. Stich and E. McCready (eds.), *Epistemology for the Rest of the World*, 215–250. Oxford: Oxford University Press.

Wierzbicka, Anna. 2018b. Minimal English as a new and transformative tool for effective health care communication in English-speaking countries. *Paper at International Symposium for Communication in Health Care*, ANU, Canberra, 13 February 2018. (online)

Wierzbicka, Anna. 2018c. Talking about the universe in minimal English: Teaching science through words that children can understand. In C. Goddard (ed.), *Minimal English for a Global World*, 168–200. Cham: Palgrave Macmillan.

Wierzbicka, Anna. 2020. The Meaning of the Christian confession of faith: Explaining the Nicene Creed through universal human concepts. In L. Iomdin and I. Boguslavsky (eds.), *From Semantic Quarks to the Universe in Alphabetical Order: In Honour of Academician Yuri Derenikovich Apresjan for his 90th Anniversary, Vol 1*. Proceedings of the V.V. Vinogradov Russian Language Institute, 2(24), 150–169. Moscow: Vinogradov Russian Language Institute.

Wierzbicka, Anna. 2021. Universal semantic primitives, fifty years later. *Russian Journal of Linguistics* 5(2); 317–342.

Wierzbicka, Anna and Cliff Goddard. 2017. Talking about our bodies and their parts in Warlpiri. *Australian Journal of Linguistics* 38(1), 31–62.

Xue, Wendi. 2016. The semantics of "uncle"-type kinship terms in Cantonese (Guangzhou) and Teochew (Jieyang). Advanced Master's thesis, Australian National University.

Ye, Zhengdao. 2010. Eating and drinking in Mandarin and Shanghainese: A lexical-conceptual analysis. In W. Christensen, E. Schier and J. Sutton (eds.), *ASCS09: Proceedings of the 9th Conference of the Australasian Society for Cognitive Science*, 375–383. Sydney: Macquarie Centre for Cognitive Science.

Ye, Zhengdao (ed.). 2017. *The Semantics of Nouns*. Oxford: Oxford University Press.

CHAPTER 4

Frame Semantics

Esra' M. Abdelzaher

1   Introduction

Fillmore's Frame Semantics is one of the founding theories in cognitive semantics. It maintains that the existence of a lexical item entails its correspondence to a schematic conceptual structure, i.e., a frame. Meaning in Frame Semantics is explored in relation to the "concepts present in the mind of the speaker" and activated in the mind of the addressee (Ackerman, Kay, and O'Connor, 2014: 757; Nerlich and Clarke, 2000: 143). Frame Semantics views language as a means of reflecting the conceptualization of the world. Experiential knowledge, therefore, represents the conceptual background that gives rise to the existence of linguistic categories (Sambre, 2010: 1). This chapter presents an overview of Frame Semantics as a cognitive linguistic theory and tool of analysis. It introduces Fillmore's initial syntactic and cognitive ideas from which the theory developed, and places emphasis on analytic examples that demonstrate the application of the theory in different fields.

The situation or the schema of meting out "punishment" for some wrong deed, according to Frame Semantics, constitutes the frame of REVENGE (the name of frames will be written in SMALL_CAPITALS). The typical participants in a frame are called frame elements and their occurrence is either core or peripheral to the understanding of the frame (frame elements will be capitalized and written in "Double_quotes"). For REVENGE, "Avenger," "Offender," "Punishment," "Injury," and "Injured_party" are core to the frame whereas the "Place" and "Time" of the event of revenge are non-core frame elements. The experience of REVENGE and its typical participants motivate the existence of some lexical units to express this situation linguistically. A lexical unit is a pairing of a word and one of its senses (lexical units will be *italicized*). *Retaliate*.v, *get even with*.v, and *revenge*.n are some of the lexical units representing the frame of REVENGE, for a speaker, and activating it, for an addressee, in natural communication. Phrases occurring in the context of these lexical units are the linguistic realizations of the above-mentioned frame elements (Fillmore, 2014: 125–130).

Fillmore introduced Frame Semantics after years of working on Case Grammar and schematic categorization of words (Section 2). Boas and Dux (2017:

2–3) argued that Frame Semantics emerged as a reaction to the drawbacks of the previously proposed Case Grammar and the inclination towards cognitive and ethnographic semantics. Also, Lakoff (2014: 252–253) considered Frame Semantics "a much-elaborated version of Case Grammar." Frame Semantics showed considerable potential for lexicography and for the implementation of the mental lexicon in a computational lexicographic resource, i.e., FrameNet.[1] (Section 3) which embodied the frame-based lexicographic approach to grammatical phenomena (Section 4). However, the application of Frame Semantics is not limited to lexicography. It is also directed to qualitative and quantitative linguistic analyses, performance of computational tasks and applied linguistic research (Section 5).

2   Historical Perspective

Fillmore spent decades theorizing a framework for meaning representation which could provide adequate lexico-grammatical description of words and sort them based on their common schematic background. Fillmore conducted his early research within the framework of transformational grammar and aimed at addressing the semantic and syntactic properties of words in order to discover language universals. This led to the proposal of a new categorization of words which was different from previous taxonomies based on the syntactic requirements of words or the syntagmatic and paradigmatic relations in semantic fields. The new taxonomy could relate words such as *hit*.v, *strike*.v and *touch*.v to each other because of the semantic roles played by their arguments, i.e., Place, Instrument and (Agent) (Section 2.1).

Later, the cognitive revolution in psychology inspired Fillmore to capture conceptual schematic coherence between words which may seem unrelated at the surface level of representation (e.g., *buy*.v, *sell*.v, *pay*.v, *cost*.v). Fillmore borrowed the concepts of "frames" and "schemas" from cognitive psychology and applied them to language and meaning representation. Frames could explain the similarities between the above-mentioned verbs at the deep semantic level, i.e., all are related to a COMMERCIAL_TRANSACTION in which there is a "Buyer," "Seller," "Goods," and "Price." These four elements which are essential components of the frame are realized differently at the surface level based on the verb used in the sentence (Section 2.2).

---

1   https://framenet.icsi.berkeley.edu/fndrupal/

Fillmore integrated the semantic and syntactic description of words with the concept of frames into a theory of linguistic knowledge representation, i.e., Frame Semantics. The theory could explain the meaning of words against the frames they are related to and describe the lexico-syntactic behavior of words in natural communication. Subsequently, Fillmore implemented the main tenets of this theory in FrameNet (Section 3.1).

2.1   *Semantically-Motivated Grammar*

In 1960s, grammarians did not appreciate the role of semantics in a linguistic theory; Fillmore himself described the semantic grounds of his approach as a drawback he must defend. He (1968a) proposed a modification to the generative transformational approach in order to achieve a higher level of universality, which was strongly motivated by "semantic considerations." Moreover, he entertained the possibility of having a "universal syntactic theory" that was "semantically justified." Unlike generative transformational grammarians, Fillmore argued that the categories of subject and direct object are not parts of the base component of the grammar which is supposedly universal; rather, they are only relevant to the description of the surface structure. Consider the following.

(1)   a. The door opened.
       b. John opened the door.
       c. The wind opened the door.
       d. John opened the door with a chisel.

At the surface level, *the door* and *John* and *the wind* fill the subject positions in (1a), (1b) and (1c) respectively. However, their semantic relations to *open* differ significantly. Whereas *the door* is the affected entity of *open* in the four sentences, *John* is the volitional actor in (1b) and (1d). *The wind* and *a chisel* are semantically understood as the force and the tool involved in the act of opening. The semantic distinction is clarified in (1d), which uses different syntactic structures but maintains the same semantic relations between *the door, John* and *open*.

Fillmore's proposal for Case Grammar considered Agentive, Dative, Factive, Objective, and Instrumental, among others, to be universally present cases, which can be realized at the surface level through noun phrases functioning as subject or object. He reformulated the phrase structure rules accordingly. For Case Grammar, the two constituents of a sentence are "modality" and "proposition" and the latter was the main focus of the analysis. A proposition is composed of a "verb" and at least "one case." The following formula in (I) represents a case feature that accepts verbs like *open*. This case feature highlights the obligatory case of Objective and the optionality of Instrument and Agentive cases (abbreviated as O, I, and A respectively). The + sign refers to the possibility of a verb having this feature while the parenthesis refers to the optionality of the case.

(I)   +[___O (I) (A)]

The concept of frames appeared within this syntactic context twice. "Case frames" denoted case environments provided by a sentence with a placeholder for the verb and "frame feature" which represented the set of possible case frames. Such frames will or will not accept the verb or, more generally, the lexical item associated with the feature. More importantly, it suggested a new categorization of verbs based on their ability to accept of case features. *Turn*.v, *rotate*.v, *move*.v, and *bend*.v seemed to share the same case feature +[___O (I) (A)] with *open*.v (Fillmore, 1968a: 23–49, 119).

The prediction of surface syntactic structure based on universal deep semantic roles or cases aroused controversy that has not been settled about the basis of the theory of grammar (Ackerman, Kay, O'Connor, 2014: 756). Boas and Dux (2017: 2) identified three main problems with the universal cases suggested by Fillmore. First, there was no linguistic test that can determine the role played by an argument. Second, the number of cases, in this proposal, abstracted from several differences between semantic roles for the sake of universality. Third, there was no one-to-one correspondence between the supposed roles and their syntactic realizations.

However, Fillmore (1968b) went on with his proposal and explored the newly introduced categorization of verbs from a predicate-argument perspective to describe the semantics and grammar of verbs. The lexical entry of a verb should adequately describe the relationship between the predicate (e.g., *open.v*) and all its possible arguments in terms of the roles the arguments play (e.g., "Agent," "Instrument"). Regardless of the surface subject-object positions of the argument, *open*.v can be represented as follows.

(II)   OPEN$_{\text{OBJECT, (INTRUMENT (AGENT))}}$

This description covered the different transitive and intransitive uses of *open* realized in (1). Whereas the formula in (I) was a universal frame within which a word may or may not fit, the representation in (II) was more predicate-specific. It was still able to capture similarities among verbs. *Hit*.v, *strike*.v, and *touch*.v, for instance, can be described in the same way. Similarly, *rob*.v and *steal*.v both have the following three roles: The person who performs the act of stealing or robbing, the entity that loses the property, and the object whose ownership is illegally transferred, but they differ in the order of the overt NP arguments realized at the surface level as well as in the obligatory grammatical functions imposed by this order. While *rob* allows the realization of the Agent who performs the act and the Dative which suffers the loss as realized in (2a), *steal* overtly expresses the Agent and the stolen Object as realized in (2b). That is to say, the lexical entry of a verb should not be based on the surface realization and the order of its arguments (373–390).

(2) a. Harry robbed a casino
     b. Harry stole a casino

One year later, Fillmore (1969) moved a step forward to analyze the semantic description of verbs, especially verbs of judgment. The proposed analysis was influenced by the work of Austin on communication, presupposition and speech acts. The description of roles was the first step to address the lexico-syntactic features of the verbs. The analysis replaced the general cases of Agent and Instrument with a more specific concept. "Role concepts" were introduced as specific and essential to the context of judging. Situation, Affected, Defendant, Judge, Statement, and Addressee were used to specifically account for this group of verbs. In addition to the description of the semantic roles relevant to each verb, the meaning and presupposition underlying each verb were described. Therefore, a lexical entry for *accuse*, for instance, is represented as follows.

(III) ACCUSE [Judge, Defendant, Situation (of)]; (performative);
       Meaning: SAY [Judge, X, Addressee];
       X= Responsible [Situation, Defendant];
       Presupposition: Bad [Situation].

The facts relevant to the description of *accuse* were recorded with reference to the "role concepts" functioning as the conditions necessary for the appropriate use of the verb. Characteristic to all verbs of judgment are the badness of a Situation and the "responsibility" of the Affected, but they differ in the description of the meaning and the statement of the presuppositions. Unlike *accuse*, the meaning of *criticize* defines X as Bad [Situation] and assumes different presuppositions. First, it presupposes the responsibility of the Defendant for the Situation. Second, it presupposes the factuality of the Situation (97–110).

This situation-oriented description was accentuated in Fillmore's (1970) discussion on the separation between the subject role and the possible semantic role played by the word in the subject position. The former is a syntactic label based on the position of the word in a sentence; the latter encompasses roles such as Agent and Instrument and is characteristic to the relation between the argument and the predicate.

He attempted to reach a correspondence between the universal cases he proposed before the analysis of judging verbs and the specific roles assumed in the judging situation. He suggested that the universal Agent function can be mapped to the role of Customer which is specific to the context of *buy*.v while Agent was mapped to Merchant in the case of *sell*.v. That was a further step towards linking verbs which were superficially unrelated (251–258). The role of sociolinguistics in a theory of grammar was further explored in Fillmore (1972: 282). He rejected the soundness of the argument about "a grammar generating a set of grammatical sentences in a language." He rather defined the job of a grammarian as the identification and description of the native knowledge (e.g., elements, structures, processes, and constraints) which enable language users to communicate successfully. Further, he committed himself to the exploration of the ways, purposes and settings of using grammars by language users.

By 1977, Fillmore had adopted a cognition-based approach to meaning. He suggested that linguistic elements reflect paralinguistic scenes. He discussed his Case Grammar proposal from a new perspective: "meanings are relativized to scenes." He added another dimension to the description of *buy*.v and *sell*.v that accounted for their similarities and differences with reference to scenes. The term *scenes* referred collectively to visual scenes, scenarios and experiences. The commercial event comprehensively covers Buyer, Seller, Money, and Goods. Each linguistic instance that conveys information about this event/situation expresses only part of the situation, i.e., the "perspective" of either the Buyer or the Seller. *Buy* and *sell* differ in the order and realization of their cases because they activate different scenes that adopt different perspectives. Hence, Fillmore added a new interpretive feature to his earlier proposals (Fillmore, 1977a: 59, 72–73).

There had been a gap between Fillmore's proposals and the assumptions of transformational grammar since his early work on Case Grammar. As the gap grew wider, Fillmore developed the construction approach to grammar, which is dominant in the current application of Frame Semantics in FrameNet. Fillmore (1988) advocated the use of grammatical constructions as the basic unit of analysis, which can lead to the discovery of both language-specific facts and language universals. He defined a grammatical construction as "any syntactic pattern" that is associated with at least one conventional linguistic function and the lexical properties relevant to its meaning and usage in a sentence. He argued that the grammatical patterns and their relevant semantic and pragmatic aspects should be equally described in Construction Grammar. The descriptive adequacy of Construction Grammar stipulated recording facts about the semantic and syntactic valence of a word. The following multi-layered valence description, of *give*.v, became core to Frame Semantics.

(IV)   GF: Subject   Object   Complement
         SR: Agent   Patient   Recipient
         MS: N   N   P[to]

The arguments of *give*.v serve the Grammatical Functions (GF) of subject, object and complement. The Semantic Roles (SR) corresponding to these functions are Agent, Patient and Recipient respectively. At the phrase level, the morphosyntax (MS) of *give*'s complements is realized as noun, noun and preposition[to]. This valence description, similar to other construction approaches, replaced "simple atomic categories" with categories labeling "complex bundles of information," used direct representation of properties instead of assumptions about the transmission of information and allowed the realization of more than one construction at the same level. It is worth mentioning that grammatical constructions can be embedded in each other, and the containment of one construction in another may impose conditions on it (Fillmore, 1988: 35–42). The transition from the representation in (I) to that in (IV) displays Fillmore's orientation towards considering the specificity of constructions with reference to their syntactic, lexical and usage-based features.

2.2   *Frames-Scenes Model of Meaning*

Fillmore emphasized that since his first use of the word "frame" in Case Grammar, he was interested in grouping verbs according to their underlying situations and associated roles (Andor, 2010: 158). A comprehensive description of linguistic elements should expose the relations among these linguistic elements, on the one hand, and between the linguistic elements of the experience they encode, on the other hand (Fillmore, 1968b: 393). However, the use of frames in an explicit cognitive sense relevant to Frame Semantics was manifested years after the introduction of Case Grammar.

Fillmore (1975) was influenced by the concepts of frames and prototypicality which were originally borrowed from cognitive psychology. Frames, in cognitive psychology, denoted "schemata or frameworks of concepts or terms" that form a coherent system and "impose structure on some aspects of human experience." However, the frame-scene model of meaning formulated a linguistic-oriented definition of frames which was different from the original use of the term in cognitive psychology. Fillmore's early use of frame referred to "any system of linguistic choices," which could be a collection of words or a choice of grammatical rules associated with particular scenes (i.e., visual scenes, common cultural scenarios, interpersonal transactions and experiences). It was the concept of scenes that was relevant to the paralinguistic schematic experience. This distinction was jettisoned at later stages of the theory.

The description of *write*.v in this model provided the following information. The frame of *write* is associated with a scene whose entities are "Writer," "Implement," "Surface," and "Product." Given that the prototypical Product of writing has to be linguistic, *write*.v was associated with the frame of LANGUAGE. In addition, the scene of linguistic communication is added to the action scene of writing when a sentence such as (3) is uttered.

(3)   I wrote a letter.

The linguistic choice of *letter* as the product of writing is associated with a scene in which a "Sender" communicates a "Message" with an "Addressee." Fillmore was not sure at that stage whether his ideas were a novelty or a redundancy (Fillmore, 1975: 123–130). However, it was clear that he maintained the ideas about the semantic relations between a predicate (e.g., *write*) and its arguments (e.g., Writer, Implement), although he displayed some terminological inconsistencies.

Fillmore (1976) introduced Frame Semantics as a theory of meaning representation. It sought to provide a uniform representation of meaning at the levels of word, sentence and text, complying with world modeling. Understanding the meaning of a word requires knowledge about the frame or scenario underlying it. When the word is used in a sentence, extra information should be available to the hearer and the speaker. In addition to the scenario, language users must understand how the lexical contents and grammatical structures of the sentence fill the details of the scenario expressed by the word.

Consider example (4):

(4)   I bought a new pair of shoes

Understanding the sentence requires knowledge about the frame of COMMERCIAL EVENT which underlies *buy*.v and understanding the relation between the noun phrase in the subject position and the role of the "Buyer," on the one hand, and between the noun phrase in the direct object position and the role of "Goods."

At this stage, the cognitive sense of "frame" was applied, while the concept of scenes was discarded. The new proposal stated that particular linguistic elements are associated in the memory with certain frames. Exposure to the linguistic element (e.g., *buy*) in the appropriate context activates the relevant frame (e.g., COMMERCIAL_EVENT). The activation of the frame, in turn, enhances access to the other linguistic elements associated with it (e.g., *cost, spend, charge*).

During language acquisition, a native speaker acquires a repertory of frames and performs mental processes on them. Therefore, the construction of an inventory of frames that have linguistic reflexes can enable effective exploration of the language system. Although Fillmore expressed his agreement with the representation of linguistic knowledge through grammar (i.e., the aspect of linguistic knowledge representable by rules) and the lexicon (i.e., item-by-item knowledge), he accentuated the importance of integrating the "social functions of language," processes of "speech production and comprehension" and speaker-context relations into the representation of linguistic knowledge (Fillmore, 1976: 20–29). In this connection, studies in neurolinguistics maintained that this internal representation of a context includes partial representations of specific events and event structures which are inferred from previously processed contextual input or a repertory of frames (Kuperberg and Jaege, 2016).

Fillmore (1977b) referred to the distinction between frames and scenes again in the explanation of several linguistic phenomena including language acquisition. According to this view, a child acquires the label of an entire situation, such as writing, before the acquisition of the labels specific to the situation's entities. Acquiring the experience of being in a room drawing a circle with a pencil precedes the acquisition of labeling the entities which are parts of the experience, such as pencil, paper and drawing. Later, the child experiences relevant scenes such as writing, sketching and printing and acquires the labels of their different parts. Before reaching the mature stage, children are not able to isolate a word from the experience in which they learned it. For example, 7-year-old children could not accept that the item labeled grapefruit can be peeled up and segmented because they acquired it in a scene in which the fruit was cut into halves with a knife and eaten with a spoon, unlike the orange which was peeled and segmented. That is why, when the children saw a grapefruit, they were able to label it correctly. However, after seeing the teacher eating it in an atypical scene to their previous experience, they called it an orange.

Also, scenes and frames can address the category-boundary challenge. Participants should not be asked about their judgments regarding the belonging of an item to a category. They should be asked about their willingness to extend the frame that is already associated with a prototypic scene to cover another scene relevant to the word under exploration or to create a new frame (Fillmore, 1977b: 62–69). Fillmore, at the early stages of formulating the theory, kept moving between the use of frames as linguistic choices associated with a scene and their use as a schematic representation of experiences.

In 1985, Fillmore confirmed the significance of interpretive frames to the theory of meaning and differentiated between language-dependent and language-independent frames. Language-dependent frames make considerable contribution to meaning, despite the dominance of language-independent frames. To elaborate, the description of containers of "soap flakes" as *large* in American supermarkets referred to the smallest size of containers while *jumbo, economy,* and *family size* are used to describe larger sizes. This association between *large* and the smallest size is not relevant to a non-linguistic frame, i.e., does not reflect world knowledge about size and proportions. It is, rather, created by language to reflect this specific situation. Frames were still able to categorize words according to their shared underlying schema. At the same time, frames could assign separate frames to semantically related words such *skip, hop* and *leap*, which reflect different schemas of pedal locomotion (226–229).

It was in 1992 that Frame Semantics witnessed a turning point. Fillmore, accompanied by the prominent lexicographer Atkins, integrated the lexico-syntactic description of words, the cognitive concept of frames and corpora in a lexicographic-oriented study of the lexeme RISK. After Fillmore's proposal of a frame-based lexicon, linguists realized the potential of adopting a frame-based approach to dictionary-making (Petruck, 2011: 1). The new proposal centralized the role of conceptual frames in grouping words together (Ackerman, Kay, and O'Connor, 2014: 757). Figure 4.1 illustrates the development of Fillmore's main ideas through the history of Frame Semantics.

The next section discusses the new frame-based perspective on the lexicon, provides an overview of the application of this view to the construction of FN and addresses some grammatical and lexicographic issues from a frame-based approach.

3   A New Perspective on the Lexicon

Fillmore and Atkins (1992: 75–77) applied the theory of Frame Semantics and corpus tools to the field of lexicography. Their idea about the imitation of the mental lexicon in a dictionary depended on making all information that speakers have about their language accessible to users in a frame-based dictionary. Pre-lexicographic decisions about marketability, space, and price of

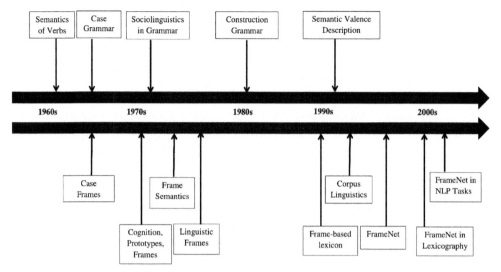

FIGURE 4.1 Fillmore's main ideas through the history of Frame Semantics.

the dictionary were not applicable to this project because the lexicon was not meant to be a trade dictionary. For the same reason, it did not rely on previously-stored information in traditional dictionaries. Adopting the framework of Frame Semantics, the new perspective on the lexicon maintained that understanding the meaning of a word depends on knowledge about the frame (i.e., cognitive structure), which motivates the concepts encoded by this word. The new lexicographic proposal included information about (a) relations between meaning and lexico-syntactic patterns; (b) relations among words evoking the same frame; (c) relations among polysemous word senses and (d) relations between the frame of the target word and any relevant frames.

They conducted a comprehensive corpus-based analysis of the lemma RISK. The study relied on hypotheses about the association of RISK with two subframes, namely, RISK_TAKING and RISK_RUNNING, and the existence of categories such as Victim, Valued Object, Harm and Actor. Fillmore and Atkins used "categories" to designate a concept similar to that of semantic roles and cases. The new term was introduced to suggest the frame-specificity of the roles played by the phrases surrounding the target word, as opposed to the previous statements about the universality of cases and semantic roles (Fillmore and Atkins, 1992: 80–84).

(5) a. He *risked* a trip into the jungle
     b. He *risked* his inheritance
     c. The board was *risking* a liquidity crisis

The frame-based analysis of *risk*.v linked the different senses of the verb to each other and linked the meaning of the word to its semantic and syntactic valence. *Risk* in (5a) denotes the performance of an act which causes a possibility of harm to oneself and it expresses a relation between an Actor (i.e., *he*) and a Deed (i.e., *a trip into the jungle*). This relation includes two valence patterns, displayed in (V). Deed can be syntactically realized as a noun phrase in the direct object position or as a gerundial object. In this case, *chance, hazard* and *venture* are relevant words to *risk*. Example (5b) displays another sense of *risk* as a verb. It refers to acting in a way that puts something in danger and therefore expresses a relation between an Actor (i.e., *he*) and a Valued Object (i.e., *his inheritance*). *Jeopardize, endanger* and *imperil* are associated with this sense of *risk*. The NP complement of the verb *risk* can correspond to a third category. Example (5c) expresses a relation between an Actor, which is *the board*, and Harm, which is *a liquidity crisis*. Harm is a "potential unwelcome outcome" and it can be syntactically expressed as nominal object or clausal complement, among others. The use of these "categories," which are parts of the frame structure in the definitions of *risk*.v, highlights the similarities and the differences between its senses (Fillmore and Atkins, 1992: 49–99).

(V)   Risk ^{D}{NP}
      Risk ^{D}{Gerund}

These ideas were further developed and implemented in the Berkeley Frame-Net Project. A dictionary entry composed of these various frame-based pieces of information was essentially different from entries in traditional dictionaries. Fillmore (2003: 263–264) identified the essentiality of frames to the explanation of meaning in FrameNet, the decisions about the price of trade dictionaries in the market and the expected patience of users of traditional dictionaries as major obstacles to the inclusion of FrameNet data in traditional dictionaries. The type of information aimed at in FrameNet is better represented in an electronic form to be used by both humans and computers. FrameNet information did not acknowledge the existence of clear boundaries between dictionary definitions and encyclopedic ones or between dictionaries and thesauri.

3.1   The Lexicographic Process in FrameNet

The traditional process of lexicography consists of analysis and synthesis stages. At the analysis stage, the lexicographer searches for and records the maximum possible number of facts about words in a form of rough notes, structured text or a database. At the synthesis stage, lexicographers extract from these facts the information relevant to the purpose of the target dictionary (Atkins, 2008: 33).

The process of lexicography in FrameNet consists of four steps. First, the vanguard, at the preparation stage, writes an initial description of the frame, proposes the semantic components of the frame, suggests a working label for each element and creates a list of the words which are expected to belong to the frame. At the second stage, the manually-recorded data by the vanguard serves as an input to the automatic sub-corpus extraction of the sentences containing the lemmas of the target words. Third, annotators select canonical examples and novel uses for each lexical unit, perform semantic role labeling and describe the phrase type and the grammatical function of each frame element. The three steps can be situated within the traditional analysis process. The final step, which is performed by the rearguard, corresponding to the traditional synthesis stage, includes review of the information recorded by the vanguard and the annotator and writing the final entry for the lemma, the definition of the frame and the description of its frame elements (Fillmore, Petruck, Ruppenhofer and Wright, 2003: 288; Baker, Fillmore, and Lowe, 1998: 86–89).

FrameNet was committed to the use of frames in explaining the meaning of words and describing the semantic valence of words. It was also committed to drawing general conclusions about word usages depending on corpus evidence. At the macrostructure level, FrameNet was designed to be a human-browsable and machine-readable database. Therefore, the storage and encoding of the information in the databases were different from its representation in the user interface. Given that the frame-based analysis proceeded frame by frame, not lemma by lemma, FrameNet created different entries to frames and to lexical units. The lexicon part of FrameNet recorded information about lexical units, i.e., a pairing of a word and a single sense. For each lexical unit, FrameNet registered information about parts of speech, definitions (primarily cited from the Concise Oxford Dictionary and occasionally written by FrameNet lexicographers), tabulated valence patterns and links to their annotated representative examples in the "lexicon." The frame database recorded the frames, their descriptions, frame elements (i.e., the last term used to encode frame-specific semantic roles) and relations to other frames in the Frame Database. The last part of the project included sentences in which the target word appears and the frame elements are realized according to the stored valence patterns. The frame of DRIVING, for instance, referred to a situation in which a "Driver" is essentially initiating and controlling the movement of a "Vehicle." In addition, "Rider" and "Cargo" are other frame elements in DRIVING. The frame inherits the structure of the general TRANSPORTATION frame. The annotated sentences in (6) displayed two patterns of *drive*.v (Fillmore, Wooters, and Baker, 2001: 11; Baker, Fillmore, and Lowe, 1998: 86–89).

(6) a. [$_D$ Kate] *drove* [$_P$ home] in a stupor
     b. Now [$_D$ Van Cheele] was *driving* [$_R$ his guest] [$_P$ back to the station]

At first, the FrameNet team planned to record statistical information about the frequency of sense-pattern relations. However, the statistical information provided in FrameNet to date is the number of the syntactic realizations of each frame element and the numbers of each valence pattern as recorded in the annotated examples. The annotation schema used in the current version of FrameNet is similar to the three-layered annotation mentioned in (IV) (Section 2.1) but replaced the term Semantic Role (SR) with Frame Element (FE) and Morph-Syntax (MS) with Phrase Type (PT). Table 4.1 displays a sample of the information recorded in the current FrameNet database about *abuse*.v and ABUSING.

TABLE 4.1 Sample of the information present in FrameNet

Information	Frame: ABUSING	Information	Lexical unit: *Abuse.*v
Description	In this frame an Abuser repeatedly treats the Victim in a cruel and violent way, including physically harming or forcing the Victim to engage in sexual activity against their will. The Victim usually lacks the power to resist or fight back. A Type of abuse may be indicated. There may also be a Degree.	Definition	FN: to cruelly mistreat, esp. physically or sexually
			ABUSING
		Frame:	
Frame Elements	Core: Abuser: subjects the Victim to repeated verbal, physical, emotional or sexual attacks Semantic Type: sentient	Frame Elements with realizations	Abuser: NP.Ext (14) Manner: AVP.Dep (1) Place: AVP.Dep (1) Time: Sub.Dep (1) Type: AVP.Dep (3) Victim: NP.Obj (15)
	Victim: the recipient of the Abuser's actions Semantic Type: Sentient		
	Non-Core: Manner: used for any description of the abuse event Semantic Type: Manner		

TABLE 4.1   Sample of the information present in FrameNet (*cont.*)

Informa-tion	Frame: ABUSING	Information	Lexical unit: *Abuse.v*		
Lexical Units	*abuse.n, abuse.v, abusive.a, batter.v, domestic violence.n, maltreat.v, maltreatment.n*	Valence Patterns	Abuser NP Ext.	Manner AVP Dep.	Victim NP Obj.
			Abuser NP Ext.	Abuser NP Ext.	Victim NP Obj.
Related Frames	Inherits from: COMMITTING_CRIME	Annotated Examples	[Abuser Parents] [Abuser who] ABUSE^{Target} [Victim their children]		

The frame-based approach was lexicographically effective in (a) identification of the information that is lexicographically relevant to a headword; (b) provision of authentic citations relating word meanings to valence patterns; (c) systematic separation of word senses and (d) categorization of word senses in a thesaurus-like style (Atkins, Fillmore, and Johnson, 2003).

3.2   *Frame-Based Lexicographic Relevance*

Within the framework of traditional lexicography, at the synthesis stage, lexicographers have to select the lexicographically relevant information to the dictionary under construction. To that end, they need to consider the needs and the skills of the target user, purposes of the dictionary and limitations of the marketing and publication processes (Rundell, 2008: 230). Lexicographically relevant information about a headword is either internal to the word (e.g., morphological, phonetic, orthographic, lexical, semantic) or external to the word and related to its connection with other words (e.g., grammatical behavior, usage information, semantic field). The inclusion of this information, as long as it is not theoretically-motivated, varies across dictionaries (Atkins, 2008: 43–47). Frame Semantics is one of the most prominent theories that can provide theoretical background for digital lexicographic projects. It can also be integrated with other cognitive semantic theories such as Conceptual Metaphor Theory and Prototype Theory to improve lexicographic practice (Abdelzaher, 2021).

FrameNet recorded lexicographically relevant information within the theoretical framework of Frame Semantics. Fillmore (2003) argued that definitions in electronic dictionaries should include (a) characterization of the frame underlying each word sense and (b) description of word-specific meaning through the parts of the frame, frame elements in particular. Although advanced users may not be interested in the description of the frame, frame description is essential to reach the second part, which defines the target word. The description of the frame is equally important to the decoding and encoding purposes. Understanding the conceptual motivation behind the existence of a word is vital to the acquisition of the knowledge about the context in which the word is typically used. For each word sense, FrameNet presents "frame-external" facts about the situation the frame expresses and "frame-internal" information about the definition of the lexical unit and the annotated sentences representing its valence patterns (267–269, 288), as previously displayed in Table 4.1.

3.3 *Corpus-Based Reliable Citations*

Atkins and Rundell (2008: 45) linked the reliability of a dictionary to its accurate reflection of natural language. A dictionary should make "generalizations about word behavior" on the basis of native usage and understanding of a word in natural communication. Corpora are argued to be authentic sources of lexicographic information. Fillmore (1992: 35–36) advocated the use of corpora and corpus tools in linguistic analysis. Although corpora can never contain all linguistic information, any corpus can reveal some linguistic facts that were not known to linguists or lexicographers. FrameNet was committed to making generalizations about the lexico-syntactic behavior of words based on corpus examples. Unlike traditional dictionaries, FrameNet provided manually-annotated examples to illustrate how each word sense is used. FrameNet used the tagged lemmatized version of the British National Corpus for its comprehensive and balanced coverage. The corpus was enriched with American newswire texts provided by the Linguistic Data Consortium and the American National Corpus (Baker, Fillmore, and Lowe, 1998: 86; Johnson and Fillmore, 2000: 56–57; Ruppenhofer et al., 2016: 9).

Citations in FrameNet not only served as authentic examples of word usage, but they served as a link between the frame-motivated meaning of the word and its usage-based lexico-syntactic patterns. The semantic part of the annotation (i.e., frame elements) provided this link between them. As a demonstration, FrameNet recorded a sense of the verb *steal* as "move somewhere quietly or surreptitiously." *Steal*.v evokes the frame of SELF_MOTION. The frame structures an experience in which a "Self_mover" moves along a "Path." "Area," "Direction," "Source," and "Goal" are also frame elements characterizing this movement (see Table 4.2). FrameNet recorded 13 valence patterns for this lexical unit and annotated 53 examples realizing them. The annotated examples (7a) and (7b) demonstrate the tabulated patterns A and B, respectively.

TABLE 4.2   Examples of the valence patterns of *steal*.v

Pattern A				Pattern B			
Frame Elements	Area	Manner	Self_mover	**Frame Elements**	Distance	Goal	Self_mover
Grammatical Function	Dep	Dep	Ext	**Grammatical Function**	Dep	Dep	Ext
Phrase Type	PP[upon]	PP[like]	NP	**Phrase Type**	AVP	PP[into]	NP

(6)   a. [$_{\text{Self\_mover}}$ It] could not *STEAL*^{Target} [$_{\text{Area}}$ upon the country unaware], [$_{\text{Manner}}$ like a thief in the night]

   b. [$_{\text{Self\_mover}}$She] grew bolder and *STOLE*^{Target} [$_{\text{Distance}}$a wee bit further] [$_{\text{Goal}}$into the garden]

The use of FrameNet's annotated sentences instead of traditional dictionary examples was recommended for better learning and memorization of words. Language learners exposed to frame-based examples performed better in paraphrasing tasks than learners who read entries totally cited from traditional dictionaries. The inclusion of frame knowledge in dictionaries had a positive effect on language learners (Ostermann, 2015: 78–117).

3.4   *Frame-Based Sense Separation*

Separation of senses in lexicography does not follow a conventional practice. Two dictionaries that belong to the same type and are addressed to the same users may display substantial differences in their separation or grouping of senses. Dictionaries may resort to fine-grained splitting of senses in some cases and a general hierarchical lumping of senses in other cases. Style guides do not usually provide instructions to inform lexicographic decisions about sense identification and separation, but Frame Semantics provides criteria for sense separation (Atkins, 2008: 41; Atkins and Rundell: 2008: 267–268; Fillmore and Atkins, 2000: 91–92, 108–109). At the cognitive level, the different senses of a word generally evoke separate frames and are, accordingly, split in various entries according to their respective frames (Fillmore, Johnson, and Petruck, 2003: 236). At the linguistic level, it is the annotation of corpus instances that presents evidence of the existence of different senses. The word sketch (i.e., corpus-driven summary of the lexical collocates in grammatical relations with the target word) for *argue.v* showed *argue against* and *argue about* as frequent and statistically significant collocations. Intuitively, FrameNet lexicographers associated *argue against* with the sense of "reasoning" and related *argue about* to the sense of "quarreling." They searched for concordance lines to confirm, refute or modify the two-sense hypothesis. Concordances suggested the existence of a third sense which was relevant to "demonstrate" or "prove," and the subject in this case is not a person (Atkins, Rundell, and Sato, 2003: 336–337; Atkins and Bouillon, 2006: 28–32).

Corpus tools provided evidence of the different behaviors of *argue.v*. Frame-Net lexicographers associated the behaviors with different senses of the word and explained each case against its conceptual schematic structure (i.e., frame). Currently, the three senses of *argue.v* in FrameNet evoke the frames of REASONING, QUARRELING, and EVIDENCE as expressed in Table 4.3.

TABLE 4.3   The three senses of *argue.v* in FrameNet

Lexical Unit	*Argue.v*	*Argue.v*	*Argue.v*
Definition	give reasons or cite evidence in support of something	to be evidence for a conclusion	exchange diverging or opposite views heatedly
Frame	REASONING	EVIDENCE	QUARRELING
Frame Elements	Addressee; Arguer; Content; Manner; Place; Medium; Support; Time	Degree; Proposition; Support	{Arguer1; Arguer2} or {Arguers}; Depictive; Issue; Manner
Co-lexical Units	*case.n, demonstrate.v, demonstration.n, disprove.v,*	*assure.v, attest.v, confirm.v, contradict.v,*	*altercation.n, bicker.v, bickering.n, disagreement.n,*

The annotated sentences in (7) evoke REASONING, QUARRELING and EVIDENCE. (7a) evokes a frame in which the sentient "Arguer" and the "Content" presented are the core frame elements while the occurrence of the sentient "Addressee," "Support," "Manner," and "Time," among others, is non-core to the understanding of the sense. (7b) activates a frame in which there is a group of people who are the "Arguers," or there are two persons represented as "Arguer₁" and "Arguer₂," and they "express incompatible" ideas about an "Issue." Therefore, the existence of the "Arguers" and the "Issue" is core to the frame whereas the "Duration," "Manner," and "Place" are non-core frame elements. Whereas

FrameNet lexicographers had already presupposed these two senses and used the corpus to check them, the third sense was exposed by the corpus. *Argue* in (7c) is "used in a non-communicative, epistemic sense." Therefore, it does not require the existence of a person to express the "Content" or an opinion about an "Issue." The core frame elements in this case are the "Proposition" which is a claim or a belief and the "Support" which is the fact or the phenomena consolidating the "Preposition."

(7)   a.   [Arguer The Government] *ARGUED*Target [Addressee before the commission] [Time last Friday]
           [Content that the killings were lawful]
      b.   [Arguer1 You] can't *ARGUE*Target [Issue politics] [Arguer2 with foreigners]
      c.   [Support The existence of the two suites] *ARGUES*Target [Degree strongly]
           [Proposition against the
           royal apartment interpretation]

Although traditional dictionaries record more than 5 senses for the verb *argue*, Atkins, Rundell, and Sato (2003: 337) described the frame-based sense splitting as extremely fine-grained and likely to be too time-consuming to be applicable to traditional dictionaries. However, the enumeration of senses was not the source of this fine-granularity. It was the method of sense separation that distinguished FrameNet senses from senses in other traditional dictionaries. Sense splitting in FrameNet depended on exhaustive manual lexicographic effort, word sketches and concordances.

Verbs have been widely studied in Frame Semantics research because they were considered prototypical frame-bearing or frame-evoking lexical units. At the early stages of the project, FrameNet focused mainly on verbs (Fillmore and Baker, 2001). However, the current status of the lexical units in the FrameNet database (5575 nouns, 5213 verbs, and 2407 adjectives) reflects the growing interest in investigating other parts of speech. The exploration of nouns within the framework of Frame Semantics is also present in current studies.

Abdelzaher and Toth (2020) used a multifaceted approach based on distributional similarity, Frame Semantics and FrameNet to define *crime*.n. The study attempted to link *crime*'s distributionally relevant words to its co-lexical units in FrameNet. However, corpus-based evidence suggested that there are four additional senses of *crime*.n that are absent from FrameNet. In addition to being an illegal act, *crime*.n denotes (a) an undesirable event which is evocative of CATASTROPHE, (b) wrong behavior which is relevant to MORALITY_EVALUATION and COMPLIANCE, (c) undesirable situation which activates

PREDICAMENT and (d) a negatively appraised characteristic which relates to the ATTRIBUTES hierarchy. The following examples illustrate each of these senses in order.

(8)   a. [Undersirable_event This small seaside village serves as a horrifying micro-cosm of massive
         ecological] CRIMES^Target happening [Patientworldwide].
      b. People are starving. It is a CRIME^Target [Actionto waste even a single grain]
      c. [ExperiencerA healthy, adoptable animal] killed for the sole CRIME^Target of [Situationbeing homeless]
      d. it sounds as if it were a CRIME^Target [Attributeto be a Mexican]

The introduced senses differ in the hierarchies they descend from, the situation they express, the type and the number of their core frame elements. *Crime*.n in FrameNet descends from the top-level frame EVENT and it typically occurs with the core frame elements "Perpetrator," which is sentient, and "Crime," which is the act forbidden by law. FrameNet does not record information about the entity that suffers from the crime in COMMITING_CRIME, although such information is present in frame elements of the inheritors (e.g., ABUSING, KIDNAPPING, THEFT). Sentences like (8a) express another situation in which there are typically an undesirable event and a patient suffering from this event. Distributional similarity and sketch differences demonstrate that *crime*.n, *disaster*.n, and *crisis*.n can be used interchangeably in the context of CATASTROPHE. The legal aspect of criminal acts and the involved intentionality of the perpetrator are absent from the scene expressed by the sense given in (8a).

The use of *crime* in (8c) is based on its distributional similarity with *problem*.n. Sketch differences and concordance functions, in Sketch Engine, reiterate the similar behavior of *crime*.n and *problem*.n in some contexts. *Problem*.n, according to FrameNet, evokes PREDICAMENT and requires the occurrence of an "Experiencer" in an undesirable "Situation." Despite the overlap of CATASTROPHE and PREDICAMENT (i.e., core presence of an entity influenced by or in an undesirable situation or event), they are hierarchically separated in FrameNet. Whereas CATASTROPHE follows from EVENT, PREDICAMENT descends *from* the top-level frame STATE. The dynamicity of the undesirable event is partially manifested in the lexical units evoking CATASTROPHE, such as *suffer*.v, *betide*.v, and *befall*.v, in FrameNet. In contrast, *have* and *be* (*in*) are frequent governors of the lexical units evoking PREDICAMENT. The two senses of *crime* in (a) and (c) are separated to maintain the ontological differences between EVENT-inherited and STATE-inherited frames.

Corpus tools suggested a fourth use of *crime*.n, 8 (d), that differs from the previous senses in its core frame elements, hierarchy, and the situation it expresses. Concordance lines displayed that *crime* can be used to refer to a permanent characteristic (not an act, event, or situation) that is not inherently negative but is negatively evaluated in a specific context.

3.5   *Thesaurus-like Grouping of Lexical Units*

Attempts to group words in dictionaries to reflect their "dependence" instead of piling them in a "confused heap" go back to Dr. Johnson's (1747) plan for a dictionary. In addition to etymology, derivation, and word classes, some dictionaries which focused on encoding purposes categorized words conceptually or thematically according to their meaning (Rundell, 2008: 232–233). Semantic fields gave rise to many of these conceptual taxonomies but they are different from the frame-based grouping. Semantic fields are based on paradigmatic and syntagmatic relations among words; accordingly, the taxonomy is a reflection of linguistic knowledge only. In contrast, words grouped in the same frame reflect a shared schematic representation. A frame, therefore, represents cultural and contextual knowledge (Nerlich and Clarke, 2000: 145).

Four criteria are established to grant lexical units the same frame membership. First, lexical units in the same frame must occur with the same number and type of arguments. Therefore, *rob*.v and *steal*.v, for instance, are now separated in the current version of FrameNet. *Rob*.v occurs with three core frame elements (i.e., Perpetrator, Victim, and Source) whereas *steal*.v occurs with four core frame elements (i.e., Perpetrator, Victim, Source, and Goods). Accordingly, *rob*.v is included in the frame of ROBBERY and *steal*.v is listed as evocative of the THEFT frame. Second, co-lexical units must bear the same semantic relations to their arguments. As an example, FrameNet states that both *attack*.v and *execute*.v occur with the same number of core frame elements which have the same semantic type (i.e., sentient). However, *attack*.v assigns the semantic relations of "Assailant" and "Victim" to its two arguments. *Execute*.v, on the other hand, assigns the roles of "Executioner" and "Executed" to its arguments. Whereas the "Executed" is killed "in retribution for a crime" he was convicted of, the "Victim" is injured because of the physical harm attempted by the "Assailant." EXECUTION also inherits the structure of REWARD_AND_PUN-ISHMENT, a frame that is totally irrelevant to ATTACK. Accordingly, *attack*.v and *execute*.v evoke different frames. Third, co-lexical units must adopt the same perspective on the frame. Whereas (9a) expresses the ENTER_AWARE-

NESS perspective of AWARENESS_CHANGE_SCENARIO, (9b) adopts the COM-ING_TO_BELIEVE perspective. Finally, co-lexical units should share similar denotations regardless of their parts of speech. For instance, *fatal*.a, *murder*.v and *genocide*.n are co-lexical units in the KILLING frame, according to the FrameNet database (Ruppenhofer et al., 2016: 11).

(9)   a. [Experiencer This   individual],   however,   is   not   [Manner suddenly] *STRUCK*Target [Content by a brilliant idea]

      b. [Cognizer We] [Time still] haven't *FIGURED*Target *OUT*Target [Content how to get the right numbers of people in the field]

In addition to co-membership, lexical units can be related to each other if they evoke frames that are related to each other. *Sin*.n, *crime*.n, and *pickpocket*.n are hierarchically linked in FrameNet because they evoke MISDEED, CRIME, and THEFT, respectively, which are linked through the inheritance relation (i.e., CRIME is an instance of MISDEED and inherits its conceptual structure, THEFT is an instance of CRIME and inherits its schematic structure). *Over-run*.v and *resist*.v activate the frames of INVADING and REPEL respectively. The former frame precedes the latter in the INVASION_SCENARIO (Ruppen-hofer et al., 2016: 79–85). Frame-to-frame relations changed through the history of frame semantics and FrameNet. Whereas the Inheritance relation has been always present, the Composition relation, for instance, changed into "Subframe of" and "Has subframes" (Ruppenhofer, Baker, and Fillmore, 2002: 360). The composition relation refers to the ability to decompose a complex frame into subframes. The new terms "subframe of" and "Has subframes" allow a bidirec-tional relation from the complex frame to its subparts (i.e., Has subframes) and from the subframes to their complex frames (i.e., subframe of). Relations among frames aimed at improving the understanding of frames and adding robustness. Figure 4.2 illustrates partial relations between some lexical units in the FrameNet database with reference to their related frames.

4   Frame-Based Analysis of Grammatical Phenomena

Fillmore fundamentally aimed at exploring the ways in which lexical units and grammatical constructions evoke frames and the realization of frame struc-tures in the sentence (Andor, 2010: 159). Therefore, FrameNet annotation iden-tifies the phrase type, grammatical function and roles played by the arguments of the predicate. Except for the subjects, the frame elements associated with the target word usually occur locally within the maximal phrase headed by

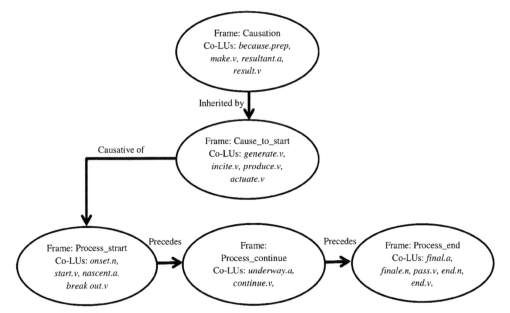

FIGURE 4.2 Partial frame-to-frame relations in FrameNet.

the target word. However, some grammatical phenomena force FrameNet lexicographers to annotate non-local constituents. FrameNet annotation is always lexicographically-motivated and the description of the semantic and syntactic valence of a word is customized for lexicographic purposes (Ruppenhofer et al., 2016: 18, 21, 31).

4.1   *Raising Constructions*

Predicates such as *seem, appear,* and *expect* represent cases of subject-to-subject and subject-to-object raising according to transformational syntax. In (10a), "Prime Minister" is hypothesized to be raised from the subject position of "appoint" to fill the object position of "expect" leaving a trace in its original subject position. Similarly, "Dublin" in (10b) was treated in transformational syntax as a case of raising the subject of "changing" to the subject position of "seems."

(10) a. They had expected the Prime Minister to appoint a third woman to his cabinet
    b. Dublin seems to be changing before my eyes

FrameNet, however, conducted a different, lexicographically-motivated analysis. It described the semantic properties of the filler of the frame element of the higher predicate (i.e., *expect.v* and *seem.v*) in a way that enables one of its arguments to be shared with the dominated target word (*appoint.v* and *change.v*). *Expect.v* evokes the frame of EXPECTATION in which the sentient "Cognizer" and the "Phenomenon" are core frame elements as displayed in (11a). "The Prime Minister" is annotated as part of the Phenomenon that was expected to happen in the future, similar to "to appoint a third woman to his Cabinet". However, *appoint.v* itself is a frame-evocative word. It essentially requires "Selector," "Appointee," "Role," "Function," and "Body." The annotation of the same sentence with *appoint.v* as the target lexical unit revealed that "Prime Minister" filled the position of the "Selector" although it is not dominated by the maximal phrase headed by *appoint.v* as exemplified in (12a).

Similarly, *seem.v* activates GIVE_IMPRESSION, which again allows one of its arguments (i.e., Phenomenon) to be shared with UNDERGO_CHANGE as reflected in (10)a and (11)b.

(11) a. [$_{Cognizer}$They] had *EXPECTED*^{Target} [$_{Phenomenon}$the Prime Minister] [$_{Phenomenon}$to appoint a
third woman to his Cabinet]

   b. [$_{Phenomenon}$Dublin] *SEEMS*^{Target} [$_{Inference}$to be changing before your very eyes]

(12) a. They had expected [$_{Selector}$the Prime Minister] to *APPOINT*^{Target} [$_{Appointee}$a third
woman] [$_{Role}$to his Cabinet]

   b. [$_{Entity}$Dublin] seems to be *CHANGING*^{Target} [$_{Manner}$before your very eyes]

The same phenomenon is applicable to modal verbs but another phenomenon is present in this case, i.e., discontinuous frame elements. There is a shared argument between the modal verb and the embedded predicate, typically the argument filling the subject position. FrameNet described this as part of the semantic representation of the modal verb that enables language users to interpret the subject of the modal verb as an argument of the VP complement. In addition, modal verbs typically realize one of their main arguments discontinuously before and after the modal verb. This discontinuity is not interpreted syntactically as a derivation from an underlying coherent form. It is rather understood as a property specific to modal predicates (Ruppenhofer et al., 2016: 22–36). See example 13.

(13) a. [$_{Possible\_event}$they] CAN^{Target} [$_{Possible\_event}$live together again]
      b. [$_{Resident}$they] can $LIVE^{Target}$ [$_{Manner}$together] again

4.2   Support Constructions

In the most straightforward case, the syntactic and semantic heads of the structure are the same. However, there are several instances in which the semantic
head of the target lexical unit is different from its syntactic head. In such cases,
the syntactic head is considered to support the semantic head. Supports are
syntactic governors of the target lexical units which express a state, event or
relation and are, accordingly, frame evocative. But supports do not have significant contribution to the meaning of the construction and they have a different
meaning outside the frame evoked by the governed lexical unit. Therefore,
the FrameNet team advocates for the argument that the semantic head is the
selector of the syntactic governor. FrameNet records *give, have* and *put up* as
supports of the lexical unit *fight*.n in the frame of HOSTILE_ENCOUNTER. The
frame evoked in (14) is not POSSESSION or GIVING. The two sentences evoke
the same frame, i.e., HOSTILE_ENCOUNTER, although different verbs syntactically govern the semantic head. The two verbs, i.e., *had* and *give*, support the
noun to project clauses. This stipulates the annotation of the subject of the support verb as one of the core frame elements, i.e., typical participant in the event
expressed by the target noun.

(14) a. [$_{Sides}$we] [had]^{Supp} a $FIGHT^{Target}$ [$_{Issue}$about something]
      b. [$_{Side\_1}$SPORTS enthusiasts representing Petersfield Chamber of Trade]
          [gave]^{Supp} [$_{Side\_2}$their opposition] a tough $FIGHT^{Target}$

It is not only verbs that can support nouns. Prepositions can function as supports of nouns, too. FrameNet displays *on* as support of *leave*.n, *for* as support
of *walk*.n and *to* as support of *piece*.n, among others (Ruppenhofer, Baker and
Fillmore, 2002: 365–368; Ruppenhofer et al., 2016: 21, 23–36).

4.3   Controllers

Controllers are also syntactic governors of frame-evoking nouns but, unlike
supports, they influence the meaning of the construction they participate in
with the frame-evocative noun. They are able to evoke their own frame, which
is typically different from the frame evoked by their adjacent noun. On the one
hand, supports do not evoke a frame and, therefore, do not have frame elements. However, the syntactic argument in the subject position of a support
verb is semantically interpreted as a frame element in the frame evoked by the
target noun. On the other hand, controllers evoke a frame and share one of their

frame elements with the lexical unit they govern. In the case of controllers of nouns, the argument in the subject position is usually the shared frame element (Ruppenhofer et al., 2016: 36–38; Fillmore, 2008: 132–136).

(15) a. [$_{Force}$it] had [suspended]^{Ctrlr} *OPERATIONS*^{Target} [$_{Area}$in Syria]
      b. [$_{Agent}$The United Nations] *SUSPENDED*^{Target} [$_{Activity}$humanitarian aid operations in Bosnia-Herzegovina]
      c. [$_{Cognizer}$He] regularly [got]^{Ctrlr} [$_{Degree}$very] *DRUNK*^{Target}
      d. [$_{Entity}$she] 'd probably started to *GET*^{Target} [$_{Final\_quality}$drunk] [$_{Explanation}$for it]

The verb *suspend* controls the noun *operations*, and, accordingly, *suspend operation* can evoke both MILITARY_OPERATION through the noun *operation* and ACTIVITY_PAUSE through the lexical unit *suspend*. *Operations* labels the subject of *suspend* Force in (15a). The alternative annotation considers *suspend* the target lexical unit and labels *operations* as part of the constituent realizing the "Activity," illustrated in (15b).

Similarly, *get drunk* is able to evoke two frames. It can evoke the frame of INTOXICATION through the controlled adjective *drunk*, demonstrated in (15c). In this case, *got* is labeled as controller and its subject is labeled as an external argument of *drunk*, i.e., "Cognizer." *Get drunk* also can evoke TRANSITION_TO_A_STATE through the controller verb *get* and assigns FINAL_QUALITY to *drunk*, (15d) exemplifies this case.

4.4   *Expletive Arguments*

FrameNet annotates several cases in which a construction requires one of its arguments to be non-referential. This includes cleft structures, especially subject extraposition. *Possible.a* evokes the frame of LIKELIHOOD, which requires the presence of a "Hypothetical_event." The "Hypothetical_event" can be realized as an external subject as displayed in (16a) or it can be extraposed while the subject position is filled with expletive *it* as instantiated in (16b). Similarly, the object position can be filled with expletive *it* whereas the original object of the sentence is extraposed. *Hate.v*, for instance, activates the frame of EXPERIENCER_FOCUSED_EMOTION. It requires the presence of an "Experiencer" who "feels intense dislike" for "Content" which can be realized as dependent object as annotated in (16c) or extraposed as represented in (16d). The third case, which requires the use of expletive *it* in an argument position, is relevant to the description of the WEATHER, displayed in (16e). Finally, existential constructions require the presence of expletive *there* in an argument position.

FrameNet created a frame of EXISTENCE, considered *there be* one of its evocative lexical units and assigned it the part of speech of a verb. The annotation of *there be* as target lexical units is shown in (16f) (Ruppenhofer et al., 2016: 42).

(16) a. [Hypothetical_event A higher quality of timely competitor intelligence] is *POSSIBLE*Target

b. It was just *POSSIBLE*Target [Hypothetical_event that the kidnappers might show it to him]

c. [Experiencer He] *HATES*Target [Content days when he can't get straight into his workshop]

d. [Experiencer She] *HATED*Target it [Content when he made her feel stupid]

e. It should have been raining, thundering, hailing.

f. But *THERE*Target still *ARE*Target n't [Entity enough ringers to ring more than six of the
    eight bells]

5   Frame Semantics and FrameNet in Current Research

Boas and Dux (2017: 6) argued that the diversity of research work based on or oriented to FrameNet is a manifestation of its quality and usability. This section reviews some of the studies that adopted a frame-based approach to the investigation of cognitive linguistic or pragmatic phenomena, the improvement of forensic linguistic research, the creation of language resources, and the performance of linguistic tasks.

5.1   *Cognitive Linguistic Research*

The frame-based approach was applied to the study of logical metonymy, conceptual metaphors and other cognitive linguistic areas of research. To demonstrate, Sweep (2010) adopted a frame-based approach to the study of logical metonymy. The study focused on one of the dominant logical metonymies, i.e., OBJECT FOR ACTION IN WHICH THE OBJECT IS INVOLVED. To elaborate, the semantics of verbs like *begin, finish* and *enjoy* is compatible with an activity or an event. However, these verbs may combine with a metonymical object typically involved in the event instead of mentioning the event itself. *Begin a book* is interpreted as "begin the activity of reading or writing a book." The study focused on 21 verbs divided into three groups, namely, aspectual (e.g., *begin, start, continue*), evaluative (e.g., *choose, enjoy, want*) and in-between (e.g., *attempt, resist, survive*). The frame-based analysis identified 13 frames triggered by these verbs. In addition, the metonymical object did not typically correspond to part of the frame evoked by the verb. It was part of a different frame.

(17) Mary began the book

Two conceptual structures (i.e, frames) are present in example (17). The first frame is ACTIVITY_START and it is evoked by *began*. It has "Agent" and "Activity" as core frame elements. Whereas "Agent" is realized by *Mary*, "Activity" is not present at the surface level. In addition, *the book* is not a filler of any frame element slot in ACTIVITY_START. It is rather part of the "Activity" which is not linguistically realized. It functions as a filler of the core frame element "Text" in the READING_ACTIVITY frame. Therefore, examples such as (17) contain an embedded structure relevant to the implicit "Activity" frame element and another main conceptual structure evoked by the main verb in the sentence, i.e., *began*.

(18) Mary interrupted John

This analysis revealed the presence of another logical metonymical relation PARTICIPANT (AGENT) FOR AN ACTION which accounts for several sentences as observed in (18). *Interrupted* evokes the frame of INTERRUPTING_PROCESS in which "Agent" and "Process" are core frame elements. On the one hand, *Mary* realizes the frame elements of "Agent." On the other hand, *John* is relevant to the "Process" which is understood as a process of talking or presenting. *John* is, therefore, the "Interlocutor" in the embedded conceptual structure of DISCUSSION.

Given the interpretative power of frames, Sullivan (2016) argued that frames can identify which parts of the metaphoric language are capable of evoking conceptual structures. Verbs, on the one hand, are dependent elements, and they evoke the source domain of a metaphor. Fillers of the frame elements, on the other hand, are autonomous, and they evoke the target domain of the metaphor.

(19) a. The lawyer devised an argument.
      b. **The lawyer devised a building.
      c. **The carpenter devised an argument.
      d. The lawyer built an argument.

The application of the conceptual metaphor THEORIES ARE BUILDINGS on a non-metaphoric sentence such as (19a) without affecting the syntactic structure is possible only through changing the verb *devise*. Replacing either of the nouns with another noun from the semantic field of building results in the odd (**), or at least non-metaphoric, sentences in (19b) and (19c). Conceptual Metaphor Theory does not provide reasons for this linguistic phenomenon. The theory is more concerned with explaining the conceptual mapping between the source and target domains than in interpreting the linguistic structures.

In contrast, Frame Semantics and Construction Grammar explain the linguistic realization of conceptual metaphors. *Build* evokes the frame of BUILD-ING which is the source domain of THEORIES ARE BUILDINGS. The meaning of *build* depends on "Agent" (who performs the building act) and "Created_entity" (which is the entity that exists after the performance of the act of building). Understanding the meaning of *build* is dependent on the meaning of the frame elements "Agent" and the "Created_entity." However, the meaning of the fillers of these frame elements, for instance *house* as filler of "Created_entity," is autonomous.

The fillers of the "Created_entity" evoke frames different from the ones evoked by the main lexical units in the sentence. *House*, for instance, evokes the frame of BUILDINGS in which "Building" is the sole core frame element whereas *argument* evokes the frame of REASONING. "Agent" is the trajectory and "Created_entity" is the landmark in this representation. To create the metaphoric sense in (19b), *argument* or *build* are fundamentally understood as denoting one of their non-central senses. The study recommended the creation of a new frame, e.g., ABSTRACT_BUILDING, to account for conceptual metaphors such as THEORIES ARE BUILDINGS. FrameNet also separates several metaphoric and non-metaphoric senses in different frames. The literal sense of *link*.v is recorded in BEING_ATTACHED and its metaphoric sense is placed in the frame of COGNITIVE_CONNECTION.

5.2   *Corpus Pragmatic Research*

In addition to the ushering of Frame Semantics towards cognitive linguistic studies, Hu and Chen (2019) used Frame Semantics to study a pragmatic aspect of language. They conducted a corpus-based study of surprise markers in published academic research. Surprise is relevant to cognition because it depends on a mismatch between what was expected and what is actually experienced. Although research articles are known for the use of non-emotive language, surprise markers were frequent in the analyzed corpus. A qualitative analysis of the concordances of *surprise* and its synonyms, antonyms and derivative forms assigned 7 frames to 439 surprise markers. EXPECTATION, STIM-ULUS_FOCUS, TYPICALITY, JUST_FOUND_OUT, EMOTION_DIRECTED, DESIR-ABILITY and STIMULATE_EMOTION were evoked by the surprise markers in the studied research articles. "Stimulus," "Result," "Explanation," and "Degree" were among the most frequent frame elements realized in the context of surprise-related frames.

A qualitative exploration of the frames and their frame elements in Frame-Net displayed that "Using," "Inheritance," and "Perspective_on/Perspectivized_ in" relations hold the frames together. In addition, some of the frame elements are common among the frames. The study, accordingly, proposed a more general schema that embraced the conceptual structures of the seven frames and reflected the most frequent frame elements in the corpus. That is why the suggested frame was classified as genre-specific.

The new frame included five core frame elements "Trigger," "Degree," "Explanation," "Resolution," and "Experiencer." Each frame element had a label that is general enough to accommodate for the several frame elements originally present in FrameNet. "Trigger," for instance, had four types based on the analyzed examples. A "Trigger" can be a relationship, attribute, behavior or phenomenon. Similarly, the "Experiencer" may be the author, a participant or another researcher. In addition, the new frame changed the status of "Degree," for instance, from non-core to core.

In this connection, Abdelzaher (2019a) addressed the negative and positive evaluation of contexts through the use of frame semantics. The study focused on violence-related frames, frame elements and lexical units. Generally speaking, the two participants in the violent context determine the polarity and the designation of the act. The same act if performed by *an army* against *an occupation force* would be positively labeled defense or resistance. If the situation was reversed, it would be perceived as attack or invasion.

She identified violence-related frames based on frame-to-frame relations, definition of frames and shared frame elements in FrameNet. Regardless of the different labels of frame elements, "Aggressor" and "Victim" were considered typical participants in violence-related frames. "Agent," "Assailant," and "Killer" in CAUSE_HARM, ATTACK, and KILLING were collectively referred to as "Aggressor" in the study. The quantitative analysis of two corpora identified HOSTILE_ENCOUNTER, ATTACK, WEAPONS, KILLING, and CAUSE_HARM among the most frequent violence-related frames.

The qualitative analysis of the fillers of "Aggressor" and "Victim" revealed the different ways by which radical groups manipulated the appraisal of violence. Although "Aggressor" is negatively perceived, fillers like *brave soldier, knights of right* and *justice* change the negativity of "Aggressor." This change was reinforced when the "Victim" was realized through negatively evaluated fillers such as *tyrants, apostates* and *injustice*.

5.3   *Forensic Linguistic Research*

Legalese usually raises problems of understanding for those who are not well versed in the legal domain and procedures. Nominalizations, passive forms and vague terms are some of the typical features hindering the comprehension of legal texts. Rathert (2006) employed frame semantics in the domain of forensic linguistics. The study called for the collaboration between jurists and linguists in the enhancement of the comprehensibility of legal texts. The application of Frame Semantics to the analysis of legal discourse enabled better understanding of the discourse.

(20) The 28-year-old Moroccan was found guilty as accessory to murder in more than 3000
cases

Frame Semantics interprets example (20) as an instance of VERDICT. "Defendant," "Charges," "Case," and "Finding" play core roles in this frame. *The 28-year-old Moroccan* is a filler of "Defendant," *to murder* fills the "Charges" frame element and evokes the frame of KILLING and *guilt* is a filler of "Finding." "Case," however, was not realized in the sentence. Modeling the meaning of the sentence in terms of frames and frame elements improves the comprehensibility of frames. Moreover, frame-to-frame relations in FrameNet enrich the relations among sentences in a text and, accordingly, enhance its comprehensibility. CRIMINAL_PROCESS in FrameNet consists of several sub-frames, namely ARRAIGNMENT, ARREST, TRIAL, and SENTENCING. It is also a sub-frame of CRIME_SCENARIO. Also, ARREST inherits the conceptual structure of INTENTIONALLY_ACT. Whereas the density of this net of frames increases the comprehensibility of legal texts, unexpressed frame elements and singletons (i.e., frames which are not related to other frames) cause comprehensibility problems.

Also, Barreira, Pinheiro, and Furtado (2017) advocated the use of Frame Semantics in conducting forensic linguistic analysis. Given the growing textual data on electronic devices and the ineffective use of keyword search, forensic experts need new tools to explore and extract crime-related information from the electronic texts submitted for forensic analysis. Forensic experts examined all frames in FrameNet and selected 113 frames which are relevant to criminal investigations, e.g., QUANTITY, Intoxicants, COMMERCIAL_TRANSACTION. The selected frames formed knowledge base called FrameFOR which is specifically constructed for forensic analysis purposes. FrameFOR increased the recall of the information relevant to forensic investigations even if the lexical unit was not present in the lexicon. To elaborate, *grams of skunk* was retrieved as an instance of QUANTITY because of the lexical unit *grams*. Although *skunk* was absent from the lexicon storing the lexical units in FrameFOR, it was identified as the filler of the "Measured_entity" frame element. *Skunk* was used by criminals to refer to a type of marijuana.

The constructed knowledge base and its dependent semantic role labeling helped forensic experts realize new words (i.e., filler of frame elements) employed by criminals to camouflage the original message. This method also increased the retrieval of the entities, people, places and times of the events.

5.4   *Creation of Language Resources*

The innovative design of FrameNet inspired several scholars to construct similar language resources. As a demonstration, Abdelzaher (2017) used FrameNet data to build a lexicon of violence. VIOLENCE in FrameNet is related to a single frame, i.e., CAUSE_HARM. Although frames like ATTACK, KILLING, and RAPE are present in FrameNet, they display no association with VIOLENCE. In contrast, the proposed lexicon contained twelve interlinked frames. For instance, ATTACK was inherited by HITTING_BEATING, CUTTING_STABBING, and SEXUAL_ASSAULT whereas WEAPONS was inherited by SHARP_WEAPONS and EXPLOSIVE_WEAPONS.

The proposed lexicon modified the conceptual structure of some frames. RAPE was generalized to include all types of SEXUAL_ASSAULT. Also, HITTING_BEATING, and CUTTING_STABBING, among others, were newly introduced as relevant to the frame of VIOLENCE. The differences between the proposed lexicon of violence and the coverage of violence in FrameNet emanated from the different schemas of violence proposed in the two resources. VIOLENCE in the new lexicon covered two situations. The first situation represented one-sided violence committed by an "Aggressor" against a "Victim." The second situation denoted the mutual participation of two sides in a violent act against each other. This new schema of violence allowed the inclusion of fighting and war situations as relevant to the conceptualization of violence. A more developed version of the lexicon was then applied in the automatic detection of violence on social media (Abdelzaher, 2019b).

Ide et al. (2008) worked on the creation of a "sharable" and "reusable" resource of annotated sentences. They planned the creation of a manually annotated sub-corpus of American English. FrameNet frames and frame elements were used in the annotation process. The process consisted of manual annotation and automatic semantic role labeling conducted by FrameNet annotators.

(21) a. [FLUID The River Liffey] FLOWS^Target [SOURCE from west] [GOAL to east] [AREA through the
center of the city] [GOAL to Dublin Bay].

   b. The River Liffey flows from west to east through the [PART CEN-TER^Target] [WHOLE of the
city] to Dublin Bay.

   c. The [LOCALE RIVER^Target] [NAME Liffey] flows from west to east through the center of
the city to [NAME Dublin] [LOCALE BAY].

FrameNet annotators conducted full-text annotation of part of the sub-corpus. Full-text annotation stipulated that all evocative words in a sentence are equally analyzed. Therefore, it resulted in multiple annotations of the same sentence. Example (21) illustrates the three frames evoked by the same sentences. FrameNet annotators also supervised the automatic semantic role labeling. Errors in the automatic labeling of semantic roles included wrong identification of the frame evoked by the lexical unit, failure to assign a frame to the lexical unit despite the existence of the frame and wrong labeling of the frame elements. FrameNet annotators conducted additional manual annotation of sentences to train the automatic labeler to overcome the most frequent errors. FrameNet-based annotations increased the "reliability" and "usability" of the sub-corpus in natural language processing tasks.

Full-text annotation provides richer information than the traditional lexicographic annotation that is extensively used in FrameNet. In turn, it requires more exhaustive effort of the annotator and increases the complexity of the semantic role-labeling task. Baker (2012) referred to the significance of full-text annotation to text understanding, detection of textual entailment, and making inferences. Because annotators analyze all lexical units in a text, the frequency of the annotated lexical units should be equal to the number of the words in the text and the frequency of the annotated senses should reflect the presence of the senses in the analyzed text.

5.5   *Performance of Linguistic Tasks*
Frame Semantics and FrameNet significantly contributed to the task of semantic role labeling in natural language processing. The task requires the identification of lexical units, assigning of the correct frame, identification of the linguistic arguments of the lexical unit and correct frame element labeling of the arguments. Ruppenhofer et al. (2013) highlighted the contribution of frame semantics to the discovery of linguistically absent but conceptually inferred arguments (i.e., null instantiations) in a sentence. The study discussed the

influence of annotating predicate-argument structure, realizing null instantiations and coreference on the performance of semantic role labeling. The
annotation of null instantiations moved the task beyond the traditional semantic labeling of linguistically instantiated arguments. It enriched the task with a
discourse dimension beyond the sentence level.

Shen and Lapata (2007) argued for the considerable impact of frame-based
semantic role labeling on text understanding. They explored its influence on
question-answer tasks. Their framework aimed at extracting answers based on
FrameNet semantic role annotations. It mainly focused on the use of FrameNet
in checking the matches between the text of the question and the words in the
automatically recalled sentences embedding the answer. FrameNet was used
to analyze the structure of the question according to the evoking lexical unit
and its semantic roles assignment. Semantic roles were automatically assigned
according to the word realizing the frame element, its semantic role and the
score (i.e., the numerical possibility of the semantic role to function as a label of
the word in the argument position). This enabled automatic matching between
the structure of the question and the structures of potential answers. Although
the application of the new frame-based method alone obtained poor results,
the authors recommended the integration of the new model with a syntax-
based system to retrieve better results.

Frame Semantics was also effective in modeling and recognizing textual
entailment. Lexical units in the same frame share the same semantic roles and
are potential sources of textual entailment, e.g., *kill* (*oneself*) and *suicide*. Similarly, frame-to-frame relations provide a good candidate for the realization of
textual entailment, for instance, the Causative_of relation links *die* and *kill* and
the Precede relation links *accuse* and *arrest*. Also, FrameNet rules generalize
the frames and frame elements over syntactic alternations. For instance, the
passive and active forms if they involve the same lexical unit are similarly annotated as evocative of the same frame.

The use of frame information in modeling and detecting textual entailment
depends on the precision and the recall of automatic semantic role labeling
and on the coverage of the FrameNet lexicon. The authors created a corpus of
entailment pairs. The sentences were annotated based on FrameNet information and enriched with textual entailment information. The corpus was used
to check the influence of frame information on textual entailment recognition. The manually annotated corpus contained additional frame information,
for entailment pairs, that was absent in FrameNet to evaluate the influence of
FrameNet coverage on the task. It also represented a manual gold standard
against which the performance of automatic semantic parsers such as Shalmaneser can be measured. The limited coverage of lexical units in FrameNet

did not result in low performance. The coverage of FrameNet was good enough to perform the task. In addition, the results recommend the use of the constructed corpus to improve the relatively low performance of Shalmaneser (Burchardt et al., 2009).

Hasegawa et al. (2011) highlighted the role of frame-to-frame relations in manual paraphrasing tasks. They provided qualitative examples of the use of co-lexical units, frame-to-frame relations and grammatical information in FrameNet in paraphrase.

(22) a. Henry wanted to be the best
      b. Henry was eager to be the best

(23) a. [Authority They] are going to *INCARCERATE*Target [Prisoner him]
      b. [Agent They] are going to *CONFINE*Target [Theme him] [to prison Holding_ Location]

(24) a. [Behavior Arguing in front of them] was *RUDE*Target of [Evaluee us].
      b. It was *RUDE*Target of [Evaluee us] [Behavior to argue in front of them].

Co-lexical units can be used interchangeably to convey similar meanings. *Want*.v and *eager*.a, as displayed in example (22), activate the DESIRING frame and occur with the same frame elements. In the previous example (22a) and (22b) are cases of paraphrase by "intersubstitutability of synonymous expressions." In addition, lexical units belonging to frames related by a FrameNet relation are good candidates for paraphrasing tasks, too. For instance, the Inheritance relation between INHIBIT_MOVEMENT and IMPRISONMENT allows the conceptual structure of the parent frame to be inherited by a second, child frame with some additional specifications. Example (23) displays the transfer from the specific instance of IMPRISONMENT in (23a) to the more general situation of INHIBIT_MOVEMENT in (23b). The similarity between the two instances is evident and explained through the Inheritance relation. Moreover, available grammatical information in FrameNet such as the different valence patterns is beneficial to paraphrasing tasks. The valence patterns of *rude*.a in the frame SOCIAL_INTERACTION_EVALUATION display several ways in which "Agent" and "Evaluee" are realized. Example (24) shows how two of these patterns are used to convey the same message. FrameNet is proved to be a valuable resource for systematic paraphrase.

6   Conclusion

This chapter presented an overview of Frame Semantics as a cognitive linguistic theory and as a tool of analysis. Frame Semantics aims at modeling
experiential world knowledge and displaying the linguistic information stored
in the mental lexicon to language users. It established a strong link between
schematic structures at the cognitive level and lexico-syntactic information at
the linguistic level. Fillmore worked on Case Grammar, explored the role of
semantics in grammar, applied concepts of cognitive psychology to language
and suggested new ways of defining words before he could formulate his theory
of Frame Semantics. A historical perspective on the ideas which led Fillmore
to the formulation of Frame Semantics was offered in Section 2.

Frame Semantics is a multidimensional theory and, accordingly, it has several applications in linguistics, lexicography and language engineering. Some of
the most outstanding contributions of Frame Semantics are salient in lexicography. Frame Semantics provided solid theoretical background to the computational lexicographic project FrameNet. FrameNet is different from traditional
lexicographic projects in several aspects, including the choice of lexicographically relevant information, the systematic separation of word senses, and the
categorization of words in frames, among others. Section 3 discussed the new
perspective on the lexicon provided by Frame Semantics and its lexicographic
realization in the FrameNet database.

Fillmore's argument for the description of the semantic and syntactic
valence of words has been one of the distinguishing features of the theory and
of FrameNet. Linking the abstract frame elements at the frame level and their
linguistic realizations at the sentence level resulted in a new description of
some grammatical information about raising predicates and support constructions, for example. Section 4 explained the frame-based approach to several
grammatical phenomena and cited illustrating examples from FrameNet.

In addition to lexicography and grammar, Frame Semantics and FrameNet
have been effective tools of analysis in diverse linguistic domains. Section 5
showed how frame information was used to advance cognitive semantic analysis, tackle pragmatic features in corpora, aid forensic linguistic research, create language resources and perform linguistic tasks computationally and non-
computationally.

References

Abdelzaher, Esra'. 2017. Compiling a cognition-based thematic monolingual lexicon: The case of violence. *Cognitive Linguistic Studies* 4: 313–329. Available at doi:10.1075/cogls.00007.abd

Abdelzaher, Esra'. 2019a. The systematic adaptation of violence contexts in the ISIS discourse: A contrastive corpus-based study. *Corpus Pragmatics* 3: 173–203. Available at doi:10.1007/s41701–019–00055-y

Abdelzaher, Esra'. 2019b. Lexicon-based Detection of Violence on Social Media. *Cognitive Semantics* 5: 32–69. Available at doi:10.1163/23526416–00501002.

Abdelzaher, Esra'. 2021. Cognitive Linguistics and Digital Lexicography. *The Routledge Handbook of Cognitive Linguistics*, 568–584. New York: Routledge. Available at doi:10.4324/9781351034708–38.

Abdelzaher, Esra', and Ágoston Tóth. 2020. Defining Crime: A multifaceted approach based on Lexicographic Relevance and Distributional Semantics. *Argumentum* 16: 44–63. Available at doi: 10.34103/argumentum/2020/4.

Ackerman, Farrell, Paul Kay and Catherine O'Connor. 2014. Charles J. Fillmore. *Language* 90: 755–761.

Andor, Jozsef. 2010. Discussing frame semantics: The state of the art. An interview with Charles Fillmore. *Review of Cognitive Linguistics* 8: 157–176.

Atkins, Sue, Michael Rundell, and Hiroaki Sato. 2003. The Contribution of FrameNet to Practical Lexicography. *International Journal of Lexicography* 16: 333–357.

Atkins, Sue, and Michael Rundell. 2008. *The Oxford Guide to Practical Lexicography*. Oxford: Oxford University Press.

Atkins, Sue, Charles Fillmore and Christopher Johnson. 2003. Lexicographic relevance: Selecting information from corpus evidence. *International Journal of Lexicography* 16: 251–280.

Baker, Collin. 2012. FrameNet, current collaborations and future goals. *Language Resources and Evaluation* 46: 269–286.

Baker, Collin, Charles Fillmore and John Lowe. 1998. The Berkeley FrameNet Project. *36th Annual Meeting of the Association for Computational Linguistics and 17th International Conference on Computational Linguistics* 1, 86–90. Montreal: Association for Computational Linguistics.

Barreira, Ravi, Vladia Pinheiro, and Vasco Furtado. 2017. A framework for digital forensics analysis based on semantic role labeling. In *2017 IEEE International Conference on Intelligence and Security Informatics (ISI)*, 66–71. Beijing: IEEE Press.

Boas, Hans, and Ryan Dux. 2017. From the past into the present: From case frames to semantic frames. *Linguistics Vanguard* 3: 1–14.

Burchardt, Aljoscha, Marco Pennacchiotti, Stefan Thater and Manfred Pinkal. 2009. Assessing the impact of frame semantics on textual entailment. *Natural Language Engineering* 15: 527–550. Available at doi: 10.1017/S1351324909990131

Fillmore, Charles. 1968a. The case for case. *Form and Meaning in Language,* volume 1: *Papers on Semantic Roles,* 21–119. Stanford: CSLI Publications.

Fillmore, Charles. 1968b. Lexical Entries for Verbs. *Foundations of Language* 4: 373–393.

Fillmore, Charles. 1969. Verbs of judging: An exercise in semantic description. *Paper in Linguistics* 1: 91–117.

Fillmore, Charles. 1970. Subjects, speakers and roles. *Synthese* 21: 251–274.

Fillmore, Charles. 1972. A grammarian looks to sociolinguistics. *Report of the Twenty-Third Annual Round Table Meeting on Linguistics and Language Studies,* 273–287. Washington: Georgetown University School of Language.

Fillmore, Charles. 1975. An alternative to checklist theories of meaning. *Proceedings of the First Annual Meeting of the Berkeley Linguistics Society,* 123–131. Berkeley: Berkeley Linguistics Society.

Fillmore, Charles. 1976. Frame semantics and the nature of language. *Annals of the New York Academy of Sciences: Conference on the origin and development of language and speech* 280: 20–32.

Fillmore, Charles. 1977a. The case for case reopened. In P. Cole and J. Sadock (eds.), *Grammatical relations,* 59–81. New York: Academic Press.

Fillmore, Charles. 1977b. Scenes-and-frames Semantics. In A. Zampolli (ed.), *Linguistic Structures Processing,* 55–81. Amsterdam: North-Holland.

Fillmore, Charles. 1985. Frames and the semantics of understanding. *Quaderni di semantica* 6: 222–254.

Fillmore, Charles. 1988. The mechanisms of "construction grammar." *Proceedings of the Fourteenth Annual Meeting of the Berkeley Linguistics Society,* 35–55. Berkeley: Berkeley Linguistics Society.

Fillmore, Charles. 1992. "Corpus linguistics" or "computer-aided armchair linguistics". In J. Svartvik (ed.), *Directions in Corpus Linguistics,* 35–60. Berlin: De Gruyter.

Fillmore, Charles. 2003. Double-decker definitions: The role of frames in meaning explanations. *Sign Language Studies* 3: 263–295.

Fillmore, Charles. 2008. Valency issues in FrameNet. In T. Herbst and K. Götz-Votteler (eds.), *Valency: Theoretical, Descriptive and Cognitive Issues,* 129–162. Berlin: De Gruyter. Available at doi: 10.1515/9783110198775.1.129

Fillmore, Charles. 2014. Frames, constructions and FrameNet. In T. Herbst, H. Schmid and S. Faulhaber (eds.), *Constructions, Collocations, Patterns,* 121–166. Berlin: De Gruyter. Available at doi: 10.1515/9783110356854.121

Fillmore, Charles, and Sue Atkins. 1992. Towards a frame-based organization of the lexicon: The semantics of RISK and its neighbors. In A. Lehrer, E. Kittay and R. Lehrer (eds.), *Frames, Fields, and Contrasts: New Essays in Semantic and Lexical Organization,* 75–102. New York: Routledge

Fillmore, Charles, and Sue Atkins. 2000. Describing polysemy: The case of 'crawl.' In

Y. Ravin and C. Leacock (eds.), *Polysemy: Theoretical and Computational Approaches*, 91–110. Oxford: Oxford University Press.

Fillmore, Charles, and Collin Baker, 2001. Frame semantics for text understanding. *In Proceedings of WordNet and Other Lexical Resources Workshop*. Pittsburgh: NAACL.

Fillmore, Charles, Christopher Johnson, and Miriam Petruck. 2003. Background to FrameNet. *International Journal of Lexicography* 16: 235–250.

Fillmore, Charles, Miriam Petruck, Josef Ruppenhofer and Abby Wright. 2003. Frame-Net in action: The case of attaching. *International Journal of Lexicography* 16: 297–332.

Fillmore, Charles, Charles Wooters and Collin Baker. 2001. Building a large lexical data-bank which provides deep semantics. *Proceedings of the Pacific Asian Conference on Language, Information and Computation*, 3–26. Hong Kong: City University of Hong Kong.

Hasegawa, Yoko, Russel Lee-Goldman, Albert Kong and Akita Kimi. 2011. FrameNet as a resource for paraphrase research. *Constructions and Frames* 3: 104–127.

Hu, Guangwei, and Lang Chen. 2019. "To our great surprise ...": A frame-based analysis of surprise markers in research articles. *Journal of Pragmatics* 143: 156–168.

Ide, Nancy, Collin Baker, Christiane Fellbaum, Charles Fillmore and Rebecca Passon-neau. 2008. MASC: The manually annotated sub-corpus of American English. *Proceedings of the 6th International Conference on Language Resources and Evaluation*, 2455–2460. Morocco: European Language Resources Association (ELRA).

Johnson, Christopher, and Charles Fillmore. 2000. The FrameNet tagset for frame-semantic and syntactic coding of predicate-argument structure. *1st Meeting of the North American Chapter of the Association for Computational Linguistics*, 56–62. US: Association for Computational Linguistics.

Kuperberg, Gina, and T. Florian Jaeger. 2016. What do we mean by prediction in lan-guage comprehension? *Language, Cognition and Neuroscience* 31: 32–59. Available at doi: 10.1080/23273798.2015.1102299.

Lakoff, George. 2014. Charles Fillmore, discoverer of frame semantics, dies in SF at 84: he figured out how framing works. *Review of Cognitive Linguistics* 12: 251–257.

Nerlich, Brigitte, and David Clarke. 2000. Semantic fields and frames: Historical explo-rations of the interface between language, action, and cognition. *Journal of Pragmatics* 32: 125–150.

Ostermann, Carolin. 2015. *Cognitive Lexicography: A New Approach to Lexicography Making Use of Cognitive Semantics*. Berlin: De Gruyter.

Petruck, Miriam. 2011. Advances in frame semantics. *Constructions and Frames* 3: 1–8.

Rathert, Monika. 2006. Comprehensibility in forensic linguistics—new perspectives for frame semantics. *Form, Structure, and Grammar. A Festschrift presented to Gün-ther Grewendorf on occasion of his 60th birthday*, 337–352. Berlin: Akademie.

Rundell, Michael. 2008. Recent trends in English pedagogical lexicography. In T. Fontenelle (ed.), *Practical Lexicography: A Reader (Oxford Linguistics)*, 221–243. Oxford: Oxford University Press.

Ruppenhofer, Josef, Charles Baker and Charles Fillmore. 2002. Collocational information in the FrameNet database. *Proceedings of the 10th EURALEX International Congress*, 359–369. København: Center for Sprogteknologi.

Ruppenhofer, Josef, Russel Lee-Goldman, Caroline Sporleder and Roser Morante. 2013. Beyond sentence-level semantic role labeling: Linking argument structures in discourse. *Language Resources and Evaluation* 47: 695–721.

Ruppenhofer, Josef, Michael Ellsworth, Miriam Petruck, Christopher Johnson, Collin Baker and Jan Scheffczyk. 2016. *FrameNet II: Extended Theory and Practice*. Online

Sambre, Paul. 2010. Framing from grammar to application. *Belgian journal of linguistics* 24: 1–15. Available at doi:10.1075/bjl.24.00int

Shen, Dan, and Mirella Lapata. 2007. Using semantic roles to improve question answering. *EMNLP-CoNLL 2007—Proceedings of the 2007 Joint Conference on Empirical Methods in Natural Language Processing and Computational Natural Language Learning*, 12–21. Prague: Association for Computational Linguistics.

Sullivan, Karen. 2016. Integrating constructional semantics and conceptual metaphor. *Constructions and Frames* 8: 141–165.

Sweep, Josefien. 2010. A frame-semantic approach to logical metonymy. *Constructions and Frames* 2: 1–32.

CHAPTER 5

Conceptual Semantics

Ronald W. Langacker

1   Basic Notions

A basic claim of Cognitive Grammar (CG) is that grammar is *symbolic*, consisting in form-meaning pairings (Langacker, 1987; 1991; 2008a). It follows that any sensible approach to grammar has to be based on meaning. In cognitive linguistics, meaning is identified with *conceptualization*, in a very broad sense of the term. It refers to any aspect of our mental experience, not just abstract concepts, but also immediate experience: sensory, motor, and emotive. Also included is apprehension of the context in all its dimensions: physical, linguistic, social, and cultural. *Semantic structures* are those conceptions which function as the meanings of linguistic elements. So semantics is part of conceptualization: the portions adapted for purposes of speech and language.[1]

How do we describe meanings? It must first be recognized that a complete and definitive description of meaning is not really possible, short of a complete description of human psychology and cognitive processing. There are several reasons for this. First, semantic structures have too many different aspects or dimensions for them all to be represented in a single formalism (e.g. a set of features, symbolic logic, or some version of formal semantics). It is a common expectation in linguistics that semantic (or other) structures should be reducible to a discrete set of symbols arranged in a certain way on a page, that a strictly formal account is in principle possible. Of course, we want to be precise, and I often use formulas, but I never think of these as being complete or definitive or as faithfully capturing the actual nature of a phenomenon. In the case of conceptualization, the meaning of many words includes a visual, auditory, or motor image. Part of the meaning of a word like *trumpet* is an auditory image of what a trumpet sounds like, and also a visual image of what one looks like. Part of the meaning of a verb like *walk* is what it feels like to walk—sensorimotor

---

1   This position has been misrepresented by various people, notably Levinson (1997: 14), who wrote that I do not distinguish between conceptualization in general and linguistic meaning. My view, rather, is that linguistic meanings are conceptualizations adapted for expressive purposes in accordance with the conventions of language.

© KONINKLIJKE BRILL NV, LEIDEN, 2023 | DOI:10.1163/_006

images. It is hard to imagine that these would be expressible in the same kind of formalism as other aspects of meaning. We need to have reasonable expectations about what linguistic meaning is like, and a realistic account has to be diverse to accommodate different kinds of phenomena.

Second, linguistic meanings are neither self-contained nor well delimited. Being built on our conceptualizations, based on our interaction with the world, they are not sharply distinct from other kinds of knowledge. There is no specific dividing line between what is linguistic and what is extralinguistic. And finally, meanings are variable and context-dependent, always shifting in use even when they have a stable and conventional basis. It is probably true that an expression is never used twice with exactly the same conceptual import.

It is generally held in cognitive linguistics that most common expressions have multiple established meanings—not just a single meaning, but a family of related meanings. These are sometimes called *senses*. Some senses are *prototypical* relative to others, and some are *schematic* relative to others. An example I've often used is the noun *ring*. Some of its senses are noted in Figure 5.1. Used out of context, it would probably be taken as referring to a circular piece of jewelry worn on the finger. That is the prototypical or basic sense, which I have indicated with a heavy-line box. More abstractly, a *ring* can be a circular piece of jewelry regardless of where you wear it (maybe an earring or a navel ring, but nowadays rings are worn in all sorts of places). More abstractly still, it could be a circular object of any sort, not necessarily a piece of jewelry. It does not even have to be an object. It can be a mark: when you drain the water from a bathtub, and there is dirt around it, we call that a ring. Observe that I use the solid arrows for relations of *schematicity* or *elaboration*; a circular entity is the schema that a circular mark and a circular object both instantiate. A circular piece of jewelry is a special case of a circular object, and a circular piece of jewelry for the finger is a special case of a circular piece of jewelry. These are all different senses of *ring*, different conventional ways of understanding it. And there are others still. Metaphorically, a *ring* can be a group of people who operate together secretly, like a smuggling ring or a spy ring. That is a kind of metaphor, a matter of viewing it as somehow circular with an interior, which goes along with the notion of secrecy. But we also describe a circular arena as a ring, e.g. a bull ring. Once established, that gets extended to rectangular arenas, as for boxing or wrestling; these are not circular, but they are still rings. There is also the schema that these share, which is just the notion arena.

These are only some of the established senses of *ring* in its use as a noun. Although their relationship seems quite evident, the range of conventional meanings cannot be predicted a priori but has to be learned through experience. They differ in familiarity (or *entrenchment*), a psychological matter, as

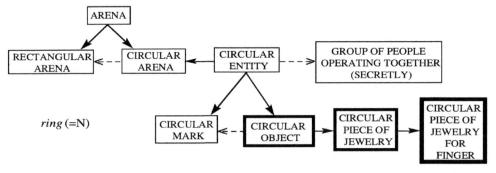

FIGURE 5.1   An expression with multiple senses.

well as in conventionality, a social matter. Owing to the possibility of extensions in different directions, there need not be an overarching schema—an abstract sense that all of them instantiate.

Figure 5.1 contains two kind of arrows, which represent kinds of categorizing relationships—a solid arrow, for *elaboration*, and a dashed arrow for *extension*. A → B indicates that A is schematic for B: A is schematic, B is specific; B elaborates A; B is an instance of A. It implies that A and B are compatible, but that B is specified in more detail (it is a finer-grained description). The import of A ⇢ B is that A is a more central or prototypical sense, B is more peripheral (e.g. in metaphor). In this case there is some conflict in meaning: B does not completely match A; it suspends certain features of A; it changes A in some way. Categorization is a broad and varied phenomenon, but at least we have to recognize these two basic types.

One kind of semantic extension is *metaphor*, as when we speak of a *smuggling ring* or a *spy ring*. Another kind is *metonymy*, e.g. the word *church*, which can designate either a building or something related to it, namely a religious group. Whereas metaphor is based on similarity, metonymy is based on association. A standard example (cited in Lakoff, 1987) is the classifier *hon* in Japanese, which prototypically is used with long thin objects, such as sticks, canes, pencils, candles, trees, ropes, and hair. But around this are clustered a variety of senses related by metonymy, such as a martial arts contest with a staff or sword. A staff or sword is a long thin object, but *hon* is used not to name or classify that object, but rather the contest or combat. Once the term is applied to martial arts contests of that sort, it can be generalized and used for something like a judo match, which does not involve a long thin object. That is a natural path of extension. Or a medical injection, where the long thin object is a needle, associated by metonymy, or a roll of tape, which can be stretched out to be a long thin object. Or a film or a movie, or a wire as a special case, and then a telephone call, by metonymic extension from a wire. Or a hit in baseball—that

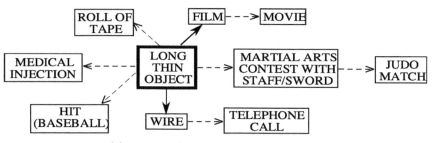

FIGURE 5.2 Semantic elaborations and extensions from a prototype.

could either be metonymy or metaphor (you hit with a bat, which is a long thin object, but usually the ball goes along a flat trajectory that resembles such an object).

This brings us back to the fundamental questions of semantic analysis: How can meanings be described? What are they made of? The CG claim that they reside in conception runs counter to a strong tradition in semantics, which holds that we cannot even talk about conceptualization because it is so mysterious. Even in fairly recent times, semantics textbooks have maintained that appealing to concepts is necessarily vague and non-empirical, hence unscientific. But in the age of cognitive science that is not really true. We have to deal with conception, because that is where meaning mainly lies, and we can do it in a principled, rigorous, and motivated way. But how?

One proposal, well known in cognitive linguistics, is the notion of *image schemas*. It is primarily due to Lakoff (1990), and though he ascribes it to CG, I regard it as problematic in some respects. In the absence of explicit definitions, I offer the following: they are schematic and imagistic concepts which are abstracted from pre-conceptual bodily experience, function as constituents of more complex notions, and provide the structure projected metaphorically to more abstract domains. The list of image schemas cited by Johnson (1987) is at best representative: container; blockage; enablement; source-path-goal; cycle; part-whole; full-empty; counterforce; link; near-far; merging; contact; compulsion; restraint-removal; count-mass; superimposition; process; collection. I will not discuss image schemas in detail, as the notion is rather vague and the examples quite diverse. They can all be recognized as basic concepts plausibly used in semantic descriptions. However, I find it more helpful to distinguish several kinds of conceptual entities each of which is "basic" in some way.

A preliminary, very general notion, is that of a *cognitive domain*: any coherent area or product of conceptualization, relative to which semantic structures can be characterized. I suggest that any expression evokes a set of cognitive domains as its basis. There are two main sorts of domains: *basic* and *non-basic*. A basic domain is cognitively irreducible, i.e. it cannot be explicated in terms of more fundamental conceptions. Prime examples are time, space, and the experiential potential of the various senses (e.g. color, pitch, taste). Most domains do invoke other conceptions and are thus non-basic. For instance, the shape conception CIRCULAR presupposes the basic domain of space, and in turn functions as a non-basic domain with respect to RING.

We have terms for basic domains, and use concepts from other domains to talk about them metaphorically, but these fall short of actual characterizations of the fundamental experience. Basic domains are not themselves concepts, but regions of conceptual potential. For instance, COLOR SPACE—a metaphorical term—is simply the set of color sensations we are capable of experiencing. A color concept, like RED or GREEN, is a non-basic domain representing a particular realization of that potential. Qualifying as non-basic domains are any sort of concept or product of conception, ranging from a simple notion like RED to something as complex as a specialist's knowledge of Chinese history. Given these broad definitions, it could hardly not be true that an expression's meaning is based on a set of domains. These do not however constitute its meaning, for this also depends on what we do with the content they provide (how we *construe* it).

The irreducibility of basic domains is only one way in which something can be "basic." We can usefully distinguish three kinds of conceptual entities, each basic in its own way, for purposes of describing linguistic meanings: (i) *minimal concepts* in basic domains; (ii) experientially grounded *conceptual archetypes*; and (iii) *maximally schematic notions* independent of specific domains.[2]

Some examples of (i) are LINE, ANGLE, and CURVATURE—minimal concepts in the domain of space. Focal colors, like RED, BLUE, and YELLOW, represent minimal concepts in color space. TEMPORAL SEQUENCING is a minimal notion in time, and the exertion of MUSCULAR FORCE, in the kinesthetic domain.

Conceptual archetypes are quite different. Among the countless examples are the conception of a physical object, the spatial motion of an object, the human face, the human body, a physical container and its contents, a whole and its parts, seeing something, holding something, handing something to someone, exerting force to effect a desired change, speaking, a face-to-face

---

2   Image schemas, as Lakoff and Johnson use the term, represent a mixture of these types, especially (ii) and (iii).

social encounter, and so on indefinitely. These are complex notions with a lot of conceptual content, but psychologically they are basic and fundamental, and while some have an innate basis, all are grounded in experience, which can make them both elaborate and hard to define. Consider how hard it is to explicitly characterize the human face, or to say what a physical object is. Despite this complexity, we are obviously equipped to deal with such entities, and come into this world expecting to find them. Archetypes thus tend to function as *prototypes* for linguistic categories, e.g. physical object for nouns, and for verbs, the exertion of force to effect a change.

Some examples of (iii) are the notions point vs. extension, contrast, boundary, change, continuity, contact, inclusion, separation, proximity, multiplicity, and group. These resemble the cases in (i) by virtue of being highly schematic, but differ in that they can be manifested in many different domains. These can be basic domains (like time, space, or color), or most any non-basic domain (ranging from the structure of a bicycle to the history of China).

Central to CG is the working hypothesis that certain fundamental and universal grammatical notions—minimally including noun, verb, subject, object, and possessive—are characterized in terms of both a prototype and a schematic meaning instantiated by all instances. Such notions involve a natural relationship between an experientially grounded *conceptual archetype*, functioning as the prototype, and a basic, presumably inborn *cognitive ability*, providing the schematic characterization. The ability, which makes it possible for structured experience to occur in the first place, is initially manifested in the archetype and then applied to other realms of experience (Langacker, 2015). While I regard this as self-evident, it is certainly not a consensus view. Most linguists would probably agree about the prototypes, but even in cognitive linguistics there are many who would not accept the schematic characterizations, which I think are equally critical.

Consider nouns. Granted that the prototype is the notion physical object, what might be the schematic definition? Since nouns are so diverse, a characterization that applies to all category members has to be independent of any particular conceptual content. Thus it is reasonably taken as consisting in a basic cognitive ability: the capacity for mental *grouping*, in which multiple entities (which may or may not be apprehended separately) are conceived as a single thing for higher level cognitive purposes. In the case of a physical object, this is obvious and automatic; it is what lets us perceive physical objects in the first place. First manifested in the prototype, it is later extended to other cases involving other realms of experience. The fundamental role of grouping is perhaps most evident in the many count nouns designating groups (e.g. *set, array, orchestra, constellation, forest, convoy, archipelago*, and so on indefinitely).

2   Cognitive Domains

The meaning of a linguistic expression consists of both conceptual content and a particular way of construing or viewing that content. As an initial example of content vs. construal, I often use the expressions in (1), which correspond to diagrams (a), (b), (c), and (d) in Figure 5.3. They share the essential content sketched in the diagram at the left: the conception of a physical container only partially filled with liquid. But although they describe the same objective situation, these expressions are semantically and grammatically very different. This is due to their selection of lexical and grammatical options, each of which imposes a certain construal on the content they invoke. So even when the content is the same, they differ in meaning.

(1)   a. the glass with water in it
       b. the water in the glass
       c. the glass is half-full
       d. the glass is half-empty

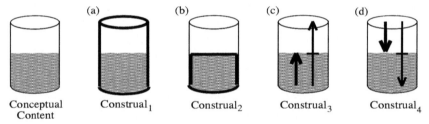

FIGURE 5.3 Alternate construals of conceptual content.

The nominal expression in (1a) designates the container, i.e. singles it out as the immediate focus of attention. I use the term *profiling* for this kind of prominence. Indicated in diagrams by heavy lines, an expression's profile is its *conceptual referent*: what it refers to within the content invoked. As construed in (1a), the container is profiled by *glass* as well as the nominal as a whole. By contrast, (1b) refers to the fluid inside. The container still figures in its meaning, but the liquid is profiled by both *water* and the full nominal. The other two expressions are clauses, which profile relationships. The key relationships are those profiled by the adjectives *full* and *empty*, as indicated by arrows in diagrams (c) and (d). Both are based on the dynamic concept of filling, in which content is added to a container until its level reaches the top. The verb *fill* profiles an event of this sort, and when used as a verb *empty* describes its reversal. The relationships profiled by the adjectives *full* and *empty* are those resulting from the completion of these events, to which *half* adds the specification that the liquid (for full) or its absence (for empty) reaches only the midpoint of the container.

The two basic aspects of linguistic meaning, content and construal, need to be examined in more detail. I describe an expression's content as residing in a set of *domains*. While this is neither a strong claim nor a precise definition, it is useful as a convenient and general way of dealing with the immense complexity of conceptual structures. The label does not indicate a particular type of conception, but rather a function: that of providing the basis for semantic analysis and description. Structures of any size or at any level of organization can serve in this capacity. Collectively, the set of domains evoked by a given expression are referred to as its *matrix*. These are not separate and discrete, like beads on a string or jars on a shelf, but are related in various ways (e.g. overlap, inclusion) and differ in salience and centrality. It is therefore hard to provide a definite inventory, or even say how many there are, as a specific number depends on how we choose to count.[3]

It is useful to go through an example in some detail, so let us consider the count noun *glass*, as in (1). A number of domains, each presupposed by the next, are central to its characterization. The referent being a physical object, there is first the basic domain of space. With an object comes the conception of a typical shape (roughly, a cylinder closed at one end). That in turn brings in the concept of a canonical orientation (long dimension aligned along vertical axis, with the closed end at the bottom). This orientation is quite helpful for the function of a glass as a container for liquid (which also involves the notions of spatial inclusion, potential motion, force, and stability through time). The container function is incorporated in the next: the role of a glass in the process of drinking, which likewise involves a number of other domains (e.g. the human body, grasping, motion with the arm, ingestion). More variable, though still fairly central, are properties such as material (usually the substance glass) and size (easily held in one hand). More peripheral to the meaning of *glass*, hence activated only in particular contexts, are many other facets of our encyclopedic knowledge of such objects (e.g. cost, washing, storage, possibility of breaking, position on a table at meals, occurrence in matching sets, method of manufacture).

All of these notions figure to some extent in the meaning of this lexeme. Figure 5.4 is an attempt to show this graphically. The ellipses stand for cogni-

---

3 I note just in passing that, since mental spaces qualify as domains, mental space configurations—including metaphoric and metonymic relations—constitute domain matrices.

tive domains. The point of diagram (a) is simply that they overlap, with some included in others, as was just indicated. The heavy-line circle represents the expression's profile (conceptual referent and focus of attention). It plays some role in all these domains and thus ties them together. The domains are shown separately in diagram (b) because it has a different purpose: to indicate that they differ in degree of centrality, hence the likelihood of being activated on a given occasion.

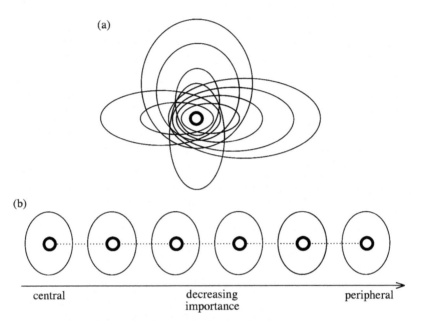

FIGURE 5.4 Relations among the domains in a matrix.

A basic question now arises. Given that all these domains are included in what we know about glasses, how much of this is linguistic, and how much a matter of general (extralinguistic) knowledge? The issue is fundamental and controversial (Haiman, 1980; Wierzbicka, 1995; Langacker, 1987: § 4.2). The traditional assumption is that just a small portion of this knowledge is specifically linguistic. Referred to as the *dictionary view* of semantics, it holds that a lexeme's meaning comprises only a particular, limited set of specifications. A basic problem is the absence of any principled way to draw the line; from language use it seems evident that any definite boundary would be arbitrary. More fundamentally, it rests on a common but highly misleading metaphor (Reddy 1979): that expressions are bounded containers with meaning as their content. An alternative that avoids these problems, known as the *encyclopedic view* of semantics, is widely adopted in cognitive linguistics. Instead of being separate and discrete, semantic structure resides in the exploitation and adaptation of conceptual structures for linguistic purposes. So on this view, all the domains discussed for *glass* have the potential to be accessed as part of its linguistic meaning.

Crucially, not all of this knowledge is equal. Mastering a lexical item like *glass* is not simply a matter of labeling a body of knowledge, but of structuring it in a particular way, such that certain specifications are by convention more central and accessible than others. This is indicated in Figure 5.4(b), where domains are shown separately (despite their overlap) and placed along a scale indicating their relative importance to the lexeme's semantic value. Ranging from highly central to quite peripheral, their position on this scale translates into the likelihood of being activated on a given occasion. Some specifications are so fundamental that they are probably evoked even when overridden by the context, others so peripheral that a special context is required for their activation. The essential point is that the likelihood and level of activation are matters of degree partially determined by contextual factors. Being neither completely fixed nor entirely unconstrained, an expression's meaning affords the conventionality and flexibility required for effective use.

The encyclopedic view has an important consequence: when examined in sufficiently fine detail, an expression is never used twice with exactly the same semantic value. Though some might find this disturbing, I regard it as being self-evident. Figure 5.5 represents two occurrences of the same expression (e.g. *glass*). As matters of established convention, we can presume that they have access to the same set of domains with the same ranking for centrality. But in terms of actual use, they are bound to differ in how they exploit this potential. As indicated by lines of different thickness, uses vary in regard to the *selection* of domains to be activated as well as their *degree* of activation. It is improbable that any two usage events would ever be exactly identical in these respects.

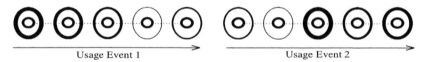

FIGURE 5.5 Variable activation of domains in a matrix.

Let us take another example, the lexical item *cat*. The sentences in (2) all involve the basic sense of *cat* but construe it very differently by highlighting various facets of its encyclopedic meaning. Its use in (a) is stereotypical, based on nothing more than central specifications pertaining to well-known properties (an

animal of certain size, of a certain shape, covered with fur, makes a characteristic sound, and so on). The others rely on more peripheral specifications that
for various reasons are accessed less commonly. Sentences (b) and (c) invoke
properties of cats manifested only on certain occasions. The interpretation of
(d) depends on specialized knowledge, and (e) on the cultural association of
cats with witchcraft and superstition. In (f)–(h), *cat-proof* indicates resistance
to cat activities with undesirable consequences: killing birds, scratching on furniture, and excretion. It can be seen that anything we know about cats has the
potential to be singled out, directly or indirectly, as a basis for linguistic meaning.

(2)   a. When she picked up the cat it started purring.
      b. He was saved by his cat-like reflexes.
      c. It was a real cat-fight.
      d. A cat is a mammal.
      e. Watch out for ladders, black cats, and broken mirrors!
      f. Is this birdcage cat-proof?
      g. Is this sofa cat-proof?
      h. Is this rug cat-proof?

The essential claim of encyclopedic semantics, the absence of any specific
dividing line between linguistic and extralinguistic specifications, would therefore seem well-motivated. The more traditional view—that there is a definite boundary—rests on a standard but inappropriate metaphor that likens
expressions to containers, which has the entailment that meanings are "in the
words." But rather than being distinct from general knowledge, the conceptions constituting linguistic meanings are accessed through it, representing
the flexible evocation and adaptation of structures largely established on other
grounds.

   This has a number of theoretical consequences. For one thing, if semantics
is included (as it has to be), language is not an encapsulated module (distinct
and self-contained), but an integral aspect of cognitive processing. It follows
that a truly exhaustive description of semantic structure cannot be achieved,
for that would require a complete account of human cognition. Finally, despite
there being patterns of composition, semantics is not fully compositional. The
meaning of a whole cannot be predicted from those of its parts, if only due to
the indeterminacy of the component lexemes.

3   Construal

Linguistic meaning is a function of both conceptual *content* and *construal*.[4] Providing the content is an array of cognitive domains, flexibly accessed and adapted to the context. Construal is our ability to conceive and portray the same situation in different ways. There are many dimensions of construal, which are subject to alternate classificatory schemes. Here we will focus on three broad classes: *specificity*, *prominence*, and *perspective*.

3.1   *Specificity*

Specificity is the level of precision and detail ("granularity") at which a structure is characterized. It was illustrated in Figure 5.1 by different senses of the lexeme *ring*: CIRCULAR ENTITY → CIRCULAR OBJECT → CIRCULAR PIECE OF JEWELRY→ CIRCULAR PIECE OF JEWELRY FOR FINGER. The notation A → B indicates that A is schematic relative to B, which is consistent with it but more specific (characterized in finer-grained detail). Distinct expressions are also related in this fashion: each noun in (3a) serves to elaborate the more schematic noun it follows; likewise for the verbs in (3b). Choosing among such options is a basic and unavoidable aspect of construal. Depending on the circumstances, for example, the sentences in (3c) could all be used for the event described by the last one. There is no requirement that the various parts of an expression be comparable in their level of specificity. Thus in (3d) the subject is schematic and the predicate quite specific, whereas (3e) is fairly specific apart from the verb.

(3)   a. thing → creature → animal → mammal → dog → poodle
        b. do → act → move → run → sprint
        c. Something happened. → An animal moved. → A dog ran into the room.
           → A dirty poodle sprinted recklessly into the kitchen of our cottage.
        d. An animal sprinted recklessly into the room.
        e. A dirty poodle entered the kitchen of our cottage.

A fundamental claim of CG is that grammar is inherently meaningful—not (as in one standard view) an autonomous formal system. Instead of belonging to separate "components," lexicon and grammar form a continuum of symbolic structures (form-meaning pairings). Specificity is pivotal in this regard.

---

4   The relation between them can be seen as a special case of figure-ground organization (Talmy, 1978).

Whereas lexical items tend to be rich in conceptual content and are often very specific, the structures ascribed to grammar are conceptually impoverished and generally quite schematic. This is however a matter of degree, and a particular line of demarcation would be arbitrary. We can see this in grammaticization: the evolution of grammatical elements from lexical sources. The process is known to be gradual, often resulting in the co-existence of "lexical" and "grammatical" uses of the same element, as exemplified by *thing* and *do*.

As a lexeme, the uses of *thing* center on the prototype PHYSICAL OBJECT (a conceptual archetype), which indicates a bounded expanse of material substance in space. When it functions grammatically as part of the indefinite pronouns *something, nothing, anything*, and *everything*, it abstracts away from these specifications, as the referent need not be physical, substantive, spatial, or bounded (e.g. *Nonsense is something she can't tolerate*). Instead it represents the schematic import of nouns, residing in the capacity for mental grouping (a basic cognitive ability). Likewise for *do*. As a lexical verb, its uses center on the prototype VOLITIONAL ACTION. It lacks this import when used grammatically as an "auxiliary" verb, where it appears in questions and in cases of negation or affirmation. There its content is limited to the verb schema, consisting in an occurrence scanned sequentially through time (Langacker, 2008b). Since they serve different functions, the lexical and grammatical variants often co-occur (e.g. *What did she do?*).

Once more, these are matters of degree. Both lexicon and grammar are meaningful, forming a continuum of symbolic structures. The meaningfulness of grammar tends not to be recognized because its semantic import resides primarily in the construal it imposes on conceptual content. However, construal is equally important in lexical meanings. The following survey will illustrate its crucial role in both lexicon and grammar.

3.2   *Prominence*

Many linguistic phenomena are reasonably viewed as matters of prominence, but since they are quite diverse, that alone is not an adequate characterization. For example, concepts in the physical realm have greater salience for us than abstract entities. A prototype is more prominent in a category than peripheral members. The discursive notions topic and focus both involve prominence, but they are not equivalent. Here we are mainly concerned with two phenomena central to grammar: profiling and trajector/landmark organization.

As the basis for its meaning, an expression invokes a certain body of conceptual content, called its *base*.[5] Within this base, it gives special prominence

---

5   There is no real distinction between its base and its matrix (i.e. the relevant set of domains). The difference (an example of construal) is that the term base contrasts with profile.

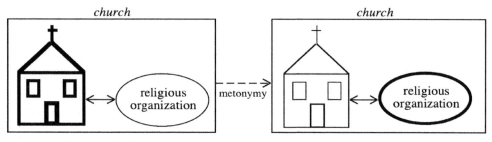

FIGURE 5.6 An example of metonymy.

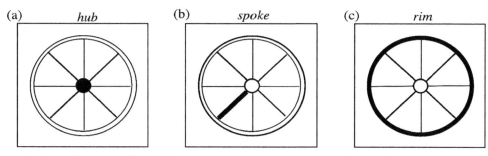

FIGURE 5.7 Alternate profiles on a base.

to some substructure, called its *profile*. The profile is a kind of focus of attention: what the expression refers to (designates) within the base. It is thus its *conceptual referent*.

Profiling is pivotal to many instances of *metonymy*, as exemplified by the alternate senses of *church*. In contemporary English, *church* refers primarily to a building, where religious organizations hold their meetings, but by metonymy, it can also refer to such an organization (e.g. *the Catholic Church*). As seen in Figure 5.6, the two senses share a base comprising overlapping portions of their matrices: domains pertaining to the building, the organization, and their association. They differ as to which facet of the base they focus as the profile, thereby making it the center of attention. This is considered an instance of metonymy to the extent that the 'building' sense is perceived as being more fundamental, so that the 'organization' sense is apprehended in relation to it.

The term metonymy applies to alternate construals of the same expression. Clearly, though, analogous semantic distinctions hold between different expressions, as shown in Figure 5.7. The terms *hub*, *spoke*, and *rim* all refer to parts of a wheel, and can only be understood in relation to its overall configuration, which serves as their common base. While they share this content, they differ from one another owing to their profiles, and also from *wheel*, which profiles the entire configuration. These specifications are far from being exhaustive of their meanings (e.g. the functions of the profiled entities are also quite important). They are however central and crucial for distinguishing them.

Further examples of profiling offer a basis for discussing a fundamental distinction, which can be viewed in several ways: from the standpoint of processing activity, from that of conception, or that of linguistic categorization. Given that processing consists of patterns of activity (most basically, neural activation), we can distinguish between *connection* and *grouping*. Connection is a matter of co-activation, where patterns overlap or influence one another. They thereby constitute a higher-order pattern, with the potential to participate as a whole (effectively as a single pattern) in further connections. I refer to this as a *grouping*. For instance, the notion of a triangle represents a grouping residing in the connection of line segments. The terms *thing* and *relationship* are respectively used in CG for conceptions residing in groupings and connections, which can be recognized as basic cognitive abilities of maximal generality. Being independent of any specific content, these are proposed as the schematic characterizations of maximally general grammatical categories (nouns and relational expressions).

Although the distinction is fundamental, things and relationships are inextricably bound up with one another: groupings are a product of connections, which often pertain to prior groupings. Since both are usually involved, the mere inclusion of a thing or a relationship does not determine an expression's category—that depends on the choice of profile, an aspect of construal. Consider the term *hypotenuse*, sketched in Figure 8(a), which refers to the side of a right triangle lying opposite the right angle. Its base is thus the conception of a right triangle, which incorporates a number of things and relationships: three line segments; their connection via overlapping endpoints; the angles they form; and for one angle, a relation of perpendicularity. An essential point is that neither the triangle nor the profiled line segment is itself an instance of *hypotenuse*. It is only in relation to one another—when the line is specifically conceived as part of the triangle—that this concept emerges. It represents a particular construal of the base obtained by imposing a certain profile.

Because it is based on the notion right triangle, the concept hypotenuse represents a *higher level of organization*. The levels discernible in a complex conception are an important factor in profiling. As indicated in Figure 8(b), both *iris* and *pupil* are higher-level notions characterized with respect to the overall configuration of the human eye. But they are also characterized in relation to the higher-level configuration comprising them both, imposing alternate profiles on this smaller base. A significant aspect of their meaning resides in their apprehension as distinct but complementary facets of this structure (hence the standard collocation *iris and pupil*). If asked to define the word *iris*, a speaker might very well describe it as the colored region surrounding the pupil; conversely, a *pupil* could be defined as the opening in the center of the iris. However, it is not obvious that either notion is more basic than the other or defined in terms of it. In CG their relationship may just be a matter of different profiles on the same conceptual content.

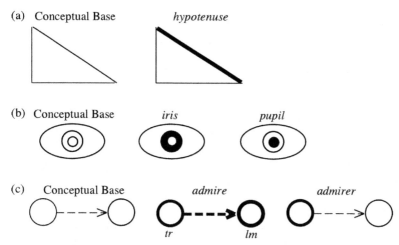

FIGURE 5.8 Effects of profiling.

By contrast, one notion is indeed based on another in a transparent instance of derivational morphology, as in Figure 5.8(c). Despite having the same conceptual content, the verb *admire* and the noun *admirer* are semantically distinct and represent different categories. Their shared base consists in a mental relationship (dashed arrow) between two individuals, such that one entertains a positive attitude toward the other. The verb *admire* profiles this relationship, including its participants.[6] Being derived from this verb, the noun *admirer* has little additional content. The main difference, the semantic contribution of *-er*, is that it shifts the profile from the relationship as a whole to the individual who entertains the attitude.

This example illustrates the central CG claim that an expression's *grammatical category* depends on the nature of its *profile* (Langacker 2008a; 2015). Fundamental in this regard is a broad division into expressions that profile *things* (i.e. groupings) and those which profile *relationships* (connections); in terms

---

6   They are included because a relationship is *conceptually dependent* on its participants, requiring them for its own manifestation. Participants are generally more *autonomous* (capable of being conceived in isolation).

of traditional classes, nouns are included in the former, while verbs, adjectives, and prepositions belong to the latter. *Admire* is a verb because it profiles an *occurrence*, i.e. a relationship followed in its evolution through time. But although it has the same content, *admirer* is a noun because it profiles a thing.

The profile-base distinction, together with the notion that grammatical category depends on profiling (rather than overall conceptual content), offers a straightforward resolution of certain issues that might seem problematic. There is first the prevalence of expressions that function grammatically as nouns even though a relationship is clearly essential to their meaning. Prime examples are body-part and kinship terms, such as those in Figure 5.9, whose *raison d'être* is to specify an entity's relation to others (its place within a larger configuration). But if nouns designate *things*, why is the standard term *relational noun* not contradictory? There is no inconsistency because the conception of a relationship, crucial though it is, merely constitutes the base with respect to which the profile—a thing—is characterized. They differ in nature: whereas the base consists in content, profiling is a matter of reference (focusing of attention).

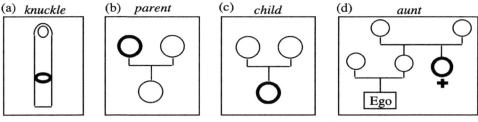

FIGURE 5.9 Relational nouns.

This view of linguistic meaning has the additional advantage of avoiding a problem of circularity that arises when one relies on verbal definitions. What, for instance, is a *parent*? The word is succinctly and accurately defined as 'a person who has a child.' But what, then, is a *child* (in the kinship sense)? It is 'a person who has a parent.' Though not wrong, these definitions alone do not get us very far. They can hardly be understood without invoking the biological and social relationships summarized by the minimal kinship configuration in diagrams 9(b)–(c). Neither word is solely defined in terms of the other, nor do their meanings consist in linguistic expressions. Rather, these notions represent alternate profiles on the same conceptual base.

Broadly defined as connections, relationships figure in the meaning of every expression, but run the full gamut in terms of salience and individuation. At one extreme, they are wholly implicit, remaining below the level of conscious awareness. Relationships are inherent even in the conception of a featureless mass of substance, e.g. *rock*, for its apprehension as such is based on assessments of continuity and identity—the registration (at some level of processing) of sameness throughout its expanse.[7] At the opposite extreme, exemplified by *admire*, are expressions in which a relationship is not only explicit but is made the focus of attention as the profile. In between are cases like those in Figure 5.9, where an unprofiled relationship provides the essential content and is therefore highly salient.

As manifestations of basic mental capacities (grouping and connection), things and relationships underpin a fundamental linguistic opposition in the form of grammatical categories based on profiling. Either can be profiled, rendered salient by being singled out as the focus of attention. But owing to their nature, this prominence is intuitively less evident with relationships than with things. The difference is most striking in the case of central instances: physical objects vs. events. A typical object is physical and directly observable, consisting in a compact, stable expanse of material substance in space. By contrast, a typical event consists in energy-driven change, and thus is transient (occurring through time), immaterial (having no substance of its own), diffuse (involving multiple participants), and observable only through its effects. An object can often be identified by pointing to it in a picture, but while a relationship may be discernible in a visual scene, it is not itself a visible entity which can be pointed to as such. As informal notations, therefore, relationships are often represented in CG diagrams by various sorts of lines and arrows meant to be suggestive of connections.

If relationships are ultimately just a matter of connection, a fundamental aspect of processing activity, they figure somehow in every conception. Whether they rise to the level of conscious awareness, and conform to our informal notion of what constitutes a "relationship," depends in large measure on the nature and prominence of the connected entities. These can be things, other relationships, qualities, or locations. If salient and apprehended separately, the connected entities are referred to as *participants*. There are also *one-participant relationships*, in which the connections hold among facets of a single entity (e.g. a shape specification) or position it with respect to a frame of reference.

Being dynamic and non-substantive, relationships are usefully thought of as residing in various kinds of *operations* describable (informally and impression-

---

7   A count noun use (a rock) also incorporates relationships pertaining to shape, size, and bounding.

istically) by terms like "assessment," "comparison," and "scanning."[8] By way of illustration, the adjectival use of *parallel* (as in *parallel rows*) profiles a relationship represented by the arrows in Figure 5.10(a). It consists in the connection of two line-like entities through a multifaceted assessment of their spatial positions: first the apprehension of separation, a matter of scanning from one to the other at every point along their extension; and based on this, comparisons registering identity throughout in the magnitude of displacement. The verb *rise*, sketched in Figure 5.10(b), designates a complex relationship comprising a change of location through time (t). Its single participant occupies successive locations along the vertical axis, with moment-to-moment comparison ("sequential scanning") indicating successively greater distance from its original position.

(a) *parallel*

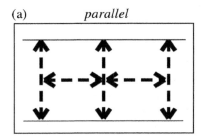

(b) *rise*

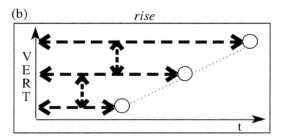

FIGURE 5.10 Profiling of relationships.

Though simplistic and at best suggestive, these descriptions may at least illuminate the characterization of relationships as complex patterns of connecting activity. They can be helpful in grasping two basic notions of CG: that grammatical category depends on an expression's profile; and that, despite their lesser salience and non-substantive nature, relationships share with things the potential to function in this capacity. So while they both profile relationships involving space, *rise* and *parallel* belong to distinct categories owing to a fundamental difference. It is claimed that a verb profiles an *occurrence* (also called a *process*), defined as a relationship *scanned sequentially*, i.e. followed step by step in its evolution through time (Langacker, 1987: § 7.1.3; 2008b). By contrast, the relationship profiled by the adjective *parallel* is viewed holistically, the entire configuration being accessible all at once (hence evident in a photograph).[9]

---

8 These refer here to implicit aspects of processing activity (as opposed to volitional actions focused as objects of conception).

9 Among the relational expressions that fail to qualify as verbs are adjectives, prepositions, adverbs, participles, infinitives, and nominalizations. Even when based on an occurrence,

As with nominal expressions (which profile things), we find relational expressions that have the same content but differ in meaning due to their choice of profile. In their basic sense, for instance, the verbs *give* and *receive* invoke as their base the conception of a canonical act of transfer. As shown in Figure 5.11, this is a complex event involving three participants in the semantic roles of agent, mover, and recipient. In either a physical or an abstract sense, the agent initiates the event by exerting some kind of force whereby the mover, originally under the agent's control, comes to be controlled by the recipient. The semantic distinction is a matter of profiling different facets of this complex interaction: *give* focuses attention on what the agent does, and *receive* on the recipient gaining control.

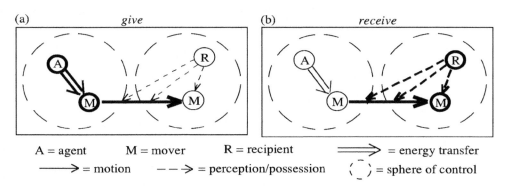

FIGURE 5.11 Alternate profiles within a complex relationship.

It should now be abundantly clear that profiling has a pivotal role in semantics and grammar. Another kind of prominence crucial in grammar pertains to the participants in a profiled relationship, which have varying degrees of salience within it. The main participant, called the *trajector* (*tr*), can be roughly characterized as the entity being located, evaluated, or described. A second participant, called the *landmark* (*lm*), is often invoked for this purpose. While these have varied semantic roles (e.g. 'agent,' 'patient,' 'mover,' 'experiencer'), it is only in their prominence per se that we find a viable basis for general definitions (schematic meanings). In the CG analysis, the trajector is thus the *primary focus of attention* within a profiled relationship, and a landmark (when present) the *secondary focus*.[10] There is also a temporal dimension to their characterization:

<hr>

they construe it holistically either by restricting its profile (e.g. *broken, admirer*) or by summation, accessing all its facets simultaneously (e.g. to *finish*, [*having*] *finished*).

10   The relation between them can be seen as a special case of figure-ground organization (Talmy, 1978).

from the standpoint of dynamic processing, the trajector is the *initial focus* in building up to a full conception of the profiled relationship (Tomlin, 1995; Langacker, 1999a).

The need to recognize trajector/landmark organization is evident from expressions that differ in meaning despite having the same content and profiling the same relationship. For example, the prepositions *above* and *below* are clearly non-synonymous,[11] but where does the difference reside? For all intents and purposes, they invoke the same conceptual base (a configuration in oriented space) and designate the same two-participant relationship (involving position along the vertical axis), so the diagrams in Figure 12 are basically alike. The semantic distinction can only be attributed to the status of the participants as primary vs. secondary relational focus. It is a matter of whether the expression is aimed at locating the higher participant or the lower one, making it the trajector, with the other participant serving as landmark (point of reference) for this purpose. In other words, *A is above B* situates A with respect to B, while *B is below A* does just the opposite.

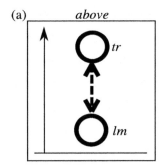 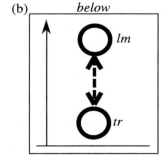

FIGURE 5.12 The semantic importance of trajector and landmark.

Evidence for this analysis is provided by discourse sequences like those in (4a)–(b). Since the question in (4a) seeks to determine the location of a certain lamp, an appropriate answer is one in which the lamp functions as trajector. The response in (i) is thus felicitous, but the one in (ii)—with the table as trajector—is not. In (4b), of course, the reverse is true.

(4) a. Where is the lamp?
     (i)   The lamp (tr) is above the table (lm).
     (ii) *The table (tr) is below the lamp (lm).

---

11   If you look up the meaning of *above* in a dictionary, and it merely says *below*, you should get another dictionary.

    b. Where is the table?
       (i)   The table (tr) is below the lamp (lm).
       (ii) *The lamp (tr) is above the table (lm).

The sequences in (5) are analogous. As seen by comparing Figures 5.12 and 5.13, they are basically the same except that *before* and *after* profile relationships in time instead of space. It is worth noting that these alternate domains correlate with a difference in participants: in terms of their actual nature, the party and the ceremony are events rather than objects. Linguistically, however, they are expressed by nouns, being construed as abstract things (like the noun *event* itself).

(5) a. When was the party?
       (i)   The party (tr) was before the ceremony (lm).
       (ii) *The ceremony (tr) was after the party (lm).
    b. When was the ceremony?
       (i)   The ceremony (tr) was after the party (lm).
       (ii) *The party (tr) was before the ceremony (lm).

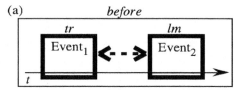 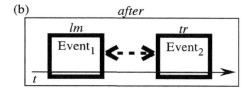

FIGURE 5.13 A temporal example of trajector/landmark organization.

Though needed for semantic purposes, trajector/landmark organization also has a basic role in grammar. In particular, the notions trajector and landmark are put forth in CG as the ultimate basis for characterizing the grammatical notions subject and object (Langacker, 1991: ch. 7). Here I will merely cite a few cases suggesting the plausibility of defining subject as initial focus, i.e. the "starting point" for conceptualizing a profiled relationship (Chafe, 1994). Only at this level of abstraction can a fully general (schematic) definition be sought.

    It is widely agreed that the prototypical subject is an 'agent,' who initiates an event and is the source of the energy that drives it. However, since subjects are not limited to relationships based on physical activity and the exertion of force, a general definition has to be quite schematic. In the case of *give* (Figure 11), the possessor's control and act of transfer need not be physical, as possession is very often experiential or social in nature. Still, the subject is the original possessor and the one who initiates the change. This is also the case with *receive*, but since only the latter portion of the overall event is profiled, it is the recipient whose control and activity is focused, making it the trajector. The relationship profiled by *admire* (Figure 5.8[c]) is primarily mental and emotive. Of the two participants, the subject is the one who originates their interaction by engaging in the mental/emotive activity comprising it. Finally, the responses in (4) and (5) represent the extreme case in which the subject's status as initial focus is not based on conceptual content—the relation between the two participants being symmetrical—but on discourse considerations. The trajector is the one just asked about, hence the starting point for a felicitous answer.

3.3   *Perspective*

Having briefly examined two basic dimensions of construal, specificity and prominence, we turn now to perspective. Of the notions under this broad heading we will consider just two: *vantage point* and *scope*.

The term vantage point is typically used in regard to vision and indicates the location from which a scene is viewed. It is thus to be distinguished from the scene itself and, within that, from whatever is being looked at. Metaphorically, we can describe these as being "onstage," with the viewer and vantage point being "offstage." In terms of the viewer's awareness, the onstage elements are explicit, functioning as "objects" of perception, whereas the viewer and its vantage point remain implicit, the former being the "subject" of perception.[12] Vision being our primary sense and a fundamental means of apprehending the world, these notions are naturally extended to other aspects of conceptual experience. Indeed, the many similarities of *per*ception and *con*ception have led to the coinage of *ception* as a term that applies to both (Talmy, 1996).

The similarities hinge on a number of correspondences between conception in general and the special case of perception. Taking vision as a metaphorical basis, a *conceptualizer* is seen as a kind of *viewer*, with the *scene* consisting in the array of *content* being attended to. Corresponding to the *subject* and *object* of perception are the *conceptualizer* and the *focus of attention* within the currently active content. And for conception in general, what counts as the *vantage point* is the conceptualizer's immediate *circumstances* (not just spatial location). Of concern here is the conceptualizing activity in linguistic expressions. In canonical language use there are two conceptualizers, the *speaker* and the *addressee*, who alternate in those roles. Their interaction is aimed at a shared apprehension of the content being expressed (the scene), within which

---

12   These must not be confused with the linguistic functions of grammatical subject and object, which focus onstage participants in a profiled relationship.

the expression's *profile* stands out as the focused object of conception. The vantage point, identified as the interlocutors and their immediate circumstances, is referred to in CG as the *ground*. These are flexibly interpreted as including not only the time and place of speaking (the "deictic center") but also such factors as the interactive situation and the expression's place in the ongoing discourse.

In their application to language, these notions come into play at different levels of organization. At one level, they pertain to the overall linguistic event, where the interlocutors function as offstage viewers with respect to the onstage content comprising the scene. They can also figure in the scene itself, as facets of the situation being described, most obviously in expressions that explicitly refer to vision (e.g. *She sees him*). But they are by no means limited to such expressions. For instance, a viewer, a vantage point, and objects of perception are all are implicit in the scene described by *the house across the street*.[13]

Even when viewing is implicit, vantage point represents an important aspect of linguistic meaning. With respect to the same conceived situation, for example, choice of vantage point can be responsible for determining what counts as the profiled relationship. The scene in Figure 14 is thus described quite differently in (6) depending on which of two vantage points is assumed: when viewed from VP_1, the rock is *in front* and the tree *behind*; from VP_2 the opposite is true.

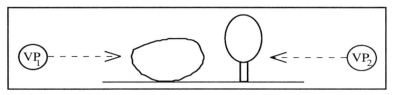

FIGURE 5.14 The effect of vantage point.

(6)   a. VP_1: The rock is in front of the tree. The tree is behind the rock.
      b. VP_2: The tree is in front of the rock. The rock is behind the tree.

An assumed vantage point can be that of any conceptualizer evident from the context: an interlocutor; an onstage viewer established in the prior discourse, as in (7a); or a generalized viewer (representing anyone who might fill that role), as in (7b). There can be multiple viewers, with the same or different vantage points. In Figure 14, the speaker might occupy VP_1, and the addressee VP_2, in

---

13   By default, an implicit viewer tends to be identified with the speaker. In that case the speaker has a dual role: as offstage subject of conception, and as a tacit element of the onstage configuration.

which case they would describe it differently, as in (6a)–(b). A key point, however, is that a description need not reflect the speaker's actual position, as we have the mental agility to adopt an alternate vantage point and imagine how the scene appears from there. To facilitate understanding, the speaker might thus choose to describe it from the standpoint of the addressee by using the expressions in (6b). Another possibility, exemplified in (7c), is a mental shift in vantage point to one not currently occupied by any viewer. If both interlocutors are at VP_1, they can nonetheless imagine and describe the scene as it appears from VP_2.

(7)   a. [He was quite familiar with the graveyard.] The headstone was in front of a small tree.
       b. In that picture, the rock is in front of the tree.
       c. [from VP_1] If we were over there [at VP_2], the tree would be in front of the rock.

In some way, and with varying degrees of salience and importance, a vantage point thus figures in the semantic characterization of most any expression. It usually remains implicit even when its role is pivotal, as in (6). Though it serves to distinguish *in front of* and *behind*, as shown in Figure 5.15, the vantage point is not itself a focused participant in the profiled relationships: neither the trajector (the entity being located) nor the landmark (with respect to which it is located). Its role pertains instead to the apprehension of their relationship—a basis for assessing it rather than part of it. The import of *in front of* is that, starting from the vantage point, the trajector intervenes in the line of sight leading to the landmark. Conversely, *behind* indicates that the landmark intervenes in the line of sight leading to the trajector. But either way, the relationship at issue is the location of the trajector and landmark relative to one another.

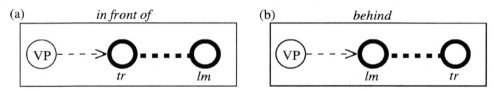

FIGURE 5.15 Vantage point vs. trajector and landmark.

Though based on space and vision, the notion vantage point is naturally extended to other domains, the most obvious being time. A simple example is (8a), sketched in Figure 16. *Next year* is the year adjacent to the current one, apprehended by looking forward from a temporal vantage point within it. And as in the case of space and vision, the presumed vantage point need not be the speaker's actual location. In (8b), the speaker adopts the vantage point of another conceptualizer—the main clause subject—in describing that person's belief.

(8)   a. Next year will be full of surprises.
       b. Sean believed that next year would be full of surprises.

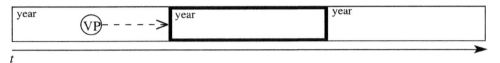

FIGURE 5.16 A vantage point in time.

A second aspect of perspective relates to another similarity between vision and conception: just as we can only see so much at a given instant, we can only conceive of so much. By rough analogy to the visual field, we can therefore posit a *scope of conception*. To be sure, the conceptual scope is much less clearly or precisely delimited, for several obvious reasons. For one thing, conceptualization varies enormously in degree of activation and its consequent salience. Moreover, much takes place below the surface; only a portion is consciously accessible to us. Nor is it possible to isolate the pattern of activity comprising a particular conception, for it draws upon many others representing overlapping domains and lower levels of organization. Finally, since an expression's meaning is complex and multifaceted, specifications of scope pertain to different facets of its structure and different semantic functions.[14]

Quite important for grammar is the distinction between an expression's immediate scope (IS) and a more inclusive maximal scope (MS). Its immediate scope is what we have described metaphorically as being "onstage," i.e. the general region of viewing attention. Its profile is the specific focus of attention within that region. The maximal scope is a larger array of conceptual content in terms of which the immediate scope is characterized. We see in Figure 17, for example, that the concept *arm*—being directly relevant for their apprehension—functions as the immediate scope for both *elbow* and *hand*, which profile different substructures within it. But *arm* is itself apprehended

14   We saw in (2), for example, that the relevant scope of conception for *cat*—the portions of its encyclopedic meaning activated for its interpretation—depends on the context (e.g. *cat-proof bird-cage* vs. *cat-proof rug*).

in relation to the body as a whole, which is thus the immediate scope for *arm* as well as the maximal scope for *elbow* and *hand*.[15]

(a) *elbow*   (b) *hand*

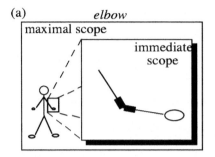 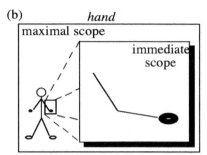

FIGURE 5.17 Scope and profiling.

Although the notion of scope is fully general, its linguistic importance is especially evident with terms for parts of the body. Such expressions reflect a conceptual hierarchy based on part-whole relations, one that speakers are quite aware of; they know, for example, that a *finger* is part of a *hand*, and a *hand* is part of an *arm*. These implicit connections are central to the meaning of body-part terms (e.g. a crucial specification of *finger* is its location and function in a hand). Their relation to one another can thus be recognized as a dimension in the organization of the English lexicon. More specifically, the profile of one expression serves as immediate scope for the next, as shown in Figure 18: the conception of an arm is the immediate scope for *hand*; the conception of a hand, for *finger*; and that of a finger, for *knuckle*. And in a global sense, the conception of the body as a whole is the maximal scope for all of these.

In addition to semantics and lexicon, immediate scope has an important role in grammar. There is first its association with the essential grammatical notion of profiling: it is only in relation to immediate scope that an expression's profile constitutes a focus of attention. It also figures more directly in grammar as something which has to be specifically mentioned in the description of grammatical constructions. One such case, exemplified in (9a), is a regular pattern in which complex body-part terms are formed by combining simpler ones.[16] It is

15   These terms, of course, are only relative. If *hand* is the immediate scope for *finger*, what
      we take to be its maximal scope can either be *arm* or *body* (as in Figure 5.18) depending
      on whether we privilege immediacy (adjacency in a conceptual hierarchy) or the promi-
      nence of a whole compared to its parts.
16   This is a special case of Noun+Noun compounds (e.g. *cat food, garage sale, mountain top*),
      which belongs to a still broader pattern of English compounding.

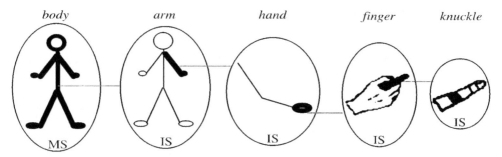

FIGURE 5.18 Vantage point, scope, and levels of organization.

regular in that the profile of the first element functions as immediate scope for
the second element: they are adjacent in the body-part hierarchy, so that skip-
ping a level is non-standard and usually not even interpretable. So in *fingertip*,
the concept *tip* is interpreted specifically in relation to a finger, even though it
is also part of a hand, an arm, and a body.

(9)   a. fingertip; fingernail; toenail; eyelash; eyelid; eyeball; wrist bone; knee-
         cap
      b. *handtip; *armnail; *legnail; *facelash; *bodylid; *headball; *arm bone;
         *legcap

A different kind of example is the progressive construction marked by *be ...
ing*, as in (10b). It applies to perfective clauses like (10a), i.e. those designating
temporally bounded events such as painting a chair; in Figure 19 an event of
this sort is represented by a horizontal line with vertical ticks to indicate its
endpoints. By itself, a perfective clause profiles the full event, including its ini-
tiation and termination. Its immediate temporal scope is thus a span of time
sufficient to encompass this occurrence. The essential feature of the progressive is that it imposes a more limited immediate scope within the temporal
boundaries of the original one. Two kinds of scope are thus distinguished in the
higher-level structure that results: a maximal scope equivalent to the immediate scope at the lower level; and a restricted immediate scope internal to it. And
since an expression's profile is the focus of attention in its immediate scope, the
higher-level expression profiles only the portion of the overall event that falls
within this time span. For this reason the progressive is often described informally as taking an "internal perspective" on events.

(10) a. He painted a chair.
      b. He was painting a chair.

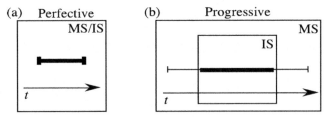

FIGURE 5.19 Maximal vs. immediate scope in time.

4   Dynamicity and Imagination

It remains to consider two aspects of conceptualization whose role in linguistic meaning is both fundamental and pervasive: *dynamicity* and *imagination*. What is meant by dynamicity is that language consists in activity, which unfolds through time, so that how it does so—its *time course*—is a basic dimension of its structure. That the meanings expressed are to a large extent based on imagination (as opposed to objective reality) is a central tenet of conceptual semantics. These factors are not unrelated, and various phenomena involve them both.

As with viewing and vantage point, we need to distinguish the roles of time at two levels of linguistic organization. On the one hand, it can figure in an expression's onstage content as a facet of the scene described. To the extent that it does—and is thus an object of conception—it functions as *conceived time*, as indicated by the arrow labeled *t* in Figure 19. On the other hand, *processing time*—the time through which conception occurs—hosts the offstage activity of the interlocutors in using an expression. Every expression requires some span of processing time for its apprehension, irrespective of whether time figures in its onstage content. By contrast, conceived time inheres in only certain expressions and varies in salience when it does. It is quite prominent in *before* and *after* [Figure 5.13], being the domain in which the profiled relationships are manifested, but does not figure at all in *above* and *below* (Figure 5.12) when they profile static configurations in space. Conceived time does figure in expressions that profile occurrences, as in (10) (Figure 5.19), since by definition these are relationships tracked in their evolution through *t*.

Because both form and meaning reside in activity, processing time has a dual nature, functioning as both *speech time* and *conception time*. Speech time is of course a fundamental dimension of phonological structure, in that elements at a given level of organization—segments, syllables, words, or larger groupings—occur sequentially. Moreover, a structure at one level consists of lower-level elements whose occurrence in a particular temporal sequence is essential to its identity (e.g. changing the order of syllables in a word yields a different word). Conception is more flexible, in that the formation of complex structures depends more on conceptual overlap than on sequence of activation.[17] But since a conceptual structure does unfold through a span of time, its time course can be recognized as a secondary aspect of its meaning. And since both involve processing time, this raises the question of how the time course of conception relates to that of speech.

The CG claim that lexicon, grammar, and discourse are symbolic in nature implies a close correlation. A symbolic structure resides in the association of a semantic and a phonological structure, either of which is able to activate the other, and usually their co-activation is automatic and roughly simultaneous. So in proceeding through a complex structure step by step, their coordinated activation is one facet of the expression's temporal organization.[18] Because this is true for both interlocutors, their access to a complex expression progresses more or less in parallel.

This coordination of speech and conception pertains to the dual role of processing time. We must also consider the relation between *processing* time and *conceived* time. The former—time as the *medium* of conception—is always involved. This does not hold for the latter, since for certain expressions—e.g. *above* and *below* (Figure 5.12)—the role of time as an *object* of conception is non-essential (either absent or peripheral). In principle, then, the temporal ordering of symbolic structures (their sequence of activation in processing time) is independent of how or whether ordering in conceived time figures in the complex conceptions they symbolize. The order of symbolization may just serve a grammatical purpose, without ascribing any particular temporal sequencing to the onstage content. In *above the table*, for example, the temporal adjacency and ordering of *above* and *the table* symbolizes their conceptual overlap in the prepositional object construction,[19] but does not itself invoke conceived time or specify temporal sequencing.

---

17   Thus a change in word order does not necessarily effect a change in onstage content. In terms of its basic structure, for instance, the following sentences describe the same conceived event: *He bought a rather expensive bracelet for his wife* vs. *He bought for his wife a rather expensive bracelet.* This does not imply semantic equivalence, as linguistic meaning depends on both descriptive content and its presentation.

18   Being automatic and inherent in every expression, a "symbolization path" of this sort tends to be taken for granted. It is in any case only one aspect of temporal organization, which cannot be reduced to a single linear pass through a complex structure. For one thing, processing runs concurrently on different time scales. It also includes such factors as recall, anticipation, interruption, and backtracking.

19   Specifically, it identifies the nominal profile with the preposition's landmark.

Prime examples of expressions that do invoke conceived time are verbs and clauses, which profile occurrences. So although the prepositional phrase *above the table* merely describes a spatial configuration, a clause derived by adding the schematic verb *be* profiles an occurrence consisting in its continuation through conceived time: *The lamp is above the table.* Thus included in the overall conception are two spans of time: that of the onstage occurrence (in conceived time), and that of the time of speaking (in processing time, a facet of the ground). These are the basis for *tense*. While they sometimes coincide ("present tense"), in general they are distinct in both duration and temporal location, e.g. *He painted a chair.*[20]

Illustrating another aspect of the relation between conceived and processing time are expressions like (11), where a series of symbolic structures each describe a separate event. The most likely interpretation is that the events occurred in the order of their description, but this is neither explicitly indicated nor strictly necessary: the speaker may simply intend to list the subject's main accomplishments, which might have been achieved in any order. That is, the sentence may or may not exhibit temporal *iconicity*, such that the sequence of event *occurrences* in *conceived* time matches the sequence of event *descriptions* in *processing* time. Whether the conceived ordering motivates the descriptive ordering or merely reflects it, their congruence no doubt contributes to processing efficiency.

(11) She found a cure for cancer, won the Nobel Prize, and was promoted to associate professor.

Temporal iconicity of this sort is far from the only source of dynamicity in linguistic meanings. Indeed, they are inherently dynamic, as they reside in conceptualizing activity which requires a span of processing time, however brief. An expression's meaning thus has a time course, irrespective of whether conceived time figures in its content. This is so even for a minimal expression describing a static situation (e.g. *above the table*, or just *table*). With longer expressions, there can be a sense of dynamicity just because facets of the scene are accessed sequentially via symbolization. This sequencing does not necessarily correlate with any ordering intrinsic to its prelinguistic conception, but

---

20   Such relationships pertain to a particular level of organization. For instance, the progressive [Figure 5.19(b)] involves two spans of conceived time: that of the full bounded event (e.g. *paint a chair*) and the profiled portion delimited by the immediate temporal scope (*painting a chair*). In a present progressive, only the latter coincides with the time of speaking: *He is painting a chair.*

should there be a potential for such a correlation, it tends to be exploited. Accordingly, a sentence like (11) is interpreted iconically by default.

Dynamicity due to sequence of symbolic access can be evident and semantically significant even for expressions that do not describe events. Rather than events, for example, the sentences in (12) describe a stable situation: a spatial configuration representing the location of a camera. It is precisely the same configuration, where the same locative structures specify the same locations related in the same manner (the camera is *on the shelf*, which is *in the closet*, which is *in the bedroom*, which is *upstairs*). But while there is no difference in their onstage content, the sentences are semantically non-equivalent owing to the conceptual experience engendered by the order of presentation: in (12a) the scene is mentally accessed by "zooming in" to successively smaller locations, and in (12b), by "zooming out" to successively larger ones (Langacker, 2020). From the standpoint of CG, this constitutes a difference in linguistic meaning, which includes not only conceptual content, but also its apprehension and construal by the conceptualizers.

(12) a. Your camera is upstairs, in the bedroom, in the closet, on the top shelf.
     b. Your camera is on the top shelf, in the closet, in the bedroom, upstairs.

As a general matter, it is quite common for static situations to be viewed in dynamic terms.[21] One manifestation of this tendency is the extension and adaptation of dynamic language for the description of static scenes. Exemplified in (13) is a much studied case known as *fictive* (or *subjective*) motion (Talmy, 1996; Matlock, 2004). In its basic sense, the verb *run* designates rapid physical movement along a spatial path. Here, though, it describes a static spatial configuration: the import is simply that the scar occupies all the points comprising the path in question. Within the scene itself, nothing actually moves or changes (there is no intimation, even, that the creation of the scar followed this path). To be sure, there is a kind of motion, though not in the scene itself. It resides instead in *mental scanning* by the conceptualizer (the offstage *subject* of conception) in apprehending the onstage structure. More specifically, it resides in *summation*, wherein each activated structure remains active as the next is accessed. So while the full path conception does have a time course, and proceeds in a certain direction (e.g. from the elbow to the wrist), the end result

---

21   This is natural both because viewing is itself dynamic, and also because a stable situation is so often perceived as either resulting from or leading to a dynamic occurrence. For instance, (12a) would most likely be used as an instruction for how to find the camera (invoking the potential for moving along a path without explicitly referring to it).

is that all the point-like locations are active simultaneously. The conceived situation is therefore stable despite the dynamic access.

(13) a. A scar runs from his elbow to his wrist.
     b. A scar runs from his wrist to his elbow.

With fictive motion we enter the vast realm of *imaginative* phenomena, whose diversity, pervasiveness, and fundamental nature belie the secondary status they have often been accorded. They are in fact essential to both semantics and grammar. We might first note the absence of any definite boundary between products of imagination, on the one hand, and what we take to be "reality," on the other hand. In the last analysis, our conception of reality—even when based on direct experience—is *mentally constructed* through interactive activity.[22] And while the label imaginative is not inappropriate, the phenomena in question are based on very general capacities also observed in more mundane expressions. They will be discussed under the broad rubrics of integration, abstraction, and disengagement.

Conceptual integration is the basis for constructing complex expressions through grammatical composition. It is a matter of smaller structures being connected by overlap (shared processing activity) to form a larger structure in which the shared structure has a dual role. For example, a prepositional phrase like *above the table* is based on overlap between the preposition's landmark (a schematic thing) and the nominal referent, so that they correspond to the same conceived entity in the profiled onstage relationship. In (12a), the "zooming in" effect is achieved by merging the location specified by one locative (e.g. *upstairs*) with the immediate scope of the next (*in the bedroom*). Because it may be only partial or schematic, the overlap specified by grammatical constructions does not guarantee full compatibility or consistency of the composite whole. For instance, the general construction responsible for *square table* and *lazy cat* also sanctions expressions that are either semantically anomalous (e.g. **square circle*) or at least run counter to normal experience (*obedient cat*).

In short, integration is a matter of degree that depends on the number of connections between two structures and the extent to which connected elements merge to form an internally consistent whole. Partial integration is a characteristic of *metaphor*, whose purpose—in contrast to basic composition—is not simply to describe an onstage situation, but to furnish a way of

---

22   Seeing a cat, for instance, is not just the passive registration of a stimulus, but consists in active visual processing (at multiple levels) as well as the cognitive activity of recognition and categorization.

understanding it in terms of something more basic (Lakoff and Johnson, 1980; Lakoff, 1990). It involves the connection of two domains, the "source" and the "target," and the projection of salient properties of the former onto the latter. To take just one example, the body is commonly invoked as a source domain: we speak of the *foot* of a mountain, the *eye* of a needle, the *shoulder* of a road, or the *neck* of a bottle. In a "live" metaphor, the integration is only partial since, in apprehending the target in terms of the source, we do not lose sight of its actual nature. The resulting structure is imaginative because the target, so construed, is not (and generally could not be) real: the *foot* of a mountain does not have toes; the *eye* of a needle cannot see.

Metaphor is one kind of *mental space configuration*, a far more general notion with broad applicability to conceptual structure (Fauconnier and Turner, 2002). A configuration can be of any size, consisting in a dynamic network of mental spaces (domains) connected by correspondences. Among these spaces, created by selective projection from others, are imaginative *blends* exhibiting varying degrees of integration. Even if it is highly fanciful, a blend may still be sufficiently coherent that its activation in conjunction with those giving rise to it serves to cast them in a different light. For instance, the once timely expression in (14) served to highlight the ability of Bill Clinton to survive attacks from political opponents. It invokes a configuration based on three aspects of general knowledge: (i) a space representing Clinton and his career; (ii) another pertaining to political conflict; and (iii) the well-known story of the Titanic and its sinking. The *if*-clause explicitly describes a blended space obtained by projecting selected properties of Clinton onto the Titanic, thereby creating an imagined Clinton-like Titanic. One can then imagine this fanciful ship colliding with an iceberg, as in (iii), resulting in the still more fanciful space (iv) in which it is the iceberg—rather than the Clintonesque vessel—that sinks. The overall function of (14) was thus to comment on the state of American politics.

(14) If Clinton were the Titanic, the iceberg would sink.

Abstraction, a second general source of imaginative structures, consists in suppressing or simply ignoring conceptual content. For example, the depiction of *iris* and *pupil* in Figure 5.8(b) abstracts away from the location of these entities in the face and the body as a whole, directing attention to just the eye (their immediate scope). An important special case is *schematization*, in which a loss of precision and fine-grained detail results in a conception of lesser "granularity." A *schema* is less specific than its *instantiations*, each of which *elaborates* it in some fashion; it is *immanent* in its instantiations, residing in facets of the patterns of activity constituting them. A main application in language is the need to posit both general *types* and *instances* of those types. In particular, it is usual for a lexeme (e.g. *cat*) to merely designate an abstracted type, whose specifications are quite schematic compared to the elaborate detail possible with instantiating expressions (e.g. *that giant yellow cat with a bad disposition*). Abstraction goes along with fictivity. Whereas an instance can be real (existing in the world), a schematic type as such is mentally constructed.

Types come under the broad heading of *generalizations*, which consist in the apprehension of recurring patterns of experience. It is by virtue of generalizations that we build up our conception of the world as having a particular structure (indeed, as having any structure at all). They can pertain to any aspect of experience, and range in scope from being local (e.g. *She drinks scotch*) to fully global (*A triangle has three sides*). In the case of language, conventionally established structures of any sort (e.g. sounds, lexemes, grammatical classes, constructions) represent generalizations abstracted from facets of occurring expressions. They are imaginative in the sense that they do not per se occur: when examined in fine-enough detail, their implementation in actual use is always more specific than the schema reflecting their commonality.

A third general source of imaginative phenomena is disengagement, in which processing activity originally confined to a particular context comes to be employed independently of it. Disengagement is closely related to abstraction, and might be viewed as abstraction away from the context. Conversely, schematization can be thought of as disengagement from the specific details of instantiating structures. Disengagement is the key factor in sensory and motor *images*, which have an essential role in conception and linguistic meaning. Central to the meaning of *cat*, for example, is a visual image (or family of images) of what one looks like, and central to the meaning of *run* is a motor image of what it feels like to do so. Such images reside in the autonomous occurrence of certain internal aspects of sensory and motor experience, being disengaged from the peripheral activity normally responsible for them. In the absence of actual perceptual or motor input, they are generally more schematic and less "vivid" than direct experience.

Another kind of disengagement relates to the scene (the onstage situation being described). A prime example is fictive motion, as in (13), where structures whose basic value pertains to physical movement through space are used instead to characterize static configurations. The structures in (15) that specify an actual case of physical motion—namely, the verb *run* and the path construction *from X to Y*—are used instead in (13) to describe the shape and location of a scar. Nothing in the scene is portrayed as moving, as the profiled occurrence is simply the continuation through time of the stable situation in which a scar simultaneously occupies all the points constituting the path. While a kind of motion is in fact involved, it does not reside in the onstage situation, but rather in the processing activity of the interlocutors, who build up a full conception of the scar by mentally scanning along it.[23] So in lieu of physical movement by an onstage mover (an object of conception), what we have is mental scanning (along the same spatial path) by an offstage conceptualizer (a subject of conception). This type of disengagement can thus be characterized as an instance of subjectification (Langacker, 1999b).

(15) He ran from his house to the park.

Through integration, abstraction, and disengagement, occurring in combinations and at many levels of organization, we construct large networks of imaginative conceptions that constitute a large proportion of the mental world that we live in and talk about. While ultimately it is grounded in immediate physical reality, the connection is often quite indirect, as it encompasses countless aspects of experience that are either non-physical (e.g. social, cultural, intellectual) or represent departures from reality (e.g. situations that are future, hypothetical, counterfactual, or merely wishful). It is common for such conceptions to incorporate fictive counterparts of real entities, expressed linguistically in the same manner. For example, the sentences in (16a) refer to a cat conceived as being real, whereas the fictive cat described in (16b)—by means of the same two expressions (*a cat* and *my cat*)—is invoked specifically in order to indicate what is *not* real.

(16) a. I have a cat. Being generous, I feed my cat tuna.
     b. I don't have a cat. If I did, I would feed my cat tuna.

It is generally not appreciated how frequently we resort to imaginative structures, even in regard to actual situations (Langacker, 2005). The fictive motion in (13) is in no way special or unusual, but represents the normal way of describing the scar; indeed, it is hard to come up with a non-fictive alternative. There are fictive versions for most any aspect of semantic organization, such as participants (e.g. the cat I don't have), events (my feeding of this cat), vantage point,

---

23   Because the scanning can proceed in either direction, the configuration can be described by either (13a) or (13b). These are equivalent in terms of the onstage situation, but semantically distinct owing to the direction of mental access.

speech acts (e.g. rhetorical questions), and conversational interaction (Pascual, 2014).

Fictive motion is one type of fictive change. Another common type involves the adjectival use of past participles, as in *broken* pencil, *scattered* marbles, and *sunken* ship. These designate the property that results from an instance of the change described by the verb stem, e.g. a *broken pencil* is one that has undergone the process of breaking. In these examples the change probably actually happened. But in others it is only fictive: most likely, a *broken line* has never been solid, *scattered villages* have never been together, and a *sunken bathtub* was built in place. In cases of actual change, the verb describes how the *final* situation relates to an *earlier* situation. In their fictive counterparts, it instead indicates how the *actual* situation relates to an imagined *canonical* situation.

Another sort of fictive change is exemplified in (17). It should first be noted that these sentences can in principle be construed non-fictively, i.e. as accurate descriptions of a somewhat fanciful conception of reality. Though unlikely, it is not impossible to imagine a company president getting younger, or trees shrinking when transported to higher altitudes. More probable, however, is an interpretation involving two levels of fictivity. The first consists in generalizing over a number of distinct situations that are alike in most respects; e.g. in (17a), each situation is that of the company having a single president, of a certain age, for some length of time. The second is a matter of invoking an imagined company president who stands for all the actual presidents without being equated with any particular one. Since there are multiple actual presidents, it may well be the case that each is younger than her predecessor. So when the global situation is viewed in terms of this fictive participant, the president *keeps getting younger*.

(17) a. The company's president keeps getting younger.
     b. The trees get shorter at higher altitudes.

The sentences in (18) illustrate some subtleties in regard to vantage point. Canonically we view things from a fixed location, but since we are mobile creatures, we can also accommodate the alternate visual experience engendered by a moving vantage point. Sentence (18a) reflects the familiar circumstance of reporting on how things appear while looking out the window in a moving vehicle. It involves a kind of fictive motion, in that the scenery is not actually rushing past, yet this movement is also real in the sense of representing what the viewer actually sees. The vantage point likewise has a dual status. The actual vantage point is real but atypical. Yet the presumed vantage point is fictive in the sense that the situation is described as if the viewer were stationary and the scene were in motion.

(18) a. I sat in the car and watched the scenery rush past me.
     b. There is a house every now and then through the valley.

Sentence (18b) also describes what things look like while traveling, but the details are different and more complex, involving several levels of fictivity. For one thing, the expression does not pertain to a particular journey, but represents a generalization over possible travel experiences—what anyone might see along the way. For a given journey, moreover, it generalizes over multiple viewing episodes occurring at different times (*every now and then*). These imagined episodes reside in equivalent experiences, so a single description applies to them all: *there is a house*. It is, of course, a different house each time. The one explicitly mentioned is a fictive participant comparable to the company president in (17a), standing for any number of actual houses without being equated with any particular one.

It should be noted that (18b) makes no direct reference to a journey, a viewer, or a multiplicity of houses. The entire complex conception is mentally constructed on the basis of fragmentary clues (*a house; through the valley; every now and then*). Except perhaps in degree, this is really not unusual, but illustrates a fundamental principle of conceptual semantics: that linguistic meanings are not "in the words" or "contained" in expressions. Rather, they are mentally constructed based on all available resources, including background knowledge, cognitive abilities, and apprehension of the context (Reddy, 1979). In short, linguistic meaning is prompted by words and overt linguistic structures, but never fully constituted by them.

References

Chafe, Wallace. 1994. *Discourse, Consciousness, and Time: The Flow and Displacement of Conscious Experience in Speaking and Writing*. Chicago: University of Chicago Press.

Fauconnier, Gilles and Mark Turner. 2002. *The Way We Think: Conceptual Blending and the Mind's Hidden Complexities*. New York: Basic Books.

Haiman, John. 1980. Dictionaries and encyclopedias. *Lingua* 50: 329–357.

Johnson, Mark. 1987. *The Body in the Mind: The Bodily Basis of Meaning, Imagination, and Reason*. Chicago: University of Chicago Press.

Lakoff, George. 1987. *Women, Fire, and Dangerous Things: What Categories Reveal About the Mind*. Chicago: University of Chicago Press.

Lakoff, George. 1990. The invariance hypothesis: Is abstract reason based on image-schemas? *Cognitive Linguistics* 1: 39–74.

Lakoff, George and Mark Johnson. 1980. *Metaphors We Live By*. Chicago: University of Chicago Press.

Langacker, Ronald W. 1987. *Foundations of Cognitive Grammar*, volume I: *Theoretical Prerequisites*. Stanford: Stanford University Press.

Langacker, Ronald W. 1991. *Foundations of Cognitive Grammar*, volume II: *Descriptive Application*. Stanford: Stanford University Press.

Langacker, Ronald W. 1999a. Assessing the cognitive linguistic enterprise. In T. Janssen and G. Redeker (eds.), *Cognitive Linguistics: Foundations, Scope, and Methodology*, 13–59. Berlin: Mouton de Gruyter.

Langacker, Ronald W. 1999b. Losing control: Grammaticization, subjectification, and transparency. In A. Blank and P. Koch (eds.), *Historical Semantics and Cognition*, 147–175. Berlin: Mouton de Gruyter.

Langacker, Ronald W. 2005. Dynamicity, fictivity, and scanning: The imaginative basis of logic and linguistic meaning. In D. Pecher and R.A. Zwaan (eds.), *Grounding Cognition: The Role of Perception and Action in Memory, Language and Thinking*, 164–197. Cambridge, UK: Cambridge University Press.

Langacker, Ronald W. 2008a. *Cognitive Grammar: A Basic Introduction*. New York: Oxford University Press.

Langacker, Ronald W. 2008b. Sequential and summary scanning: A reply. *Cognitive Linguistics* 19: 571–584.

Langacker, Ronald W. 2015. On grammatical categories. *Journal of Cognitive Linguistics* 1: 44–79.

Langacker, Ronald W. 2020. Nested locatives: Conceptual basis and theoretical import. In W. Lowie et al. (eds.), *Usage-Based Dynamics in Second Language Development*, 207–223. Bristol, UK: Multilingual Matters.

Levinson, Stephen C. 1997. From outer to inner space: Linguistic categories and non-linguistic thinking. In J. Nuyts and E. Pederson (eds.), *Language and Conceptualization*, 13–45. Cambridge, UK: Cambridge University Press.

Matlock, Teenie. 2004. The conceptual motivation of fictive motion. In G. Radden and K. Panther (eds.), *Studies in Linguistic Motivation*, 221–248. Berlin: Mouton de Gruyter.

Pascual, Esther. 2014. *Fictive Interaction: The Conversation Frame in Thought, Language, and Discourse*. Amsterdam: John Benjamins.

Reddy, Michael J. 1979. The conduit metaphor—A case of frame conflict in our language about language. In A. Ortony (ed.), *Metaphor and Thought*, 284–324. Cambridge, UK: Cambridge University Press.

Talmy, Leonard. 1978. Figure and ground in complex sentences. In J.H. Greenberg (ed.), *Universals of Human Language*, volume IV: *Syntax*, 625–649. Stanford: Stanford University Press.

Talmy, Leonard. 1996. Fictive motion in language and "ception." In P. Bloom, M.A. Peterson, L. Nadel and M.F. Garrett (eds.), *Language and Space*, 211–276. Cambridge, MA: MIT Press.

Tomlin, Russell S. 1995. Focal attention, voice, and word order. In P. Downing and M. Noonan (eds.), *Word Order in Discourse*, 517–554. Amsterdam: John Benjamins.

Wierzbicka, Anna. 1995. Dictionaries vs. encyclopedias: How to draw the line. In P.W. Davis (ed.), *Alternative Linguistics: Descriptive and Theoretical Modes*, 289–315. Amsterdam: John Benjamins.

CHAPTER 6

Embodied Semantics

Daniel Casasanto

1   What Is Embodied Meaning?

What does it mean for meaning to be *embodied?* The term "embodiment" is used in many ways, and by multiple communities of researchers (Wilson, 2002). In perception research, "embodiment" can mean the sense of where one's own body ends and the rest of the world begins (Longo et al., 2008). In artificial intelligence, "embodiment" is the project of endowing robots with biologically inspired mechanisms of learning and behavior (Anderson, 2003; Brooks, 1990). More broadly, "embodiment" can mean the belief that the mind is shaped by our bodily experiences (Varela et al., 1991), or the observation that bodies and minds affect each other (Niedenthal, 2007). This chapter focuses on a notion of embodiment that is of particular relevance to theories of linguistic meaning, which has revolutionary implications for research on minds and brains: an idea that will be referred to here as the *embodied simulation hypothesis.*

According to the embodied simulation hypothesis, part of the meaning of a word (or a phrase, or a sentence) is a *simulation* of its referent, implemented in neural and cognitive systems that support perception, action, and emotion. Three variants of this hypothesis were proposed in parallel in 1999, by the psychologist Lawrence Barsalou (Barsalou, 1999), the neuroscientist Friedemann Pulvermüller (Pulvermüller, 1999),[1] and by the philosopher Mark Johnson and the linguist George Lakoff (Lakoff and Johnson, 1999). These proposals were not identical, but they overlapped to a remarkable extent. Together, these three publications have been cited more than 30,000 times, and have generated hundreds of theoretical papers and thousands of experimental studies. This chapter aims: (i.) to explain the embodied simulation hypothesis; (ii.) to review ways in which it has (and has not) been tested effectively; and (iii.) to outline some remaining challenges for the embodied simulation hypothesis.

---

1   Pulvermüller (1999) did not use the term *simulation,* but his proposal is nevertheless a seminal version of the embodied simulation hypothesis described here. The phrase "embodied simulation hypothesis" is intended as a generic term that encompasses key elements of the hypotheses framed by Barsalou (1999), Pulvermüller (1999), and Lakoff and Johnson (1999).

2   What Is a Simulation?

A simulation is a pattern of neural and cognitive activity that corresponds to our experience of an entity in the world outside of your mind (e.g., seeing a cat), but crucially, simulations occur when you are *not* currently experiencing that entity (i.e., when you are not seeing a cat, but only thinking about a cat or understanding the word *cat*). How is a simulation different from other notions of thinking or understanding? Simulations are posited to occur in neurocognitive (i.e., neural / cognitive) systems that are responsible for our primary experience of the external world: most notably, systems for perception and motor action, which were long believed to be separate from systems for thinking and constructing linguistic meaning (Fodor, 1983).

In order to understand the construct of *simulation*, it is first necessary to understand how information flows from the world into the mind, and what kinds of neurocognitive systems are responsible for this flow of information. People interact with their environment via multiple input and output *modalities*. A modality is a channel through which we experience or act upon the world. When we interact with a cat, we can *see* its shape, *hear* its purr, *reach out* our hand to *touch* its fur, and *feel* the happiness of communing with a pet (assuming we like cats). Each of these perceptual, motor, and emotional components of our 'cat' experience is implemented initially in a different *modality-specific* neurocognitive system. A system is modality-specific if it is highly specialized for a single input or output modality (e.g., vision). Modality-specific regions of the brain have spatially constrained locations, are largely segregated from each other, and are highly selective for processing information in one modality or another: *visual cortex* for sight, *auditory cortex* for sound, *somatosensory cortex* for touch, *olfactory cortex* for smell, *gustatory* cortex for taste, *motor cortex* for performing actions, and structures in the limbic system for forming emotional responses to stimuli.[2]

As the 'cat' example illustrates, our primary experiences often involve more than one kind of modality-specific input. Initially, this input is segregated:

---

2 Primary sensory and motor cortices are essential for perception or action in a given modality (e.g., *seeing* is not possible without activity in visual cortex). However, it would be a mistake to believe that these modality-specific cortices are *sufficient* to support perception or action; each primary cortex is only one critical part of a distributed network of brain areas needed, for example, to transform sensory input into conscious perceptual experience. Here, we focus only on the primary and secondary sensory and motor cortices (e.g., motor cortex and premotor cortex) because these are the only parts of their distributed networks that are modality-specific; therefore, they are the only parts of the network that are useful for distinguishing between embodied and disembodied theories experimentally.

The cat's visual appearance is processed in visual cortex; the sounds that the cat makes are processed in auditory cortex, etc. Information from these separate modality-specific regions is then integrated in multimodal regions of the cerebral cortex called *convergence zones* (Barsalou et al. 2003; Damasio 1989). Convergence zones are not modality-specific; rather, they receive inputs from various modality-specific systems. Each episode of interacting with a cat results in patterns of modality-specific neurocognitive activity during the process of perception (e.g., seeing the cat) or action (e.g., petting the cat). Then, with the help of non-modality-specific brain structures (which will not be discussed extensively here, e.g., the hippocampus), this transient modality-specific activity leads to the formation of longer-lasting memory traces, that are stored in non-modality-specific convergence zones. These long-term memory traces are built out of modality-specific information that accumulates over the course of an individual's experiences, but they are stored in non-modality-specific brain areas.[3]

This sketch of how information flows from the outside world into our minds (via modality-specific systems) and produces long-term memory traces (stored in non-modality-specific brain areas) should be largely uncontroversial; this account is shared by both embodied and 'disembodied' theories, alike. These theories diverge, however, concerning how our long-term memory traces get used during thinking and linguistic meaning construction.

According to "disembodied" 20th-century theories of concepts and semantics, not only are words' meanings *stored in* non-modality-specific brain areas, they are also *retrieved from* these same areas when we need to use our stored knowledge. One area long believed to be the locus of our "mental dictionary" is the left Temporal cortex (Hagoort, 2005): a non-modality-specific brain area that integrates information from various modality-specific cortices. On this view, visual cortex, auditory cortex, and motor cortex *do* play a role in language,

---

3 An alternative to the term "modality-specific" is "unimodal"; there is no clear distinction between these two terms so, for most purposes, they should be treated as synonyms that both designate brain tissue that is highly specialized for processing information in a single perceptual or motor modality. The term "non-modality-specific" has several near synonyms: amodal (not associated with any modality); multimodal (processing inputs from multiple modality-specific regions); polymodal (presumably an exact synonym for multimodal); supramodal (somehow transcending modality (i.e., amodal), or incorporating different modalities (i.e., multimodal)). Some authors may intend for there to be subtle distinctions between these near synonyms; however, these distinctions are rarely made clear, and are not widely agreed upon across authors. Brain regions are sometimes designated as "bimodal" or "trimodal" (i.e., integrating input from exactly two or exactly three modalities): These regions can be considered to be a subset of non-modality-specific regions.

but that role is limited to processing the *forms* of words. It is uncontroversial that the auditory cortex is crucial for perceiving the auditory forms of words that you hear, that the visual cortex is crucial for perceiving the orthographic forms of words that you read, and that the motor cortex is crucial for producing the articulatory forms of words that you speak with your mouth or sign with your hands; both disembodied and embodied theories agree upon these facts about perceiving and producing the forms of words. The theories disagree, however, about the role that modality-specific brain areas play in constructing a word's meaning. According to the "disembodied" theories of language, these modality-specific perceptual and motor cortices are crucial for processing the forms of words, but they play no role in processing their meanings. This belief was virtually unquestioned until the turn of the 21st century.

By contrast, according to the embodied simulation hypothesis, modality-specific brain areas play important roles in processing *both* the forms of words and their meanings. The 'cat' example, above, illustrates how information about cats enters our minds, passing from various modality-specific brain areas during perception to non-modality-specific brain areas for long-term storage. Simulation involves, essentially, running this process in reverse.

When we hear the word *cat*, this acoustic input from the ear is first processed in the auditory cortex; this auditory signal is then classified as an instance of the English wordform /*kaet*/, and this word form classification process involves left Temporal lobe structures near the auditory cortex: specifically, structures that have been traditionally associated with the "mental dictionary" (Pulvermüller, 1999). Both embodied and disembodied theories may agree on this word form classification process, but they diverge concerning the extent of the role that these left Temporal lobe structures play in language and thought. According to the traditional "disembodied" view, the Temporal lobe contains complete lexical entries (i.e., entries in the mental dictionary), including words' forms, morphosyntactic roles, and—importantly—their meanings.[4] According to the embodied view, however, the left temporal cortex is the locus of *some* kinds of information about words, most crucially their *forms*, but is not the locus of words' (complete) meanings. Rather, once a word form has been identified, it cues modality-specific simulations in the relevant perceptual or motor cortices, which constitute the word's meaning. (On moderate versions of this hypothesis, simulations *partly* constitute the word's meaning.)

---

4 Adherents to this long-held majority view of language in the brain acknowledge that semantic information is likely to be distributed over various non-modality-specific brain areas, but maintain that the left temporal lobe is particularly "crucial for lexical-semantic processing" (Hagoort, 2005: 421).

Once the word form /kaet/, has been identified, various aspects of the context determine which particular simulations will (or will not) be run: The relevant "context" may include the linguistic context, social context, the physical context in which the word is perceived, as well as the language user's own history of using this word form previously (Willems and Casasanto, 2011). In the linguistic context, "My pet cat is a white Angora," naming a breed known for having exceptionally soft fur, the simulations that get triggered may involve somatosensory areas that perceive touch with the fingers, and motor areas that allow us to plan and execute the action of petting a cat with our hands, as well as low-level visual areas that allow us to perceive the animal's shape and higher-level visual areas that are involved in perceiving color. If, instead, the linguistic context were, "The black cat dashed across the road," then in addition to simulations in visual areas for perceiving shape and color, simulations may also be triggered in high-level visual areas involved in perceiving motion and speed (Wallentin et al., 2011).[5] Alternatively, if the context were a jazz musician commenting that, "Our drummer is a cool cat," it remains an open question whether any simulations related to a small furry animal would be triggered, at all; instead, a different set of simulations would likely be triggered, since the referent of this figurative expression is a drum-playing human.

Typically, simulations are *implicit*, meaning that the simulations, per se, are not available to consciousness (even though language users are usually conscious of hearing and understanding the words whose referents are being simulated). Listeners would not actually perceive the attributes of a cat, even when hearing this word form causes them to simulate these attributes in perceptual cortices: Experiencing a percept in the absence of any perceptual input is a hallucination. Likewise, even though listeners' understanding of *cat* may include motor simulations of what their hands do when they pet a cat, they are unlikely to actually perform these hand actions. It is unclear, at this time, *why* we don't perform the actions that we simulate (e.g., whether the actions are never fully programmed by the motor cortex, or whether they are programmed but inhibited). What is clear, however, is that even when listeners (or readers)

---

5   As these "cat" examples illustrate, simulations are posited to occur in all of the contextually-relevant modality-specific cortices, in parallel. This process is sometimes referred to as a "multimodal simulation." This label, however, is potentially confusing: Most likely, authors using the term "multimodal simulation" *do not* mean that the simulation is being implemented in multimodal (i.e., non-modality-specific) brain areas. Rather, this term is used to indicate that multiple, distinct, modality-specific simulations are being run in parallel (e.g., in visual cortex, auditory cortex, etc.).

understand a sentence like, "I pet the cat," they do not typically start involuntarily petting a cat (or petting the air, if no cat is present). Furthermore, in most instances of rapidly understanding ongoing speech, listeners do not form a conscious mental image of the cat (see Willems et al., 2010 for a discussion of mental simulation vs. mental imagery).

3   Testing the Embodied Simulation Hypothesis

In order to design an experimental test of the embodied simulation hypothesis, two fundamental criteria must be met. First, it must be clear what *competing hypothesis* embodied simulation is being tested against: If the experimental results turned out to confirm the embodied simulation hypothesis, what alternative hypothesis (or null hypothesis) would be disconfirmed?[6] Second, the competing theories must make *contrasting predictions* about the behavior or brain activity in the experimental participants. Designing experiments that satisfy both of these criteria—where competing hypotheses make contrasting predictions—has been more challenging than many researchers realized (Dove, 2009; Machery, 2007).

3.1   *First Successful Tests:* Where *Does Simulation Happen in the Brain?*
The first successful tests of embodied simulation, that satisfied both of these criteria, were conducted by Freidemann Pulvermüller and colleagues (Hauk et al., 2004; Pulvermüller, 2005). Pulvermüller's team identified a prediction that follows from the embodied simulation theory but does not follow from the disembodied alternative: Understanding sentences that refer to actions should selectively activate modality-specific parts of the motor system that are necessary for planning and/or executing these actions. To test this prediction, Hauk, Johnsrude, and Pulvermüller (2004) introduced a new experimental paradigm

---

6   The *disembodied* theory of semantics described in Section 1 can be considered to be an *alternative hypothesis* against which embodied simulation is being tested in many studies. However, the disembodied theory can also be considered to be the *null hypothesis* in these studies: that which the relevant community of researchers would continue to believe if the experiment in question had never been done, or if it produced no interpretable results. Often, when testing a new hypothesis (e.g., embodied semantics) against an established hypothesis (e.g., disembodied semantics), the alternative hypothesis is coextensive with the null hypothesis. Here, what the relevant community of researchers would continue to believe in the absence of evidence that semantics is embodied would be: that semantics is disembodied (i.e., linguistic meaning relies on neurocognitive systems that are distinct from the systems that support our direct perceptual, motoric, and affective interactions with the environment).

using Functional Magnetic Resonance Imaging (fMRI). With fMRI, researchers can track changes in cerebral blood flow that accompany neural activity, and can determine which parts of the brain are associated with which mental activities (e.g., understanding a sentence). Hauk et al. (2004) tested participants while they were engaged in two separate tasks: a cognitive task, and then a motor task. The cognitive task was silently reading sentences with action verbs referring to either foot actions (e.g., *kick*), mouth actions (e.g., *lick*), or hand actions (e.g., *pick*). In the first part of the study participants read these sentences while lying still in the fMRI scanner, *not* moving any of these body parts. In the second part of the study, they were instructed to move their feet, mouth, and hands. The cognitive task was of primary interest: The goal was to determine what brain areas were active while participants read about hand, foot, and mouth actions. The motor task was not testing any hypothesis, per se. Rather, it served as a *functional localizer*: a task that allows researchers to identify, in individual subjects' brains, regions that are known to serve a behavioral function. In this case, the goal was to identify the areas of the motor cortex that enable foot, mouth, and hand actions. In the context of this study (and subsequently many others), these motor areas served as *regions of interest* (often abbreviated *ROIs*): brain regions that are already known to serve a particular function (e.g., programming motor actions), which guide researchers' search for the locus of a cognitive function of interest (e.g., the semantics of action verbs).

The motor cortex is organized in a way that makes this brain area particularly useful as a testbed for embodied simulation. Stretched out over part of the cerebral cortex is a *somatotopy* (i.e., a body map). Each part of our bodies corresponds to a patch of motor cortex that controls this body part's movements, and neighboring body parts (e.g., thumb, index finger) correspond to neighboring parts of the cortex. A secondary motor area, the premotor cortex (involved in planning motor actions), has roughly the same somatotopic organization as the primary motor cortex (necessary for executing motor actions). This somatotopy allows for precise prediction of where in the brain simulations should and should not be found: Foot verbs should preferentially activate foot areas of motor and premotor cortex (more than they activate mouth or hand areas); hand verbs should preferentially activate hand areas of motor and premotor cortex (more than they activate mouth or foot areas); etc.

Hauk, Johnsrude, and Pulvermüller (2004) found that action verbs cued a somatotopic pattern of brain activity. Activity cued by the foot, mouth, and hand sentences overlapped with activity found in the foot-, mouth-, and hand-action regions of interest. This result was predicted by the embodied simulation hypothesis but not by the disembodied alternative, according to which the somatotopic motor areas should play no role in understanding sentences or representing the meanings of verbs.

This result has been replicated and extended by multiple studies testing for "semantic somatotopy" cued by action verbs in the motor and premotor cortices (for reviews see Fischer and Zwaan, 2008; Willems and Casasanto, 2011). Beyond the motor system, analogous results have been found for perceptual simulations driven by language about perceptible things: Understanding color words activates visual areas specialized for color perception (Simmons, et al., 2007); understanding words for fragrant things activates olfactory perception areas (González et al., 2006); understanding sentences about motion events activates visual areas specialized for motion perception (Wallentin et al., 2011). Together, these fMRI studies provide an initial body of evidence that supports the embodied simulation hypothesis by showing that modality-specific perceptual and motor areas are selectively activated by language referring to our perceptual and motor experiences.

3.2   When *Does Simulation Happen in the Brain?*

Studies that use fMRI to show *where* language-driven activity in the brain is happening have answered a first important question: Does activity in modality-specific perceptual and motor areas correlate with the process of computing the meanings of words (and sentences) that refer to perceptuo-motor experiences? But these studies leave open a further question: *When*, precisely, is this language-driven modality-specific activity happening? FMRI is not a suitable tool for addressing this question. After a stimulus (e.g., a word) is presented to an experimental participant, neurons that are receptive to that stimulus begin responding almost instantaneously. However, as mentioned above, the fMRI signal does not index neural activity directly: It indexes changes in cerebral blood flow that occur in response to stimulus-driven neural activity. These changes in blood flow may peak four to five seconds after the neural event that necessitated them. Given this lag in the blood flow response (which is somewhat variable and depends on many factors), fMRI does not allow researchers to determine precisely how much time has passed between the presentation of a stimulus and the brain's response to it.

Why does timing matter with respect to the embodied simulation hypothesis? Simulations are posited to be the stuff of thought, and the stuff of linguistic meaning (or, at a minimum, *some of* the stuff of thinking and meaning construction). Much of our thinking happens fast, on the order of tens or hundreds of milliseconds, as does much of ordinary language understanding. Therefore, to be the stuff of cognition and semantics, simulations would need to happen *fast.*

How fast do people understand words? A neurolinguistics literature that pre-dates the embodied simulation hypothesis provides some precise information, and sets a lower "speed limit" for how fast simulations would need to happen in order to fulfill the role in our mental lives that embodied simulation theorists posit. For more than four decades, researchers have used Electroencephalogra-phy (EEG) to measure electrical signals generated by the brain in response to linguistic stimuli. According to this literature, readers can understand a word, and determine whether a newly-presented word is sensible in its linguistic con-text, in about 400 milliseconds (Kutas and Hilyard, 1980). Therefore, for simu-lations to be the stuff of meaning, they would need to occur in less than 400 milliseconds. Do they? In order to answer this question, researchers need a tool that has better temporal precision than fMRI and also greater spatial precision than EEG (which can indicate precisely when a neural event occurred but does not typically give precise information about where it occurred).

To determine how long it takes to generate a modality-specific simulation, Pulvermüller and colleagues used a third kind of brain imaging, which com-bines high spatial resolution (like fMRI) with high temporal resolution (like EEG): Magnetoencephalography (MEG). MEG measures the weak magnetic fields that are induced by electrical currents flowing through neurons. Pulver-müller and colleagues determined the instant when spoken action verb stimuli could be uniquely identified, and measured how much time elapsed between word form identification (in the left Temporal lobe, near auditory cortex) and the appearance of somatotopic activity in the motor system (e.g., activity in foot-motor areas for verbs like *kick*). Results showed that somatotopic motor simulations could be detected within tens of milliseconds after word form iden-tification, suggesting these simulations were indeed happening fast enough to play the role in linguistic meaning construction that is posited by the embodied simulation hypothesis (for a review of relevant MEG studies see Pulvermüller, 2005).

3.3   *Do Simulations Play a Causal Role in Understanding Words?*

Results from fMRI studies show that modality-specific brain areas are activated in response to linguistic stimuli, and MEG studies show that this activation happens fast enough to be relevant to the process of linguistic meaning con-struction. Do these results demonstrate that meaning is represented, at least in part, in neurocognitive systems for perception and action? No, these results lay the groundwork for such a conclusion, but they do not license this conclusion, per se. Why not? Because typical brain imaging studies can only demonstrate a *correlation* between patterns of brain activity and patterns of thinking, and *correlation does not imply causation.*

Inferring a causal relationship, for example, between somatotopic motor activity shown in fMRI and MEG studies and the comprehension of action verbs would be an error in statistical reasoning. In order to test for a causal relationship, a different kind of experiment is needed. An illustration of what kind of studies can only show correlation (like the brain imaging studies reviewed above), and what kind of further study is needed to support causal inferences: Medical studies often test for correlations between a behavior and a medical outcome. Imagine a study that tested thousands of people who drink caffeine and found that the more caffeine they reported drinking the more likely they were to have a heart attack. A tempting conclusion would be: Caffeine causes heart attacks. But this imaginary study would not license this conclusion: There could be a strong correlation between caffeine and heart attacks even if there were no causal relationship, at all. For instance, the real causal factor could be: Stress. Maybe people with more stressful jobs: (a) drink more caffeine to keep themselves motivated, and also (b) have more heart attacks because *stress* causes heart attacks, not caffeine.

In order to determine whether there is a causal relationship between caffeine and heart attacks a second type of medical study would need to be conducted: a randomized controlled trial (RCT). Whereas correlational studies measure naturally-occurring relationships between two variables (e.g., caffeine consumption, heart attacks), RCTs intervene on naturally-occurring relationships, manipulating one variable in order to determine how it influences the other. To test the caffeine-heart attack relationship, our imaginary medical researchers could randomly assign groups of participants to different *treatments* (e.g., caffeine drinking, no caffeine drinking) and then measure whether there was a difference in the number of heart attacks between the two groups, post-treatment.

How can a RCT study help researchers test for a causal relationship between modality-specific brain activity and linguistic meaning construction? To determine whether activity in modality-specific areas plays any causal role in language understanding, it is necessary to manipulate activity in these brain areas and measure whether this intervention on the brain influences how participants process the meanings of words. One tool for directly manipulating brain activity in healthy experimental participants is Transcranial Magnetic Stimulation (TMS). With TMS, researchers can place a magnetic coil on the scalp and pulsate a magnetic field in order to selectively increase or decrease neural activity in the cortical area beneath the coil. Willems et al. (2011) used TMS to modulate activity in the hand areas of participants' left or right premotor cortex. After treatment, participants performed a standard task known to elicit activation of words' meanings called a *lexical decision task*: For each stimulus shown, participants judged whether the stimulus was a real English verb or a meaningless pseudo-verb (e.g., *to wunger*), as quickly as possible. Only responses to the real verbs were of interest. Each verb either referred to a manual action that is typically performed with one's dominant hand (e.g., to write) or a non-manual action (e.g., to wander). The experimenters reasoned that, if motor simulation consists in partially preparing the brain's motor system to perform the action named by the verb, then only the *left* premotor hand area would be involved in simulating the manual actions (since the left hemisphere of the brain controls the right hand, and all of the participants were right-handed). Furthermore, neither premotor hand area would be involved in simulating the non-manual actions, since the hand area only programs hand actions (not actions with other parts of the body). The results supported these predictions: Stimulating the left premotor cortex (but not the right premotor cortex) influenced how quickly participants could respond to the manual verbs (but not the non-manual verbs). This finding provided some of the first evidence that somatotopic motor activity plays a causal role in processing action verbs' meanings.[7]

3.4.1 How Embodied Semantics Cannot Be Tested
This chapter focuses almost exclusively on studies using methods from Cognitive Neuroscience, which allow questions about embodied semantics to be addressed by examining relationships between neural and cognitive activity. Another related body of studies has emerged over the first two decades of the 21st century which uses behavioral methods from Cognitive Psychology. This body of research, which includes thousands of experiments, has been omitted from this review of foundational evidence for embodied semantics because, in most cases, these studies do not accomplish their goal of testing the embodied simulation hypothesis.

In one influential study from this behavioral literature, Zwaan and Yaxley (2003a) showed participants pairs of words, one presented above the other, which named pairs of objects that have canonical vertical positions with respect

---

7   Pulvermüller et al. (2005) conducted a similar TMS study prior to Willems et al. (2011), but the pattern of data they obtained made the results hard to interpret with respect to the embodied simulation hypothesis. Other studies have used a different kind of TMS protocol in which single magnetic pulses are applied to motor cortex while participants process limb-specific action verbs (e.g., write, kick), and muscle activity in the relevant limb is measured (e.g., Papeo et al., 2009). These single-pulse TMS studies do not support direct inferences about a causal role for the motor system in processing language because the dependent measure (that which is influenced directly by the TMS treatment) is a measure of muscle activity, not of language processing.

to each other (e.g., *cup, saucer*). The experimenters compared how long participants took to judge whether the words were related to each other, depending
on whether the arrangement of the words on the computer screen matched the
canonical positions of their referents (e.g., cup above saucer) or mismatched
their canonical positions (e.g., saucer above cup). Participants judged words
faster when their relative locations on the screen matched their referents' typical locations in the world. This result is often interpreted as evidence that
participants understand the meanings of words referring to visible objects, at
least in part, using modality-specific simulations of the referents, implemented
in visual cortex. Yet, in addition to this embodied explanation for Zwaan and
Yaxley's (2003a) match-mismatch effect, there are also clear disembodied alternative explanations.

To Zwaan and Yaxley's (2003a) credit, the authors acknowledged these alternatives, suggesting the following as one plausible disembodied explanation for
their match-mismatch effect, which would not implicate any modality-specific
brain areas in the process of constructing and comparing the words' meanings. For the pair of stimulus items (1) BRANCH presented above ROOT, or
(2) ROOT presented above BRANCH, the authors suggested that:

> (A) spatial "tag" is attached to each word. In a semantic network, a con-
> cept like BRANCH would have a link with concepts such as *top*, given that
> branches are typically found in the top parts of trees. As a consequence,
> for the pair in (1), TOP would be attached to BRANCH and BOTTOM
> to ROOT, whereas the reverse would happen in (2). In the case of (2),
> this would yield a conflict between the spatial tags and the information in
> semantic memory. This conflict would delay the activation above thresh-
> old of the concept pair, thus delaying the response.
>
> ZWAAN and YAXLEY, 2003a: 957

Zwaan and Yaxley (2003a) also acknowledged that similar results had been
obtained years before the embodied simulation hypothesis had been formulated (MacLeod, 1991), which were necessarily motivated and explained by disembodied theories of language. To the authors' further credit, Zwaan and Yaxley (2003b) conducted a subsequent study in which they attempted to resolve
the ambiguity of these results by grounding their experimental predictions in
patterns of brain activity that would be compatible or incompatible with an
embodied account.

Zwaan and Yaxley's (2003a) study, and thousands of behavioral studies like
it, failed to test the embodied simulation hypothesis effectively *not* because
of idiosyncratic aspects of the particular experiments, but rather because of

their violation of a general principle of experimental design. In order for an experiment to distinguish between two competing hypotheses (e.g., embodied semantics, disembodied semantics), the competing hypotheses must make contrasting predictions. If two hypotheses both predict the same pattern of results (for different reasons), then obtaining this pattern is uninformative: The result supports both the hypothesis that the experimenters hoped to confirm *and* the hypothesis that they hoped to disconfirm. Although it is possible to design purely behavioral studies that test the embodied simulation hypothesis effectively (e.g., Shebani and Pulvermüller, 2013; Escámez et al., 2020), most behavioral tests of embodied semantics to date share the same fatal flaw: The competing hypotheses do not make contrasting predictions. In principle, it is possible that nearly any cognitive function could be implemented in *either* modality-specific systems or non-modality-specific systems in the mind; behavioral results are generally compatible with either of the in-principle possibilities. Therefore, in general, studies using methods from Cognitive Neuroscience have been more successful than behavioral studies at generating predictions that are capable of confirming one account of semantics (either embodied or disembodied) and disconfirming the alternative, on the basis of whether the predicted patterns of neural activity are found in modality-specific brain areas or only in non-modality-specific areas.

3.4   *Summary and Open Questions*

Together, studies using fMRI, MEG, and TMS established a body of evidence that confirmed key predictions of the embodied simulation hypothesis, and challenged the "disembodied" alternative that dominated theories of language in the mind and brain through the end of the 20th century. Modality-specific brain areas including the visual cortex, auditory cortex, and motor cortex, which have long been known to play a crucial role in perceiving and producing the forms of words, now appear to be involved in instantiating the meanings of words, as well. Beyond showing that these modality-specific brain areas are active during language understanding via fMRI studies, researchers have used MEG to show that activity in modality-specific areas happens quickly enough to meet the requirements of rapid, online language processing, and therefore to play the role in linguistic meaning construction that simulation theorists posit. Beyond showing a correlation between modality-specific brain activity and language understanding, studies using TMS provide preliminary evidence that modality-specific areas play a causal role in processing word meaning.

The majority of the studies reviewed here were conducted during roughly the first decade of the 21st century. These studies validated the most fundamental tenets of the embodied simulation hypothesis. During the subsequent decade, in addition to replicating and incrementally extending these foundational studies, researchers have turned to questions for which no complete answer has yet emerged. For example: *How much* of meaning is embodied in modality-specific simulations? Intervening on modality-specific brain areas has been shown to produce small changes in response times (Willems et al., 2011) or accuracy (Gijssels et al., 2018) in judging relevant words, but there is little evidence that modulating modality-specific brain activity has any substantial influence on the process of meaning construction (cf., Escámez et al., 2020).

Another open question concerns the extent to which semantic representations differ between individuals and groups as a result of their differing bodily experiences. If thinking and language understanding is (partly) constituted by simulations of our own perceptuo-motor experiences, then do people with different kinds of bodies who perceive or act upon the world in systematically different ways, also think differently in corresponding ways? A body of research has shown that, indeed, people with different kinds of bodies construct predictably different feelings, object representations, mental images, and word meanings, and these thoughts are implemented in predictably different modality-specific brain areas (Casasanto, 2011). Yet, this research on the "body-specificity" of language and thought remains in its early stages, in part because only one bodily difference between individuals (i.e., their handedness) has been extensively explored.

Perhaps chief among the open questions about embodied simulation is: How can modality-specific simulations represent abstract concepts, like time, justice, or happiness? Concrete objects like cats can be represented via perceptual simulations; concrete actions like throwing can be represented via motor simulations. But how can we use perceptual or motor simulations to represent abstract ideas of things we can never perceive with the senses or act upon with the muscles? Three potential solutions have been pursued by researchers, but none of these pursuits has been particularly successful. First, perhaps abstract ideas can be embodied via metaphorical mental representations (Lakoff and Johnson, 1999)? For example, suppose the abstract notion of *understanding* were conceptualized, in part, via the concrete action of *grasping*, as suggested by expressions like "she grasped the idea." If so, then at least part of the semantics of *understanding* could be a motor simulation of grasping, in the hand motor areas that support literal grasping. Although this possibility remains plausible and well-motivated, numerous experimental tests have failed to provide any clear support for it. Whereas literal sentences like "she grasped the knife" reliably activate somatotopic hand areas, metaphorical sentences like "she grasped the idea" do not (for a review see Casasanto and Gijssels, 2015).

According to another proposed solution, perhaps abstract ideas can be embodied via simulation of the complex situations in which these ideas are experienced and used (Barsalou, 1999). For example, perhaps *justice* can be understood via simulating a courtroom scene? Yet, this proposal faces both in-principle and empirical challenges. In principle, a courtroom scene could be simulated in rich multi-modal detail (like an audio-video recording in one's brain and mind), but *still* the person experiencing this courtroom simulation would not necessarily understand justice. Empirically, the study that has tested the embodiment of "situation models" most directly did not report any clear modality-specific brain activity corresponding to situation model construction, even for concrete concepts (Simmons et al., 2008).

According to a third proposal, perhaps abstract concepts are embodied via simulations of affective (i.e., emotional) experiences (Meteyard et al., 2012)? Consistent with this proposal, abstract words are statistically more likely than concrete words to have affective content as part of their semantics (Kousta et al., 2009). Yet, this proposal also faces a priori and empirical challenges. A priori, this proposal is not likely to be a complete answer to the problem of embodying abstract concepts (and the corresponding word meanings) because many abstract ideas have no clear emotional charge (e.g., time, neutrality, multiplication, quark, etc.) Empirically, this proposal is hard to evaluate with respect to the embodied simulation hypothesis because the brain structures that support our primary experience of emotions (e.g., the amygdala) are multifunctional and non-modality-specific.

Ultimately, the resolution to these and other outstanding questions will determine whether the discovery of modality-specific simulations simply modifies 20th-century theories of concepts and semantics in the brain and mind, or revolutionizes them.

References

Anderson, Micheal L. 2003. Embodied cognition: A field guide. *Artificial Intelligence* 149(1): 91–130.

Barsalou, Lawrence W. 1999. Perceptual symbol systems. *Behavioral and Brain Sciences* 22(4): 577–660.

Barsalou, Lawrence W., W. Kyle Simmons, Aron K. Barbey and Christine D. Wilson. 2003. Grounding conceptual knowledge in modality-specific systems. *Trends in Cognitive Sciences* 7(2): 84–91.

Brooks, Rodney A. 1990. Elephants don't play chess. *Robotics and Autonomous Systems* 6(1–2): 3–15.

Casasanto, Daniel. 2011. Different bodies, different minds: the body specificity of language and thought. *Current Directions in Psychological Science* 20(6): 378–383.

Casasanto, Daniel and Tom Gijssels. 2015. What makes a metaphor an embodied metaphor? *Linguistics Vanguard* 1(1): 327–337.

Damasio, Antonio R. 1989. Time-locked multiregional retroactivation: A systems-level proposal for the neural substrates of recall and recognition. *Cognition* 33(1–2): 25–62.

Dove, Guy. 2009. Beyond perceptual symbols: A call for representational pluralism. *Cognition* 110(3): 412–431.

Escámez, Omar, Daniel Casasanto, Gabriella Vigliocco and Julio Santiago. 2020. Motor interference changes meaning. In S. Denison, M. Mack, Y. Xu and B.C. Armstrong (Eds.), *Proceedings of the 42nd Annual Conference of the Cognitive Science Society*.

Fischer, Martin H. and Rolf A. Zwaan. 2008. Embodied language: A review of the role of the motor system in language comprehension. *Quarterly Journal of Experimental Psychology* 61(6): 825–850.

Fodor, Jerry A. 1983. *The modularity of mind*. Cambride, MA: MIT press.

Gijssels, Tom, Richard B. Ivry and Daniel Casasanto. 2018. tDCS to premotor cortex changes action verb understanding: Complementary effects of inhibitory and excitatory stimulation. *Scientific Reports* 8(1): 1–7.

González, Julio, Alfonso Barros-Loscertales, Friedemann Pulvermüller, Vanessa Meseguer, Ana Sanjuán, Vicente Belloch and Cesar Ávila. 2006. Reading cinnamon activates olfactory brain regions. *Neuroimage* 32(2): 906–912.

Hagoort, Peter. 2005. On Broca, brain, and binding: a new framework. *Trends in Cognitive Sciences* 9(9): 416–423.

Hauk, Olaf, Ingrid Johnsrude and Friedemann Pulvermüller. 2004. Somatotopic representation of action words in human motor and premotor cortex. *Neuron* 41(2): 301–307.

Kousta, Stavroula-Thaleia, David P. Vinson and Gabriella Vigliocco. 2009. Emotion words, regardless of polarity, have a processing advantage over neutral words. *Cognition* 112(3): 473–481.

Kutas, Marta and Steven A. Hillyard. 1980. Reading senseless sentences: Brain potentials reflect semantic incongruity. *Science* 207(4427): 203–205.

Lakoff, George and Mark Johnson. 1999. *Philosophy in the flesh: The embodied mind and its challenge to western thought*. New York: Basic Books.

Longo, Matthew R., Friederike Schüür, Marjolein P.M. Kammers, Manos Tsakiris and Patrick Haggard. 2008. What is embodiment? A psychometric approach. *Cognition* 107(3): 978–998.

Machery, Edouard. 2007. Concept empiricism: A methodological critique. *Cognition* 104(1): 19–46.

Meteyard, Lotte, Sara Rodriguez Cuadrado, Bahador Bahrami and Gabriella Vigliocco.

2012. Coming of age: A review of embodiment and the neuroscience of semantics. *Cortex* 48(7): 788–804.

Niedenthal, Paula M. 2007. Embodying emotion. *Science* 316(5827): 1002–1005.

Papeo, Liuba, Antonino Vallesi, Alessio Isaja and Rafaella Ida Rumiati. 2009. Effects of TMS on different stages of motor and non-motor verb processing in the primary motor cortex. *PloS One* 4(2): e4508.

Pulvermüller, Friedemann. 1999. Words in the brain's language. *Behavioral and Brain Sciences* 22(2): 253–336.

Pulvermüller, Friedemann. 2005. Brain mechanisms linking language and action. *Nature Reviews Neuroscience* 6(7): 576–582.

Shebani, Zubaida and Friedmann Pulvermüller. 2013. Moving the hands and feet specifically impairs working memory for arm- and leg-related action words. *Cortex* 49: 222–231.

Simmons, W. Kyle, Vimal Ramjee, Michael S. Beauchamp, Ken McRae, Alex Martin and Lawrence W. Barsalou. 2007. A common neural substrate for perceiving and knowing about color. *Neuropsychologia* 45(12): 2802–2810.

Simmons, W. Kyle, Stephan B. Hamann, Carla L. Harenski, Xiaoping Hu and Lawrence W. Barsalou. 2008. fMRI evidence for word association and situated simulation in conceptual processing. *Journal of Physiology-Paris* 102(1–3): 106–119.

Varela, Francisco J., Evan Thompson and Eleanor Rosch. 1991. *The Embodied Mind: Cognitive Science and Human Experience*. Cambridge, MA: MIT press.

Wallentin, Mikkel, Andreas H. Nielsen, Peter Vuust, Anders Dohn, Andreas Roepstorff and Torben E. Lund. 2011. BOLD response to motion verbs in left posterior middle temporal gyrus during story comprehension. *Brain and Language* 119(3): 221–225.

Willems, Roel M. and Daniel Casasanto. 2011. Flexibility in embodied language understanding. *Frontiers in Psychology* 2(116).

Willems, Roel M., Ivon Toni, Peter Hagoort and Daniel Casasanto. 2010. Neural dissociations between action verb understanding and motor imagery. *Journal of cognitive neuroscience* 22(10): 2387–2400.

Wilson, Margaret. 2002. Six views of embodied cognition. *Psychonomic Bulletin & Review* 9(4): 625–636.

Zwaan, Rolf A. and Richard H. Yaxley. 2003a. Spatial iconicity affects semantic relatedness judgments. *Psychonomic Bulletin & Review* 10(4): 954–958.

Zwaan, Rolf A. and Richard H. Yaxley. 2003b. Hemispheric differences in semantic-relatedness judgments. *Cognition* 87(3): B79–B86.

CHAPTER 7

Simulation Semantics: How the Body Characterizes the Mind

Nian Liu

1   Introduction

Meaning is at the center of the study of language and the mind. After all, conveying meaning is the reason why humans have language and why our children need to acquire language. But how do people make meaning of language? How do we discern the meaning of a speaker or a writer from a string of sounds or a sequence of letters or characters?

The traditional view of meaning holds that our minds are abstract, logical, and rational, and most linguists holding that view believe that language is a system of abstract and logical symbols that are internal to our minds. To understand the referent of a word (that is, the thing the word refers to) or the meaning of a sentence, we use our mental definitions for them, or *Mentalese*, a hypothetical language in our mind, in which concepts and propositions are represented without words. The mental definitions of words match up to things in the real world, and in that way we make meaning of words. The theory of Mentalese could explain how a word and its referent in the real world are connected and understood in our mind (Fodor, 1994). However, this theory has several limitations. For example, it cannot explain how we learned Mentalese in the first place. We surely do not learn it with our first language, because understanding words in any language depends on our knowledge of Mentalese. This suggests that Mentalese is innate. But those abstract mental symbols need to be grounded in the real world to be meaningful. How can an innate mental language be connected to the real world of actions and physical objects?

To address such questions, some cognitive psychologists (e.g., Barsalou, 1999) propose a different perspective on the human mind. They argue against the traditional view of the mind-body relationship and suggest that meaning might be much more intertwined with our experience in the real world. In Barsalou's view (1999; 2008), comprehension involves simulation of our past experiences, which is the core element in the process that allows us to derive meaning from linguistic input. Because meaning in minds has everything to do with our own bodily experiences, language comprehension is not about decoding abstract mental symbols but rather a process of mentally creating scenery and actions based on our expansive conceptual knowledge of the world and our idiosyncratic experiences of interacting with the world. The theory of meaning that grew from the embodiment simulation hypothesis of language comprehension is called simulation semantics (Feldman and Narayanan, 2004), an emerging hypothesis to explain how people understand language.

Simulation semantics posits that language comprehension automatically engages mental simulation of the content described in language. More specifically, mental simulation subjectively resembles perceptual or motor experiences that people have when interacting with the real world, but it occurs without the presence of the associated perceptual stimuli or motor actions. To construct meaning, people create mental simulations of the content of utterances they encounter. With neuroimaging and fine-tuned experimental measures of reaction time, eye gaze, and hand movements, we are able to test the simulation semantics hypothesis (e.g., Bergen and Chang, 2005; Feldman and Narayanan, 2004; Gallese and Lakoff, 2005; Glenberg and Kaschak, 2002; Zwaan 1999; Zwaan et al. 2002).

The past two decades have witnessed burgeoning research on simulation semantics and, more generally, the embodiment account of language comprehension (see books such as Pulvermüller, 2003; Bergen, 2012; Fincher-Kiefer, 2020). This chapter introduces and discusses theoretical accounts of the simulation semantics hypothesis and evaluates them in light of recent empirical evidence.

2   Visual Simulations

2.1   *What to Simulate*
According to the claims of simulation semantics, in order to understand a word that describes an object, people recreate the details of the object using the same parts of the brain that are used for vision; they see the object with their mind's eye. A series of behavioral studies by Zwaan and colleagues, as well as other scholars (Stanfield and Zwaan, 2001; Zwaan et al., 2002; Simmons et al., 2007; Zwaan and Pecher, 2012), have found that merely hearing an object mentioned evokes visual simulation of the object's properties, such as orientation, shape, and color.

Stanfield and Zwaan (2001: 153–156) designed an elegant experiment investigating whether language comprehenders have access to perceptual information during reading. They had participants read sentences describing objects with specific orientations, such as *John put the pencil in the cup* and *John put the pencil in the drawer.* The participants' task was to decide whether a picture shown immediately after each sentence depicted the object mentioned in the sentence (in this case, a pencil). The key manipulation was that the orientation of the object in the picture either matched or mismatched the orientation implied in the sentence. That is, in the matching condition, participants saw a picture of a vertical pencil after reading about a pencil being put in a cup, or they saw a picture of a horizontal pencil after reading about a pencil being put in a drawer. Conversely, in the mismatched condition, participants saw a picture of a horizontal pencil after the sentence describing a pencil being put in the cup, or a picture of a vertical pencil after the sentence describing it being put in a drawer. In both the matching and mismatching conditions, the answer should be "yes," because the object described in the sentence was shown in the picture regardless of its orientation. Participants also saw filler sentences in which no pictured object was mentioned and thus the correct response would be "no." As expected, Stanfield and Zwaan found that participants' reaction times were different when the object's orientation was matched and mismatched. Participants were faster to press the "yes" button when the orientation of the object in the picture matched the orientation of the object implied by the sentence, suggesting that people automatically construct mental images of objects in specific spatial orientation implied by a verbal description.

This is compelling evidence supporting the simulation semantics hypothesis, because no explicit word in the sentences, such as "vertical" or "horizontal," indicated that the object should be in a specific orientation. However, despite the absence of verbal cues, a compatibility effect[1] was observed, which shows that the participants created the right image in their mind by applying their expansive knowledge of the world to their reading. Based on these findings, it is reasonable to propose that language comprehension is not (at least not fully) about activating abstract symbols. Instead, processing language involves dynamically constructing the appropriate mental experience of the scene.

Beyond orientation, there are of course other details that a word or sentence implies which could induce mental simulation. Zwaan and colleagues conducted two other experiments using the same sentence-picture verification task (Zwaan et al., 2002). This time, they manipulated the shape rather than the orientation of the object mentioned in the sentence. For example, an egg in a

---

1   The compatibility effect occurs here when a person responds more quickly when the orientations of the mentioned object and the pictured object are compatible, and more slowly when the orientations of the mentioned object and the pictured object are incompatible.

refrigerator normally implies a different shape from an egg in a skillet (see Figure 7.1). As in the previous experiment, participants identified the object more quickly when the shape of the depicted object matched the implied shape of the object in the sentence.

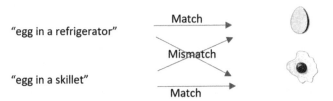

FIGURE 7.1   Different shapes of an egg: in a refrigerator versus in a
                     skillet and their matching and mismatching phrases.

Both experiments seem to suggest that people automatically construct visual details of objects mentioned in a linguistic input. However, in real life, people are rarely asked to judge whether a picture shows an object mentioned in a sentence. So, these experiments' specific tasks might have focused participants' attention on the object and caused them to consciously build a mental image of it.

To eliminate this possibility, the researchers followed up with a slightly modified experiment. This time, participants were asked to read a sentence and then name an object shown in a picture, rather than pressing a button to indicate whether the picture showed an object mentioned in the preceding sentence. For instance, participants simply said "egg" when an egg was shown in a picture, after reading a shape-manipulating sentence mentioning an egg in a refrigerator or in a skillet. The findings replicated the previous experiments' results: even when the shape of the object was irrelevant to the task at hand, participants responded more quickly when the shape of the depicted object matched the shape implied in the preceding sentence. In fact, participants could focus only on the noun and complete the task without fully understanding the sentence, yet their responses were still faster when the two shapes matched, showing that people mentally simulate object properties even when the task does not require them to do so.

Connell (2007) used the same sentence-picture matching method to learn whether people also simulate color, another salient feature of objects. In his experiment, people read sentences that implied a color for a given object. For example, *Sarah stopped in the woods to pick a leaf **off the ground*** implied an orange leaf, whereas *Sarah stopped in the woods to pick a leaf **off a tree*** implied a green leaf. The researcher expected to find a compatibility effect; that is, participants would respond more quickly when the color of a pictured object matched the color implied by the previous sentence. However, the study found the opposite result: people responded more quickly in the mismatching condition and more slowly in the matching condition. To explain this, Connell suggested that color, because it is unimodal (i.e., it can be perceived by one sense) might be less salient or stable than multimodal properties such as shape and orientation. Therefore, when the perceptual input mismatched the simulation (seeing an orange leaf after reading about a green leaf), there is minimal interference, because people would suppress color to simulate shape and orientation. This is in line with findings of other studies suggesting that color is a less accessible visual property than orientation and shape. For instance, children learn to use color to distinguish objects relatively later than they learn to use shape (Wilcox, 1999). Moreover, color information decays in memory more quickly than shape does (Vandenbeld, 2002). It is worth noting that the incompatibility effect reported in Connell's experiment does not mean people did not perform mental simulation of color; if that were the case, the study would have yielded a null effect, with no difference in reaction times. This experiment's intriguing and unexpected result suggests that more research on color is needed.

In a more recent study on color, Zwaan and Pecher (2012) found a matching effect that was almost the perfect opposite of Connell's results. They conjectured that the color effect "is weak and might go in any direction" (Zwaan and Pecher, 2012: 8). A similar and more recent study (Hoeben et al., 2017) confirmed the matching effect and found that it was stronger when the picture's degree of color saturation was greater. This suggests the perceptual richness of mental simulations during language comprehension.

These studies all indicate that when hearing or reading language about objects, people "see" that object with their mind's eye by mentally simulating it. Furthermore, the simulations produced during language comprehension are sensitive to object properties, including but likely not limited to orientation, shape, and color.

2.2   *Where to Simulate*

The previous section presents empirical evidence about *what* is mentally simulated when we read or hear a sentence about an object. But *what* is just part of the story. Our brain also needs to understand *where*—that is, the object's location. Bergen, Lindsay, Matlock, and Narayanan (2007) explored whether an object's location was simulated during language comprehension. In their first experiment, they asked participants to listen to recorded sentences in which spatial location was implied by subject nouns, as in sentences (1a) and (1b). The subject nouns in these sentences (*ceiling* and *ground*) are objects with canonical location in the upper or lower region of vision.

(1)   a. The **ceiling** cracked. [upness-associated noun]
      b. The **ground** shook. [downness-associated noun]

After listening to the sentence, participants saw a shape (a circle or square) appear on the computer for a very short time period (200 milliseconds). Their task was to decide whether they saw a square or circle by pressing the appropriate button. The key manipulation was the location of the shape on the computer screen. For all the experimental sentences, the shape appeared in either the upper or the lower part of the screen. The experimenters expected to find an interference effect: that is, participants would be slower to perceive a shape located in the same location (upper or lower part of the visual field) as the object mentioned in the sentence, and quicker to perceive a shape located in the opposite location. The results confirmed their expectations. People were much slower to identify the shape when it appeared in the same location where the just-mentioned object would canonically appear. This is because mentally simulating the location of an object uses the parts of the brain responsible for actual vision. When we mentally simulate "ceiling," which would normally appear in the upper location, while also perceiving a shape appearing in the same location, the two processes compete for the same resources. These results show that during language comprehension, people automatically simulate spatial details of the objects.

Bergen and colleagues (2007) found similar results in a study that replaced subject nouns with motion verbs showing upwardness or downwardness, such as *climbed* and *fell* in sentences (1c) and (1d).

(1)   c. The mule **climbed.** [verb indicating upward motion]
      d. The glass **fell.** [verb indicating downward motion]

Participants listened to sentences that described upward or downward motion, and this interfered with their ability to perceive a shape that appeared in the same region on the screen. This suggests an inhibition effect, which occurs when activities requiring the same part of the brain happen simultaneously.[2]

---

2   The inhibition effect and the facilitation effect occur for the same reasons but with different timing. When congruent stimuli are processed simultaneously, interference occurs due to competition for the same resources. However, when congruent stimuli are processed consecutively (one task following the other), facilitation occurs because one activity has primed the other.

These results demonstrate that people mentally simulate spatial information implied in a sentence, and this can be triggered by both subject nouns and motion verbs.

Similar results were found by Kaschak and colleagues (2005), whose experiment used sentences implying four kinds of directionality of motion, as shown in sentences (2a) through (2d).

(2) a. The steam rose from the boat. [upward-motion]
     b. The sand poured through the hourglass. [downward-motion]
     c. The dog was running towards you. [towards-motion]
     d. He rolled the bowling ball down the alley. [away-motion]

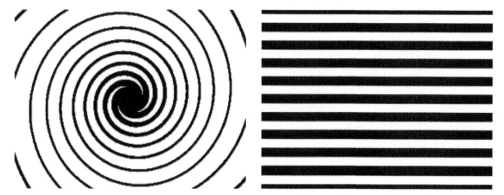

FIGURE 7.2 left: Spiral stimulus for "towards" and "away" displays; right: Horizontal bar stimulus for "up" and "down" displays.
FROM KASCHAK ET AL. 2005; USED BY COURTESY

While listening to these sentences, participants were shown visual displays that created illusory motion matching or mismatching the motion direction described in the sentence. (Static versions of the stimuli creating visual motion are shown in Figure 7.2). The participants' task was to complete a sentence sensibility task (All of the experimental sentences were sensible compared to filler sentences such as *The rib dropped a fire*). As in the study conducted by Bergen and colleagues (2007), they observed a mismatching effect. People's responses were slower when the sentence motion and the visual motion were of the same direction (such as hearing *The dog was running towards you* while seeing visual cues creating towards-motion). This finding confirms that people construct simulation of the content of the sentences they hear and also suggests that such simulations are not general, but highly specific.

Converging results have been reported from studies using different methodologies, including eye-tracking studies (e.g., Spivey and Geng, 2001; Johansson et al., 2006). Spivey and Geng (2001) were the first to conduct a simulation semantics study observing eye movements. In their experiment, participants' eye gazes were recorded as they listened to instructions to imagine visual scenes while looking at a blank white projection screen. Participants were not assigned any particular task and were unaware that their eye movements were being recorded. They were also unaware that listening to the scene descriptions was part of the study; they were told that this was the "break" between the "real" experiment sessions, so that they would behave as naturally as possible. The descriptions they heard introduced various directionality of objects or events, such as upward, downward, leftward, and rightward (see Table 7.1).

TABLE 7.1   Stories used in Spivey and Geng (2001)

Upward story	*Leftward story*
"Imagine that you are standing across the street from a 40-story apartment building. At the bottom, there is a doorman in blue. On the 10th floor, a woman is hanging her laundry out the window. On the 29th floor, two kids are sitting on the fire escape smoking cigarettes. On the very top floor, two people are screaming."	"Imagine a train extending outwards to the left. It is pointed to the right, and you are facing the side of the engine. It is not moving. Five cars down is a cargo holder with pink graffiti sprayed on its side. Another six cars down is a flat car. The train begins to move. Further down the train you see the caboose coming around a corner."
Downward story	*Rightward story*
"Imagine you are standing at the top of a canyon. Several people are preparing to rappel down the far canyon wall across from you. The first person descends 10 feet before she is brought back to the wall. She jumps again and falls 12 feet. She jumps another 15 feet. And the last jump, of 8 feet, takes her to the canyon floor."	"Imagine a fishing boat floating on the ocean. It's facing leftward from your perspective. At the back of the boat is a fisherman with a fishing pole. The pole extends about 10 feet to the right beyond the edge of the boat. And from the end of the pole, the fishing line extends another 50 feet off to the right before finally dipping into the water."

Spivey and Geng found that participants spontaneously looked at the regions on the blank screen where the object and events would appear in the scene described. The explanation is that when people listen to stories about events that take place in a particular location, they mentally construct simulations of objects in that same location. In the process, people "act out" the simulations by moving their eyes to "see" the mental images they have constructed. Interestingly, when participants were asked to recall those stories, the same eye movement patterns were observed, even when no verbal cues were presented. Because eye movements are not under conscious control, these experiments show that mental simulation during language comprehension is automatic.

People simulate scenes of motion as well as static scenes. Richardson and colleagues (2003) asked people to listen to sentences describing either vertical motion (e.g., *The ships sinks in the ocean*) or horizontal motion (e.g., *The miner pushes the cart*) and then perform the shape verification task of identifying a circle or square, as in the study of Bergen and colleagues (2007). In addition to the upper and lower parts of the screen, the shape could appear along the horizontal axis to the left or right side. As expected, Richardson and colleagues observed an interference effect: After hearing *The ships sinks in the ocean*, participants took longer to identify a circle or square either in the upper or lower parts of the screen (along the same vertical axis) than on the left or right of the screen (along the horizontal axis). This leads us to conclude that when objects are described as being in motion, people mentally represent the trajectories of the described motion. Zwaan and colleagues (2004) further demonstrated that the simulation constructed was not static but dynamic, including motions. They had people listen to sentences describing a ball moving toward or away from them (e.g., *The pitcher hurled the softball to you* or *You hurled the softball to the pitcher*). After hearing the sentence, participants saw two pictures of the ball in quick succession, with the second picture showing the ball either slightly larger or slightly smaller than the first picture. This created the illusion of movement toward or away from the observer. The researchers predicted that participants would respond more rapidly when the implied movement of the ball matched the motion described in the sentence. The reasoning is that if a person performs dynamic embodied simulation of the motion indicated in the sentence, the relevant parts of the brain have been activated, so the person should be quicker to subsequently identify an object moving in the same direction. This experiment's results confirmed the researchers' predictions.

The evidence we have explored so far all points in the same direction: when processing language, we simulate seeing the scenes and objects being described. The scenes we recreate are detailed and dynamic, based on our bodily experience of interacting with the world.

3   Motor Simulations

We have learned that when people process language about objects and motions, they perform visual simulations using the same brain circuitry dedicated to actual vision. This raises a related question: Does language about actions trigger people to perform actions in their mind? A series of experiments by Glenberg and Kaschak (2002) investigated this question and reported the action-sentence compatibility effect (or ACE), which served as the basis for many subsequent studies in this field.

In the original ACE experiments (Glenberg and Kaschak, 2002), participants read or listened to sentences denoting particular types of action, such as motion toward or away from the body, as in *Andy handed you the pizza* or *You handed Andy the pizza*. Then they made sensibility judgments (deciding whether the sentence made sense or not) by pressing a button that required them to move their hand either toward or away from their body. The motion described by the sentence could thus be either compatible or incompatible with the hand motion they had to perform. Participants were quicker to respond when the described action and the performed action were compatible, a phenomenon called the action-sentence compatibility effect. The explanation for this finding is that performing actions involves a particular set of muscles, which are driven by a particular set of neurons in the brain's motor cortex. Understanding language about actions also activates the same set of neurons. Because the two processes—action-language processing and physical action—engage the same motor control structures consecutively, participants respond more quickly than when the two processes occur simultaneously and compete for use of the brain's motor control structures, which induces the inhibition or interference effect, as in some of the previously mentioned experiments.

Findings from ACE studies suggest that action execution and action-language understanding share underlying neurocognitive mechanisms. Moreover, when the subject noun "you" is replaced by a third person, such as *Mary* or *John*, the same pattern of interaction was observed (Bergen and Wheeler, 2005), suggesting that people use their motor systems to understand language about action in general, not just language about their own actions. Furthermore, motor simulations are detailed. People seem to activate affordances[3] representing what they can do with a certain object when they process the noun denoting that object. In two visual word recognition tasks, a group of researchers

---

3   Affordances are properties of objects that show users the actions they can take. For instance, a button can be designed to look as if it needs to be turned or pushed.

Matching verb	Run	Scratch
Same effector	Kick	Hold
Different effector	Drink	Stumble

FIGURE 7.3 Action verbs and images involving different body parts.

FROM BERGEN, LAU, NARAYAN, STOJANOVIC, AND WHEELER, 2010; USED BY COURTESY

investigated whether an object's affordances were simulated in language comprehension (Siakaluk et al., 2008). They created two lists of words based on people's rating about how easy or difficult it would be to interact with the objects.
For instance, *mask* was a word with high body-object interaction (BOI) rating,
meaning that people consider masks easy to interact with. *Ship*, on the other
hand, belonged to the low BOI rating list. The researchers then asked another
group of people to judge whether words from the two lists, together with some
pseudo-words, were real English words. People were faster at identifying high-
BOI words (such as *mask*) as real words and slower with low-BOI words (such
as *ship*).[4] Once again, the results support the theory of simulation semantics.
When reading a noun, merely deciding whether it is a real word involves extensive knowledge about how to physically interact with the object it denotes. The
easier it is to interact with the object and thus activate the motor simulation,
the faster we can understand the word.

Another line of experimentation, known as "the knob," provided further evidence about how the motor system encodes fine details of hand movements
(Zwaan and Taylor, 2006). The researchers used a knob to replace keyboard
buttons in their experiment. A knob about 1 inch in diameter was mounted
in a box. The knob could be turned either clockwise or counterclockwise up
to sixty degrees, and when it reached either of those positions, the computer
recorded the participant's response, much like a keypress. Participants listened
to sentences that implied clockwise rotation, like *Dennis turned on the lamp*, or

---

4 Frequency, length, concreteness, and a variety of factors of the chosen words were controlled.

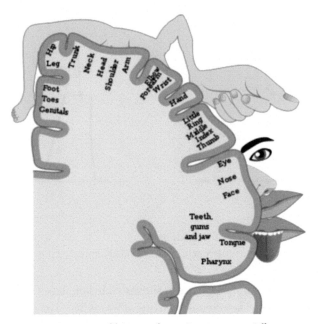

FIGURE 7.4 A cortical homunculus, or "cortex person," illustrating the concept of a representation of the body lying
within the brain.
FROM WIKIPEDIA, RETRIEVED DEC 21, 2020

counterclockwise rotation, like *Eric turned down the volume.* They then had to
rotate the knob in one direction or the other to indicate whether the sentence
was sensible. Zwaan and Taylor reasoned that if the comprehension of sentences describing manual rotation produced motor simulation, then it should
affect the subsequent hand movements: same-direction rotations should yield
faster responses than different-direction rotation. That was exactly what they
found, a variant of the ACE, once again suggesting that people create detailed
motor simulations in comprehending language about hand movements.

At around the same time, several other researchers conducted studies testing diverse types of motor simulation about other parts of the body. From a
sentence sensibility test (Buccino et al., 2005), we learned that reading sentences describing hand actions (e.g., *turning a key*) slowed people's responses
more if they had to push a button with their hand than if they had to do so
with their foot. Likewise, after reading foot-action sentences (e.g., *kicking a
chair*), participants' responses were slower if they had to push a button with
their foot rather than their hand. Bergen and colleagues (2010) designed an
image-verb matching experiment in which participants were presented with
an image (see Figure 7.3) followed by a written verb and asked to decide as

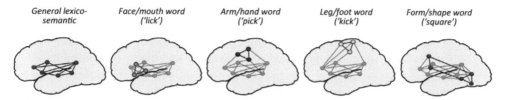

| General lexico-semantic | Face/mouth word ('lick') | Arm/hand word ('pick') | Leg/foot word ('kick') | Form/shape word ('square') |

FIGURE 7.5   The grounding of concepts in motor brain systems: the motor representations of different parts of the body are located in different parts of the motor systems.
FROM PULVERMÜLLER, 2013; USED BY COURTESY

quickly as possible whether that verb was a good description of the image. The images and verbs depicted actions associated with different body parts— mouth/face (e.g., *smile*), hands/arms (e.g., *punch*), or feet/legs (e.g., *kick*). Participants took longer to decide that a verb was not a good description of an image when the action it described and the action the image depicted used the same body parts (matching condition) than when they used different body parts (mismatching condition). This study demonstrated that accessing the meanings of action verbs activated motor simulations specific to the relevant body parts.

In addition to the behavioral studies discussed, neural evidence also provides strong empirical support for motor simulation. Along the motor cortex, the areas specializing in different body parts are arranged in different areas (Figure 7.4).

Even fine-grained semantic differences between action-related words are manifest in motor activation. Words referring to actions typically performed with a particular part of the body (for example, *lick*, *pick*, and *kick*) activate motor and premotor areas in a somatotopic manner. The areas of motor cortex involved in leg motion are more widely dispersed than those involved in arm motion or face motion (see Figure 7.5). If understanding words about actions engages the same neurons that govern actual physical actions, then it should take longer for us to understand leg-related words than arm-related and face-related words, because it simply takes more time for signals to travel a longer neural distance to activate the entire network. A group of German researchers (Pulvermüller et al., 2001) confirmed that verbs denoting actions performed with different body parts were processed in different regions of the motor cortex and at different speeds: face-related words elicited the fastest average response, followed by arm-related words and leg-related words. Although the difference was small (about 10 milliseconds), it was statistically significant. Furthermore, Tettamanti and colleagues (2005) have shown through functional brain imaging that passively listening to sentences describing mouth *versus* leg *versus* hand actions activated different parts of the premotor cortex.

A more recent study supports simulation semantics theory's predictions concerning the nature and specificity of motor simulation during language comprehension. Willems and colleagues (2010) predicted that if understanding linguistic input truly involved creating visual and motor simulation based on one's own experience, then the simulations should differ for different populations that interact with the world in different ways. They tested people with different handedness, predicting that understanding words of hand motion (e.g., *throw* or *pick*) should induce activation of different brain regions for right- and left-handed people. In an fMRI scanner, participants performed a lexical-decision task and a mental imagery task. As expected, the brain activity of the two groups showed contrasting patterns correlating to their dominant hand. The variation in simulation found here is important, because it suggests that we use our idiosyncratic mental resources to construct meaning, so the simulations induced by the same word could vary for different people. For this reason, language cannot be abstract symbols referring to same referent for different people.

In short, behavioral and neuroscience studies have consistently shown that language describing motor actions activates motor systems (see also Helbig et al., 2006; Masson et al., 2008; Kiefer and Pulvermüller, 2012). When processing language, people automatically simulate many details of described actions, such as which direction to move, how to rotate their hand, which hand to use, and what other body parts would be involved. Such simulations involve the same parts of the brain that are used when people perform actual actions.

4   Grammatical Constructions and Mental Simulation

In the previous sections, we have read about research on how language drives mental simulation. People perform mental simulations of the visual and motor content of utterances. Moreover, empirical work has confirmed the intuitive notion that content words such as subject nouns and main verbs contribute specific details about the objects, events, and states to be simulated. We have also seen indirect evidence that the way individual words are arranged also contributes to our simulations. For instance, in the ACE experiment, whether a pencil is vertical or horizontal depends not on any single word, but on all parts of the sentence, including the verb, which shows how to interact with the pencil (e.g., *put*), and the prepositional phrase, which shows the endpoint of the interaction (e.g., *in a cup*). Therefore, the content words are not the only parts of an utterance that contribute to language-driven mental simulation. How do linguistic elements other than words, such as grammatical structures, contribute to meaning?

It is important to investigate the role of grammar in language-driven mental simulation for three reasons. First, to the extent that grammar directs and configures mental simulation, it can be shown to contribute, perhaps indirectly, to meaning. Second, most theoretical schools treat grammar, and language in general, as structurally and functionally distinct from other neurocognitive systems—the so-called "modularity" of syntax or of language (e.g., Fodor, 1983). If grammar can be shown to interact with perceptual and motor systems that support mental simulation, it becomes more difficult to support this view of modularity. Third, grammar is a unique human capacity that holds inherent interest for its potential to reveal characteristics of human cognition. For instance, argument structure constructions indicate how people should construe a described event in simulation.

To English speakers, there is a very subtle semantic difference between the two sentences *You handed Andy the pizza* (ditransitive structure[5]) and *You handed the pizza to Andy* (caused-motion structure). Theoretical linguistics predicts that no two grammatical forms should be fully equivalent in their meaning.[6] In this case, the ditransitive structure emphasizes the transfer of possession, whereas the caused-motion form focuses on the path of transfer (Goldberg, 1995). This has been confirmed by experimental evidence from Kaschak and Glenberg (2000). In two of a series of experiments, they asked people to read pairs of sentences such as (3a) and (3b) below, followed by an inference statement. Their task was to mark which of the two sentences most strongly implied the inference.

Experimental sentences:
(3)   a. The old man cupped the boy some popcorn to calm him down. (ditransitive)
      b. The old man cupped some popcorn to calm the boy down. (caused-motion)

Inference statements:
(4)   a. The boy got the popcorn. (transfer of possession)
      b. The old man acted on the popcorn. (act-on)

---

5   This is also known as double-object structure.
6   This is known as the principle of no synonymy, or the principle of non-equivalence of grammatical forms.

Internal/Performing   External/Performing

FIGURE 7.6 Sample images showing internal versus external view.
FROM IN BRUNYÉ ET AL., 2009; USED BY COURTESY

The novel design was that the verbs employed—cupped, in this example—were denominal verbs (derived from nouns) used in a nonstandard way that implied an innovative meaning, which would not bias participants towards either inference statement. If people took into account of the meaning conveyed by the argument structure (and not the verb), then they should choose the sentence consistent with the inference statement. As predicted, people overwhelmingly chose the ditransitive sentence (3a) when shown the transfer of possession inference (4a). This clear preference indicates that people are sensitive to the meaning implied by syntactic constructions. A follow-up paraphrasing task replicated the results using a more natural setting of testing.

Grammar can also modulate people's perspective and influence how they simulate a scene (Borghi, Glenberg, and Kaschak, 2004). For example, grammatical person (first person *I*, second person *you*, third person *he*) may prime people to take different angles in language-driven simulation. Brunyé and colleagues showed that grammatical person could affect what perspective participants' adopt in a mental simulation (Brunyé et al., 2009). Participants read event descriptions such as *I am slicing the tomato*; *you are slicing the tomato*; *she is slicing the tomato* and then verified whether a picture matched the event. The researchers found that people responded significantly faster when the perspective induced by the grammatical person in the description matched that of the subsequent picture. More specifically, when people processed third-person language (e.g., *she is slicing the tomato*), they were more likely to mentally represent the described scenario from the viewpoint of an outside observer (adopting an external perspective) than from that of an experiencer (adopting an internal perspective). By contrast, second-person language (e.g., *you are slicing the tomato*) was more likely to induce an internal perspective.

What would happen if no linguistic cues were used to specify perspective? Connell and Lynott (2007) reported that people could simulate the content of a sentence without adopting a specific or a single perspective and even simulate parallel representations from different perspectives. Sato and Bergen (2013) looked into this question by replicating the study of Brunyé and colleagues (2009) using the Japanese language. As Japanese is a pro-drop language in which personal pronouns can be omitted from a sentence, they were able to test whether sentences without subject pronouns drove mental simulations to incorporate a particular perspective. To do so, they asked participants to read two sentences that set the context before moving to the critical sentence, such as (5) below.

(5)   I am/you are a deli employee
       I'm/You're making a vegetable wrap
       Right now, (I/you) am/are slicing a tomato[7]

The researchers found that when pronouns were present, like in English, the sentences facilitated identification of an image matching the described perspective. But when the subject pronoun was omitted, so that the sentence did not explicitly mention the subject, the effect disappeared. However, native speakers of Japanese automatically and easily tracked the protagonist of an action even when it was not explicitly mentioned as a subject pronoun in a sentence. The researchers concluded "the mental content of the null subject may not be integrated into mental simulation in the same way as it would be if explicitly mentioned." (Sato and Bergen, 2013: 372) This disparity prompted calls for future investigation into the exact effect of zero anaphor on simulation.

Aspect is a characteristic of the different stages of an event; for instance, whether it is ongoing or completed. Grammatical aspects are among the best-studied linguistic elements in terms of their effects on mental simulation. A simulation-based account would predict that grammatical aspects should contribute to language-driven mental simulation. In English, the most widely studied aspects are the progressive and the perfective. Linguists claim that the progressive aspect (such as *The boy is walking to the store*) accentuates the internal structure of an event, whereas the perfective aspect (such as, *The boy has walked to the store*) highlights the end-state or results of an event (Comrie, 1976; Dowty, 1977; Langacker, 1983).

Do grammatical aspects modulate mental simulations and create simulations with different details? A study by Madden and Zwaan (2003) was among

---

7 This example is made up for convenience to parallel the one used in the study by Brunyé et al.

the first to investigate the relative contribution of grammatical aspects on language-driven simulations. They had participants read either progressive or perfective sentences (*The boy was lighting the fire* or *The boy lit the fire*), then presented a picture depicting the event in either an ongoing or a completed state (see Figure 7.7). The experimenters found that after reading perfective sentences, participants responded to completed-state pictures faster than ongoing-state pictures, suggesting that scenes of completed events were constructed in mental simulation when the perfective aspect was used to describe an event. In other words, the perfective aspect increases the end-state focus of a described event. However, the researchers found no such effect when testing the progressive sentences, explaining that "the lack of effect ... suggests that each reader represents an in-progress event at varying stages of completion."

FIGURE 7.7 Sample pictures depicting events as in progress (left) and completed (right).

FROM MADDEN AND ZWAAN, 2003; USED BY COURTESY

Bergen and Wheeler (2010) reported complementary findings on the progressive aspect. They employed the ACE paradigm and asked people to read sentences denoting manual actions toward or away from their body. Their innovative addition was to manipulate the sentences' grammatical aspect. If the progressive aspect enhances simulated focus on the ongoing action, it should then produce an ACE. Their results confirmed their prediction—progressive sentences reliably facilitate actions compatible with the described motion, but perfective sentences produce no effect on compatible or incompatible actions. This suggests that the progressive aspect prompts people to mentally simulate the central part of an event.

Following this line of research, Liu and Bergen (2016) investigated whether the final location of an action was represented in simulation. Modifying the ACE paradigm, they conducted a location-sentence compatibility experiment. In their experiment, no hand movements were required; instead, participants held their fingers on the response button either close to or far from the body.

Participants' task was to read sentences implying an ending location close to the body, such as *Lisa is adjusting her glasses*, and sentences implying an ending location far from the body, such as *Terry is pushing the elevator button*. The sentences were in either the progressive or the perfective aspect. If an action's final location is part of the nucleus of the event, then the progressive aspect should augment its effect in simulation; conversely, if the final location is part of the end-state of an event, then a location-sentence compatibility effect (LCE) should be observed with perfective sentences. The researchers found that participants did simulate the locations implied in the sentences, but only when the sentences used the progressive grammatical aspect.

The studies discussed in this section reveal that content words such as nouns and verbs provide details about entities and what to simulate, but grammatical constructions also play a role in mental simulation by contributing meaning of their own. Grammar, by providing higher-order instructions in combining and constraining words, influences how we produce embodied simulations.

5   Abstract Concepts and Simulation

So far, we have seen compelling evidence about processing language about concrete concepts. We create perceptual and motor simulations of the content of language based on previous experience. But processing abstract concepts presents challenges to the simulation account of language understanding. Simulation semantics predicts that our knowledge is represented by a recreation of our previous bodily experiences of interacting with the world. But how do people represent abstract concepts that are intangible and never physically experienced? What kind of simulation, if any, is involved? Can we comprehend abstract concepts using the same embodied simulations that we perform to understand concrete concepts?

Some of the studies mentioned in the previous section included abstract language in their testing materials, with mixed results. Some evidence suggests that abstract and concrete language activate similar simulations. Richardson and colleagues (2003) found that abstract verbs implying vertical or horizontal motion (e.g., *respect* and *argue*) activated spatial representation just as concrete verbs do (e.g., *lift* and *push*). But in their LCE study, Liu and Bergen (2016) found that sentences denoting abstract transfer, such as *Darlene is transmitting the orders to the front lines* were processed much more slowly and might induce different kinds of motor simulations than sentences describing concrete transfer, such as *Christina is pouring the water into the sink*. Moreover, sentences with abstract upward or downward directionality (*The cost climbed* vs. *The quantity fell*) showed neither a compatibility nor an inference effect, as was observed using their concrete counterparts (*The mule climbed* vs. *The glass fell*) (Bergen et al., 2007). These null effects are in line with theories claiming that simulation semantics cannot account for the comprehension of abstract concepts (Dove, 2009; Chatterjee, 2010). However, it is possible to solve this problem by investigating language structures that commonly are used in daily life to present abstract concepts: metaphors.

We tend to describe abstract concepts through concrete ones, such as *life is a journey*, an example of metaphor. Conceptual metaphor theory (Lakoff and Johnson, 1980) proposes that metaphor is not a purely linguistic device, but rather a conceptual device that maps across domains of knowledge[8] and is integral to how we understand the world (Lakoff, 1993). Accordingly, the embodied metaphor hypothesis proposes that we conceive of abstract concepts in terms of concrete concepts (Gibbs, 2006). Lakoff (2014) further posits that metaphors are neural circuits connecting two brain regions, a concrete (source domain) region, and an abstract one (target domain).

Behavioral evidence for conceptual metaphor theory was reported in an early behavioral study (Gibbs, Bogdanovich, Sykes, and Barr, 1997). The experimenters asked participants to read stories that ended in one of the three final expressions, such as (6a), (6b), and (6c), and measured participants' reaction time in completing a lexical decision to a related word (e.g., *heat*) or unrelated word (e.g., *lead*). As predicted, only metaphorical idioms showed a priming effect (faster reaction time). The results revealed that processing metaphorical language primed people to activate the actual source domain (in this case, *heat*, as in the "anger is heat" metaphor). The converse is also true. Wilson and Gibbs (2007) demonstrated that people were faster to understand a metaphorical phrase, such as *push an argument*, when they had just performed or imagined performing a matching body action (e.g., a pushing movement). Both studies suggest that understanding metaphorical language involves mental simulation as induced by concrete language.

(6) a. metaphorical idioms (e.g., he blew his stack)
     b. literal paraphrases (e.g., he got angry)
     c. control sentences (e.g., he saw many dents)

---

8 According to the conceptual metaphor theory, each metaphor involves two conceptual domains: a target domain that is abstract and relatively difficult to understand (e.g., *life*) and a source domain that is concrete and can be mapped onto (e.g., *journey*). The mapping is unidirectional (e.g., *Life is a journey* but not *Journey is a life*). There may be multiple mappings for a particular abstract concept (e.g., *Life is a show; Life is a box of chocolates*).

A study by Zanolie and colleagues (2012) provided both behavioral and neu-rological support for conceptual metaphor theory. They examined whether comprehending metaphors about power activates vertical spatial representa-tion. In their first experiment, participants saw words displayed in the center of a screen. Their task was to identify whether the word denoted a powerful per-son (e.g., *king*) or powerless person (e.g., *servant*). After each decision, a letter (*p* or *q*) appeared in the upper or lower part of the screen. Participants were asked to identify the letter as quickly and accurately as possible. If understand-ing power words activated vertical dimensions, then spatial attention should be directed to the corresponding visual field immediately after word recogni-tion, facilitating the identification of letters that appear in the matching loca-tion. As predicted, participants responded faster when the location of the letter was congruent with the perceived power of the preceding word—when a let-ter appeared at the top of the screen after the word *king* or the lower part of the screen after the word *servant*. This suggests that accessing the meaning of abstract power words activates the concrete domain of space. The researchers' second experiment replicated the result using event-related potential (ERP) as real-time measure. Once again, they observed attention shifts consistent with the power metaphor.

Bardolph and Coulson (2014) tested words whose verticality (up/down) was either literal (e.g., *ascend/descend*) or abstract (e.g., *delight/agony*). These words were presented on a screen while participants performed actual hand movements following directions that were either compatible or incompatible with the direction implied by the words. They found that comprehending both literal and abstract words showed positive ERPs, suggesting that people were sensitive to the connection between the source domain and the target domain in the "good is up" metaphor. More interestingly, the compatibility effect for lit-eral words appeared within 200 to 300 milliseconds after their onset, whereas the metaphorical compatibility effect did not occur until at least 500 millisec-onds after their onset. This argues against the strongest version of embodied simulation theory, which claims that literal and abstract words evoke similar sensorimotor processing (e.g., Gallese and Lakoff, 2005). However, although sensorimotor activations caused by metaphorical language take longer than those caused by literal language, they do occur, but they might be constrained by context and the nature of task (Lebois et al., 2015).

Fictive motion is another category of metaphorical language, and investi-gating it may shed light on the nature of simulation about abstract language. Fictive motion sentences use motion through space to describe the static spa-tial arrangement of an object that is incapable of moving. Matlock (2004) found that people use their mind's eye to simulate motion through space following the implied fictive motion in sentences such as *The road runs through the valley*. In this study, when the sentences implied difficult terrain or a slow speed of travel, participants' reaction times increased accordingly. Richardson and Matlock (2007) further confirmed that such simulations produce related eye movements. When hearing a fictive motion sentence (e.g., *The books run along the wall*), people spent more time looking along the axis implied by the motion than when hearing a static sentence (e.g., *The books are on the wall*). So, when reading about fictive motion, people simulate motion in their mind. It seems that fictive motion might work as metaphors do, by inducing simulation of one thing while understanding something else.

However, some other investigations present divergent evidence. Sometimes neurons dedicated to certain actions are not activated when understanding abstract concepts using corresponding action words (e.g., Aziz-Zadeh and Damasio, 2008; Raposo et al., 2009). For example, an fMRI study showed that passively reading metaphorical phrases such as *kick off the year* or *bite the bullet* did not necessarily activate brain structures specialized for those actions (Aziz-Zadeh and Damasio, 2008). But findings from other studies with adapted methodology support the embodied metaphor hypothesis. When metaphorical actions were shown to participants one at a time, so that the presentation and processing were incremental, the parts of the brain that control the corresponding body parts were activated (Boulenger, Hauk, and Pulvermüller, 2009). Moreover, less familiar metaphorical idioms trigger greater sensory motor activation than conventionalized metaphorical idioms (Desai et al., 2013; Pulvermüller, 2013). Conventionalized metaphors are those that have become so common that most language users do not think of them as metaphors. For instance, *bite the bullet* is such a commonly used metaphor that when people hear it, they rarely create simulations of the action *biting* or the object *bullet*.

The research literature does not support a particular conclusion regarding whether and how mental simulation is performed in understanding abstract concepts. Clearly, a definitive answer awaits further work. But it is clear that people perform simulation in understanding some metaphorical language, and more with innovative metaphors than conventionalized ones.

Although we do not know exactly how metaphorical language is understood, several strands of research converge on a deep connection between the source and target domains of metaphorical language. It seems that we tend to think about abstract concepts through concrete concepts even in non-linguistic tasks, as the change of physical context affects people's understanding of metaphorical language. For example, time is very commonly discussed in spatial terms, such as *The future is **ahead of** us* or *Next Wednesday's meeting has been **moved forward** two days*. However, this spatialized representation of time can be ambiguous. When people hear *Next Wednesday's meeting has been moved forward two days*, they may think about themselves as moving forward through time and therefore assume the meeting will be on Friday. On the other hand, they may think of time as coming toward them, and thus assume the meeting will be on Monday. Boroditsky and Ramscar (2002) presented this ambiguous "Wednesday meeting" question to people as they engaged in different types of everyday spatial activities. They found that the further along in a lunch line people were (experiencing more forward spatial motion), the more likely they were to think of themselves as moving through time, hence to say the meeting had been moved to Friday. The researchers asked the same question of visitors at an airport, comparing the responses of people arriving from a flight, people waiting to depart on a flight, and people waiting to pick up arrivers. They found that arrivers were more likely than departers to think of themselves as moving through time and to say the meeting was moved to Friday. Furthermore, departers were more likely to answer "Friday" than those waiting to pick someone up. This suggests that our understanding of the abstract domain of time is closely dependent on the more experience-based domain of space, such that standing in a lunch line or making an air journey would change our perspective in viewing about time (Boroditsky and Ramscar, 2002).

More interestingly, even seemingly unrelated bodily experiences with the source domain modulate people's opinion about and reaction to the target domain, such as personality. For example, Williams and Bargh (2008) found that participants rated a described person as significantly "warmer" when the participant was holding a warm cup of coffee rather than a cold cup of coffee. The researchers argued that the physical sensation of warmth gave rise to feelings of cognitions of psychological warmth (see also, Zhong, and Leonardelli, 2008; Landau, Meier, and Keffer, 2010). The important takeaway point is that the connection between abstract and concrete concepts is deeply situated in our mind, even beyond language.

6   The Nature of Mental Simulation

How exactly does simulation work? Do we have control over it? How soon does it begin after we start to read or hear a sentence? How long does it last? And do we revise it to recreate the correct scene or action when we encounter an ambiguous sentence, such as *the horse raced past the barn fell*?[9]

---

9   This is also known as a garden-path sentence, which is a sentence that upon first reading would likely induce wrong interpretation due to the reader's incorrect parsing. "Garden path" refers to the saying "to be led down the garden path."

First, mental simulation is automatic. It is worth noting the differences between mental imagery and mental simulation. Both are imagery and actions we perform in our mind without direct external stimulus. But mental imagery is a conscious process and can be used and even trained, such as to meditate, practice sports, and so forth. By contrast, like most of the other functions of the brain, language-driven mental simulation is neither necessarily intentional nor available for conscious introspection. For example, in the studies of shape, orientation, and color mentioned previously, Zwaan and Pecher (2012) tested participants' mental imagery ability to eliminate the possibility that the effects being found were due to mental imagery rather than mental simulation. They found that the size of the matching effect did not correlate with participants' ability to perform mental imagery, suggesting that the effects they found resulted from non-conscious mental simulation, not conscious mental imagery. Neurophysiological imaging experiments provide direct observation of how rapidly neural systems in the motor cortex are activated during action word recognition. For instance, Pulvermüller and colleagues (2005) found that brain signals occurred as early as 150–200 milliseconds after the action words were recognized as unique lexical item, suggesting that word-evoked simulation is not post-comprehension but rather happens during meaning comprehension. As discussed in previous sections, metaphorical language simulations also occur automatically during language comprehension (within about 500 milliseconds), although more slowly than during literal language comprehension (Bardolph and Coulson, 2014).

Second, simulation happens early and incrementally. It can happen as soon as a person starts to hear or read a word. When being shown pictures of different objects, people tend to move their eyes more to the picture showing the object with the same beginning sound upon hearing an initial letter (Allophenna, Magnuson, and Tanenhaus, 1998). As for sentences, people's perceptual and motor circuitry starts to create simulations as soon as linguistic input provides information to simulate. In one of the series of the knob experiments mentioned above (Zwaan and Taylor, 2006), the researchers slightly changed the setting and asked participants to turn the knob to present the sentence frame by frame (with a single word or a phrase on each frame) and measured how much time they spent reading each frame. They found that participants' reading time for verbs was faster when the knob rotation direction matched the direction of rotation implied by the sentence. This suggested that as soon as a verb appeared that implied a rotation, people mentally simulated rotation in that direction. Taylor, Lev-Ari, and Zwaan (2008) extended this finding using the same procedure with different testing materials. They presented sentences with ambiguous rotation directions (e.g., *The carpenter turned the screw*) until the clarification came in the subsequent sentence (e.g., *The boards had been connected too tightly*). The researchers again found a compatibility effect, but it appeared with any word providing distinguishing information (in this case, *tightly*). In addition, research on negation revealed that two stages of simulations were involved in understanding negated sentences. People first simulate counterfactual scenes, which are subsequently suppressed or modified, followed by activation of the factual scene, suggesting that the simulation process is incremental (Kaup, Lüdtke, and Zwaan, 2006). In other words, people do not wait until the end of a sentence to mentally build a scene or to simulate an action; they do so as soon as a word, any word, provides distinguishing information to simulate.

Third, simulation is ephemeral. The knob experiment showed that as soon as the frame with distinguishing information ended, there was no measurable matching or mismatching effect. Sato, Shafer, and Bergen (2012) replicated this finding using the sentence-picture-verification paradigm from the shape experiment by Zwaan and colleagues (2002). The experimental setting was the same except that the sentences were presented in Japanese, a Subject-Object-Verb language in which verb comes last in a sentence.[10] No sentence-image shape compatibility effect was found at the end of the sentence. But when participants were shown the image right after the noun but before the sentence-final verb, the matching effect appeared as predicted—the Japanese speakers responded faster when the shape implied by the image and the sentence matched, just as in the English version of the study, but the effect simply did not last long. The fact that any compatibility effect disappears by the end of the sentence in the Japanese shape experiment suggests that simulation is short-term effect.

7   Conclusions, Challenges, and Future Developments

In this chapter, my overall purpose has been to highlight results from behavioral and neuroimaging studies to show that people create mental simulations in response to language. Language comprehension is grounded in bodily actions and involves modality-specific sensorimotor simulations. More specifically, when we process linguistic information such as words, grammatical structures, and abstract language, our perceptual and motor systems are recruited to

---

10   e.g.,   *Nana-ga reezooko-nonakani tamago-o ireta.*
         Nana   fridge-inside   egg   put
         Nana put the egg inside the fridge.

mentally simulate the content described by the linguistic information. When we read or hear words or sentences about objects, our minds use our previous experience to create visual properties of those objects, such as shape, orientation, color, and details about how to interact with the objects. Similarly, our comprehension of words or sentences about actions entails activation of the motor systems used to perform those actions with specific body parts. Grammatical structures contribute to meaning comprehension by guiding our attention to focus on different aspects of the events being simulated. Language structures involving abstract concepts, such as metaphors and fictive motion, are understood through concrete concepts. In that process, the corresponding concrete domains are activated and simulated, but the simulations seem to be less detailed and occur later. Although not discussed extensively in this chapter, comprehending words and sentences involving emotion entails an internal simulation of the emotion state (e.g., Havas, Glenberg, and Rinck, 2007).

From this large body of compelling evidence, it is reasonable to conclude that meaning is not simply about abstract mental symbols. People generate meaning in their minds, using the same brain circuitry they use to see and act, based on their individual experiences. The recreated experiences are grounded, modality-specific, substantially varied, and subjectively real.

Like many other theoretical hypotheses, simulation semantics theory is not free of challenges. One criticism of research on simulation involves the experimental methods and materials. Different methods have not provided convergent results, and supporting findings have not been replicated (see, for example, Postle et al., 2008). More crucially, most of the studies tested only individual words or sentences, whereas everyday language comprehension does not happen in such a decontextualized way. To learn exactly how meaning is created, we would need to study it in a broader and more natural context involving extended discourse (Zwaan, 2014). Some newer studies have responded to this concern, but more research is required to fully capture the nature of language-driven simulations in the real world (Nijhof and Willems, 2015).

Moreover, the nature of abstract-concept simulation is the focus of a current debate among simulation semantics scholars. How similar or different is the simulation induced by abstract language and concrete language? Besides mental simulations, are there other infrastructures and mechanisms involved in abstract-concept processing? We have seen empirical support showing that some abstract concepts are grounded in sensorimotor systems through the linguistic device of metaphor. Bardolph and Coulson (2014) showed that simulation evoked by abstract language did occur in language processing, but its timing was different from simulation evoked by concrete language (see also Liu and Bergen, 2016). This argues against the strongest view of the embodiment account of language comprehension. Nonetheless, it is still not clear whether simulation semantics alone can fully account for abstract language comprehension.

The last issue to be addressed is fundamental: whether simulation plays a causal role in language comprehension. To date, most studies have focused on when a particular kind of simulation would happen, and in what way; few studies have focused on the functional role of simulation. But there is behavioral evidence showing that impairing people's ability to construct simulations interferes with their ability to understand language (Kaschak et al., 2005), as well as empirical examples of language dysfunction caused by body impairment (e.g., Havas et al., 2010). Havas and colleagues found that women who had just received facial Botox injections for treatment of frown lines were much slower to understand sentences describing sad and angry emotions (but not happy emotions) compared to their pre-injection comprehension times. This shows that blocking bodily actions, such as facial expressions, impairs language processing that invokes the simulation associated with those actions. This is strong evidence supporting the idea that mental simulation is integral to language comprehension. Combining evidence from both sides, a more tempered version of embodiment simulation might be needed to explain the discrepancies. Zwaan (2014) proposed that both symbolic representations and grounded representations of meaning were involved in language. The two forms are active simultaneously, and multiple factors, such as reading goals and linguistic ability, will determine which form of representation is dominant.

Clearly, there is still much to learn about mental simulation, and the controversial issues discussed here require further clarification in future research. However, the simulation semantics approach has given rise to new impetus to work on models of language understanding (e.g., Zwaan, 2004). In the future, new experiments with innovative methods will likely offer new and exciting avenues for investigating how we make meaning out of language.

References

Allopenna, Paul D., James S. Magnuson and Michael K. Tanenhaus. 1998. Tracking the time course of spoken word recognition using eye movements: Evidence for continuous mapping models. *Journal of Memory and Language* 38(4): 419–439.

Aziz-Zadeh, Lisa and Antonio Damasio. 2008. Embodied semantics for actions: Findings from functional brain imaging. *Journal of Physiology-Paris* 102(1–3): 35–39.

Bardolph, Megan and Seana Coulson. 2014. How vertical hand movements impact brain activity elicited by literally and metaphorically related words: an ERP study of embodied metaphor. *Frontiers in Human Neuroscience* 8: 1031.

Barsalou, Lawrence W. 2008. Grounded cognition. *Annual Review Psychology* 59: 617–645.

Barsalou, Lawrence W. 1999. Perceptual symbol systems. *Behavioral and brain sciences* 22(4): 577–660.

Bergen, Benjamin K. 2012. *Louder than Words: The New Science of How the Mind Makes Meaning*. New York: Basic Books.

Bergen, Benjamin and Nancy Chang. 2005. Embodied construction grammar in simulation-based language understanding. In J.O. Östman, and M. Fried (eds.), *Construction Grammars: Cognitive Grounding and Theoretical Extensions*, 147–190. Amsterdam: John Benjamins.

Bergen, Benjamin, Ting-Ting Chan Lau, Shweta Narayan, Diana Stojanovic and Kathryn Wheeler. 2010. Body part representations in verbal semantics. *Memory & Cognition* 38(7): 969–981.

Bergen, Benjamin K., Shane Lindsay, Teenie Matlock and Srini Narayanan. 2007. Spatial and linguistic aspects of visual imagery in sentence comprehension. *Cognitive Science* 31(5): 733–764.

Bergen, Benjamin and Kathryn Wheeler. 2010. Grammatical aspect and mental simulation. *Brain and Language* 112(3): 150–158.

Boroditsky, Lera and Michael Ramscar. 2005. Listening to action-related sentences modulates the activity of the motor system: a combined TMS and behavioral study. *Cognitive Brain Research* 24(3): 355–363.

Boulenger, Véronique, Olaf Hauk and Friedemann Pulvermüller. 2009. Grasping ideas with the motor system: semantic somatotopy in idiom comprehension. *Cerebral Cortex* 19(8): 1905–1914.

Brunyé, Tad T., Tali Ditman, Caroline R. Mahoney, Jason S. Augustyn and Holly A. Taylor. 2009. When you and I share perspectives: Pronouns modulate perspective taking during narrative comprehension. *Psychological Science* 20(1): 27–32.

Buccino, Giovanni, Lucia Riggio, Giorgia Melli, Ferdinand Binkofski, Vittorio Gallese and Giacomo Rizzolatti. 2005. Listening to action-related sentences modulates the activity of the motor system: a combined TMS and behavioral study. *Cognitive Brain Research* 24(3): 355–363.

Comrie, Bernard. 1976. *Aspect: An Introduction to the Study of Verbal Aspect and Related Problems*, volume 11. Cambridge, UK: Cambridge university press.

Connell, Louise. 2007. Representing object colour in language comprehension. *Cognition* 102(3): 476–485.

Connell, Louise, and Dermot Lynott. 2009. Is a bear white in the woods? Parallel representation of implied object color during language comprehension. *Psychonomic Bulletin & Review* 16(3): 573–577.

Desai, Rutvik H., Lisa L. Conant, Jeffrey R. Binder, Haeil Park and Mark S. Seidenberg. 2013. A piece of the action: modulation of sensory-motor regions by action idioms and metaphors. *NeuroImage* 83: 862–869.

Dowty, David R. 1977. Toward a semantic analysis of verb aspect and the English 'imperfective' progressive. *Linguistics and Philosophy*: 45–77.

Feldman, Jerome and Srinivas Narayanan. 2004. Embodied meaning in a neural theory of language. *Brain and Language* 89(2): 385–392.

Fincher-Kiefer, Rebecca. 2019. *How the body shapes knowledge: Empirical support for embodied cognition.* American Psychological Association.

Fodor, Jerry A. 1994. *The elm and the expert: Mentalese and its semantics.* Cambridge, MA: MIT press.

Fodor, Jerry A. 1983. *The Modularity of Mind.* Cambridge, MA: MIT press.

Gallese, Vittorio and George Lakoff. 2005. The brain's concepts: The role of the sensory-motor system in conceptual knowledge. *Cognitive Neuropsychology* 22(3–4): 455–479.

Goldberg, Adele E. 1995. *Constructions: A construction grammar approach to argument structure.* Chicago: University of Chicago Press.

Gibbs Jr, Raymond W. 2006. Metaphor interpretation as embodied simulation. *Mind & Language* 21(3): 434–458.

Gibbs, Raymond W., Josephine M. Bogdanovich, Jeffrey R. Sykes and Dale J. Barr. 1997. Metaphor in idiom comprehension. *Journal of Memory and Language* 37(2): 141–154.

Glenberg, Arthur M., and Michael P. Kaschak. 2002. Grounding language in action. *Psychonomic Bulletin & Review* 9(3): 558–565.

Hauk, Olaf, Ingrid Johnsrude and Friedemann Pulvermüller. 2004. Somatotopic representation of action words in human motor and premotor cortex. *Neuron* 41(2): 301–307.

Havas, David A., Arthur M. Glenberg and Mike Rinck. 2007. Emotion simulation during language comprehension. *Psychonomic Bulletin & Review* 14(3): 436–441.

Havas, David A., Arthur M. Glenberg, Karol A. Gutowski, Mark J. Lucarelli and Richard J. Davidson. 2010. Cosmetic use of botulinum toxin-A affects processing of emotional language. *Psychological Science* 21(7): 895–900.

Helbig, Hannah Barbara, Markus Graf and Markus Kiefer. 2006. The role of action representations in visual object recognition. *Experimental Brain Research* 174(2): 221–228.

Johansson, Roger, Jana Holsanova and Kenneth Holmqvist. 2006. Pictures and spoken descriptions elicit similar eye movements during mental imagery, both in light and in complete darkness. *Cognitive Science* 30(6): 1053–1079.

Kaschak, Michael P. and Arthur M. Glenberg. 2000. Constructing meaning: The role of affordances and grammatical constructions in sentence comprehension. *Journal of Memory and Language* 43(3): 508–529.

Kaschak, Michael P., Carol J. Madden, David J. Therriault, Richard H. Yaxley, Mark Aveyard, Adrienne A. Blanchard and Rolf A. Zwaan. 2005. Perception of motion affects language processing. *Cognition* 94(3): B79–B89.

Kaup, Barbara, Jana Lüdtke, and Rolf A. Zwaan. 2006. Processing negated sentences with contradictory predicates: Is a door that is not open mentally closed?. *Journal of Pragmatics* 38(7): 1033–1050.

Kiefer, Markus and Friedemann Pulvermüller. 2012. Conceptual representations in mind and brain: theoretical developments, current evidence and future directions. *Cortex* 48(7): 805–825.

Kosslyn, Stephen M., Giorgio Ganis and William L. Thompson. 2001. Neural foundations of imagery. *Nature Reviews Neuroscience* 2(9): 635–642.

Lakoff, George. 1993. The contemporary theory of metaphor. *Metaphor and Thought* (2nd ed.). Cambridge, UK: Cambridge University Press.

Lakoff, George. 2014. *The All New Don't Think of an Elephant!: Know Your Values and Frame the Debate*. Hartford: Chelsea Green Publishing.

Lakoff, George and Mark Johnson. 2008. *Metaphors We Live By*. Chicago: University of Chicago press.

Landau, Mark J., Brian P. Meier and Lucas A. Keefer. 2010. A metaphor-enriched social cognition. *Psychological Bulletin* 136(6): 1045.

Langacker, Ronald W. 1982. *Remarks on English aspect. Tense-aspect: Between semantics and pragmatics*: 265–304. Amsterdam: John Benjamins.

Lebois, Lauren AM, Christine D. Wilson-Mendenhall and Lawrence W. Barsalou. 2015. Are automatic conceptual cores the gold standard of semantic processing? The context-dependence of spatial meaning in grounded congruency effects. *Cognitive Science* 39(8): 1764–1801.

Liu, Nian and Benjamin Bergen. 2016. When do language comprehenders mentally simulate locations?. *Cognitive Linguistics* 27(2): 181–203.

Madden, Carol J. and Rolf A. Zwaan. 2003. How does verb aspect constrain event representations?. *Memory & Cognition* 31(5): 663–672.

Mannaert, Lara N. Hoeben, Katinka Dijkstra and Rolf A. Zwaan. 2017. Is color an integral part of a rich mental simulation?. *Memory & Cognition* 45(6): 974–982.

Masson, Michael E.J., Daniel N. Bub and Christopher M. Warren. 2008. Kicking calculators: Contribution of embodied representations to sentence comprehension. *Journal of Memory and Language* 59(3): 256–265.

Matlock, Teenie. 2004. Fictive motion as cognitive simulation. *Memory & Cognition* 32(8): 1389–1400.

Nijhof, Annabel D., and Roel M. Willems. 2015. Simulating fiction: individual differences in literature comprehension revealed with fMRI. *PLoS One* 10(2): p.e0116492.

Postle, Natasha, Katie L. McMahon, Roderick Ashton, Matthew Meredith and Greig I. de Zubicaray. 2008. Action word meaning representations in cytoarchitectonically defined primary and premotor cortices. *Neuroimage* 43(3): 634–644.

Pulvermüller, Friedemann. 2013. How neurons make meaning: brain mechanisms for embodied and abstract-symbolic semantics. *Trends in Cognitive Sciences* 17(9): 458–470.

Pulvermüller, Friedemann. 2005. Brain mechanisms linking language and action. *Nature Reviews Neuroscience* 6(7): 576–582.

Pulvermüller, Friedemann, Markus Härle and Friedhelm Hummel. 2001. Walking or talking?: Behavioral and neurophysiological correlates of action verb processing. *Brain and Language* 78(2): 143–168.

Pulvermüller, Friedemann, Yury Shtyrov and Risto Ilmoniemi. 2005. Brain signatures of meaning access in action word recognition. *Journal of Cognitive Neuroscience* 17(6): 884–892.

Raposo, Ana, Helen E. Moss, Emmanuel A. Stamatakis and Lorraine K. Tyler. 2009. Modulation of motor and premotor cortices by actions, action words and action sentences. *Neuropsychologia* 47(2): 388–396.

Richardson, Daniel and Teenie Matlock. 2007. The integration of figurative language and static depictions: An eye movement study of fictive motion. *Cognition* 102(1): 129–138.

Richardson, Daniel C., Michael J. Spivey, Lawrence W. Barsalou and Ken McRae. 2003. Spatial representations activated during real-time comprehension of verbs. *Cognitive Science* 27(5): 767–780.

Sato, Manami and Benjamin K. Bergen. 2013. The case of the missing pronouns: Does mentally simulated perspective play a functional role in the comprehension of person?. *Cognition* 127(3): 361–374.

Sato, M., Amy J. Schafer and Benjamin K. Bergen. 2012. Mental representations of object shape change incrementally during sentence processing. *Language and Cognition* 5(4): 345–373.

Siakaluk, Paul D., Penny M. Pexman, Laura Aguilera, William J. Owen and Christopher R. Sears. 2008. Evidence for the activation of sensorimotor information during visual word recognition: The body–object interaction effect. *Cognition* 106(1): 433–443.

Solomon, Karen Olseth and Lawrence W. Barsalou. 2004. Perceptual simulation in property verification. *Memory & Cognition* 32(2): 244–259.

Spivey, Michael J. and Joy J. Geng. 2001. Oculomotor mechanisms activated by imagery and memory: Eye movements to absent objects. *Psychological Research* 65(4): 235–241.

Stanfield, Robert A. and Rolf A. Zwaan. 2001. The effect of implied orientation derived from verbal context on picture recognition. *Psychological Science* 12(2): 153–156.

Simmons, W. Kyle, Vimal Ramjee, Michael S. Beauchamp, Ken McRae, Alex Martin and Lawrence W. Barsalou. 2007. A common neural substrate for perceiving and knowing about color. *Neuropsychologia* 45(12): 2802–2810.

Taylor, Lawrence J., Shiri Lev-Ari and Rolf A. Zwaan. 2008. Inferences about action engage action systems. *Brain and Language* 107(1): 62–67.

Tettamanti, Marco, Giovanni Buccino, Maria Cristina Saccuman, Vittorio Gallese, Massimo Danna, Paola Scifo, Ferruccio Fazio, Giacomo Rizzolatti, Stefano F. Cappa, and

Daniela Perani. 2005. Listening to action-related sentences activates fronto-parietal motor circuits. *Journal of cognitive neuroscience* 17(2): 273–281.

Vandenbeld, Lisa Anne. 2002. *The Decay Characteristics of Size, Color, and Shape Information in Visual Short-term Memory.* PhD dissertation, University of British Columbia.

Wheeler, Mark E., Steven E. Petersen and Randy L. Buckner. 2000. Memory's echo: Vivid remembering reactivates sensory-specific cortex. *Proceedings of the National Academy of Sciences* 97(20): 11125–11129.

Wilcox, Teresa. 1999. Object individuation: Infants' use of shape, size, pattern, and color. *Cognition* 72(2): 125–166.

Williams, Lawrence E. and John A. Bargh. 2008. Experiencing physical warmth promotes interpersonal warmth. *Science* 322(5901): 606–607.

Willems, Roel M., Peter Hagoort and Daniel Casasanto. 2010. Body-specific representations of action verbs: Neural evidence from right-and left-handers. *Psychological Science* 21(1): 67–74.

Wilson, Nicole L. and Raymond W. Gibbs Jr. 2007. Real and imagined body movement primes metaphor comprehension. *Cognitive Science* 31(4): 721–731.

Zanolie, Kiki, Saskia van Dantzig, Inge Boot, Jasper Wijnen, Thomas W. Schubert, Steffen R. Giessner and Diane Pecher. 2012. Mighty metaphors: Behavioral and ERP evidence that power shifts attention on a vertical dimension. *Brain and Cognition* 78(1): 50–58.

Zhong, Chen-Bo and Geoffrey J. Leonardelli. 2008. Cold and lonely: Does social exclusion literally feel cold?. *Psychological Science* 19(9): 838–842.

Zhong, Chen-Bo and Katie Liljenquist. 2006. Washing away your sins: Threatened morality and physical cleansing. *Science* 313(5792): 1451–1452.

Zwaan, Rolf A. 2004. The immersed experiencer: Toward an embodied theory of language comprehension. *Psychology of learning and motivation* 44: 35–62.

Zwaan, Rolf A. 1999. Embodied cognition, perceptual symbols, and situation models. *Discourse Processes* 28: 81–88.

Zwaan, Rolf A. and Diane Pecher. 2012. Revisiting mental simulation in language comprehension: Six replication attempts. *PloS one* 7(12): p.e51382.

Zwaan, Rolf A. and Lawrence J. Taylor. 2006. Seeing, acting, understanding: Motor resonance in language comprehension. *Journal of Experimental Psychology: General* 135(1): 1.

Zwaan, Rolf A., Robert A. Stanfield and Richard H. Yaxley. 2002. Language comprehenders mentally represent the shapes of objects. *Psychological science* 13(2): 168–171.

Zwaan, Rolf A., Carol J. Madden, Richard H. Yaxley and Mark E. Aveyard. 2004. Moving words: Dynamic representations in language comprehension. *Cognitive Science* 28(4): 611–619.

PART 2

Basic Issues

∴

CHAPTER 8

A Usage-Based Analysis of the Semantics/ Pragmatics Interface

Mira Ariel

1 Introduction

We process language extremely fast. Yet, interpreting utterances is a complex process which cannot be explained only by reference to our knowledge of the grammar and the lexicon. Since linguistic utterances are open to multiple interpretations the addressee needs to rely on extralinguistic competencies in order to interpret the utterance according to the speaker's communicative intention. The immediate discourse context, as well as shared socio-cultural assumptions, provide useful bases for drawing inferences as to the speaker-intended message (Ariel, 2008, 2010, Carston, 2002, Grice, 1989, Sperber and Wilson, 1986/1995).

The pioneering theory integrating the coded with the inferred is Grice's (1989) Cooperative principle, which serves as a trigger for deriving what he called conversational implicatures. Grice distinguished between 'what is said,' the linguistic meaning, and the pragmatically derived Particularized and Generalized conversational implicatures. Particularized conversational implicatures are proposition-level inferences indirectly conveyed by the speaker, on top of and separate from 'what is said,' as in:

(1)   ALINA: My hair's dirty,
              I have it pulled back in a ponytail (SBC: 006).[1]

Showing up for a party not looking her best, Alina has been told that she's looking very chic. She then responds with (1), implicating that 'I am looking quite the opposite of chic.' This Particularized Conversational implicature is clearly separable from the meaning of the assertion(s) that gave rise to it (e.g., *My hair's dirty*).

---

1   SBC stands for the Santa Barbara Corpus of Spoken American English (Du Bois et al., 2000–2005), based on which I have argued for the Usage-Based semantic/ pragmatic interfaces outlined below.

But semantic/pragmatic interfaces take place at the word level as well. Consider the different interpretations of *short* in (2) and *hair* in (3):

(2) a. NICK: your legs are so **short**, (SBC: 057)
     b. FRED: it's on a twelve-month repayment,
                   which is relatively **short**, (SBC: 014)
     c. LYNNE: ... She had like on this .. really ... p- kinda **short** shirt, (SBC: 001)
     d. MILES: the one had on a real real **short** skirt. (SBC: 002)

The linguistic meaning of *short* is contextually narrowed in each of the examples in 2(a-d). *Short* specifies quite a different length for legs (a, depending on who their owner is too) and for debt payments (b). Even short shirts (c) and short skirts (d) express different lengths. The same is true for another everyday term, *hair* (3). It is narrowed to 'head hair' in (a-c), but refers to chick's hair in (d). The *hair* in (b) is actually interpreted as a 'hairdo,' whereas in (c) it's a few detached hairs:

(3) a. KENDRA: ... My **hair** looks like a ⟨X mess X⟩. (SBC: 042)
     b. JULIE: ... Too many teeth and **hair** [(Hx)=]. (SBC: 056)
     c. KEVIN: Looks like !Wendy's **hair** is on it (Hx). (SBC: 013)
     d. AMY: ... they were .. losing all of their .. **hair**. (SBC: 039)

Note that the role of pragmatic inferences in (2) and (3) is different from that of the implicature in (1). Here the inference does not function as an indirect additional speaker message. Rather, it gets integrated with the linguistic meaning to form the very concept intended by the speaker. This is also true for so-called Generalized Conversational implicatures, on which I base my claims here about an appropriate, Usage-Based approach to the question of semantic/pragmatic interfaces.[2]

Even if they have recognized the viability of a semantics/pragmatics dividing line and interface Cognitive linguists have tended to ignore or downplay the issue(Lakoff, 1987; Talmy, 2000). Langacker (2000) has even argued that this division of labor is untenable, but I take exception to this view (see my brief argumentation in the next section).

---

2 Generalized Conversational implicatures are ones routinely triggered by specific expressions (e.g., *some*), where the specific context plays no role in their derivation, although it can work to cancel them.

2   Distinguishing the Semantic from the Pragmatic

Addressees must combine their linguistic competence with their rational infer-encing abilities in order to enrich the semantic representations they derived with ad hoc contextual inferences. But can we distinguish between these two products and processes? Can we equate between the linguistic and the seman-tic and between the extralinguistic and the pragmatic? Following Grice (1989), the consensus among semanticists and pragmatists has been that we should and we can. Semantics according to many Grice followers specifies all and only the truth conditions associated with some proposition, namely the basis for our truth judgments vis-a-vis some relevant state of affairs. Pragmatics was then defined as "the rest" of meaning. Whereas semantic meanings that do not cor-respond to the relevant state of affairs render the proposition false pragmatic violations trigger a different effect, that of inappropriateness.

Clearly, however, the more criteria we can use to distinguish between seman-tics and pragmatics the more robust and psychologically real the division of labor must be. Indeed, a long list of criteria has been offered in the litera-ture (see Ariel, 2010: Chapter 2 for a survey). Table 8.1 lists some of the main ones:

TABLE 8.1   Distinguishing between semantics and pragmatics

Criterion	Semantic meaning	Pragmatic meaning
Context role	Context-independent	Context-dependent
Truth conditions	All and only truth con-ditions	No truth-conditional meaning
Explicitness	Explicit	Implicit
Relevant unit of analysis	Syntactic clause	Discourse (beyond the clause)
Nature of generalization	Linguistic code	Extra-linguistic inference

Unfortunately, while each criterion divides up meanings into two distinct cat-egories, the sets are not identical for different criteria. In other words, many phenomena that are defined as e.g., semantic according to some criterion may very well be defined as pragmatic according to some other criterion. Moreover, not all criteria reflect well our pre-theoretical intuitions as to the linguistic ver-sus the extra-linguistic divide. I discuss many such problems in Ariel (2010: Chapter 3). Here I mention just a few cases where various criteria are incom-patible with each other.

Consider *after all*, for example, as in:

(4)   MONTOYA: I mean how can (H) Doctor ~Montoya say that Latinos have
                     no, =
                     no real power, ((1 LINE OMITTED))
                     After all,
                     (H) they have two people that are cabinet members,
                     .. they have (H) supervisor here in Los Angeles,
                     they have city council people in Los Angeles, (SBC: 012)

The proposition modified by *after all* has a clear explicit content: "Latinos have two cabinet members, a supervisor, as well as city council people in Los Angeles." But *after all* too makes a contribution here. It (implicitly) indicates that the assertion it modifies is already known by the addressee. This is why it would be strange to utter:

(5)   ?? ... **After all**, we have solved the Covid 19 problem.

The assertion in (5), highly relevant in a discussion on allowing international flights, may be true or false. But even if it's true, (5) is not (currently) acceptable because the speaker has no basis to assume that the expressed assumption is known, let alone accepted by her addressees.

    Now, how does *after all* fare on the semantics/pragmatic criteria in Table 8.1? The function of *after all* is definitely pragmatic according to the explicitness condition: The '(given) information status' condition on *after all* is not part of the 'what is said' representation of the relevant proposition. It is implicit. *After all* is also pragmatic in that its contribution (Givenness) is not truth-conditional. This can be seen quite clearly when we consider a potential addressee responding with:

(6)   That's not true!

What this addressee is asserting is that it's not true that "Latinos have two cabinet members, a supervisor, as well as city council people in Los Angeles," not that this assertion does not constitute Given information.

    However, is the Givenness condition context-dependent? Not really. Even in the absence of a relevant context, speakers know that *after all* indicates a piece of Given information. In other words, the interpretation associated with *after all* is context-independent. In the same vein, the addressee need not consider clause-external units in order to figure out the meaning of *after all*. Most crucially, the association between *after all* and the Givenness condition is completely conventional, an integral part of speakers' linguistic competence. We certainly cannot derive the 'Givenness' condition from an explicit message of something like "after everything (has been considered)." So, all in all, *after all* meets two pragmatic criteria and three semantic criteria. Is it then semantic or pragmatic?

Truth-conditionality is considered the most important criterion for distinguishing between semantic and pragmatic meanings. So, in light of the incompatibility above, one could consider it to be the only criterion. In this case, *after all*'s contribution is clearly pragmatic. But, it turns out that truth-conditionality is actually not an appropriate condition. The various interpretations of *short* and *hair* in (2) and (3) have already demonstrated how lexical meanings must be contextually adapted in order to determine the speaker's intended message (its truth-conditional content). The examples in (7) show that whole syntactic strings too may be pragmatically recovered:

(7)   ALINA: and the next thing she know,
              there's !Mike=.
              on the --
              .. on= TV.
              And she goes,
              ⟨VOX (GROAN) VOX⟩.
              (H)= ... (TSK) And of course !Jo=hn,
              who's **just as ba=d,**
              is sitting there going,
              ⟨VOX oh=,
              did you see !M=ike,
              your ex-boyfriend VOX⟩?
              (H) But he's **no better.**
              ... (SWALLOW) He does other goofy things. (SBC: 006).

Alina is talking about two men, the ex-boyfriend (Mike), and the current boyfriend (John) of some woman (Linda). She's comparing the two, twice. But note that the comparison is both syntactically and semantically incomplete. Alina says that John is "just as bad" and "no better," but she never mentions Mike in these sentences. It is the contextual relevance of comparing the two boyfriends that prompts the addressee to choose Mike as the missing term of comparison, rather than the speaker herself, Linda, or anybody else for that matter. These enrichments are definitely pragmatic, and indeed the comparison with Mike is implicit, context-dependent, requires the consideration of extra-clause content, and does not involve any linguistic code. There is no grammatical convention that dictates how we should add the conceptually missing term. If so, the enrichment involved in (7) is pragmatic according to all the criteria above except for truth-conditionality (While it may be true that 'John is just as bad as Mike' it may be false that 'John is just as bad as Linda,' for example, or vice versa).

We've reached a dead end: The criteria offered as distinguishing between the semantic and the pragmatic do not consistently apply to phenomena taken as pragmatic ('Givenness,' enrichment inferences) and many interpretative aspects meet some semantic and some pragmatic criteria (see Ariel, 2010: Chapter 3 for detailed discussion, including of unquestionably grammatical phenomena which nonetheless meet at least some pragamtic criteria). In fact, the criteria themselves conflict with each other. If we choose truth-conditionality we have to ignore a basic distinction between linguistic versus extra-linguistic competencies. The interpretation of *after all*, which is no doubt pragmatic on the truth-conditionality criterion is at the same time no doubt linguistically encoded, since it's dictated by the lexical make-up of the expression. Should we ignore this linguistic code we will have no way of accounting for its use as a Given information indicator, because there is nothing in the immediate context nor in our encyclopedic knowledge that would account for it?

A similar problem will arise if we insist on defining the completions in (7) as linguistic interpretations because they contribute to the truth-conditional content of the relevant propositions. Such an assumption requires us to specify the linguistic conventions that account for these interpretations, but none are available. In other words, insisting on truth-conditionality as the single criterion for distinguishing two interpretative processes (semantic versus pragmatic) fails to offer any account for the natural (and fast) interpretative process.

The solution offered by some linguists (Prince, 1988; Sperber and Wilson, 1986/1995 inter alia) was that the semantics/pragmatics division of labor be reduced to the distinction between coded and inferred meanings. A code directly and automatically associates between some linguistic form and some function (a meaning most often). This association is conventional. Inferences connect between some form and some function too, but in a nonconventional manner. The form/function association here is indirect, mediated by inferences based on general cultural assumptions made salient in the specific context.

Language on this view is first of all a system of codes. Linguistic semantics, therefore, includes those meanings which are derivable by the lexicon and the grammatical rules. Pragmatics is the result of a totally different cognitive process. It's an extra-linguistic phenomenon because inferences are relevant to us not only in connection with interpreting language. We always engage in inferencing. When we think, when we act, and yes, also when we use language.

But then, speakers intend their addressees to process both semantic and pragmatic messages. Are the differences between them significant? Cognitive linguists have long argued against many theoretical dichotomies commonly assumed in linguistics: lexicon versus grammar, synchrony versus diachrony, lexical versus encyclopedic content, competence versus performance, as well as the semantics/pragmatics divide.[3] Langacker (2000) does subscribe to a conventional versus nonconventional use, which is precisely the dividing line between semantics and pragmatics here advocated. But he argues that any attempt to sharply distinguish between conventional and nonconventional uses as linguistic versus extralinguistic acts is arbitrary. Langacker is definitely correct in observing that linguistic change, often the result of entrenchment or routinization (he considers the example of a computer *mouse*), presents clear evidence that the borderline between pragmatics and semantics can and is often enough crossed. Linguists may not always be able to pinpoint where on the pragmatics-to-semantics cline some function is with respect to some expression. Even interlocutors seem to consider at least some pragmatically derived interpretations on a par with linguistically encoded meanings:

(8) *Le-ma   yesh   shmone raglaim ve-holex   al ha-rosh?*
     To-what there.are eight   legs   and-walks on **the-head?**
     "What has eight legs and walks on the head?" (Hebrew, 17 May 2002)

(8) works as a hard riddle because it's quite impossible to think about an animal with 8 legs which walks on its head. It makes no difference to the addressee that it is only through inference that we learn that it is the *animal's* head here that is referred to.

But note the following exchange, which demonstrates the distinct interactional statuses associated with semantic versus pragmatic interpretations:

(9)   MA (San Francisco):   I'd like to leave a message for X.
      Hotel Operator (New York): I'll connect you to their room.
      MA: No, no. I don't want to wake them up. **It's
                                  midnight** in New York!
      Operator: No, **it's not.**

---

3 Incidentally no distinction was drawn between semantics and pragmatics by structural and
   early generative grammarians too.

MA: What time is it there?
Operator: **It's 11:53** (13 October 1998)

When MA tells the hotel operator that she'd rather leave a message for the hotel guests she explains that she doesn't want to wake the guests up, since it's late. Thus, just like the riddle asker is sure to be interpreted as saying 'its head' she actually intends a pragmatically loosened interpretation of *midnight*, something like 'late, more or less midnight.' But then, note the operator's response, which flatly denies MA's claim that it is midnight in New York. The operator is definitely not a cooperative speaker. She should have taken MA's utterance as referring to 'around midnight', which is, then, a true statement, of course. My point is, however, that the fact that *midnight*'s *linguistically encoded* meaning is exactly 12 a.m. makes it possible for the operator to deny that it's midnight, when the corresponding state of affairs is 'close to midnight'. The linguistic code has an extremely solid basis, even in the face of a clearly reasonable pragmatic adaptation of it. This is why it can be insisted on when contextually inappropriate. Pragmatically inferred interpretations are cancelable. Linguistic meanings are not.

In fact, it turns out that the solution for the riddle in (8) is "lice," which indeed have 8 legs, but most certainly do not walk on their own heads. Of course, they do walk on people's heads, which is why it's a legitimate riddle. The reason why this "wise-guy" riddle is acceptable is that the meaning of *the head* as '*some* head,' although definitely misleading, can be insisted upon because it's the linguistically encoded meaning of the expression. This is why the following version of the riddle, where 'its head' is linguistically encoded is *not* acceptable (with 'lice' as a solution):

(10) ~*??le-ma yesh   shmone raglaim ve-holex   al   ha-rosh   shelo?*
       To-what there.are eight   legs   and-walks on **the-head his**?
       "What has eight legs and walks on its head?"

The cancelation of the inferred meaning in (10) is not available for the linguistically encoded 'its head,' which is why this made-up riddle doesn't work.

Thus, the fact that there are some borderline semantics/pragmatics cases does not mean that the distinction is not significant for many or even most expressions. As I have argued in Ariel (2008; 2010), (i) semantic and pragmatic interpretations involve different cognitive processes,[4] and (ii) they are associ-

---

4 Consider the trivial fact that a second language learner must learn the linguistic conventions

ated with different interactional statuses. This is why we do need the distinction after all.

Assuming, then, that speakers' messages are conveyed by a combination of codes and inferences, how can we determine which elements of the interpretation are coded and which are inferred? Which are conventional and direct and which are indirect and derived only ad hoc? The examples so far have not been challenging for the semantics/pragmatics division of labor. Clearly, the completions needed to understand Alina's comparisons are not the product of some grammatical formula. Similarly, *after all*'s givenness cannot be indirectly inferred, and has to be stipulated as its lexical meaning.

This chapter, however, focuses on harder cases, on three types of function words. As we see below, it is not always self-evident whether a specific meaning (component) is coded or inferred. Indeed, the meeting places between the semantic and the pragmatic have prompted lively debates between linguists. I will argue that the Gricean minimalist approach to meaning (see § 2) is not always justified.[5] A Usage-Based approach to the question is not committed to assuming either minimal or maximal meanings. My case-by-case approach shows that sometimes the current minimalist analysis is right (for *and*, § 3). But at other times, (for *most*, see § 4) a more informative meaning must be posited (incorporating into linguistic meaning elements considered pragmatic inferences), and sometimes (*or*, see § 5) the linguistic meaning not only reverses the consensual division of labor between semantics and pragmatics, it is in fact also more minimal.

3   Minimalists: Torn between Code versus Inference and Truth-Conditionality

In principle, a semantic code versus pragmatic inference division of labor is consensual. Nonetheless, (i) different linguists apply it with different rigor. Some researchers (e.g., Grice and Griceans) can't help but analyze at least a subset of pragmatic inferences as part of the semantic meaning (those responsible for at least some truth-conditional meanings). I advocate a strict code versus inference application. (ii) While researchers generally agree on the overall 'con-

---

of the foreign language, but not the pragmatic inferences nor the pragmatic interpretations involved in natural uses of the foreign language.

5   The minimalist approach assumes as minimal as possible lexical core meanings, leaving to pragmatic inferences any interpretative aspects that can be contextually derived by reference to a set of pragmatic principles.

veyed meaning,' they do sometimes differ with respect to the product of the semantics/pragmatics interface, namely the contextually appropriate reading.

Since the claim was that we don't even always have pre-theoretical intuitions regarding interpretations being clearly coded or clearly inferred, the Gricean turn offered a theoretical principle for relegating some interpretation to code or to inference. This principle hinges on theoretical economy. Occam's Razor principle stipulates that given an association between some linguistic form and some interpretation which can be accounted for either as a code (e.g., a lexical meaning) or as a rational inference (as some implicature) based on a minimal code enriched by plausible contextual assumptions, the latter, pragmatic account is to be preferred.

Consider the following:

(11) ALINA: !Cathy and !Jawahar don't understand how to mix their friends at all.
⟨⟨MIC … They don't understand,
that it's also okay,
.. not to have .. (H) **everybody** MIC⟩⟩ at the same party (SBC: 006).

Clearly, Alina does not intend to refer to 'every person in the universe.' *Everybody* must receive a narrower reading, probably referring to 'all of Cathy and Jawahar's friends.' In principle, one could propose that *everybody* is ambiguous between a strong 'absolutely all' meaning and a weaker, context-relevant subset meaning. But in this case, Occam's Razor dictates that if we can derive one of the meanings from the other via pragmatic inference then the derivable meaning should be analyzed as a pragmatic meaning. In this case, of course, it's more reasonable to select the absolute meaning as the lexical one. It's quite plausible to view Alina as exaggerating the facts, conveying the message that the friends invited to Cathy and Jawahar's parties is tantamount to 'inviting everyone in the world.' If so, the addressee must narrow the absolute meaning, taking it as a mere starting point for constructing the speaker-intended set of invitees.

The *everybody* case in (11), just like the comparison cases in (7) are relatively straightforward cases, since it's relatively easy to tease apart the lexical meaning and the derived meaning. But these are cases where some linguists have been tempted to incorporate what are clearly pragmatic inferences into the semantic 'what is said' representation. The real motivation behind this step is no doubt the relevance to the truth conditions here (there's a clear difference between 'everybody' and 'all of Cathy and Jawahar's friends'): Griceans very much wanted to equate between the linguistic and the truth-conditional.

The justification for the move was that while definitely pragmatic in nature, these inferences are *grammatically* triggered. In fact, they are mandated by the grammar, it was claimed. Lack of space prevents me from arguing against this position. The reader is referred to Carston (2002) and Ariel (2008; 2010) for why this Gricean position is untenable.[6]

The Gricean proposal went further than potentially ambiguous cases such as *everyone*, interpreted differently in different contexts. Grice proposed to divide up aspects of interpretations which seem to constitute wholes, in other words, ones where we cannot necessarily find contexts where one meaning was intended as opposed to others where another meaning was intended. Consider:

(12)   KEN: (H) So I eat the local food,
                    and get deathly ill (SBC: 015).

Ken's conveyed meaning here is something like 'I eat the local food **and therefore** I get deathly ill.' Grice proposed to divide up the interpretation of *and* into two components: One component is responsible for Ken's commitment to the truth of both 'I eat the local food' and to 'I get deathly ill.' The other component is responsible for the causal interpretation between the two events. The first is lexical, the second is only pragmatic. According to Grice, then, the semantics contributed by *and* is that the two conjoined propositions are true. Whether and how the two propositions are relevant to each other is a pragmatic matter, left to implicatures. Unlike the *everyone* case, the two meanings here co-exist.

The meanings of scalar expressions such as *nine, warm, some* and *most* too, were split into a minimal semantic component versus an implicated enrichment. For example:

(13) a. FRED: he said they got **two** ladies for **nine** counties, (SBC: 014)
      b. LENORE: I know the Caribbean is incredible.
         JOANNE: (H) beau- --
                     .. beautiful @blue --
                     @@@@,
                     blue water,
                     and and,
                     (H) **warm** water, (SBC: 015)

---

6   The reason why semantics cannot be equated with truth-conditionality is that inferences (pragmatics) may very well contribute truth-conditional aspects and conventional (linguistic) expressions may carry meanings which do not affect the truth-conditional content of the

Although it's quite counter-intuitive to identify two separate components within the meaning of these expressions (*nine* seems to mean 'exactly 9' etc.), the proposal was that *nine*'s lexical meaning is 'at least 9,' and hence, it's possible that the actual number is more than 9 (say '10'), and *warm* means 'at least warm' which is why it's possible that it's actually 'hot.' In other words, the lexical meaning only specifies one component of the relevant meanings here, the absolute minimum, the lower bound of the relevant interpretation. The reason for this move was that linguists wanted to make sure that the above propositions would count as true should the actual number be higher than nine etc.

Still, we clearly don't interpret *nine* as 'at least 9,' but rather, as 'exactly 9,' and the same is true for *warm*. The solution was that the upper-bounds ('no more than 9,' 'no more than warm') would be contributed by pragmatic implicatures (Generalized conversational implicatures, in this case). These would be derived by the addressee because he would reason that had the speaker meant, say '10' or 'hot' they would have said so. Since the speakers chose not to use the more informative expressions, the addressee can infer that they had no intention to convey the stronger meanings. We then have a formula for combining the linguistic code with the relevant pragmatic inference in an additive manner in order to derive the total reading:

TABLE 8.2   Deriving the conveyed meaning of *nine* and *warm*

Expression	Lexical meaning	Scalar implicature	Intended reading
Nine	'at least 9'	'no more than 9'	'exactly 9'
Warm	'at least warm'	'no more than warm'	'exactly warm'

Finally, the interpretation of adversative *but* too was split between two components. Consider the following:

(14)   LYNNE: ... She's a tiny girl,
                  but,
                  boy I tell you,
                  she's got ar=ms the size of --
                  .. (H) they're hu=ge. (SBC: 001)

_____

proposition. Deictic expressions are a prime example of the former type of cases, and so-called conventional implicatures (e.g., *after all* above) exemplify the problem in the other direction.

Lynne uses *but* to indicate that the conclusion that follows from the subsequent proposition contradicts the conclusion supported by the initial proposition. Specifically, 'she's a tiny girl' leads to the pragmatic conclusion that 'she is not strong.' But 'her arms are huge' supports the opposite conclusion, that she *is* strong. According to the Gricean proposal, *but* is composed of two separate elements: (i) 'and,' which guarantees a speaker commitment to both propositions, and (ii) 'contrast' (which, following Anscombre and Ducrot, 1977 I define as opposite argumentative directions). According to Griceans, the first component 'and' is *but*'s semantic meaning, whereas 'contrast' is its pragmatic meaning.

Of course, there is a difference between the pragmatic implicatures above and the one associated with *but*. No rational inferencing is here involved, and no reference to contextual assumptions is needed. Just like 'givenness' for *after all*, so is 'contrast' part and parcel of the speaker's linguistic knowledge of *but*. Still, this 'contrast' is irrelevant for the truth conditions of the proposition in (14). Should someone believe that there is no contradiction between being a tiny woman and having huge arms, they would nonetheless consider (14) true (provided each of the conjuncts is true). Thus, once again, for Griceans, when there's a conflict between the truth-conditionality criterion and another criterion, here conventional code, truth-conditionality wins out—see again the discussion around (11). Since 'contrast' is not truth-conditional, it is not semantic. And if it is not semantic it must be pragmatic. Still, since no rational inference is here involved, Grice opted for a hybrid term, "conventional implicature".

Grice did not opt for splitting the meaning of many expressions only to satisfy Occam's Razor principle. Economy can hardly motivate a routine enrichment process, which is more complex in that it requires a preliminary accessing of a lexical layer, which is then enriched by a Generalized conversational implicature. The motivation behind this step is that truth-bearing elements can be associated with precise logical symbols, which specify precise truth conditions. $\wedge$, for example, the linguistic meaning of 'and' and 'but' specifies that the relevant propositions are true provided each of the conjuncts is true, and false otherwise (i.e., should just one proposition be true and the other false, for example). Such a logical representation is not available for the various coherence inferences associated with *and* (see 1 and § 3) or with the 'contrast' involved in *but*.

The separation between truth-conditional meanings and non truth-conditional (pragmatic) meanings was deemed necessary in order to explain what linguists took to be intuitive truth judgments that e.g., a proposition about *nine* is true even if the state of affairs is such that 'ten' etc. These truth judgments, which were consensually agreed on by linguists and philosophers were said to reveal the pragmatic nature of e.g., the upper bound on numerals. As befits a pragmatic inference, this upper bound can be cancelled if deemed incompatible with the relevant state of affairs. Of course, the semantic lower bound cannot be cancelled, which means that there is a solid difference between the lower and the upper bounds, which justifies the analysis of the former as semantic and the latter as pragmatic.

Sections 3–5 compare these minimalists' proposals for the semantics/pragmatics interface with my Usage-Based analysis of the interfaces. The approaches differ with respect to scalars (§4) and *or* (§5), but converge on the analysis of the semantics/pragmatics division of labor for *and* (§3).

4   *And*: A Convergence between the Minimalist and the Usage-Based Analyses of the Semantic/Pragmatic Interface

While I will later argue that the minimalist analysis is not right for many expressions, this does not mean that there are no expressions where a dual layer analysis is appropriate. This is the case for *and*. As already mentioned, Grice reduces *and* to the logical operator ∧, which provides its truth-conditional meaning, namely, that the speaker commits to the truth of both conjuncts. As befits such a logical operator, the order of the propositions does not make a difference (a is the original example):

(15) a. Lunch is ready,
          and Peres is the president. (June 13, 2007).
     b. ~Peres is the president, **and** lunch is ready.

However, natural language conjoined sentences are not always reversible:

(16) a. ALINA: we were gonna s- --
                       take it out **and** send it back to the factory, (SBC: 006).
     b.   ~??We were gonna send it back to the factory **and** take it
                       out.

In (16a) Alina talks about a plan to take out the radio from their car in order to send it back to the factory (since it was broken). Clearly, Alina meant that taking out the radio was to precede sending it back to the factory, which is why the (b) version is odd.

Indeed, speakers sometimes intend their addressees to interpret conjoined sentences as temporally ordered. One could then analyze *and* as ambiguous between the logical ^ and 'and then.' A quick look at natural discourse, however, reveals that polysemy is not the right analysis here. Consider the following examples:

(17) a. REBECCA: he sits through all the testimony,
                        and he just sort of shakes his head, (SBC: 008)

   b. KEN: (H) So I eat the local food,
                        and get deathly ill. (SBC: 015).

   c.   You say either (eether) **and** I say either (eye-ther) (Fred Astaire,
                        Let's call the whole thing off).

   d.   Messy, **and** proud of it (spotted 2.28.2006).

   e. MONTOYO: American democracy is dying,
                        ... **and** I want you to try to think .. of why. (SBC 012)

There is a temporal relation between the events depicted in the two conjoined propositions in (17a). But it's a different temporal relation from the one in (15). The first event spans over a continuous period, during which the second one takes place at specific intervals. There is no earlier and later events, nor is there a full overlap between the two (which may very well be the case in other examples). (b) manifests a causal connection. In (c) the speaker juxtaposes two contrasting facts. (d) (on a baby's bib) introduces two facts which are expected to be incompatible with each other, the speaker's point being that despite common assumptions, the two states of affairs *are* compatible with each other. In (e) the first clause introduces a background assumption which the addressees need to take into account while trying to comply with the speaker's request in the second clause.

(18) shows a parallelism between the conjoined propositions, each of which supports the very same conclusion (that the addressee is sick):

(18)   KEN: your blood's all shot,
                 and you have the liver of a ninety-year-old (SBC: 015)

The same is true for (19):

(19) My client entered (Israel) legally **and** he was born here and you know that it's his right to be here (Originally Hebrew, *Haaretz*, Jun. 18, 2010).

Interestingly, (19) manifests a clear temporal relation: The client must have been born in Israel before he entered Israel (again). Still, the reversed order chosen by the lawyer does not cause the oddity we witnessed in (15b). This is so because unlike the narrative told by Alina, where one event follows another, this is an argumentative piece of discourse, where the lawyer is listing separate arguments supporting a single conclusion, namely, the client has a legal right live in Israel.

Thus, we have seen *and* conjoin two propositions which manifest a variety of coherence relations: 'and then,' 'contemporaneously but at intervals,' 'causal,' 'contrast,' 'concessive compatibility,' 'background/foreground,' and 'parallel arguments.' All of these, I should note, by no means exhaust the potential for coherence relations between conjoined clauses. There is no sense in compiling a "complete" list of such potential relations and stipulating it as a list of ambiguous meanings of *and*, because the list is infinite. In fact, even if it were finite, a very long list is not cognitively reasonable, for it's just as easy to ad hocly derive the relation as a relevant inference as it is to go through a very long list and pick the reading appropriate for the specific context.

In sum, the Usage-Based analysis supports the minimalist analysis for *and* since the number of inferences potentially triggered by *and* is not only vast, it is sometimes also innovative.[7]

5   Scalar Expressions: A Usage-Based Analysis of the Semantic/ Pragmatic Interface

I now wish to argue that the minimalist analysis does not always provide the best semantics/pragmatics interface analysis, however. This is so for *or* (see §5) and for scalar expressions, the topic of this section. First, Occam's Razor is aimed at economy, but in fact, corpus counts show that the overwhelming majority of scalar quantifiers are not only lower-bounded but also upper-bounded (e.g., Ariel, 2004). Hence, the split between the lower and the upper bounds imposes an additional processing step for the overwhelming majority of cases; in fact, for all of them.

More importantly, splitting the interpretation of numerals, scalar adjectives, as well as quantifiers, misses the intuitive representation speakers have for

---

7   Note, however, that agreeing on the nature of the lexical meaning of *and* does not necessarily mean that we have to accept the conversational implicature status assigned to the *and*-triggered coherence relations, as analyzed by Grice. In Ariel (2012) I argued that while some such inferences are indeed Particularized conversational implicatures, some are explicated inferences (following Carston, 2002: Chapter 3), and yet others are mere Truth-Compatible inferences (see §4).

these expressions, where *nine* and *warm* and *some* do not actually combine two separate meaning components. According to Recanati's (1989) 'Availability principle,' these two meaning components are not available to speakers as separate components. Speakers represent the interpretation of these expressions as wholes.[8]

Last, contra assumptions made by Griceans, it's not true that the upper-bound is irrelevant to truth conditions (recall that conversational implicatures are not supposed to determine truth conditions). The empirical turn in linguistics brought forth experimental results which showed that quite a few experimental participants do judge scalar expressions (e.g., *some, most*) false with respect to a state of affairs in which 'all' is the case. In other words, many participants determined the truth value of propositions containing scalar expressions not only by reference to the truth of the lower bound, but also by reference to the truth of the upper bound. Such findings have weakened the motivation for the Gricean analysis, which just took it for granted that as a conversational implicature, the upper-bound interpretation doesn't participate in the truth-conditional content of the proposition, since it can be cancelled. Had this been true, it would have indeed been appropriate to separate it from the meaning component that does determine the truth conditions, namely, the lower bound.

Usage-Based linguists set out from the assumption that since language is shaped by the use speakers make of it the basis for theoretical proposals about language must be based on actual language use. Based on corpus research, mostly the Santa Barbara Corpus of Spoken American English (Du Bois et al., 2000–2005), I have proposed that scalar expressions can be analyzed as expressing a single circumbounded meaning (including both a lower and an upper bound) (Ariel, 2008: Chapter 3). This of course straightforwardly accounts for the natural interpretation of default uses of e.g., *most*, as in the following:

(20) **MOST** UCSB students have 0 ... 1 ... 2 ... 3 or 4 drinks per week (4000 don't drink at all) (An anti-drinking ad at UCSB, February 2002).

---

8 Recanati's argument is that the upper-bound components cannot be conversational implicatures, since speakers are aware of these as separate interpretations. They are therefore what I have called "explicated inferences," i.e., inferences that combine with lexical meanings into a single interpretation. I have taken a further step, arguing that the upper bound is actually part of the lexical meaning (Ariel, 2004; 2015).

The addressor in (20) is taken to assert that a majority (51–99%) of UCSB students drink up to 4 drinks a week. On my circumbounded analysis, there is no need to rely on an upper-bounding implicature here.[9]

But then, assuming a circumbounded lexical meaning predicts a false judgment in face of a state of affairs in which the upper bound does not apply. Still, some participants do judge such assertions under such circumstances as true. In order to explain such judgments I have proposed an additional type of inference, Truth-Compatible inferences. Truth-Compatible inferences (i) do *not* fall under the speaker's communicative intention (unlike conversational implicatures, which *are* speaker-intended, even if indirectly so). But they are nonetheless (ii) potentially compatible with her intended message.

(21) exemplifies a Truth-Compatible inference which is unrelated to scalar expressions, since I have argued that this concept is relevant to interaction in general:

(21)   REBECCA: .. do you guys have the cash to pay for it right now? (SBC: 008)

Rebecca is a prosecutor who summoned a witness in order to prepare her for testifying in court. The witness (and her partner) had to drive her quite a distance to attend the meeting, and Rebecca is asking them if they have the cash to pay for parking. Of course, parking will cost a rather small amount of money, so a potential inference the addressees may derive is that 'according to Rebecca, the addressees are too poor to be able to afford to pay the parking fee (for which they will be reimbursed later).' First, Rebecca clearly has no intention that the addressees draw this (potentially insulting) inference, even though she may very well subscribe to its validity. Note that she did not phrase her question as in (11), where I substituted *cash* for *money* and I deleted *right now*:

(22) Do you guys have the **money** to pay for it?

The reason for Rebecca's choice of (21) over (22) is precisely because she presumes to ask her addressees about the cash they have right now, and not about their general financial situation, money they have in the bank, for example. After all, even well-to do people may find themselves short of cash. Nonethe-

---

9   Of course, interlocutors in addition (pragmatically) narrow down the range of such vague quantities. See Ariel (2004) for preferred values for *most*.

less, a sensitive addressee might infer the Truth-Compatible inference that Rebecca thinks that 'the addressees are too poor to afford the parking fee.' In other words, this inference is compatible with what Rebecca said, although it's definitely not a speaker-intended inference (an implicature).

Now, Truth-Compatible inferences can easily explain the truth judgments associated with scalar *warm* and *nine* (as well as *some* and *most*). According to my analysis *nine* in (23) means 'exactly 9':

(23) They got two ladies for **nine** counties (SBC: 014)

To explain the variable truth judgments of participants judging *nine*'s truth in view of a '10' state of affairs I propose that some participants would, but other would not, adopt the Truth-Compatible inference in (24):

(24) 'Ten counties' is compatible with 'nine counties,' since 'nine counties' are included in 'ten counties.'

Some participants might reason as follows:

(25) a. The speaker committed to nine counties exactly.
      b. Even though the actual state of affairs points to 'ten counties,' the difference between nine and ten counties is not significant *in this context*.
      c. Hence, I will take into account the Truth-Compatible inference in (23) and confirm (24) as true.

Other participants might reason as follows:

(26) a. The speaker committed to nine counties exactly.
      b. The actual state of affairs points to 'ten counties,' and the difference between
          nine and ten counties is significant *in this context*.
      c. Hence, I will not take into account the Truth-Compatible inference in (23) and I
          will not confirm (24) as true.

Note that such a theory can naturally account for why a state of affairs in which '40 counties' are actually involved might change the ratio of truth versus false judgers of (23). Although '40' is just as compatible with 'nine' as 'ten' is, the chances for participants to consider the difference between '9' and '40' as insignificant are quite smaller.

In other words, it turns out that a truth judgment considered sharp and semantic (*nine* is absolutely true when 'more than nine' is the case), is neither sharp nor semantic. It varies between participants and it varies depending on how relevant the gap is between the speaker-intended meaning and the actual state of affairs (where the value is higher).

If that's the case, we should actually reverse the semantics/pragmatics division of labor for scalar terms, such as *nine*, as in Table 8.3:[10]

TABLE 8.3   A comparison between the Gricean and the usage-based analysis of *nine*

	Semantic meaning = truth-conditional	Pragmatic inference	Common reading
Griceans	'at least 9'	GCI: 'no more than 9'	'exactly 9'
Usage-Based	'exactly 9'	TCI: 'A value higher than 9 is compatible with 9'	'exactly 9'

I should emphasize that the TCI applies only when the truth-judger faces a state of affairs which diverges from the speaker-intended meaning ('exactly 9'), and even then, only optionally so. Also, on my analysis, a participant who judges *nine* as true when the state of affairs is say '10' does not "retroactively" adjust the speaker-intended meaning of *nine* to 'at least nine.' The meaning remains put. It's just that this particular participant happens to find '10' to be compatible with '9' in the relevant context. In other words, whereas on the Gricean account the GCI is added onto the lexical meaning to create the speaker-intended reading, on my account the TCI is *not* added on. It only serves to mediate between a speaker-intended '9' and a state of affairs of '10.' Finally, note that on the Gricean analysis it is the common interpretation (an upper-bounded 9) that is derived by combining two meaning components (the lower and the upper bounds). On my account the common interpretation directly corresponds to the lexical meaning, and it is rather rare circumstances that prompt the derivation of the TCI after the fact.

The assumption of TCIs makes a much more intuitive semantics/pragmatics interface analysis possible, one which doesn't split up a unified meaning into two components. It also defines the common meaning as the semantic meaning (cognitive economy), and it provides for an explanation why judging the

---

10   GCI stands for Generalized conversational implicature, and TCI stands for "Truth-Compatible inference."

truth of scalar expressions is unstable (for different participants, for different contexts) when the relevant state of affairs shows a higher value.

In sum, the minimalistic approach (in all its varieties) offers a reduction of certain linguistic expressions, such as numbers and scalar quantifiers, to their counterpart logical operators, which offers a precise formulation of their assumed semantics, but forces a pragmatic derivation of the actual reading at least in the majority of cases. The Usage-Based approach proposes that the semantic/lexical meaning of scalar expressions receives both a lower and an upper bound. Judging such expressions true when the state of affairs shows a higher value does not change the speaker-intended meaning, although the TCI allows for a 'true' judgment.

6   *Or*: A Usage-Based Analysis of the Semantics/Pragmatics Interface

I have so far argued that a Usage-Based approach converges with the minimalist theory on the semantics/pragmatics division of labor with respect to *and*, but not with respect to scalar expressions. I have not disputed the readings associated with *and* nor with scalar expressions, however. This section on *or* argues both against the semantics/pragmatics division of labor and against the contextual readings associated with *or*.

Two main interpretations of *or* are commonly discussed in the literature. In the inclusive reading the speaker commits to the truth of at least one of the options, and possibly to both. (27) fits such an interpretation:

(27)   GILBERT: *She got sick and tired of,*
... you know,
turning on the news,
and seeing another ... corrupt man,
or another,
..you know.
..another scandal breaking out. (SBC: 012)

It's definitely possible that the woman discussed by Gilbert got sick and tired of seeing both another corrupt man and another scandal. This interpretation exemplifies the linguistic meaning of *or* according to minimalists, i.e., when no inference modifies it.

The second reading is exclusive, where the speaker commits to one and only one of the specified alternatives. The following is supposed to exemplify this reading, since 'king' and 'queen' are mutually exclusive:

(28)   NORA: *Wonder who was the ruler.*
                in nineteen ten.
        DIANE: *Who was the king or queen?*
        NORA: *Mhm.*
        LORI: *I don't know.* (SBC: 023)

Such interpretations are usually analyzed as derived from the linguistic inclusive meaning. According to Griceans, we start out with the inclusive semantic meaning of 'king or queen or both.' We then combine this meaning with a GCI that 'not both king and queen,' to derive the reading of 'either king or queen, but not both.' We return to these examples below, but first, let's examine two examples which cast doubt on the Gricean approach:

(29)   S: *At a certain stage part of the shares were transferred to the children before*
           going out on the stock exchange or they were returned and divided up or
           partly returned I don't remember ... you have our prospectus here (*Originally Hebrew, Lotan, 1990*).

The interesting point about (29) is that the speaker does not actually commit to even one of the specified alternatives he raises. This is why (29) can be paraphrased by (30), which indeed doesn't commit the speaker to any of the alternatives:

(30)   ... It's possible that they were returned and divided up, it's possible that they *were partly returned I don't remember.*

The reason why (30) is an appropriate paraphrase of (29) is that the relevant reading here is neither exclusive nor inclusive, but rather, what Ariel and Mauri (2018) called 'Raised options.' In such cases, the speaker raises alternative hypotheses without committing to any one of them being true. When S says he doesn't remember he doesn't mean that he doesn't remember which of the alternatives he mentioned is correct, but rather that he doesn't remember what happened. Indeed, he asks the addressees to check the facts according to the prospectus they have.

Examples such as (29) are not very common in SBC (only 8.9%), but the reading triggered by examples such as (31) is very frequent:

(31)   ROY: *saving the whale,*
                or saving uh ... the .. polar bea[r,
        PETE: [*Right ... **Pandas**],*
        ROY: *or making sure there's enough] grizzly bears,*
                that's fine. (SBC: 003)

Seemingly, Roy's *ors* could be read as inclusive *ors*, which then means that at least one and possibly all the listed animals are included in his assertion. Pete's response, however, testifies that this is not quite Roy's intention. Note that Pete first confirms Roy's first contribution, but then, he goes on to offer an altogether different animal ('Pandas'). The reason why it's legitimate (and cooperative) of Pete to assume that Roy actually intends to include Pandas as well is that the relevant reading here is Higher-level category (see Ariel and Mauri, 2018). Using a Higher-level category *or* construction the speaker introduces alternatives which in fact constitute exemplars of some higher-level category, and it is that category that the speaker refers to. Thus, whale, polar bear and Grizzly bear are all members of a category of 'Endangered animals.' No wonder, then, that Pete can agree with Roy and add a different animal which is also endangered (Pandas). SBC revealed that Higher-level category *or* constructions are the most frequent *or* constructions (23.2%).

Having introduced the Higher-level category reading, let us now go back to examples (27) and (28). I used the first one in a questionnaire I administered to participants, who were asked to choose between two responses to A (B_1 or B_2):

(32) A: She got sick and tired of turning on the news, and seeing a corrupt man, or a scandal breaking out.
        B_1: I can understand her. It's depressing to watch the news these days.
        B_2: I can understand her. Both of those things are awful.

B_2 is the predicted response if the intended reading is inclusive (at least one of the alternatives and possibly both). 11% of the participants chose it. But all the others preferred the B_1 response, because the specific alternatives explicitly mentioned are not actually crucial. They merely serve to exemplify the single, higher-level category of 'political scandals' which the speaker intends to express. In fact, the same is true for (28), where the speaker wishes to refer to 'the monarch.' The speaker is not interested in the gender of the monarch. She uses *king or queen* to avoid using the rather marked lexeme *monarch*. Indeed, 'king' and 'queen' each exemplify the higher-level category of 'monarch.' If so, the seemingly inclusive example (27) turned out to actually exemplify a Higher-level category *or* construction, as did the seemingly exclusive example (28).

Are there then any examples which manifest the assumed 'exclusive' and 'inclusive' readings? There certainly are examples which would be classified as 'exclusive,' such as (33):

(33)   ALINA: Right next door is !Ted !Rich,
                      who's uh=,
                      .. (H) one of the biggies at MTM,
                      .. (TSK) **or**,
                      Lorimar **or** MGM, (SBC: 006)

Ariel and Mauri (2018) have dubbed such examples as 'Narrowed' cases. A speaker uses a 'Narrowed' *or* construction when she is not in a position to commit to a single option. Instead, she narrows down the options to just a few. The reading we have offered for this construction is 'one of the alternatives' (one of MTM, Lorimar, and MGM). Now, we chose not to call this use 'exclusive,' because the exclusive reading includes a denial of the 'both alternatives' option. We find no justification for such a denial, which is *not* speaker-intended. According to our analysis, the 'both options' does not arise, and hence, need not be cancelled.

Before I address the question of *or*'s lexical meaning let's consider one other example:

(34)   KEN: And I guess goldfish **or** g=uppies,
                    get the brunt of everything.
                    .. (H) Poor guys. (SBC: 015)

Ken here is actually saying that:

35   I guess goldfish **and** guppies get the brunt of everything.

In other words, *or* functions here as a conjunction (as if it were an *and*), the speaker actually committing to *all* three alternatives.

Table 8.4 summarizes the examples considered above according to how many of the alternatives the speaker commits to:

TABLE 8.4   Speaker commitment to *or* alternatives

Obligatory	Ø	1	All
speaker	All options are raised as	One of the alternatives	All the alternatives
commitment	possibilities/ examples only	is necessarily true	are necessarily true
Example no.	16, 17, 18, 20	22	24

Assuming our analysis is correct, we can use *or* when the speaker commits to a single alternative, to all alternatives or to none of them. Two questions arise. (1) Can we derive all these readings from the assumed 'inclusive' lexical meaning? (2) Assuming we can, is this the optimal analysis? Table 8.5 presents the (in)compatibility between the inclusive meaning and the three types of readings, classified according to the number of alternatives committed to by the speaker:

TABLE 8.5   (In)compatibility with the inclusive meaning

Obligatory speaker commitment	1	All	Ø
	One of the alternatives is necessarily true	All the alternatives are necessarily true	All options are raised as possibilities/ examples only
Compatibility with inclusive meaning	**Compatible**	**Incompatible** (reading is stronger)	**Incompatible** (reading is weaker)

It looks like the Narrowed reading, according to which one alternative is true, can theoretically be derived from the inclusive meaning, since the inclusive meaning allows for this possibility (via a 'not both' scalar GCI). The conjunctive reading ('both alternatives') will have be derived by strengthening the inclusive meaning. It's not enough to avoid the derivation of the 'not both' implicature, because its absence only allows for the *possibility* of 'all alternatives.' This is weaker than the conjunctive reading which specifies that 'all' is *necessarily* true. The most problematic cases are the ones where there is no necessary commitment on the speaker's part to any one of the alternatives. Whereas for the conjunctive reading we need to add a speaker commitment to additional alternative(s), for the Raised options and for 'Higher-level category' readings we have to *cancel* a semantic meaning (since 'inclusivity' requires commitment to at least one alternative). Cancelling a semantic component, however, is not an interpretative step allowed by the Gricean theory, nor by any other theory, since that would entail that speakers can deny having said things that their message expressed semantically.

Ariel and Mauri's conclusion was that the linguistic meaning of *or* cannot be defined by reference to the number of speaker-committed alternatives. *Or*'s lexical meaning must be compatible with a speaker commitment to 0, 1, or all alternatives. We have argued that *or* only encodes an instruction to the addressee to construe the listed options as alternatives to one another. In other words, just like *after all, or* too doesn't specify truth conditions, but rather a processing procedure (see Ariel and Mauri, 2019 for a definition of 'alternativity').

The so-called exclusive reading, we suggest, actually corresponds to three distinct readings (see Ariel and Mauri, 2018 for details). The so-called inclusive reading, we claim, is not to be found, in fact. Not one example was such that the speaker committed to an at least one alternative and possibly all *as a speaker-intended message*. Still, what if Ted Rich (in example 33, here repeated) happens to work at two or even all three studios

(36)   ALINA: Right next door is !Ted !Rich,
                       who's uh=,
                       .. (H) one of the biggies at MTM,
                       .. (TSK) **or**,
                       Lorimar **or** MGM, (SBC: 006)

On our analysis, Alina intends 'one of MTM, Lorimar, and MGM.' But this does not mean that addressees (or experiment participants) will necessarily determine that Alina's proposition is false under such circumstances. Participants should vary in their judgments, some confirming her proposition as true. But once again, this does not mean that Alina is retroactively seen as having intended an 'inclusive' reading for these participants. Instead, on our account some participants view a state of affairs in which MTM, Lorimar and MGM is the case as compatible with a claim that 'one of MTM, Lorimar, and MGM' is the case. Such participants reason that this theoretical truth compatibility is acceptable in the specific context, namely, that the difference between 'one of ...' and 'all of' is not crucial. Of course, other participants may reason that this difference *is* context-relevant, and hence, refuse to take into account the TCI. They will then judge the proposition false. But our main point was that no matter what the truth judgement of participants is vis a vis an 'all' state of affairs, the reading remains the Narrowed 'one of.'

Summing up, § 5 argued against the consensus regarding *or*. I offered a radically different semantics/pragmatics division of labor here. According to minimalists *or*'s linguistic meaning is 'inclusive' and its actual readings are predominantly 'exclusive' or 'inclusive'. According to the Usage-Based approach, however, *or*'s linguistic meaning is only procedural, 'alternativity,' and it has a richer set of contextual readings. I here mentioned 'Raised options,' 'Higher-level category,' 'Conjunctive,' and Narrowed readings (but see Ariel and Mauri, 2018 for others).

7   Conclusions: A Usage-Based Semantics/Pragmatics Interface

Most Cognitive linguists have either ignored or downplayed the question of semantics/pragmatics interfaces. Such a stance seems justified in view of the fact that interlocutors' messages combine semantic with pragmatic interpretations, where the difference between them is often enough not discourse-relevant. But I have proposed that drawing the linguistic/extralinguistic dividing line is crucial for any theory that aspires to *explain* how humans produce and comprehend natural language utterances. Effective communication mobilizes two rather different cognitive competencies: (i) mastery of conventional form/function correlations (codes) and (ii) ability to go beyond these codes in a more creative manner, using our general rational reasoning abilities, which we equally use in noncommunicative acts. Moreover, there are cases where the semantics/pragmatics distinction is in fact discourse-relevant in that interlocutors do not assign semantic and pragmatic interpretations the same status (recall that only pragmatically derived interpretations are cancelable).

This is why there is universal consensus around the code versus inference division of labor. But the differences between the Gricean minimalists (see again note 5) and Usage-Based analyses of the semantics/pragmatic interface discussed above show that even when researchers agree about the importance of the code versus inference distinction as a basis for the linguistic/extralinguistic divide they do not necessarily agree on specific linguistic analyses for specific expressions. Mostly they do not agree on the allocation of meaning components to semantics versus pragmatics.

Now, most linguists impose additional criteria on the code versus inference distinction, primarily that semantic meanings must in addition be 'truth-conditional' and 'minimalistic' (based on Occam's Razor economy principle). The most important point about a Usage-Based semantics/pragmatics interface is that it has no apriori theoretical commitments about the semantics/pragmatics divide. It straightforwardly follows natural language *use* in applying the linguistic/extralinguistic distinction between codes and inferences. My proposals above are all based on thorough investigations of the relevant expressions in spoken corpora (most prominently SBC), and are often corroborated by questionnaire results (*some, most, or*). The analyses are bottom-up, and they led me to question (i) the semantic core, (ii) the pragmatic inferences, and sometimes even (iii) the overall reading (for *or*) commonly assumed for the expressions here analyzed.

A Usage-Based analysis does not make any assumptions about the "nature" of linguistic semantics, except that it is linguistic, namely, that it associates forms and functions in a conventional manner. Hence, semantic meanings may be conceptual (*most, nine*), but they may be merely procedural (*after all, but, or*). They may carry only a minimalistic meaning (*and*), but they need not be minimalistic (scalar expressions are circumbounded rather than only lower-bounded on my analysis).

For these Usage-Based analyses to work two crucial consensual assumptions had to be abandoned. First, the "inherent" connection between semantic codes and truth-conditionality. We must give up on the idea that semantic meanings are only dedicated to conceptual and truth-bearing elements. The second assumption we must let go of is that truth judgments necessarily reflect pure truth-conditional meaning. I have argued that truth judgments take into account not only the speaker-intended message, but also Truth-Compatible inferences. The latter may mediate between some meaning and some state of affairs which does not fully correspond to it. Once some gap is allowed between the speaker-intended message (e.g., 'a proper subset majority' for *most*, 'one of the alternatives' for *or*) and 'true' judgments in light of a divergent state of affairs ('all' for *most*, 'all alternatives' for *or*), a more intuitive, holistic analysis could be offered for e.g., *nine, some, most*, and *warm*.[11] It also made possible a single (procedural) meaning for *or* ('alternativity'), which is impossible when the number of committed alternatives is used to define *or*'s lexical meaning.

Acknowledgments

The research here reported was supported by an Israel Science Foundation grant (1398/20).

---

11   The analysis can also explain why different interlocutors might vary in their truth judgments.

References

Anscombre, Jean-Claude and Oswald Ducrot. 1977. Deux *mais* en Français. *Lingua* 43: 23–40.

Ariel, Mira. 2004. Most. *Language* 80: 658–706.

Ariel, Mira. 2008. *Pragmatics and Grammar*. Cambridge, UK: Cambridge University Press.

Ariel, Mira. 2010. *Defining Pragmatics*. Cambridge, UK: Cambridge University Press.

Ariel, Mira. 2012. Relational and independent *and* conjunctions. *Lingua* 122: 1682–1715.

Ariel, Mira. 2015. Doubling up: Two upper bounds for scalars. *Linguistics* 53: 561–610.

Ariel, Mira and Caterina Mauri. 2018. Why use *or*? *Linguistics* 56: 939–994.

Ariel, Mira and Caterina Mauri. 2019. An 'alternative' core for *or*. *Journal of Pragmatics* 149: 40–59.

Carston, Robyn. 2002. *Thoughts and Utterances: The Pragmatics of Explicit Communication*. Oxford: Blackwell.

Du Bois, John W., Wallace L. Chafe, Charles Meyer, Sandra A. Thompson, Robert Englebretson and Nii Martey. 2000–2005. Santa Barbara corpus of spoken American English, parts 1–4. Philadelphia: Linguistic Data Consortium.

Grice, H. Paul. 1989. *Studies in the Way of Words*. Cambridge, MA: Harvard University Press.

Lakoff, George. 1987. *Women, Fire, and Dangerous Things: What Categories Reveal about the Mind*. Chicago: University of Chicago Press.

Langacker, Ronald W. 2000. A dynamic usage-based model. In M. Barlow and S. Kemmer (eds.), *Usage-based models of language*, 1–63. Stanford: CSLI Publications.

Prince, Ellen F. 1988. Discourse analysis: A part of the study of linguistic competence. In F.J. Newmeyer and R.H. Robins (eds.), *Linguistics: The Cambridge survey*, volume II: *Linguistic theory: Extensions and implications*, 164–182. Cambridge, UK: Cambridge University Press.

Recanati, François. 1989. The pragmatics of what is said. *Mind and Language* 4: 295–328. (Reprinted in Davis (ed.), 97–120.).

Sperber, Dan and Deirdre Wilson. 1986/1995. *Relevance*. Oxford: Blackwell.

Talmy, Leonard. 2000. *Toward a Cognitive Semantics*, volumes I–II. Cambridge, MA: MIT Press.

CHAPTER 9

Encyclopedic Knowledge and Linguistic Meaning

Patrick Duffley

1   Introduction

"Questions about the exact nature of linguistic as opposed to non-linguistic knowledge have been asked for as long as humans have studied language, be it as linguists, philosophers, psychologists, language teachers, semioticians, cognitive scientists, whatever. The distinction has been maintained and defended by some, attacked and abandoned by others" (Peeters, 2000: 1). Thus, on the one hand, in the modular view of the mind characteristic of the generative grammar tradition, a strict distinction between linguistic and non-linguistic knowledge has been practiced. On the other hand, cognitive linguists have argued that natural language reflects general cognitive mechanisms rather than the autonomous structures of a specialized language faculty. In the spirit of this view of language, Ronald Langacker (1987: 154) has famously argued that "the distinction between semantics and pragmatics (or between linguistic and extralinguistic knowledge) is largely artifactual," and that "the only viable conception of linguistic semantics is one that avoids such false dichotomies and is consequently encyclopedic in nature." Langacker holds the distinction between dictionary and encyclopedic content to be not only impossible to make, but fundamentally misconceived as well, since linguistic expressions are not meaningful in and of themselves but only through the access they provide to stores of world-knowledge that allow us to make sense of them.[1]

At the basis of this view is the fact that a given linguistic expression allows an indefinite number of specific interpretations depending on the situation to which it is applied: Langacker gives as an example the sequence *The cat is on the mat*, which stereotypically describes a situation where a mat is spread out on the floor and a cat is lying on it. Even with such a simple utterance, he argues, there is a potential for almost infinite variability, as the cat can be of any size, color or species, the mat can be of any size or color, the cat can be in an indefinite number of different positions on the mat, etc. It is also possible that the

---

1   The origins of this position go back to Haiman (1980: 331), who argued that "the distinction between dictionaries and encyclopedias is not only one that is practically impossible to make, but one that is fundamentally misconceived."

mat is rolled up in a bundle and the cat is lying on top of it. The sequence could be used as well in a mat-maker's workshop when a weaver has just finished decorating a mat with a cat motif. One could even imagine a human wrestler engaged in an exhibition match with a defanged tiger who has just succeeded in pinning the tiger's shoulders to the floor of the ring. The possibilities are endless. According to Langacker, this shows that the meaning of a complex expression cannot be determined out of context as a regular compositional function of the meanings of its component lexical items but must take into account knowledge of the real world.

From the encyclopedic nature of contextual meaning, Langacker deduces the encyclopedic nature of linguistic meaning, which he sees as contextual meaning that has been generalized and established as conventional through repeated use. In reply to the objection that this would entail that the meaning of a word like *banana* would have to include everything that the speaker knows about bananas, he invokes the criterion of centrality: not all facets of our knowledge of an entity have equal status; some are so central that they cannot be omitted (e.g. the fact that bananas are yellow when ripe), whereas others are peripheral and irrelevant to linguistic usage (e.g. the fact that my pet dog used to like bananas). However there is no specific point along the graded scale of centrality that can be non-arbitrarily chosen to demarcate linguistic meaning from extralinguistic (i.e. encyclopedic) knowledge.

This chapter aims to discuss various issues pertaining to the view that there is no distinction between linguistic and extralinguistic knowledge and that the only viable conception of linguistic semantics is necessarily encyclopedic in nature, which implies that there is no boundary that can be drawn between a word's meaning, on the one hand, and knowledge that we might have about its referent, on the other. It will also address the question as to whether the encyclopedic view of linguistic meaning applies to all words in the lexicon or only to some.

2   Is There Such a Thing as Non-encyclopedic Meaning?

As a starting-point for the discussion, it is worth noting that Langacker himself seems to recognize the existence of a kind of meaning whose encyclopedic status is problematic. He terms this type of meaning 'schematic' and describes it in the following way:

> By schematization, I mean the process of extracting the commonality inherent in multiple experiences to arrive at a conception representing a

higher level of abstraction. Schematization plays a role in the acquisition of lexical units, if only because their conventional forms and meanings are less specific than the usage events (i.e. the actual pronunciations and contextual understandings) on the basis of which they are learned. For example, the basic sense of *ring*—roughly 'circular piece of jewelry worn on the finger'—is schematic relative to the conception of specific rings in specific contexts, which vary in such details as size, material, identity of the wearer, and so on. Schematization can be carried to different degrees, depending on the diversity of the elements it is based on. Since *ring* is also used for adornments worn in other places than on the finger, we can posit for it the more schematic value 'circular adornment worn on the body,' with respect to which 'circular piece of jewelry worn on the finger' constitutes an elaboration or specific instantiation. Still more abstractly, *ring* can mean 'circular object' (consider the rings in gymnastics) or even just 'circular entity' (e.g. the ring of dirt left around a bathtub).

LANGACKER, 2008: 17

The cognitive process invoked by Langacker in this passage involves moving away from the concrete material world of our sense experience into the abstract realm of ideas. In the case of *ring*, this process can take us even further from material reality than the notion of 'circular entity' identified in the passage above, as illustrated by a use of this noun such as (1) below:

(1)   A ring of suspicion is tightening around Michele's father, stepfather, and her football hero brother, and Lillie's quest for justice will reveal the deadly lies hidden behind the closed doors of her town, and her past.

https://www.simonandschuster.com/books/No-Way-Home/Patricia-MacDonald/9781451607482[2]

This sense retains only the idea of being surrounded on all sides by something, and that something is not necessarily circular. One can go even further in the direction of abstractness in uses of *ring* such as *a ring of criminals*, where there is only the idea of being closely linked together to form a group with a continuous outer boundary that admits no outsiders inside it. A further step towards abstractness in the domain of circular sorts of things can be observed with the adjective *round* in the phrase *a round number*. What real-world roundness is involved in a use such as this? Moreover, some linguistic units seem to have a

---

2   Retrieved on March 6, 2023.

meaning which is completely abstract or schematic, one clear example being the determiner *any*, whose uses manifest no real-world reference or gradations in concreteness whatsoever. Langacker (2005: 188) describes the meaning of this word as a mental process of random selection of a referent from a reference mass, a characterization that makes it seem impossible to argue that there is any encyclopedic meaning at all associated with this lexical unit. According to Langacker's own descriptions, therefore, at least some linguistic items seem to have purely non-encyclopedic meaning.

3   The Relation between Encyclopedic and Non-encyclopedic Meaning in Langacker's Framework

In other cases, Langacker applies both the encyclopedic and non-encyclopedic meaning models to the very same linguistic item, arguing that it vehicles both an abstract schema and an encyclopedic prototypical content (2013: 17 ff.). (He sees the difference between a schema and a prototype as that between a categorization in which the target satisfies all of the specifications of the category standard, and one in which only some of the standard's specifications are satisfied.) Thus the grammatical category NOUN has as its schematic meaning (THING), which is defined as "a region in some domain" (1987: 189), a categorization satisfied by all nouns; its prototypical meaning, on the other hand, is "physical object," which is only true of the central members of the category (2013: 34). This might seem contradictory however: if each of the members of the schematic category of NOUN instantiates all of the specifications of the category standard, they do not instantiate only part of them; consequently, there should be no distinctions in centrality among members of a schematic category. Langacker opts however for a maximalist view of meaning that can involve both schematicity and prototypicality at the same time for the same item.

This is the case, for example, of the noun TREE whose meaning is illustrated by the lexical network below (Langacker, 1987: 383):

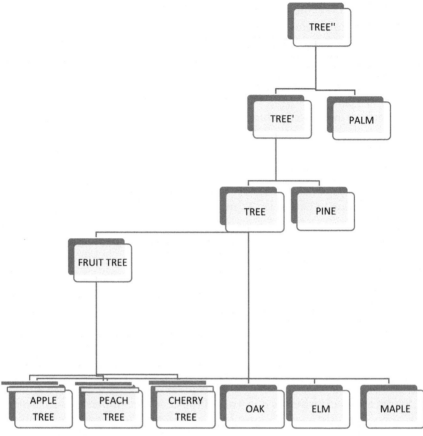

FIGURE 9.1   The lexical network for the noun *tree*
COURTESY OF RONALD LANGACKER

The lowest subschema, [TREE] in the second level from the bottom is argued to
correspond to trees with branches and leaves, the next highest schema, [TREE']
to trees with branches and foliage consisting of either leaves or needles, and the
top superschema [TREE"] to trees with or without branches and with foliage
that can be in the form of fronds, leaves, or needles. Langacker argues that
different nodes in the schematic network are activated in the five uses listed
below:

(2)   a.   Look at that tree!
      b.   There are trees along the river.
      c.   How many trees are there in this orchard?
      d.   The trees in the forest are mostly oaks and pines.
      e.   A palm is a tree.

He maintains that a speaker who utters (2a) mentally activates a node from among the second-level nodes, which could be [APPLE TREE], [PEACH TREE], [CHERRY TREE], [OAK], [ELM], [MAPLE], [PINE] or [PALM]. The utterance of (2b) with respect to elms, maples, and peach trees would activate the schema [TREE] corresponding to trees with branches and leaves, which Langacker describes as the "prototype" schema. In the case of (2c)–(2e), the respective schemas would be [FRUIT TREE], [TREE'] and [TREE"]. One might wonder however what evidence can be produced to authenticate the conceptual reality of such a complex network of schemas and subschemas for the word *tree*. All we can say for sure is that the speaker utters the sign /*tree*/ in all of the cases listed in (2) above. This indicates that they see all of the referents in question as trees, i.e. as having something in common. The differences between them, real as they may be botanically, do not seem to be significant linguistically.

4   The Relation between Encyclopedic and Non-encyclopedic
       Meaning in Evans' Lexical Concepts and Cognitive Models Theory

Another cognitive linguist who implements the hypothesis that linguistic expressions are not meaningful in and of themselves but only through the access they provide to stores of encyclopedic knowledge is Evans (2009). Unlike Langacker, however, his Lexical Concepts and Cognitive Models Theory posits a strict distinction between the "linguistic system" (home of the Lexical Concept) and the "conceptual system" of non-linguistic knowledge to which words provide access (home of the Cognitive Model). According to Evans, the conceptual system is analogue with bodily experience, i.e. it consists of stored perceptual and subjective states, including information derived from sensory-motor perception, proprioception, introspective states such as emotions, the visceral sense, and cognitive states. This experience-analogue system is designed to be accessed through the linguistic system, which is made up of much more abstract Lexical Concepts. Lexical Concepts have the following characteristics: (1) they are highly schematic and organized in terms of binary, ternary, or closed-set oppositions (i.e. they are "parameterized"); (2) they do not give rise to simulations or imaginary re-enactments of perceptual and subjective states (they are "non-analogue"); (3) they are used to point to entities in the denotational, cognitive or contextual domains (they are referential); and (4) they are associated with knowledge of which other lexical concepts regularly co-occur with them (they have a collocational profile).

Evans' attempt to separate out the "linguistic" from the "conceptual" is plagued however by pervasive confusion surrounding the meanings of the terms "conceptual" and "concept." Conceptual Structure is claimed to be populated by "Cognitive Models," and is opposed to linguistic structure, which is described as being populated by "Lexical Concepts." The use of the term "conceptual" with reference to cognitive models and of "concept" with reference to linguistic structure would seem to indicate however that both are conceptual in nature. Evans states nevertheless (p. 105) that "while conceptual structure has to do with conceptual (i.e. non-linguistic) content (...), semantic structure has to do with linguistic content," which implies that in his model linguistic content is not conceptual. This is confirmed in the next paragraph, where conceptual content is equated with records of bodily experience: "conceptual content provides records of perceptual states ... (it) encodes information that parallels the multimodal body-based (perceptual, motoric, subjective, etc.) experience that it constitutes a representation of." A footnote specifies that "conceptual content is not an exact record of the multimodal states that are captured; rather, it is somewhat attenuated." This way of describing things is baffling however: not only does it imply a reduction of the conceptual to the perceptual, but it also leaves one wondering exactly what the nature of the content of the linguistic structure and its component Lexical Concepts might be. The latter is described as "schematic," "non-analogue" and as "an abstraction over multimodal content" (pp. 105–106), but it is also placed on a continuous scale of cognitive content along with Cognitive Models, being contrasted with the latter in terms of "rich versus schematic content" (pp. 105–106). This seems to imply that both Lexical Concepts and Cognitive Models are conceptual in nature, the former being simply more abstract than the latter. What is more, according to the traditional sense of "concept," the more abstract linguistic content would have a greater claim to being called conceptual than Cognitive Models would, while in Evans' terminology only Cognitive Models receive this designation.

Further perplexity is engendered by the application of the term "lexical" to the content of linguistic items as defined by Evans. In his discussion of the Lexical Concepts of [SLIPPER] and [CHAMPAGNE], the "lexical" linguistic content of *slipper* is described as encoding merely the highly abstract notions of THING + UNIPLEX SPATIAL STRUCTURE, and that of *champagne* as only encoding the bare concepts of THING + MULTIPLEX. Uniplexity and multiplexity are terms from Talmy (2000: 48–50) and stand for "conceptual singularity" and "conceptual plurality" across both space and time; non-countable substances like champagne, and collectives like furniture, are considered to be multiplex. The notions of a slipper being a type of footwear worn at home at times of the day when one is seeking relaxation, and of champagne being a bubbly alcoholic beverage of a certain kind served and drunk in a particular way on certain sorts of occasions, are treated as non-linguistic:

> Such knowledge is based on abstracting across episodic experiences—
> that is, experience which is personal and situated, including personal
> observation—as well as cultural experience, or knowledge gleaned
> through narrative, story, and so on. As such, knowledge of this sort is
> extremely rich in nature, and hence is conceptual—that is, non-linguistic.
>
> EVANS 2009: 109

Surprisingly, what is treated here as "lexical" corresponds to what most linguists would call "grammatical" (cf. Bybee and Pagliuca, 1985: 59–60), and the traditionally recognized lexical meaning is portrayed as non-linguistic.

This manifests an underlying confusion in Evans' model as to what is really "linguistic" and what is not. Why should meaning have to conform to the structuralist-type template of being parametrized and possessing the extremely high degree of abstraction that Evans attributes to it in order to qualify as "linguistic"? This postulate seems reminiscent of the Two-Level Semantic approach of Bierwisch (1983a; 1983b) and Lang (Bierwisch and Lang, 1989; Lang, 1993), which draws a sharp distinction between Semantic Form, on the one hand, and Conceptual Structure, on the other: the former is a formalized representation of the basic features of a lexical item containing both the grammatical information that specifies how the word contributes to the formation of syntactic structures, plus a set of variables and parameters whose value is determined by reference to Conceptual Structure; the latter consists of language-independent systems of knowledge that mediate between language and the world as construed by the human mind (Lang and Maienborn, 2011). Evans seems to be adopting a similar position to that of Two-Level Semantics in treating only schematic, clearly non-encyclopedic content as linguistic meaning.

5   How to Deal with the Underdetermined Nature of Linguistic Meaning?

At this point, we can pause and take stock. It appears undeniable that some linguistically-signified meaning is encyclopedic in nature: a word like *banana* uncontroversially evokes knowledge derived from our real-world experience of buying, storing, and eating this kind of fruit. On the other hand, some linguistically-signified meaning is also clearly non-encyclopedic: a word like *any* signifies a mental operation whose exclusive home is the internal realm of the mind. Interestingly, the tension observed above in Langacker's and Evans' attempts to come to grips with linguistic meaning in a cognitive framework runs parallel to a similar tension in other schools of semantics concerning whether linguistic meaning is underdetermined or not, which shows that Cognitive Semantics is not alone in struggling with this question. Some non-cognitive linguists, mainly in the Relevance Theory tradition (e.g. Carston, 2002), hold that the semantic information encoded by a sentence underdetermines its propositional meaning: sentences can express different propositions in different contexts even after the reference of their indexical constituents has been resolved. According to Carston and similarly-minded analysts, the reason why sentences do not have full-fledged propositional contents is that some of their constituent parts (words and morphemes) do not have determinate, stable contents capable of forming parts of propositions. Thus, the genitive in *Joe's car is fast* can stand for the relation *being the property of*, as well as the relations *being driven by, having been bet on by, having been built by*, etc. And in the sentence *The leaves are green*, the adjective *green* can stand for a certain color that the leaves possess intrinsically or for a color that they display exteriorly because they have been painted green (Travis, 1996). Carston has made various suggestions as to what linguistic meaning might actually be in this type of perspective: it may consist in mere pointers to conceptual space (Carston, 2002); it may be abstract and similar in nature to syntactic information (Carston, 2008); it may be too schematic to even qualify as conceptual (Carston, 2012). Travis (1996: 451) sums up this intuition in a nutshell: "what words mean plays a role in fixing when they would be true; but not an exhaustive one."

Ruhl (1989) is one of the few authors to have actually cashed this sort of view out in detail by an analysis of the minutiae of attested linguistic usage. He examines hundreds of actual uses of a number of basic English verbs such as *break, bear, hit, kick*, and *slap*, and argues that these words have a single, highly abstract meaning which eludes consciousness:

> General abstract meanings elude consciousness; the interpretations of the conscious mind by necessity are oriented toward reality, and are thus not purely semantic, but compounds of both semantic and pragmatic (= encyclopedic). The general abstract meaning is unconscious, providing the foundation for more specific conscious distinctions.
>
> RUHL, 1989: 51

The inability of the conscious mind to grasp such meanings is argued to be due to the fact that "consciousness cannot hold all the possibilities at once, and thus must selectively partialize" (Ruhl, 1989: 125; 134–135). He makes the following points regarding the differences between general abstract unconscious meaning and particular concrete conscious import:

- conscious thought partializes, operating by separating something from context and treating it as self-contained;
- conscious awareness is like a spotlight, seeing figures better than grounds, divisions better than continuities, brief and dynamic events better than lengthy and static conditions, the mid-sized rather than the very small or the very large;
- consciousness fixes on nouns (the stereotypic "basic" word class), particularly those that refer (the stereotypic use of language) to the mid-sized type of discrete and movable objects (the most stereotypic reality);
- consciousness is analytic (the stereotypic kind of knowing) and is capable of distinguishing within the consciously isolated self-contained entity an infinity of parts, conditions, processes, and attributes;
- consciousness is concerned with reference, the fit of language, and reality.

To give a specific example, Ruhl (2002) argues that the meaning of the verb *break* involves only the highly schematic notion of a change of state from unity to non-unity. This basic meaning gets modulated in discourse through its interaction with other words, one of the most important being the direct object of the verb, which can denote a physical object (3), a physical entity that is not an object (4), a state (5), a legal prohibition (6), and even a level of performance in golf (7):

(3)   He broke all the dishes, cups, plates.

(4)   A water spider whose feet print but do not break the gliding water membrane.

(5)   A splash broke the silence.

(6)   Whether the patient breaks the law.

(7)   Those were the only golfers to break par.

The very same direct object can be construed moreover either as affected (8) or as effected (9):

(8)   They brought the dogs down to the creek, to where the fugitive broke the trail.

(9)   Moose break many trails through the snow.

Ruhl concludes that "language carries much less meaning than we usually assume" and that "we store only minimal word meaning, using any other available means, both semantic and pragmatic, to construct the particulars" (2002: 171), his contention being that "a word's semantics should concern what it contributes in all contexts" (1989: 87).

6   The Risk of Excess Underdetermination

Wary of the risk of excess underdetermination latent in an approach such as Ruhl's, Tuggy (2003) argues on the other hand that polysemy is rampant in natural language, and that even though polysemous meanings are related in systematic ways and context is necessary for the establishing of these meanings and for choosing among them, this does not warrant omitting them from the lexicon. He adduces the following arguments to support this position: there are holes in the pattern of uses of a word, in that not all reasonably expected meanings obtain (we do not use the verb *break* to refer to the introducing of a change of state from unity to non-unity into a piece of cloth, for example, where only the verb *tear* is appropriate); near-synonyms and translation equivalents exhibit differing ranges of meaning that cannot be predicted from a single meaning (the verb *casser* is not used to refer to infringing the law in French); context often does not provide enough information to account for what speakers intend and hearers understand (the context of a baseball game is not sufficient of itself to account for the meaning of 'curve' conveyed by *The ball broke over the inside corner of the plate*). These facts require integrating into the lexicon information such as the sense expressed by *break* when applied to the motion of a baseball.

Even among more formally-minded semanticists, some hold that all lexical meaning is encyclopedic or thick rather than schematic or monosemic. Pustejovsky (1995) argues for example that the lexicon entry for all lexical items consists of four different levels:

1.   **Lexical typing structure:** gives an explicit type for a word positioned within a type system for the language
2.   **Argument structure:** specifies the number and nature of the arguments of a predicate
3.   **Event structure:** defines the event type of the expression and any sub-eventual structure it may have
4.   **Qualia structure:** provides a structural differentiation of the predicative force of a lexical item.

The fourth level of Qualia structure is inspired by Moravcsik's (1975) inter-pretation of Aristotle's four causes (formal, material, final, and efficient) and thus represents an integration of certain types of world knowledge into lin-guistic meaning.

Motivation for positing Qualia structure as part of a word's lexical meaning comes from the analysis of polysemous nominals and adjectives (see Puste-jovsky and Anick, 1988). It is proposed by this approach that there is a hidden event in the lexical representation associated with nouns denoting objects that are made for a particular purpose such as *door* and *book*, this event being defined as the characteristic activity that realizes the purpose of the object. Some examples of hidden events for artifactual nouns are given below:

(10) a. a door is for "walking through"
     b. a window is for "seeing through"
     c. a book is for "reading"
     d. a beer is for "drinking"
     e. a cake is for "eating"
     f. a car is for "driving"
     g. a table is for "putting things on"
     h. a desk is for "working on"
     i. a pen is for "writing with"

According to Pustejovsky and Anick, the reason for including a hidden event in the lexical representation of these nouns is that in certain syntactic con-texts this event appears to be present in the interpretation, even though it is not expressed in the syntax. For example, in (11) below what is finished is the activity of drinking, but this information is not overtly expressed:

(11) They finished the beer. (drinking)

On the other hand, the hidden information is not arbitrary, but depends on the semantics of the noun. For example, in (12) what is finished is the activity of eating, not of drinking.

(12) They finished the cake. (eating)

A similar phenomenon can be observed in the adjective-noun constructions in (13) below, where the adjective modifies an activity associated with the noun. For example, a comfortable chair is a chair which is comfy to sit in, comfortable shoes are shoes that are pleasant to wear or to walk in:

(13) a. a comfortable chair (to sit in)
  b. comfortable shoes (to wear, to walk in)

The claim that the knowledge that chairs are for sitting in and shoes for wearing on one's feet should form part of the meaning of the words *chair* and *shoe* does not appear highly controversial.[3]

Other authors recognize the existence of rich, non-schematic meaning but do not adopt a formal meaning-template like Pustejovsky's four-level model. Foraker and Murphy (2012), for example, reject the hypothesis that there could be a schematic meaning for a term such as *school*, as it does not seem possible to find anything in common between the 'building' and the 'institution' sense of this word; they propose a multi-facetted definition that is not reducible to Pustejovsky's categories: "building where children are educated in an institutional setting, run by a principal directing a staff of teachers." Vicente and Martínez-Manrique (2016) argue that the lexical meaning of a word is a complex package of conceptual information that the word activates in a stable way, but that what the word contributes to the particular truth-conditional content of a particular utterance is not its entire lexical meaning, but only certain parts or aspects thereof.

This seems to leave us with two contradictory models of lexical meaning: a thick, non-schematic, encyclopedic model in which what the word contributes to the particular content of an utterance is not its entire lexical meaning but only certain parts or aspects thereof; and an under-determined, thin, schematic model in which the entire lexical meaning is present but needs to be fleshed out by contextual modulation in order to generate a truth-evaluable content or a fully comprehensible message. At face value, the two models would seem contradictory when applied to the same item, as the same meaning cannot be both abstract and concrete at the same time and in the same respect. The question is raised therefore as to whether there is any way to reconcile these two seemingly contradictory views of linguistic meaning.

---

3 Langacker (1984: 184–185) handles these interpretations in terms of active zones, the active zone of 'chair' with respect to 'comfortable' being the process of sitting in it, the active zone of 'shoes' with respect to 'comfortable' being the process of wearing them or walking in them, the active zone of 'beer' with respect to 'finishing' being the process of drinking, while the active zone of 'cake' with respect to 'finishing' is the process of eating. He postulates polysemy between the sense of *finish* when construed with a gerund and that observed when this verb is construed with a noun corresponding to the landmark of the process denoted by the gerund: *finish* + gerund profiles a process in which the trajector is a THING and the landmark a PROCESS; *finish* + noun profiles a process in which both the trajector and the landmark are THINGS.

7   Navigating the Waters between Underdetermination and
         Overdetermination

Two sorts of answers to this question are found in the literature. On the one
hand, as seen above in the discussion of the word *tree*, Langacker argues that
the two models can both apply to the same item at the same time. In this maximalist position, a lexical entry contains everything ranging from frequency
information about the contexts in which an item occurs to abstract schemas
that underly all of its uses, including things like taxonomical, prototypical,
metaphorical, and metonymic information as well. Here is an example of the
application of this model to the verb *run* from Langacker (1991: 267):

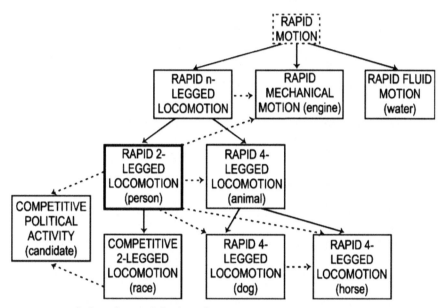

FIGURE 9.2 The lexical network for the verb *run*
         COURTESY OF RONALD LANGACKER

On the other hand, Vicente (2017) argues that the two models apply to different items in the lexicon: some meanings are encyclopedic or "thick" (typically
nouns); others are schematic or "thin" (Vicente argues this for verbs). Regarding
the distinction between these two types of words, he writes:

> (...) we do not seem to store as much information about verb denotations
> as we do about kinds of objects. As Carey (2009) puts it, kind-concepts are
> "inductively deep" (see also Millikan [2000] on the difference between
> substances and classes). Event-type concepts, in contrast, do not allow

for so many inductive inferences. If I am told that there was a cutting event, there is not much that I can infer (that is, unless I am told what was cut). So it looks like the information stored in event-type concepts, being sparser, will not typically allow for there being parts or aspects to be selected. Another, second, reason to think that verb polysemy may be of a distinctive kind is that verb senses typically look like specifications: 'cut the grass' typically denotes an action where the grass is cut in its length, while 'cut the cake' typically denotes an action where the cake is cut into pieces. The different senses of, e.g., 'school,' do not look like specifications of a more general, abstract, meaning in this same way (it could be held that school-the-building specifies the meaning of 'school,' but it is difficult to say that what it specifies is a general, abstract, meaning). That is, whereas the regular polysemy that we find in some nouns cannot be accounted for in terms of common cores (Klepousniotou et al., 2008), or properly underspecific (vs. overspecific) representations [Frisson, 2009], the different senses of verbs do seem to share some features and so to have a common core. I have argued elsewhere (Vicente, 2018) that this is due to the fact that the polysemy that verbs typically display is metaphor-based, whereas the regular polysemy patterns that nouns such as 'school' display is metonymy-based. Lastly, noun-polysemy is typically bounded, whereas verb polysemy seems relatively unbounded: the senses of a verb can extend in innumerable ways.

    VICENTE, 2017: 240–241

In Vicente's view, these two types of meaning interact in the utterance to produce a richer, more specific sentential content capable of determining the sequence's truth-conditions.

In Vicente's eyes, then, the distinction between a dictionary containing linguistic knowledge and an encyclopedia comprised of extralinguistic facts runs along the line between different types of words. Ruhl formulates a similar distinction:

For the most primary words, like *of*, the definition is almost totally linguistic; as a member of the closed class of prepositions (and a primary of that class), its 'value' is in effect not to refer but to set a framework. Its dictionary status is thus high, its encyclopedic status low. On the other hand, for a word like *tiger*, the linguistic status will be minimal; what is most crucial are the properties of tigers, extralinguistic facts. Thus, *tiger*'s definition will be largely pragmatic (= encyclopedic). As a 'natural kind word,' its 'value' will be to refer. Its dictionary status will be low, its encyclopedic status high. These are but two relatively polar extremes of a continuum; the mix of semantic and pragmatic information will vary for each word, depending on its systematic status. Those that are highly systematic will be correspondingly part of closed classes; those that are minimally systematic will be part of open classes.

RUHL, 1989: 182

As Ruhl observes, however, the distinction between primary and non-primary words is not a sharp one, but involves gradation.

Some authors hold however that a distinction can be made for one and the same word between the word's meaning and knowledge that we might have about its referent. In this respect, Riemer remarks regarding the noun *frog* that:

> (...) all of us know many things about frogs, but something seems wrong about regarding all this information as part of the *meaning* of *frog*. Examples of information about frogs that it would seem absurd to claim as part of the *meaning* of *frog* include the facts that there is a famous fairy story in which a frog is an enchanted prince waiting to be released by the kiss of a princess, that frogs are often (and somewhat offensively) associated by English speakers with French people, or that the Australian water-holding frog burrows underground and surrounds itself in a transparent cocoon made of its own shed skin. There are many English speakers who do not know these things about frogs, but who can correctly refer to frogs. This contrasts with speakers of other languages, or with learners of English who have not yet learned the word *frog*, who may know these things about frogs, but do not yet know what the English word *frog* means. It would seem, then, that there is a firm line between knowledge of a word's meaning and knowledge of factual information about the word's denotation.

RIEMER, 2010: 100

He goes on to quote Langacker's postulate that the distinction between linguistic and extralinguistic knowledge is largely artifactual, observing that both the fairy-tale frame and the association of the word *frog* with French speakers can be argued to be linguistically significant in the sense of being required knowledge in order to be able to interpret certain utterances, as is the case in *He may be a Frog, but no princess is kissing him*. He raises the objection however that if any random piece of encyclopedic knowledge that becomes relevant to the linguistic behavior of a word in one of its uses must be incorporated into its definition, the dictionary would have to grow bigger and bigger all the time and would end up looking more like an encyclopedia, with the result that "the supposed processing benefits of concision in lexical representation would disappear." He concludes:

> Since any fact known about a referent may become linguistically significant, the traditional linguistic semantic project of describing the lexical entry associated with each lexeme becomes an unending task, each lexical entry being, in principle, infinite.
>
> RIEMER, 2010: 105

Since the memory capacity of the ordinary speaker is obviously finite, some limit must therefore exist between linguistic meaning and encyclopedic knowledge. But where to draw the line?

8   Langacker's Semiological Principle

An important element for the solution to this dilemma can be found in Langacker's semiological principle. This principle states that the fundamental role of language is to allow "the symbolization of conceptualizations by means of phonological sequences" (Langacker, 2000: 1). This means that the role of the linguistic sign is to evoke in the mind of the hearer a shared conceptualization that is associated with this sign in the minds of the members of the speech community to which the speaker and hearer belong. Consequent upon this principle, the ultimate criterion for the conventionalization of cognitive content as linguistic meaning is the permanent association, in the mind of practically all speakers in a linguistic community, between a given linguistic sign and a stable notional content, whether the latter be encyclopedic or non-encyclopedic in nature. In a particular case, it may be difficult to determine whether a certain piece of knowledge is permanently associated with a given linguistic sign in the mind of the speakers of a linguistic community or not. As regards the noun *frog*, for instance, this linguistic sign does seem capable of calling to mind for the great majority of ordinary English speakers the notions of being something that can turn into a prince when kissed by a princess and of being a derogatory term for a French person. The following uses found on the Internet are predicated on the widespread knowledge of this cognitive content:

(14) We're not presented with a bunch of frogs and just ONE prince or princess.
       thestir.cafemom.com/love

(15) I'm not from Quebec, I'm in the Ottawa Valley. We hate frogs here.
      http://archive.4plebs.org/pol/thread/84374149/[4]

The situation seems different however for the knowledge of the scientific name of the frog (*Anura*), or the knowledge of the fact that the Australian water-holding frog burrows underground and surrounds itself in a transparent cocoon made of its own shed skin, or of the fact that frogs do not have to drink because they absorb water through their skin: these are things that only batrachologists know.

One characteristic of encyclopedic meanings constituted of world-knowledge shared by a linguistic community which makes them tricky to define is the fact that they are subject to temporal, geographical, and inter-speaker variation. To give an example of temporal change, sometime since the moment at which the chemical composition of water was discovered by the Italian physicist Amadeo Avogadro in 1811, the meaning of the word *water* as possessed by the ordinary speaker has incorporated the chemical formula H_2O. When exactly this occurred is difficult to determine, but at present everyone knows this fact about water, so it must be treated as part of the meaning of this word. As an example of geographical variation, the meaning of the word *kangaroo* is much richer for an Australian than for a Canadian, and probably includes the fact that these animals are collision hazards on the highway, as reflected by the fact that there were 8,000 car collisions involving kangaroos in Australia in 2019, representing 4.5% of all automobile accidents in the country. Regarding inter-speaker variation, within the same family my mother used to refer to partridges using the -*s* plural, whereas my father, who hunted these poor little creatures as game, would always designate them as *partridge*, the zero plural reflecting the collectivizing, de-individualizing view of the hunter familiar with the species (see Hirtle 2009: 96–100 for an analysis of the meaning of the bare plural in this type of usage).

Interestingly, a view of meaning based on Langacker's semiological principle that defines it relative to an observable linguistic sign and a particular linguistic community also allows a more realistic understanding of a special class of nouns that has long presented a challenge to semantic analysis: the category of proper names. Viewed from the abstract level of the worldwide Anglosphere, a proper name is practically meaningless: Mill proposed almost two centuries ago (1843) that proper names have a denotation but no connotation, i.e. they provide no information concerning the attributes of what they refer

---

4   These two instantiations were accessed on March 22, 2021.

to but merely designate an individual. Based on the observation that proper names correspond to Rosch (1977)'s basic-level categories (i.e. we have specific proper names for dogs, but not for cocker spaniels), Van Langendonck (2007: 86) claims that such basic-level concepts are "the only (presupposed) lexical meaning that proper names seem to have at the level of established convention." Thus all the name *Ronald* would mean is 'human male.' Proper names do not usually function on the level of the global English-speaking community however, outside of a few cases like *Einstein, Beethoven,* and *Hitler.* Rather, they operate on the level of the sub-community of people who know the person bearing the name. Just as *kangaroo* has a richer meaning for the linguistic sub-community of Australians, so *Ronald Langacker* has a richer meaning for the smaller sub-community of linguists and other people who know him. Consequently, the way a proper name is treated in a dictionary does not reflect the way it exists in the mind of a natural-language speaker. Since a dictionary cannot know individuals and is meant to reflect only the conceptual content attached to the linguistic sign by a very broad range of speakers of a language, mental content concerning individuals in local sub-communities is irrelevant to the lexicographer. However, one should not conclude from this that proper names are meaningless or practically without meaning. If they are used by a speaker, it is because not only he or she, but also the addressee, attaches similar content to them. Since it is clear that the association of a proper name with a unique entity is not made on the spot at the moment of speech, it can be argued to be semantic, in the sense of involving a stable relation between a linguistic sign and a mental content in a certain linguistic community. From this perspective, the meaning of a proper name does determine its denotation, as the fact of being associated in the speaker's mind with the memory of a unique individual will imply the restriction of the denotation to that individual. Proper names, even of public figures, represent the richest encyclopedic meanings in a language: research into the proper name *Harry Potter* in Twitter data between 2007 and 2017 (Frazer-McKee, 2020) found 250 unique knowledge structures associated with this linguistic sign concerning story characters, plot events, holidays, words and phrases, locations, games, weather, music, physical objects like wands, etc.

The definition of linguistic meaning that emerges from the semiological principle is thus that it concerns any mental content that is stably associated with a linguistic sign in the minds of a community of speakers. This view of linguistic content is defended by Wierzbicka (1995) and Goddard (1998); the latter defines linguistic knowledge (p. 14) as "essentially shared between all the speakers of a language, whereas real-world knowledge is not." Linguistic meaning thus cannot be defined in abstraction from a linguistic sign: this leads to the fragmentation of linguistic units into artificial logico-semantic categories, as in the analyses of *any* that categorize it as a Negative Polarity Item equivalent to the existential quantifier in some of its uses (*I don't need any help*) and as a Free Choice Item related to the universal quantifier in others (*Any help would be welcome*). Nor can it be defined in abstraction from a language community, as there are linguistic signs that only have content in smaller sub-communities, such as proper names and words that have different content attached to them in different regional varieties of a language (e.g. *bonnet* in British English referring to what North Americans call the hood of a car). Some mental content attached to linguistic signs is undeniably encyclopedic in nature, but even in these cases there still remains a distinction between linguistic and encyclopedic content, in that the former corresponds only to world-knowledge that is shared by the majority of the linguistic community and so is evocable in the minds of just about anybody in that community by means of the linguistic sign. Thus the chemical formula for water is now part of linguistic content; the chemical formula for sugar is not.[5]

9   A Second Look at Non-encyclopedic Meaning

Having laid the foundation for distinguishing between linguistic and extralinguistic knowledge for those words whose linguistic meaning is encyclopedic in nature, we can now return to consider more closely linguistic units whose meaning is non-encyclopedic. Based on the observation that all encyclopedia entries belong to the class of nouns or noun phrases, there would seem to be a distinction between this part of speech and other word-types as far as the kind of meaning they express is concerned.[6] This suggests it is perhaps the case that all non-noun word-types have thin, schematic meaning, i.e. verbs, adjectives, adverbs, prepositions, conjunctions and determiners, only nouns being capable of having thick non-schematic content. The special status of nouns jibes nicely both with Otto Jespersen's (1924) theory of grammatical ranks, which differentiates between primaries, secondaries and tertiaries, and with Langacker's (1987) analysis of verbs, adjectives, and prepositions as relational predications. Thus, for Jespersen, in *extremely tall tree*, the noun *tree* is a primary, modified by a secondary, the adjective *tall*, which is in turn defined by a tertiary, the adverb *extremely*; on the syntactic level, the subject is a primary, as is the noun *houses*

---

5   It is $C_{12}H_{22}O_{11}$.
6   There are a few adjectives like *hydrochloric* in the encyclopedia, but they occur only as part of noun phrases like *hydrochloric acid*.

in *big houses*, and the verb a secondary, like the adjective *big* in the same construction. Langacker (1987: 212–220) analyzes nouns as instances of THING and treats verbs, adjectives, and prepositions as relational, i.e. as needing to be elaborated by nouns. There is thus a basic conceptual dependency of all other types of words upon the noun. All this suggests that it is no accident that Vicente feels the rich conceptual knowledge conveyed by nouns to account for the concrete meaning that the verb expresses in a particular use in which it is predicated of a particular nominal subject.

It should be noted nonetheless that not all nouns have thick meaning. There are a considerable number of them that are semantically thin, for example the words *thing, object, topic, idea, stuff, junk, mess, ground, lump, hill, rock, shape, texture, smell, taste, quantity, quality, ease,* and *difficulty.* Langacker (1987: 218) treats the noun *part* as a relational noun that profiles only a schematically characterized internal region of a larger entity. On the other hand, verbs, adjectives and adverbs all have more schematic meaning compared to the corresponding nouns, as can be seen from cases where verbal, adjectival, and adverbial forms are derived from a nominal stem. Thus the verb *to man* in *The firefighters manned the pumps* means 'to operate as human personnel' and the firefighters could all be women;[7] *a manly attitude* is one manifesting the stereotypical male qualities of courage and strength, and could be shown by a woman just as well as by a man; the adverb *manlily* in (16) below applies the stereotypical qualities of courage and strength to the manner in which the pretending is to be performed and these qualities could also apply to someone who is not a man, as illustrated by (17) below where the hugger is not the mother:

(16) My first idea was to get a coach to Alton Towers and treat Helen to a day out there where I would manlily pretend that the rides did not affect me, before throwing up afterwards.

ANDY DALE. 2012. *First Years—Piranhas in the Bedroom*, p. 311

(17) The affectionate babysitter hugged the children motherlily before putting them to bed.

In addition, it should be observed that the schematic (thick)/non-schematic (thin) distinction does not coincide perfectly with the encyclopedic/non-encyclopedic dichotomy. Some schematic meanings correspond to bits of

---

7   Deverbal nouns are usually thin (e.g. *a walk, a talk, a look*), but can accrue encyclopedic meaning when they involve metonymical extensions to concrete things, as has occurred with the word *drink* which can denote an alcoholic beverage in uses such as *Would you like a drink?*

knowledge distilled from our experience of the world. This is the case, for example, with an adjective like *squirrelly*, which retains only one aspect typical of a squirrel's behavior, its nervousness.

Langacker's analysis of *run* cited above raises a further question: might there be various degrees of schematicity? What if the schema for *run* was a bit less abstract than that postulated by Langacker ("rapid motion") and corresponded to something like 'continuous movement like that of an animal moving in rapid locomotion mode.' All of the nodes in the network except the 'competitive political activity' sense could then be derived from this schema with the help of contextual cues. Tuggy's considerations on verbal polysemy suggest that some schematic meanings are stored along with information about the sorts of things the schema is conventionally applied to, so that facts such as the custom of using the verb *run* to refer to competitive political activity and the verb *break* to refer to infringing the law are permanently associated with these linguistic signs in English. One might perhaps argue that this kind of content is not *stricto sensu* part of the meaning of the word but rather information about what the meaning of the word is conventionally applied to; whatever the case, the speaker must possess such knowledge in order to use the word properly. The general issue raised by these considerations is the question of what economy measures the mind might have to implement with respect to word meaning given the fact that human memory-storage capacity is finite.

10 How Context Interacts with Different Types of Meaning

Context would seem to interact with the two types of meaning in two different ways in the production of the overall message conveyed by an utterance. The effect of context on schematic items is to pragmatically enrich their meaning, so that for example the abstract verb *take* is understood to refer to the more specific action of stealing in a use such as *The thief took the jewels*. With semantically thick items, on the other hand, context restricts their import to the particular aspect of the complex knowledge network that is relevant to the speaker's communicative intention. Thus in *Your cell phone is an elephant*, only the notions of size and ungainliness are exploited from the complex knowledge network that constitutes the meaning of this noun, which also includes things like the fact that elephants have trunks and tusks and are native to Africa. Analysts who apply the thin-meaning model to thick-meaning words may be mystified by phenomena such as how the word *school* could ever have an abstract meaning that is somehow indeterminate between the notions of 'building' (*to be in the school*) and 'state of engagement in instructional activities' (*to be in school*). These two things are connected metonymically however by the real-world fact that we construct certain buildings in order to provide shelter and separation into teachable groups for people while they are engaging in instructional activities. The application of the thick-meaning model to thin-meaning words, on the other hand, may lead to the unjustified attribution of distinct senses to a word that are based on distinct scenarios in the real world rather than on linguistic-semantic distinctions. Thus, for instance, in spite of the fact that he treats linguistic meaning as abstract and non-analogue with respect to human experience, Evans slips into this practice in his analysis of certain adjectives and verbs. For example, he treats the adjective *long* as having "at least two conventionally established lexical concepts"—[EXTENDED IN HORIZONTAL SPACE], as in *a long stick*, and [EXTENDED DURATION], as in *a long kiss* (Evans, 2009: 299). This amounts however to treating as part of the adjective's lexical concept a piece of knowledge about the real-world referent which is evoked by the meaning of the noun following *long*. Similarly, Evans (2009: 145) distinguishes four different lexical concepts for the single verb *fly* in the uses illustrated in (18)–(21) below:

(18) The bird is flying in the sky. [SELF-PROPELLED AERODYNAMIC MOTION]

(19) The pilot is flying the plane. [OPERATION OF ENTITY CAPABLE OF AERODYNAMIC MOTION]

(20) The child is flying the kite. [CONTROL OF LIGHTWEIGHT ENTITY]

(21) The flag is flying in the breeze. [SUSPENSION OF LIGHTWEIGHT OBJECT]

As pointed out by Murphy (2011: 394), however, no convincing justification is provided for the distinction between these four distinct lexical concepts, and it looks more like the verb is contributing the same meaning in all four uses but its arguments are modifying the overall message conveyed. Thus the notion of 'operation' or 'control' can be argued to derive from the transitivity of (19) and (20), with the idea of 'operating' and 'capability of aerodynamic motion' coming from the difference between planes and kites (although one might argue that a kite is just as capable of aerodynamic motion as a plane is). Similarly in (18), the notion of 'self-propulsion' seems due to the nature of birds, while in (21) those of 'suspension' and 'lightweight object' stem from the nature of flags. This illustrates the methodological utility of taking into account the fact that verbs are unlike nouns in that they tend to have more schematic meaning, so that one must be more careful to properly motivate proposals of polysemy when analyzing verbs.

11   Conclusion

What can be concluded from this survey of the discussions surrounding the question of the encyclopedic nature of meaning in cognitive semantics? First off, one can say that not all linguistic meaning is encyclopedic and that not all encyclopedic knowledge is linguistic meaning: on the one hand, it is quite clear that the meaning of words like *any* or *of* does not constitute knowledge about the world; on the other, it is also clear that the encyclopedic knowledge of the fact that frogs do not have to drink because they absorb water through their skin is not part of the meaning of the word *frog* for the ordinary speaker of English. Secondly, although not all schematic meaning is non-encyclopedic, all non-encyclopedic meaning is schematic: the schematic meaning of the adjective *squirrelly* is derived from our encyclopedic knowledge of the characteristic behavior of squirrels; the meanings of words like *any* that are not derived from knowledge about the world are necessarily schematic however. These distinctions are summarized in Table 9.1 below:

TABLE 9.1   Overlap between schematicity and encyclopedicity

	Schematic	Non-schematic
encyclopedic	*squirrely*	*squirrel*
non-encyclopedic	*any*	

As indicated by the table, within schematic meaning it is necessary to distinguish various degrees of schematicity: the meaning of *squirrelly* is thus more concrete and less schematic than that of *any*. The ultimate criterion for the conventionalization of cognitive content as linguistic meaning, however, is the permanent association, in the mind of practically all speakers in a linguistic community, between a given linguistic sign and a stable notional content, whether the latter be schematic or non-schematic, encyclopedic or non-encyclopedic in nature. Langacker's semiological principle provides the key to answering the question as to whether all linguistic meaning is encyclopedic or not—the answer is that it is not. However, this principle also problematizes somewhat the same author's claim that there is no specific point along the graded scale of cognitive content that can be non-arbitrarily chosen to demarcate linguistic meaning from encyclopedic knowledge. While this statement is true of cognitive content considered in and of itself—as shown by the scientific character of the chemical formula for both water and sugar (which is now part of the first word's meaning but not of the second one's)[8]—it is not true of this content in its relation to a linguistic sign: either a given cognitive content is associated with a given linguistic sign in the minds of the speakers of a given linguistic community or it isn't—at a given point in history, it's an all-or-nothing affair. The ultimate arbiter is the linguistic usage of the ordinary speakers belonging to the linguistic community in question, which implies that meaning can only be determined by the observation of usage.

References

Bierwisch, Manfred. 1983a. Formal and lexical semantics. *Linguistische Studien* 114: 56–79. Bierwisch, Manfred. 1983b. Major aspects of the psychology of language. *Linguistische studien* 114: 1–38. Bierwisch, Manfred and Ewald Lang (eds.). 1989. *Dimensional Adjectives: Grammatical Structure and Conceptual Interpretation*. Berlin: Springer.

Bierwisch, Manfred and Robert Schreuder. 1992. From concepts to lexical items. *Cognition* 42: 23–60. Bybee, Joan and William Pagliuca. 1985. Crosslinguistic comparison and the development of grammatical meaning. In J. Fisiak (ed.), *Historical Semantics: Historical Word-Formation*, 59–83. Berlin: Mouton de Gruyter.

Carey, Susan. 2009. *The Origin of Concepts*. New York: Oxford University Press.

Carston, Robyn. 1991. Implicature, explicature, and truth-theoretic semantics. In S. Davis (ed.), *Pragmatics*, 33–51. Oxford: Oxford University Press.

Carston, Robyn. 2002. *Thoughts and Utterances*. London: Blackwell.

Carston, Robyn. 2008. Linguistic communication and the semantics/pragmatics distinction. *Synthese* 165: 321–345.

Carston, Robyn. 2012. Word meaning and concept expressed. *The Linguistic Review* 29: 607–623.

Condit, Celeste M. 2010. Public understandings of genetics and health. *Clinical Genetics* 77: 1–9.

---

8   Although one must also recognize that the understanding of 'H_2O' is not the same for a chemist as for an ordinary speaker, just as the understanding of 'genetic' is not the same for a doctor as for a patient (see Condit, 2010; 2011; Vogh and Courbon, 2018).

Condit, Celeste M. 2011. When do people deploy genetic determinism? A review pointing to the need for multi-factorial theories of public utilization of scientific discourses. *Sociology Compass* 5: 618–635.

Evans, Vyvyan. 2009. *How Words Mean*. Oxford: Oxford University Press.

Foraker, Stephani and Gregory L. Murphy. 2012. Polysemy in sentence comprehension:
effects of meaning dominance. *Journal of Memory and Language* 67: 407–425.

Frazer-McKee, Gabriel. 2020. *The Semantics and Pragmatics of Proper Names in Adverbial Degree Constructions in English: a Corpus Driven Contribution*. MA thesis, Laval
University.

Frisson, Steven. 2009. Semantic underspecification in language processing. *Language
and Linguistics Compass* 3: 111–127.

Goddard, Cliff. 1998. *Semantic Analysis. A Practical Introduction*. Oxford: Oxford University Press.

Haiman, John. 1980. Dictionaries and encyclopedias. *Lingua* 50: 329–357.

Hirtle, Walter H. 2009. *Lessons on the Noun Phrase in English*. Montreal: McGill-Queen's
University Press.

Jackendoff, Ray. 1992. *Languages of the Mind*. Cambridge, MA: MIT Press.

Jespersen, Otto. 1924. *The Philosophy of Grammar*. London: Allen and Unwin.

Klepousniotou, Ekaterini, Debra Titone and Carolina Romero. 2008. Making sense of
word senses: the comprehension of polysemy depends on sense overlap. *Journal of
Experimental Psychology: Learning, Memory and Cognition* 34: 1534–1543.

Lang, Ewald. 1993. The meaning of German projective prepositions: A Two-Level
Approach. In C. Zelinsky-Wibbelt (ed.), *The Semantics of Prepositions: from Mental
Processing to Natural Language Processing*, 249–292. Berlin: Mouton de Gruyter.

Lang, Ewald and Claudia Maienborn. 2011. Two-Level Semantics: Semantic Form and
Conceptual Structure. In C. Maienborn, K. von Heusinger and P. Portner (eds.),
Semantics: An International Handbook of Natural Language Meaning, volume I, 709–
740. Berlin: Mouton de Gruyter.

Langacker, Ronald W. 1984. Active zones. *Proceedings of the Tenth Annual Meeting of
the Berkeley Linguistics Society*: 172–188.

Langacker, Ronald W. 1987. *Foundations of Cognitive Grammar*, volume I. Stanford:
Stanford University Press.

Langacker, Ronald W. 1991. *Concept, Image, and Symbol. The Cognitive Basis of Grammar*. Berlin: Mouton de Gruyter.

Langacker, Ronald W. 2000. *Grammar and Conceptualization*. Berlin: Mouton de Gruyter.

Langacker, Ronald W. 2005. Dynamicity, fictivity, and scanning: the imaginative basis of
logic and linguistic meaning. In D. Pecher and R.A. Zwaan (eds.), *Grounding Cognition: The Role of Perception and Action in Memory, Language and Thinking*, 164–197.
Cambridge, UK: Cambridge University Press.

Langacker, Ronald W. 2008. *Cognitive Grammar: A Basic Introduction*. Oxford: Oxford University Press.

Langacker, Ronald W. 2013. *Essentials of Cognitive Grammar*. Oxford: Oxford University Press.

Machery, Edouard. 2009. *Doing Without Concepts*. Oxford: Oxford University Press.

Mandler, Jean. 2004. *The Foundations of Mind*. Oxford: Oxford University Press.

Mill, John Stuart. 1843. *A System of Logic*. London: Longmans.

Millikan, Ruth. 2000. *On Clear and Confused Ideas*. Cambridge, UK: Cambridge University Press.

Moravcsik, Julius M.E. 1975. "Aitia" as generative factor in Aristotle's philosophy. *Dialogue* 14: 622–638.

Murphy, Gregory L. 2011. Review of Vyvyan Evans, *How Words Mean*. *Language* 87: 393–396.

Peeters, Bert. 2000. Setting the scene: Some recent milestones in the lexicon-encyclopedia debate. In B. Peeters (ed.), *The Lexicon Encyclopedia Interface*, 1–52. Amsterdam: Elsevier.

Pinker, Steven. 2007. *The Stuff of Thought*. London: Penguin Books.

Pustejovsky, James and Peter Anick. 1988. *The Semantic Interpretation of Nominals*. Brandeis University: Brandeis University Computer Science Technical Report.

Pustejovsky, James. 1995. *The Generative Lexicon*. Cambridge, MA: MIT Press.

Riemer, Nick. 2010. *Introducing Semantics*. Cambridge, UK: Cambridge University Press.

Rosch, Eleanor. 1977. Human categorization. In N. Warren (ed.), *Studies in Cross-Cultural Psychology*, 1–49. London: Academic.

Ruhl, Charles. 1989. *On Monosemy*. Albany: SUNY Press.

Ruhl, Charles. 2002. Data, comprehensiveness, monosemy. In W. Reid, R. Fichte and N. Stern (eds.), *Signal, Meaning, and Message. Perspectives on Sign-based Linguistics*, 171–189. Amsterdam: John Benjamins.

Talmy, Leonard. 2000. *Toward a Cognitive Semantics*, volume I: *Concept Structuring Systems*. Cambridge, MA: MIT Press.

Travis, Charles. 1996. Meaning's role in truth. *Mind* 105: 451–466.

Tuggy, David. 2003. The Nawatl verb *kïsa*: A case study in polysemy. In H. Cuyckens, R. Dirven and J.R. Taylor (eds.), *Cognitive Approaches to Lexical Semantics* (Cognitive Linguistics Research 23), 323–362. Berlin: Mouton de Gruyter.

Van Langendonck, Willy. 2007. *Theory and Typology of Proper Names*. Berlin: Mouton de Gruyter.

Vicente, Agustin and Fernando Martínez Manrique. 2016. The big concepts papers: A defense of hybridism. *British Journal for the Philosophy of Science* 67: 59–88.

Vicente, Agustin. 2017. What words mean and express: semantics and pragmatics of kind terms and verbs. *Journal of Pragmatics* 117: 231–244.

Vicente, Agustin. 2018. Polysemy and word meaning: an account of lexical meaning for different kinds of content words. *Philosophical Studies* 175: 947–968.

Vogh, Kendall and Bruno Courbon. 2018. 'For me, it was very genetic': usage de termes issus du domaine de la génétique dans le discours en ligne de diabétiques anglophones. In C. Roche (ed.), *TOTh 2016. Terminologie & Ontologie: Théories et Applications*, 83–103. Chambery: Éditions de l'Université de Savoie.

Wierzbicka, Anna. 1995. Dictionaries and encyclopedias. How to draw the line. In P.W. Davis (ed.), *Alternative Linguistics. Descriptive and Theoretical Modes*, 289–315. Amsterdam: John Benjamins.

CHAPTER 10

Meaning and Intersubjectivity

Magdalena Rybarczyk and Michael Stevens Pérez

1 Intersubjectivity in Cognitive Semantics

Cognitive semantics considers meaning in terms of the cognitive functions and resources that make language possible. But since, and arguably even before, Gärdenfors's (1999) proclamation that "The prime slogan for cognitive semantics is: Meanings are in the head" (21), cognitive semantics has been charged with incorporating a broader view of cognition. If approaches to cognitive semantics are to hew tightly to usage-based models of language, meaning must be understood not merely as arising out of individual perspectivization, but also an individual's embodiment and socio-cultural milieu. Perhaps equally important, is the emergence of meaning between interacting cognizers, an issue which did not receive due attention at the inception of the cognitive linguistic enterprise. Though the body has been acknowledged as motivating linguistic expressions from the very beginning, until recently, there was an implicit separation of an individual mind from embodied and intersubjective dimensions of communication. Broadly speaking, intersubjectivity as a concept attempts to account for how much a speaker involves others in constructing his or her utterances. Recent cognitive perspectives view intersubjectivity as an individual's ability to mentally represent or show apprehension of another mind (see section 2), and study the degrees to which conventionalized forms take into consideration interpersonal, social, and even cultural positionings (e.g. Brems, Ghesquière, and de Velde, 2014). In spite of these efforts, cognitive semantic examinations often implement a narrow understanding of *mind* by not considering the situatedness of the body and emotions in the linguistic analysis of intersubjectivity.

Inheriting the mental character of language, cognitive linguistics attempts to account for how language is accomplished through basic cognitive functions. Such a view commits cognitive linguistics to a perspectival account of meaning—it is more or less relative to individual minds. If all meaning is to a certain degree subjective, i.e. mediated by the minds of speakers, then what does it mean that something is expressed objectively? This becomes a matter of usage and construal, in how linguistic expressions are made to be objectively understood in moments of use (see Langacker, 2001; 2008). In another sense, objectivity in language is achieved through both the anthropological and institutional dimensions of language. While cultural embeddedness and local flavors enrich human experience in unique ways, there are certain possible universal conditions that all humans share—spatial, temporal, and anatomical. Cognitive linguists have aspired to identify the motivation of these conditions for language (cross-linguistic variability notwithstanding: see e.g. Talmy, 1975; 1985; Casad and Langacker, 1985). Such work is exemplified in attempts to map out basic mental structures that are presumed to derive from experience—e.g. mental spaces, image schemas, metaphorical mappings (Fauconnier, 1994; Johnson, 1987; Lakoff, 1987).

Much of this previous work deals with the relation between thought and language by taking them as separate entities, with distinct but overlapping mechanisms of use. This chapter seeks to go beyond cognition and meaning in the head, and entertain the question of cognition in interaction. In viewing language, thought, and emotion as tightly linked, a path is carved out for illuminating how linguistic expressions do not merely reflect cognitive motivations, but form part and parcel of the resources for shaping a shared world. We expand on these assumptions by illustrating some of the ways language enacts an embodied intersubjectivity.

Intersubjectivity is a fascinating but challenging notion for cognitive semantics, with several philosophical and applicative interpretations, each with different explanations behind language motivation. A specific problem that arises for linguistics is in accounting for how language users draw on common ground to construct meaningful utterances. Research domains in the social realm have tried to solve this problem by seeking out empirically verifiable ways for how expressions transparently share common ground, for example in the analytical methods employed by researchers in Conversation Analysis (e.g. Schegloff, 1992; Raymond, 2019), as well as in corporeal actions, e.g. in the deictics of gesture (McNeill, 2005: Section 4.4; Ishino, 2007). From the cognitive domain, some effort has been made to draw attention to intersubjective encodings in conventionalized forms, e.g., in work on diachronic processes into intersubjectification (Traugott and Dasher, 2002), the presence of speaker vs. addressees in epistemic modality (Nuyts, 2001), and in studies on viewpoint (e.g Dancygier and Sweetser, 2012). Questions remain, however, on how to analyze intersubjectivity as a motivator for language in moments of use. One of the primary challenges is in observing in language the attention that interlocutors give to one another, i.e. in demonstrating transparency of each other's intentions, knowledge, and emotional states. Verhagen (2015) suggests that a way to move forward is to see language use as a form of group cognition, where the shared goals of the activity result in actions that can be accounted for only by higher order ascription of the event, i.e. joint actions giving rise to distributed cognition (238). Linguistically speaking, transparency bears a relationship to how utterances are marked for interpretation (Nuyts, 2014: 59). Intersubjective marking relates to what others have called the *argumentative* nature of language (see Anscombre and Ducrot, 1983; Verhagen, 2015: Section 3). Both Langacker and Talmy develop argumentativity into their frameworks by drawing attention to the fact that all linguistic expressions are contextually dependent and hence designed for joint attention. Talmy (2017), for instance, outlines the targeting properties of demonstratives and gestures in cueing attention (see also Talmy, this volume). Both demonstratives and gestures are taken up for analysis in this chapter (see Section 4).

We therefore argue that in order to give an analysis of meaning in language, it is important to know as much of the context as possible—the goals, reasons, and events that led to the situation coming forth (see Waugh, Fonseca-Greber, Vickers, and Eröz, 2007 for a similar point about empirically researching the complexity of discourse). The relationship between interlocutors (and their relationships with others), whether personal, familial, or professional, also gives insight into the dynamics of how speakers construct their utterances intersubjectively. An array of factors shape the trajectory of how expressions are constructed over the course of a conversation, and thus have valence in what is meaningful. In this chapter, we explore how a cognitive semantics can be pursued beyond subjective perspectivalism, by reconsidering the notions of embodiment and common ground. We suggest that, unless the mind is recognized as embodied and shared, evoking the notion of intersubjectivity merely in terms of mental experience by individual cognizers restricts access to essential aspects of meaning-making. Given the shared, layered, affective, and corporeal experiences of everyday life, meaning emerges in the immediacy and pre-reflective situatedness of human interaction. These become revealed in the analysis of an *embodied* intersubjectivity, i.e. both the a priori intercorporeality of existing in a shared world, and the pursuit and achievement of intersubjective alignment. As Zlatev (2016) points out, "Armed with the concept of embodied intersubjectivity ... body and sociality are interlocked from the start, freeing us from the need to choose one or the other" (187). We thus make the case that, far from being *in the head*, meaning is shaped through its interaction with people, things, and the world, and that the body and meaning are interwoven in a "knot of living significations" (Merleau-Ponty, 1945/2012: 153; see also Johnson, 2007).

Section 2 provides a summary of intersubjectivity as used for the analysis of language and communication, which relates to intersubjectivity within context-sensitive discourse events, and intersubjectification as a diachronic process. Section 3 takes a step back to uncover some of the philosophical roots of intersubjectivity as a concept. We recognize, following Zlatev's project (2010; 2016; 2018), that unpacking some of the philosophical underpinnings of cognitive linguistics reveals the phenomenological conceptions which can guide our understanding of intentionality and intersubjectivity in cognitive linguistics. We explore some of these phenomenological underpinnings and discuss the theoretical distinction between intersubjectivity and intercorporeality. While this distinction has bearing on ontogenetic development of communicative sense-making, we find that the terminology of *embodied intersubjectivity* both expands our understanding of intersubjectivity in meaning, and also allows for comprehensive understanding of the motivational factors for construal in corporeal, i.e. holistic, sense-making. In Section 4, we expand analytically how embodied intersubjectivity plays a role in the construction of utterances. We first make the case for a methodology based on the collection of reformulations in order to gain access to alternate construals from natural and goal-oriented data. We then explore research into attitudinal and affective dimensions of construal, specifically as manifested in Polish demonstratives and possessive pronouns, followed by an analysis of the embodied intersubjectivity of concept development during peer talk in a second language classroom.

2   Intersubjectivity in Language and Communication

With the foundational premises of CL linking language directly to experience, intersubjectivity has been implied from CL's inception. However, until the turn of the millennium a majority of cognitive linguists were by and large preoccupied with explaining language structures in light of an individual's cognitive abilities (Langacker, 1999a: 4; Geeraerts and Cuyckens, 2007: 5), which only recently have increasingly been recognized as inherently social ("social cognitive abilities" in Croft, 2009; "individuated shared mind" in Zlatev, 2008). The focus on the conceptualizer came as a response to an objectivist semantics and stemmed from an assertion that language does not describe the objective world, but rather reflects a speaker's (subjective) perception of it (Croft and Cruse, 2004: 1–3). Thus, from the beginning, cognitive linguists consented that semantics is experientially based and motivated by the human body and cognition (Johnson, 1987; Lakoff, 1987; Langacker, 1987). What follows is that these same cognitive processes govern language use as visual perception, reasoning, or motor activity.

Following from Langacker's (1987; 1991) development of Cognitive Grammar, an essential cognitive ability is the capacity to portray the same referent—an object, a state of affairs, or an event—by alternate means, corresponding to different ways of conceptualizing the referent in question. Different ways of viewing a particular referent are analytically handled in Cognitive Grammar with the notion of *construal* and its various dimensions, for example, perspective, specificity, or subjectivity (Langacker, 1995). While linguistic construal refers to the specific structuring of an utterance by an individual language user, the "viewing" we are concerned with here is by the interlocutors when they jointly focus attention on a specific referent in specific interactive circumstances. The speaker initiates an act of meaning-making by selecting a linguistic expression that invites the addressee to a co-conceptualization. Consider the semantically non-equivalent expressions in (1), which—among multiple other possibilities—can be used to refer to the same individual.

(1)   Mary, my teacher, your daughter, our friend, a woman

Each of the referring expressions in (1) guides the conceptualizers towards a different perspective on the elements of the scene, i.e. a different structuring (construal) of conceptual content, which prompts different meanings (Langacker, 1987; 2008). Although meaning does not reside in linguistic expressions, but in concrete acts of use (Langacker, 1987; Fauconnier, 1994; Tomasello, 2003; Zlatev, 2016), the point is that linguistic form is invested with specific meaning potential. Co-referential expressions *meaningfully* differ with respect to various dimensions of construal, three of which are selected here for explanatory purposes.

  a. Specificity: *Mary* vs. *a woman*
     Mary is more specific than *a woman*, as it identifies the referent with more precision ('a woman called Mary').
  b. Perspective: *my teacher* vs. *your daughter*
     Perspective is multifaceted, its most obvious aspect being the "vantage point," i.e. the position from which the scene is perceived (Langacker, 1987: 122–125). The possessive pronouns *my* and *your* select the speaker's and the hearer's vantage point respectively.
  c. Subjectivity: *Mary* vs. *our friend*
     In Langacker's terminology, subjectivity pertains to the asymmetry between the conceptualizer and the intended object (Langacker, 1985; 1999b). The use of *Mary* retains maximal subjectivity of the ground (the conceptualizers remain a detached observer) and maximal objectivity of the object of conception. In contrast, the use of the possessive *our* reduces the subjectivity of the ground, by selecting a joint conceptualizer as a reference point via which attention is established with the referent of *our friend*.

These (and other) construal operations are also realized at the level of gesture and body movement (see Kok and Cienki, 2016).

Even non-linguists might agree that the expressions in (1) are not interchangeable. When asked about selection criteria, they might even say that reference is contingent on who is talking and/or to whom they are talking. While this may not be the whole story, it pinpoints the intersubjective nature of both communication and language. At one level, a given speaker apprehends the specific interactive circumstances, including the identity of the hearer, their common ground and shared knowledge. At another level, the speaker surveys the set of conventionalized expressions and selects one that best serves their purpose (Rybarczyk, 2015; see also Möttönen, 2016). In making a choice, the speaker must ensure that the addressee recognizes the choice (for successful communication to take place). For example, in the case of a proper name, the speaker who uses *Mary*, knows a referent of *Mary* and is aware that for this selection to be meaningful, the addressee must also be able to bring to awareness the same referent upon hearing the proper name *Mary*. Moreover, the addressee knows that the speaker knows, both the referent and the discursive conventions of using a proper name (Zlatev, 2018; Verhagen, 2015). Thus, linguistic communication rests on substantial shared knowledge at the level of both life and language. As an instance of joint action, it uses linguistic convention as a coordinating device (see, e.g., Verhagen, 2005: 3; Croft, 2009: 401). As noted by Möttönen (2016), "the criterion according to which a particular expression is selected for any use must pertain to the manner in which that expression conveys meaning between multiple subjects" (221). Thus, analysis of intersubjectivity falls on a spectrum of the conventionalization of language, from the shared understanding of linguistic signs to the locality and contingency of inference in specific usage events.

On a usage-based account of linguistic knowledge (Langacker, 1988; Barlow and Kemmer, 2000; Tomasello, 2001; 2003), conventionalized expressions are abstracted from actual instances of language use. As such, they often retain traces of the interactive circumstances in which they were acquired (Rybarczyk, 2015), and "a construal that corresponds to a given expression may, therefore, have conventionalized effects that adjust the relationship between the utterer and the recipient" (Möttönen, 2016: 223; see also Verhagen, 2005; 2015; Rybarczyk, 2015). Much of the work in cognitive linguistics has focused on a comparative analysis of co-referential linguistic construals, rather than on their spontaneous selection in discursive context, but it is the latter that brings the social dimension of language and cognition to the fore (see section 4).

Intersubjectivity, inherent in any act of communication, may be explicitly coded in linguistic form. Since Verhagen's (2005) analysis of negation, matrix clauses of complementation, and concessive conjunctions, a whole range of other constructions, from modals to conditionals, have been accounted for as encoding aspects of intersubjective coordination (see Boogaart and Reuneker, 2017 for an overview). Verhagen (2005) compared construals such as *possible* and *not impossible* and argued that their non-equivalence lies in that the first establishes a relation between the subject and the object of conception, while the latter a relation at the level of the *group* conceptualizer (and in this sense it is explicitly intersubjective). Verhagen (2015) proposes that with such intersubjective construals, the participants exert argumentative influence on each other's cognitive systems by managing perspectives and triggering specific inferences (236). Rybarczyk (2015) identified a specific demonstrative plus proper name construction in Polish that communicates at the level of the conceptualizer, and tested recipients' responses to it in a forced choice task (184–188). What she calls the "familiarity" use of the Polish proximal demonstrative *ten* is employed when the speaker wants to communicate *I think you should know who I am talking about because of some discourse knowledge we share* (186). Note that this shared knowledge is already implicit in the use of a proper name or the proximal demonstrative alone. The Polish *ten* + proper name construction emphasizes that the speaker believes her specific interlocutor should be familiar with the intended referent. Thus, an aspect of intersubjective coordination is made explicit. The results of the experiment suggest that the hearer recognizes the speaker's comment on their mutual ability to coordinate cognitively (i.e. the hearer knows that the speaker believes that the hearer knows). Whether or not we accept that language use is essentially aimed at "mutual influencing" (Verhagen, 2008: 307), intersubjectivity as grammaticalized in language merits further scrutiny.

Even when linguistic expressions do not evoke the conceptualizers or reference a consideration of multiple perspectives, they are still understood intersubjectively. Verhagen (2015) postulates three types of such intersubjective linguistic meanings:

> deictics invoke the most immediate evidence available to interlocutors, the speech event itself; proper names invoke a wider source of evidence: shared personal history; common nouns and verbs invoke the widest source: a shared culture.
>
> 243

Let us match Verhagen's distinctions to the referring expressions *Mary* and *your daughter*. The possessive pronoun *your* is a deictic term (a "grounding predication" in Langacker's terminology) that makes reference to the shared communicative situation by selecting the hearer and co-conceptualizer as a reference point that gives access to an intended referent. The intended referent of the proper name *Mary* can be successfully singled out if it is salient in the interlocutors' shared history. The kinship term *daughter*, a common noun, as shared within a culture, may invite certain inferences in accordance with a specific cultural model of a family. While these distinctions might be helpful for description and analysis of language, it is important to note that in ongoing communication, the different types of shared knowledge are blurred, conflated, or even transformed. Grounding elements such as possessives or demonstratives usually occur with nouns (*your daughter*) and can also occur with proper names (*my Mary*). A proper name can be used with a pointing gesture to identify a person in the immediate context of a speech event, in which case the referent may not be present in the speech participants' personal history. Most importantly, the choice itself that the speaker makes between *Mary* and *your daughter* is guided by a synthesis of interactions with the intended referent, with the specific addressee, and with the semantic potential of the expressions, all of which are experienced intersubjectively. Consider for a moment why a speaker might choose *your daughter* over *Mary* to refer to the hearer's daughter. She needs to consider both the specific discursive context and the two linguistic construals "entrenched as socially sanctioned perspectives" (Zlatev, 2016: 563; see Möttönen, 2016). The speaker's need for contextual consideration entails that intersubjectivity is multifaceted, bearing an intimate, two directional relationship between intentionality and normativity. That is, between a speaker's specific usage and bearing towards an event, and the conventions through which language conveys meaning (Zlatev, 2018: Section 4; see also Sambre, 2012).

3 The Phenomenological Approach to Intersubjectivity

In the philosophical literature, intersubjectivity generally refers to the situation of two agents coming into synchrony in some way, i.e. into epistemic, perceptual, or emotional alignment. The question lingers, however, of how it is possible for two minds to orient to a shared understanding, and thus achieve and maintain that alignment. In philosophy this is known as the problem of other minds, specifically addressed in phenomenology as a primary dimension of experiential consciousness (Gallagher and Zahavi, 2012). Living beings are pre-oriented towards each other with specific forms of sense-making that entail each other's immediate comprehension of the other as a conscious and experiencing self (Husserl, 1931/1960). Such an experience involves not only the physical space of an encounter, but people's relation to their own bodies and that of one another. In other words, embodiment cannot simply play a motivational factor when it emerges in analysis, but rather permeates the conceptualization and contextualization of a given encounter. There is thus a notion of an intersubjective disposition towards not just other minds, but towards the world and embodiment itself. For there to be any analysis in the study of intersubjectivity, the contingency of interactive context must be considered in the constraining of meaning and the co-regulation of behavior that is observable in communicative events.

For the speaker and hearer relation, this co-regulation drives the construction of utterances, where interlocutors are embedded along a temporal continuum of looking back and projecting forward (Sambre, 2012: 202). Such a notion suggests that cognition involves an active, ever-evolving intelligence and knowhow of language and of the body (Di Paolo, Cuffari, and De Jaegher, 2018). In order to account for the embodied nature of consciousness, Merleau-Ponty (1945/2012) sets forth the distinction between the body as object, and the lived body as proprioceptive experience, the distinction having special implications for the nature of intersubjectivity.

Merleau-Ponty (1945/2012; 1968) emphasized that human embodiment does not entail the perception of the body as an inanimate object, but as animating and animated by engagement in the world (i.e. a "living body"). That is, the body is the background through which we experience the world, and through our actions treat it with sense. Our embodiment, which is "eminently an expressive space" (Merleau-Ponty, 1945/2012: 147) is part of that human condition which finds us "condemned to sense" (ibid: xxxiv). "The principal regions of my body" Merleau-Ponty tells us, "are consecrated to actions, the parts of my body participate in their value, and the question as to why common sense places the seat of thought in the head is the same as the question of how the organist distributes musical significations in the space of the organ" (ibid.: 147). It would appear then that it is not just embodiment, but embodied action that is the seat of sense-making, not only in the grounding of meaning, but in the entanglement of action and interaction between different bodies in space.

There is therefore primarily an intersubjectivity in the treatment and engagement with the world as meaningful, which becomes extended through empathy in our interaction with other people (Zahavi, 2001). Merleau-Ponty's account is thus a respecification of intersubjectivity into "intercorporeality" (Heinämaa, 2013). Such a respecification extends the phenomenological account of intentionality towards a view of cognition as a thinking *of* and *with* the body, exhibiting dynamic, transformative engagement in a social world (see also Arnheim's (1969) notion of "visual thinking"). This transformative account has come to be known as the *enactive* view of cognition: the "enactment of a world and a mind on the basis of a history of the variety of actions that a being in the world performs" (Varela, Thompson, and Rosch, 1991: 9). In other words, cognition entails how we carry out meaning in and through our actions as human beings. Merleau-Ponty's reconception of embodiment thus furnishes a renewed analysis of construal in language.

The implication that intercoporeality has for language entails a holism and immediacy in the experience of communicative acts, in contra-distinction to a symbolic understanding of language and thought, which draws on notions of mental representation and simulation in the explanation of meaning. In contrast, Merleau-Ponty's analysis eschews the need for any mentalistic explanation, because we know what to do and what to say based on a repertoire of experience, which informs our dispositions. As Merleau-Ponty (1945/2012) explains:

> In order for me to understand the other person's words, I must 'already know' his vocabulary and his syntax. But that does not mean that the words act by arousing 'representations' in me, which could be associated with them and which, when taken together, could eventually reproduce in me the speaker's original 'representation.' I do not primarily communicate with 'representations' or with a thought, but rather with a speaking subject, with a certain style of being, and with the 'world' that he aims at. Just as the significative intention that initiated the other person's speech is not an explicit thought, but rather a certain lack that seeks to be fulfilled, so too is my taking up of this intention not an operation of my thought, but rather a synchronic modulation of my own existence, a transformation of my being.
>
> 189, quotes in original

Thus, any encounter with another person is pre-linguistically and pre-reflectively charged with the readiness for shared recognition. Such immediacy obviates the need for reflection, representation, and simulation, because through embodied perception "we are able not only to embody the other while the other simultaneously embodies us, but also embody ourselves in the same way as we embody the other. Our body can be a subject or object for us in the same way as the other can be one" (Meyer, Streeck, and Jordan, 2017: xx). Expression is itself the enactment of intersubjectivity, of joint senses of space, time, and participation (Sambre, 2012; Meyer et al., 2017).

Intercorporeality should be seen as not only an analytically useful distinction from intersubjectivity, but as encompassing the background to further possible subjectivities and objectivities. For instance, as Andrén (2012) indicates, the achievement of inference about the experience and thoughts of other beings demands a certain skill set, likely developed in early childhood in observation of other bodies and enactments with one's own (see also Zlatev, 2008, on the embodied co-evolution of intersubjectivity). For research on communication and meaning in social actions, intercorporeality has begun to take hold as a distinct operational framework, such as in the synchronization of bodies in martial arts (Stukenbrock, 2017; Kimmel and Rogler, 2018) and in how participants in psychotherapy sessions emotionally align (Jensen, Trasmundi, Bloch, and Steffensen, 2019).

Specific to spoken language, intercorporeality can be shown to be expressed in acts of gestural sense-making, where the speaker (or gesturer) gives treatment to the ensuing discourse through a multimodal gestalt (Müller, 2016). That is, where the very act of gesturing draws attention to the materiality and sociality of the world-at-hand (Meyer et al., 2017). This is the case not only with gestures that point to something in space, but also depictive and metaphorical practices of gesture, where an imagistic hand configuration invites the speaker to visually examine an uttered, but not-visible, referent (Streeck, 2009; Talero, 2012). Like verbal language, gestures range in the degree of subjectivity that they construe (Kok and Cienki, 2016), and can reflect conventions for directionality and viewpoint of particular languages (Haviland, 2000; Núñez and Sweetser, 2006; Núñez, Cooperrider, Doan, and Wassmann, 2012). Gestures also exhibit the corporeal nature of grammar, as shown in their synchrony with verbal language in spoken discourse (Kendon, 2004; Ladewig, 2014; McNeill, 2016; Harrison, 2018). But given their intercorporeal nature, in that human bodies share in the experience of habitual actions, gestures can explicitly demonstrate attentiveness to intersubjective intentionality. For example, Ishino (2007) showed how speakers change the directionality of their pointing gestures depending on the position of their addressees. Gesturers can also use their repertoire of experience in fashioning visualizations for abstract concepts, such as in philosophy lectures (Stevens and Harrison, 2019) and academic discourse (Rosiński, 2018; Stevens, 2021). For instance, in examining depictive gestures in academic interactions, Stevens (2021) found that gesturers refashion their depictions motivated by the anticipation of misunderstanding, but according to anatomical, environmental, and cognitive affordances that are encountered in moments of use. Research along the lines of cognitive semiotics (e.g. Trevarthan, 2012; Zlatev and Blomberg, 2016) has developed the corollary notion of embodied intersubjectivity, to draw attention to the complementarity of embodiment and sociality (Zlatev, 2017). In the following section, we explore some of the ways embodied intersubjectivity permeates and motivates construal in interaction.

4 Embodied Intersubjectivity: From Theory to Practice

4.1 *Observing Reformulations for Intersubjectivity in Construal*

Taking an embodied intersubjectivity perspective on meaning has implications for methodology and data collection. If linguistic conventions are deeply rooted in embodied, socially and culturally situated discourse, and meaning-making occurs in interaction, then studying construal outside of its interactive ecology addresses its meaning only partially. Communication, as argued by Zlatev (2018), is not only a matter of establishing joint attention, but rather requires an achievement of a basic shared intentionality. Zlatev (2018) proposes that intentionality as meaning be recognized at different levels, from life to language, that coalesce as sedimented structures in reciprocal relations to one another, with linguistic conventions "emerging from and constraining, but not determining, subject-world interactions" (in abstract).

The research discussed in this section models a methodology for accessing a wider spectrum of intersubjective processes via reformulations. Reformulated utterances provide empirically constructed alternating construals (Deckert, 2017) and reveal how multimodal structuring is enacted for the purpose of communication (see also Croft, 2009: 415–418). Aspects of the context, such as the identities of the interlocutors or the specific setting do not merely contextualize, but rather *enliven* the linguistic construals, resulting in meaning-laden episodes that are not reducible to the symbolization of the individual elements involved. To keep developing, future research in cognitive semantics should not only acknowledge that certain aspects of meaning are accessible only through authentic interactional data, but also use such data as a primary source of knowledge about intersubjective meaning and meaning construction. This approach leads to insights that are not readily available when studying construal outside of interaction. For example, research by Rybarczyk (2015), selectively summarized in section 4.2, extends the cognitive linguistic account of demonstratives and possessives by investigating them in specific interactive frames (where the identities of the speech participants and their interpersonal relationships are known) and in repeated reference to the same individual. While Rybarczyk focuses on specific linguistic constructions but adds a non-linguistic variable to the analysis, Stevens (2021) (see section 4.3) offers an investigation of concept development in longer stretches of talk. As participants 'analyze' the same concepts in multiple explanations, they develop and adjust their verbal and gestural construals based on contextual affordances and the experience of interacting with other subjects (see also Rosiński, 2018). Capabilities for intersubjective alignment are displayed in multiple domains as interlocutors make use of time, space, the affordances of the body, and the possibilities granted by verbal expressions (which themselves are abstracted from embodied and intersubjective interactions).

4.2   *Construal, Relationships, and Unfolding Attitudes*

This section presents a sample from empirical research into intersubjectivity as enacted with grammatical means of expressing attitude and/or emotion (Rybarczyk, 2015). It aligns with the growing body of work that acknowledges the role of the affective level of human interaction (see Foolen, 2012 and the sources quoted therein; see also Jensen et al., 2019). It also links to the CL developments in multimodality and conceptual metaphor (see, for example, Matthews and Matlock, 2011; Górska, 2020, 2021). If language is inherently intercorporeal, acquired by a living, feeling body in its relation to the environment and to other people, then it must be interwoven with bodily experience and, as a socio-cognitive phenomenon, essential to mediating human situatedness.

Rybarczyk (2015) investigates an interplay between speaker awareness of other people and her/his choice of expressions to refer someone to a third party. Rybarczyk focuses on nominal grounding elements in Polish, specifically demonstratives and possessives, and argues that an investigation of these forms in specific interactive frames, where the identities of the conceptualizers are known and their social situatedness is part of the analysis, reveals that their usage is interlocked with the intrinsically relational nature of human beings, including "the desire to share emotions and/or attitudes with others" (Tomasello, 2008: 210). The main function of nominal determiners is often expressed in how efficient they are in directing the conceptualizers' attention to an intended entity. In interaction, however, nominal determiners are often selected based not only on their efficiency but also on their potential to manage the social and interpersonal relationships and induce attitudes in an ever-evolving intersubjective reality. This is perhaps most transparent when a grounding element is used optionally, such as with proper names, or in a referring expression substituting a more conventional form; for example, in choosing *our son* in the interpersonal context in which a proper name would normally be used. Thus, to fully address whether and how referential choices with demonstratives and possessives impact conceptualization of attitudes and social/interpersonal situatedness, two steps need to be taken:

1.   Find any patterns that may exist in the use or non-use of these forms, and the nature of the speaker-hearer relation as well as the interlocutors' relations with the referent (convention).

2.   Investigate their (non-default) uses in dynamic discourse and observe how the structuring they carry interacts with the semantic import of other

linguistic forms as well as with the lived experience beyond language (intentionality).

The first serves to interpret the second, while the second serves to update the first (see Zlatev, 2018).

Although the same conceived entity can be mentally accessed from several perspectives, the choice is not always arbitrary. For example, the choice between assuming the speaker's or the hearer's vantage point to talk about a family member is often motivated by the kind of relationship between the speech act participants and this individual (Rybarczyk, 2011; 2015). The choice of a particular vantage point positions the interlocutors in relation to one another as well as in relation to the referent. Departures from the default often signal attitudinal or affective values. Consider the choice between a proper name (*Piotrek*) and a referring expression with a kinship term in the exchange in which parents are talking about their son (Rybarczyk, 2015: 120–123).

(2)   a. Piotrek has problems at school.
      b. Our son has problems at school.

The possessive in (2b) momentarily brings the parents into the focus of attention, and in combination with the kinship term *son* invites a host of inferences about shared responsibility, the need for action, or other contextually constructed meanings. While *our son* creates a mental space in which both parents are together with their son, another referential option—*your son*—places the speaker outside of this space and changes the affective value of the whole utterance (see Rybarczyk, 2015: 174–176).

Possessives can be used in discourse to manipulate the perspective from which an intended referent is observed. They evoke a reference point dominion (Langacker, 1991; 1993)—a mental space whose boundaries establish a grouping of participants—and can be used to communicate positive or negative emotions and/or attitudes by manipulating who belongs in it (Rybarczyk, 2015). Such uses are abundant in the documentary *Solidarni 2010* (*In Solidarity* 2010), filmed in the streets of Warsaw directly after a plane crash that killed the Polish president Lech Kaczyński and everyone else onboard (Rybarczyk, 2015: 149–162). The filmmakers interviewed the mourning nation whose repeated reference to the president in this emotional context shows a pattern in construal which seems to correspond to the political sympathies of the speakers. Many supporters of Law and Justice (a political party favored by president Kaczyński) speak of him as *mój prezydent* "my president" in the documentary, while authors of the comments posted under the film on YouTube (see Stankiewicz 2010), who mostly represent the opposition, favor a more objective construal.

Several comments, for example the one quoted in (3), express dissatisfaction with the referring expression "my president" (which they correct to "our president") due to its implication that those who did not vote for Lech Kaczyński had no right to mourn his death.

(3)   A Prezydent był *naszym Prezydentem*, wszystkich Polaków, każdemu Polakowi było źle z tym co się stało niezależnie od tego jakie miał poglądy polityczne ...

The President was *our President*, the president of all Poles. Every Pole felt bad about what happened, whatever their political views ...

The implication formulated above may seem exaggerated, but the comment in (3) hints at this interpretation and a larger context (the whole documentary, other footage of the event, the comments people made privately) supports this discursive meaning of *mój prezydent* 'my president.' This powerful excluding potential of the pronoun "my" could be noted by considering authentic interactional material in the full richness of the context which brings this potential to life. The exclusion is communicated by pragmatic inference prompted by the speaker opting out from the use of the plural pronoun "our."

Like possessives, demonstratives are also interpreted by making reference to the conceptualizers—although they do not explicitly reference the interlocutors, their meaning is expressed in the proximity (or lack of proximity) to the ground. Motivated by the human bodily and perceptual experience, demonstratives are good candidates for emphatic usage based on an intercorporeal metaphor INTIMACY IS CLOSENESS (Grady, 1997). Rybarczyk (2015) analyzes the attitudinal uses of demonstratives and possessives in Polish in terms of a multi-dimensional personal sphere: "a core personal sphere" that encompasses a fairly stable set of an individual's relations (family, friends, inalienable possessions) and a "transient personal sphere" that "hosts a complex net of short-term connections and emotional reactions to specific entities on specific occasions of interacting with them" (61). The entities in the transient personal sphere are perceived close enough to the speaker to affect her/him, often in a negative way.

From analyses of dialogues against the richness of their social and interpersonal background, both demonstratives and possessives serve as personal space builders. In Polish, the proximal demonstratives *ten/ta/to* contrast with the first person possessive pronouns along the dimension of interpersonal distance, measured by inclusion or lack of inclusion in the core personal sphere. When *ten* is used to modify a proper name, it either signals that the referent is familiar but does not belong to the interlocutors' core personal spheres, or it helps to express some emotion or attitude towards an individual (including an interpersonally close individual). Compare (4a) and (4b), where the referring expression *ta Dorota* can point to the speaker's sister only in the second context.

(4) a. W sobotę była u mnie *ta* Dorota.
         "(*This*) Dorota visited me on Sunday."
     b. Już mnie *ta* Dorota denerwuje.
         "(*This*) Dorota is really getting on my nerves now."

In a neutral context, the Polish *ta* 'this' serves as an instruction to search for an individual called Dorota outside of the interlocutors' core personal spheres (4a). On the other hand, the demonstrative can be used in an emotionally emphatic construction, such as (4b), in which case it removes the referent from the core personal sphere and places her in the transient personal sphere to express some contextually evident affective meanings. It communicates at once distance and proximity. This rhetorical potential of the proximal demonstrative is enacted in dynamic discourse, motivated by the human need to form affiliations with others via sharing feelings and attitudes (see Tomasello, 2008).

It is noteworthy that constructions with the proximal demonstratives to refer to the Polish president were extremely rare in the documentary film *In Solidarity 2010*, and no examples were found with an optional demonstrative. This avoidance may suggest that the speakers of Polish are intuitively aware of the intersubjective component of the demonstrative and its potential to communicate interpersonal distance and/or a negative attitude towards the referent, which in the context of the tragic plane crash was culturally inappropriate. Furthermore, recall that many speakers in the documentary chose to emphasize that the president belongs to their core personal sphere. It thus comes as no surprise that they should avoid a non-obligatory use of the Polish proximal demonstrative which often stands in direct contrast to this sentiment; "Systematic avoidance of certain canonical referring expressions in a specific interactive frame may be as meaningful as the usage of other variants" (Rybarczyk, 2015: 195).

Considering the intercorporeal roots of language, we can explore whether the interpersonal and affective/emotional distance associated with the construals under analysis has impact on reasoning about physical space. This correlation can be tested in experimental work using multimodal tasks, for example, verbalization-primed drawing or visually primed verbalizations as have been used in studies in conceptual metaphor (Matthews and Matlock, 2011; Winter and Matlock, 2013). In an experiment inspired by Matthews and Matlock (2011), participants read stories that involved a perspectival manipulation (*ta* 'this' vs. *moja* 'my') in person reference, and then performed a visual task in which they made decisions about the location of the referent in physical space (Rybarczyk, 2015: 177–183). Both grounding predications were added optionally to modify a proper name resulting in a grammatically coded comment on affective and/or interpersonal distance. The verbal cuing affected decisions about the referent's spatial location with respect to the speaker in the following ways: (i) in a neutral scenario, participants generally chose a proximal location when primed with inclusion within the core personal sphere (*moja Ula* "my Ula"), (ii) in a scenario which implied slight annoyance towards the referent on the part of the speaker, participants clearly enacted affective proximity within the transient personal sphere (*ta Patrycja* "this Patrycja"). The results, firstly, confirm that linguistically coded social situatedness (expressed lexically in Matthews and Matlock, 2011, and expressed grammatically here) and people's respective spatial location are interrelated in a bi-directional manner. Secondly, although

> distance is clearly relevant to the characterization of meanings encoded by possessives and determiners, (…) it is important to understand that these forms interact with the background to unfold different layers of spatial reasoning, switching between proximal and distal perspectives on entities within various layers of the personal sphere.
>
> RYBARCZYK, 2015: 183

Cognitive Linguistics has provided detailed accounts of linguistic construals. Future research should address how these construals interact with one another in *sequences* of multimodal talk investigated in the richness of their interactive ecologies. A sample of such empirical work is presented in the remainder of this section.

4.3   *The Sequentiality and Intercorporeality of Construal in Concept Development*

While much of the previous work on intersubjectivity has shown how particular constructions become reused for different degrees of alignment, this section explores the process of reaching understanding of a referent through empirically observable alternate construals. Like the examples seen in Section 4.2, the construals of a referent gleaned from authentic, *in situ* data provide access to conceptualizations at the emergent level of discourse (see Etelämäki and Vispää, 2014; Rybarczyk, 2015), and therefore the analysis of the examples in this section draws on elements of interaction research (see Stevens, 2021; Zima and Brône, 2015; Herlin and Visapää, 2016). We show how aspects of the ground, i.e. the task at hand and its participants, have bearing on the dynamic conceptualization of a particular topic. We thus observe the interrelatedness of embodied intersubjectivity and intersubjective alignment, in which layers of embodied meaning (Zlatev, 2018) become *externalized* towards the achievement of a co-conceptualization. As conversational analysts have argued for some time, speech acts are not to be understood as intentions in the minds of speakers that are manifested in linguistic structures; they are brought into being by interlocutors coordinating a shared understanding of what it means to greet, discuss, agree or disagree, provide an explanation, etc. (Schegloff, 2007). We thus observe intentionality in the goal-directedness and design that is displayed in the sequence of utterance construction, and not only in the semantics of linguistic forms, or in the minds of interlocutors.

One of the key contributions of ethnomethodology for social research is the notion of participant inference and action ascription in interaction (see Garfinkel, 1967). What this amounts to is that in sequences of talk, speakers reveal their own *analyses* of the situation. At the most basic level of interactional meaning, a speaker's response to an interlocutor reveals their understanding of what was said, conferring an ad hoc characterization of the discourse. One classic example is the greeting. When a speaker formulates a recognizable greeting, their addressee's response displays the meaning as it was understood to them (Schegloff, 2007). Likewise, for talk oriented around concept building, speakers reveal their analyses in the unfolding of talk as they build a conceptualization of their topic, sometimes referred to as *ad hoc categorization* in formulation (Hauser, 2011; see Schegloff, 1972). Stevens (2021) explores the ways intersubjective analysis plays a role in construal in examples of topic formation and gestural depiction. The speaker-analysis account of utterance formation has parallels with the argumentative assumption of utterances (see Anscombre and Ducrot, 1983): speakers fashion their utterances in order to elicit possible responses. As interlocutors build their utterances, their unfolding construals afford and constrain possibilities for elaboration.

This section presents sample data and analysis from research on verbogestural reformulations in second language concept development as observed in explanation discourse (Stevens, 2021).[1] The examples come from a classroom task in which students were paired to explain a given stimulus. Hence the context involves peers in interaction in epistemic asymmetry to one another (Heritage, 1984). Additionally, as spoken language usage events (Cienki, 2015), the

---

1   Data for these examples comes from the second language multimodal corpus of Chinese Academic Written and Spoken English (CAWSE). See Stevens, Chen, and Harrison (2020) for details. Requests for corpus materials can be accessed at https://cawse.transcribear.com/

students' explanations are interspersed with an array of embodied actions and non-lexical sounds not witnessed in carefully crafted written and/or hypothetical examples. Aspects of spoken language such as stops and restarts, prosodic contouring, and disfluencies can all have influence on the contingency of construal. Furthermore, these explanations display various degrees of embodied involvement in the task, where explainers often use hand configurations as techniques of depiction (Streeck, 2009). Also, as introduced in Section 3, the analysis of gestures in interaction offers a rich ecology to explore intersubjective alignment, especially in the analysis of joint attention to manual gestures. Rather than being conventional symbols or ritual performances, gestures exhibit the primacy of embodied intentionality and meaningful directedness within and towards a spatiotemporal world.

The contingencies of construal, including dynamic gestures, can thus be observed in reformulated talk. Consider how speakers can trial their characterizations of a topic-at-hand when given the opportunity to explain, presenting alternate construals both within their explanations and across subsequent trials. For instance, in excerpt (5), the explainer has been given the topic *tectonic plates*, and is tasked with explaining the types of fault lines different plates create in the Earth's crust. This particular stimulus proves to be difficult for the student, who displays at various times his uncertainty with the topic. With his peer's intervention, he is able to give more detail to his topic in subsequent iterations. The referent that becomes re-construed is highlighted with bold type.

(5) a. (Corpus file: mcht1617expo3ug2)

  02 A: er the (.) this this essay said (.) told us the

  03   **fault** (.) **fault** of the (.) vertical and (.) hori-

  04   horizontal (6) er it hh ex- describe describe the (5)

  05   three er (5) three types of the **normal faults** (1) er

(5) b. (mcht1617expo7ug2)

  08 A: err (.) ok (2) thi- this article is about hh the (.)

  09   about the **geography** (.) errr and (2) lots (.) **fault**

  10 → of (1) **fault** of the: <shakes head> hh (.) hh (13.2)

  11 C: it maybe maybe i (.) i talk to you first <laughs>

     (22 lines omitted)

  33 A: hh er er i think my too (.) too difficult for me (1)

  34   err (4) <shakes head> it's about the (.)

  35   the **movement** of the horizontal (.) er three types of the

  36   (3) fault (.) er one is (3) strike

37   <whispers> slip (3) hh
            +hand gesture: two flat palms down+
38 C: → **oh (.) oh it's about the earth (.) to movement**
            +two flat palms, moving side-to-side+
39 A: **movement** yeah
            +two flat palms, with some motion+

(5)   c.   (mcht1617exp10ug2)
       071 A: err er yeah (.) my article is about the er **earth** (1)
       072   → er the (1) er: **earth movement** of the (.) it can be
       073   → (.) divided by two **block block** of the (.) **earth** (.)
                         +power grip palm down isomorphic to
                         'block'+

Contextual factors bolster the identification of transformational motivations. For instance, when a previous participant interjects with candidate interpretations, which then become "borrowed" or reused for a new construal. In the excerpt above, alternations in the specificity of the referent appear to be interactionally motivated. The explainer begins by referencing the topic with specific details (5a), in this case in reference to *fault lines*. In the second iteration (5b), he subsequently generalizes the topic to *geography*, followed by the addition of *movement*, and in silence displays a two handed, palms down gesture (line 38). This gesture appears to motivate intervention by his addressee. While mimicking the explainer's hand movements, the addressee adds the term *earth* to create the compound *earth movement*, and simultaneously alters the original gesture by adding a side-to-side motion. This new terminology and gestural uses become taken up by the explainer in the third iteration at various points in his explanation (see 5c). The topic, as negotiated and interrogated in its level of precision, is demonstrated as contingent, given the attenuation of its construal in the different iterations of the explanation. The specificity of the topic is only understood from the perspective of the analyst, who can verify the various instances of use in each iteration. However, for the speaker the relation of specificity between iterations can be displayed in the ways that their subsequent construals provide new patterns for structuring the elaboration of the topic.

   A more complex example illustrates how the emergent, goal directed, and intersubjective nature of construal changes the trajectory of elaboration. In the alternate characterizations of the topic *flower reproduction*, the explainer, A, uses an anthropomorphic analogy in her explanation. For instance, in (6a), A characterizes the sex organs of the flower as the 'functional parts' for reproduction—*stamen* and *pistil*. The pistil contains the ovaries of the female component of the flower, but the explainer treats this aspect as requiring further specification when she elaborates into *mother*. Having traced a circular form in the air with her pen while uttering *ovary*, A simultaneously displays a form and projects the ensuing shape which she creates with her hands as she utters 'mothers' (Fig. 10.1a). The introduction of the *mother* analogy articulates a conceptual space to give further detail to the explanation—the pistil contains the ovary just as a mother does.

(6)   a. (mcht1617exp19ug2)

007 A:	**hh reproduction of a flower contains** two er main	
008	two parts [erm]	
009 B:	[nods mhm]	
010 A:	and er functional part is **stamen** and er	
011 A:	**postil** (.) postil er (.) mm (.) yes (.)	
017 A:	stamen [and pistil]	
018 B:	[oh yeah] it's (.) oh (.)	

((lines 019–031 omitted))

032 A:	er and (.) er and the st- er pistil
033	contains . er . ovary (.) ovary er just like er
	+*traces circle in air with pen*+
034	mo- **mothers** er (.) [erm]
fig 10.1:	|a--------------------------
035 B:	[uhuh]
036 A:	(.) ⟨nods⟩ you [know ⟨smiles⟩ uhuh:]
037 B:	[⟨laughs⟩]
038 A: →	mm **where . babies . stayed** [until]
039 B:	[er yeah er] yes [yes err]
fig 10.1:	|b-----------|
040 A:	[yes ovary]

a. two hands, laterally forming a rounded shape

A: "mothers"

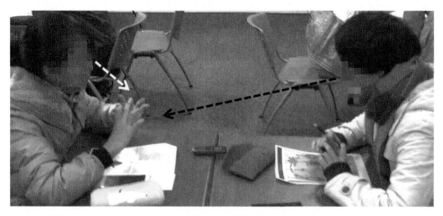

b. more precise version of (a), fingertips touching for a complete ovular shape

B: "yes er:"

FIGURE 10.1 Exchange of *ovary* gesture between explainer (A, right) and addressee (B, left).

Gaze plays a significant role in guiding the construal of gesture and verbalization. As A produces her circular gesture for 'mothers', B gazes at A's hands, but as A repeats the gesture several times, B first recreates the hand configuration, and then lifts her hands as the exchange reaches a point of fulfilled alignment on depiction of the specific term 'ovary' (Fig. 10.1b).

When paired with a new peer in (6b), A grounds the explanation in her identification as a female, and uses *herself* in place of mother for the construction of a new analogy. While other aspects of her reformulated explanation have interplay with the trajectory of her construal, we focus on her characterization of the reproductive organs. In this instance A chooses to draw these elements on a page for her addressee, C, in lieu of her previous method of using manual gestures.

(6)   b. (mcht1617exp25ug2)

112 A:	ok ok i er talk about my my article is about (.)
113	biography bio- (.) err (.) a flower's reproduction
115 C:	flower's repo-duction
116 A:	reprodu- yeah [er]
117 C:	[er] (.)
118 A:	do you know that hh (.)
119 C:	a flower
120 A:	yes a flower's (.) ⟨laughs⟩ a hh pregnant flower
121 C:	[oh i know ok ok ⟨smiles⟩]
122 A:	[⟨laughs⟩]
123 A:	[⟨laughs⟩ mm it's about two parts [mm]
124 C:	[⟨⟨nods⟩mm⟩]
125 A:	and the first is stamen and next is er er ste- mm
126	mmm pistil ok
127 C:	crystal
128 A:	pistil
129 C:	oh pistil ok ⟨nods⟩
130 A:	do you know pistil
131 C:	no=
132 A:	=⟨laughs⟩
133 C:	i want you explain to me
134 A:	the stamen (1) hh it's difficult to explain it to
135 →	you um (1) let's **if i am a flower**
136 C:	mm
137 A:	and the stamen (1) belongs to my boyfriend
138 C:	mm
139 A:	**and the pistil belong to me**
	+points to self+
140 C:	mm
141 A:	you know that [⟨laughs⟩]
142 C:	[ok ok ok ok (.) go on] (1)
143 A:	and the er in the pistil at the bottom of the pistil
144	there is a overal (1.2) [oval]
145 C:	[o-:]
146 A:	[oval] oh vee aye
	+draws a circle and points to drawing+

After initially offering her original construal, formulating the term *pregnant flower*, A reformulates her analogy in terms of herself as a female, for which a pointing gesture is sufficient to index. In Cognitive Grammar terms, the formulation serves to invite the addressee to an imagined scenario without explicitly referring to human sex organs. This can be gleaned through the overt displays of mutual embarrassment, in the form of laughter, between A and C (initially at lines 120–123, then again at lines 141 and 142). Such contextual factors enrich the analysis by offering possible explanations for the selection of terms and scenarios. In this case, the invocation of the gender roles appears salient for both the speaker's *pregnancy* analogy (A is female), and her and her addressee's possible embarrassment (because C is male).

Speakers can also attend to different aspects of a (multimodal) construal for the benefit of maintaining thematic stability, as in example (7), in which an explainer refashions his gestures coupled to the word *dream*. In this example, the speaker is attempting to explain the philosophy of *Idealism* by analogizing the *world of ideas* with the act of *dreaming*, thus drawing on a shared experience. As he says *maybe the dream*, he gestures using a palm-up open hand (Fig. 10.2a). His addressee looks at him blankly (pause in line 28), after which the explainer repeats the term *dream* while pulsing the open palm. The explainer repeats the term two more times but changes his gesture to a point to the head, and then holds the point while twirling his finger after his addressee fails to show understanding (lines 29 and 31, Figs. 10.2b, c). In the transcript for this example, the pauses are placed in bold type to draw attention to the speaker, A's, attendance to his addressee B's comprehension, or lack thereof.

(7) (mcht1617exp20ug2)

```
28 A:      maybe another example maybe the dream (0.5)
fig 10.2:          |-----------------------a---------------------------|
29         the dream [(1)            ]
           |a----------------------------|
30 B:                     [<⟨whispers⟩ dream>]
31 A:      dream (1) dream
fig 10.2:  |b-------------c-------|
32         the in the evening you make a dream (0.5)
fig 10.2:          |a--------------------b--------------|
33 B:      ⟨nods⟩
```

a. palm up   b. head point   c. head point with circu-
                                                   lar twirl

"maybe the **dream ... the**   "dream"   "dream"

FIGURE 10.2 Explainer refashions gestures as he repeats the word 'dream'.

Only after the fourth repetition and lack of response does the explainer refor-
mulate a verbo-gestural gestalt by elaborating the analogy with a contextual
scenario (Fig. 10.3). The pauses on the part of explainer demonstrate attention to his addressee's space for response, possibly to display understanding,
seek clarification, or merely process the utterance. When a lack of appropriate
response is given, the explainer redesigns his gestures, demonstrating intercorporeal analysis of the situation as a trouble in gesture, and not in the utterance
of "dream" (Stevens, 2021).

a. palm-down   b. head point and nod
"the (.) in the **evening**"   "**you** make a **dream**"

FIGURE 10.3 Speaker reformulates a scenario and verbo-gestural gestalt
           to elicit understanding of his analogy *dream* for *Idealism*.

The examples show how parties in explanation reuse, upgrade, refashion and restructure the co-conceptualization of a referent in that explanation. Rather than being an individual cognitive imposition of perspective, construal is publicly accountable in interaction, where interlocutors draw on repertoires of skillful conduct to navigate affordances for interaction. These types of studies illustrate that, at least in spoken discourse, construal is an accomplishment of multiple cognitive motivations, and that decomposing them out of context might blind the analysis to possible meanings (see Stevens, 2021; Stevens and Harrison, 2019, for more analysis into the enactive construal of gesturing).

5 Conclusion

In this chapter, we explored intersubjectivity in language by taking the reader through the use of this notion in cognitive linguistics, as well as making the case for extending the analysis of intersubjectivity to the wider, and we argue, more encompassing view of embodied intersubjectivity. We examined certain distinctions related to the transparency and explicitness of intersubjectivity in language. For instance, the approach advocated by Langacker (2008) presumes an intersubjectivity in the notion of common ground that interlocutors share in a common discourse space. Specifically, Langacker develops the concept as the firmament upon which all language events occur. Other researchers, such as Verhagen (2005; 2007), Rybarczyk (2015), and Möttönen (2016), have extended Langacker's conception of commonly oriented ground to examine intersubjectivity as not merely implicit in construal, but as motivating the construction of specific types of utterances. Consideration of another person can also be explicitly coded in linguistic form as a result of intersubjectification, whereby through normative, paradigmatic change, words and phrasings come to be understood as indexing intersubjective alignment and/or the perspectives of other people.

As Zlatev (2016) points out, however, returning to the philosophical roots of our modern understanding of intersubjectivity beckons us to reexamine the implicitness of intersubjectivity in the attenuation of the construal of utterances. This is done by a return to Merleau-Ponty's (1945/2012) conception of intentional, embodied perception, and his notion of intercorporeality (Merleau-Ponty, 1968), leading to a renewed understanding of intersubjectivity as simultaneously individually embodied and co-situated. On this account, although the terms intersubjectivity and intercorporeality have been used in different analytical contexts, they are merely different construals of the same phenomenon, i.e. the interrelation of multiple "lived bodies," which for the sake of clarity (and to avoid privileging the mental over the physical or reversely) can be termed embodied intersubjectivity (Zlatev, 2017). Embodied intersubjectivity entails the body as taken for granted not merely in influencing the encoding of experience over time (see Lakoff and Johnson, 1980), but also in shaping the characterization of language in specific contexts of use. If cognitive linguistics, following developments in enactive cognition (Varela et al., 1991; Thompson, 2007; Di Paolo, et al., 2018; inter alia), embraces the lived experience as both guiding and transforming meaning and communication, several research threads can be tied together. The transformational power of experiential action, including communication, fits well with studies that reveal the bidirectional nature of metaphors. For example, Matthews and Matlock (2011) and Rybarczyk (2015) show how distance coded linguistically impacts judgments about physical distance between interacting subjects. Furthermore, studies in multimodality that investigate image-schematic analogies between language, music, and visual arts increasingly note that social and cultural situatedness complements the embodied experience (see Górska, 2020: 5–7; Górska, 2014). Thus, the theory of image schemas is currently being extended to view embodied experience as experience derived not from *having* a body, but from *encountering the world as bodied beings*: living, feeling, and thinking through the body in culturally grounded societies.

In considering the intercorporeal nature of human experience in language, we can observe how speaker utterances and embodied actions, such as gestures, are construed for mutual understanding, thus enabling a particular construal to be mutually recognizable and its meaning to be co-conceptualized. To better observe intersubjective contingencies in action, the study of reformulated utterances gives access to alternate construals of a referent, as we illustrate in the analyses given. These analyses show how "the sharing of affective, perceptual, and reflective experiences between two or more subjects" (Zlatev, 2008: 215) in interaction motivates how speakers fashion their utterances for joint attention. Studying the interplay of construals in actual encounters thus expands the theory of meaning, and generates testable hypothesizes that can be investigated in different methodologies. We suggest that going forward in exploring intersubjectivity in meaning, cognitive linguistics has to (i) revisit the phenomenological accounts of intersubjectivity, (ii) respond to developments in theories on cognition, and (iii) develop appropriate methodologies.

Acknowledgments

We wish to thank Elżbieta Górska and Gustavo Gómez Pérez, as well as two anonymous reviewers, for their insightful comments on an earlier draft of this chapter. Any remaining flaws or errors are solely our own.

References

Andrén, Mats. 2012. The social world within reach: Intersubjective manifestations of action completion. *Cognitive Semiotics* 4(1): 139–166. Available at https://doi.org/10.1515/cogsem.2012.4.1.139.

Anscombre, Jean-Claude and Oswald Ducrot. 1983. *L'argumentation dans la langue*. Brussels: Editions Mardaga.

Arnheim, Rudolf. 1969. *Visual Thinking*. Berkeley: University of California Press.

Barlow, Michael and Suzanne Kemmer. 2000. *Usage-based models of language*. Stanford: Center for the Study of Language and Information.

Boogaart, Ronny and Alex Reuneker. 2017. Intersubjectivity and grammar. In B. Dancygier (ed.), *The Cambridge Handbook of Cognitive Linguistics*, 188–206. Cambridge, UK: Cambridge University Press. Available at https://doi.org/10.1017/9781316339732.013.

Brems, Lieselotte, Lobke Ghesquière and Freek Van de Velde. 2014. Intersections of intersubjectivity. In L. Brems, L. Ghesquière and F. Van de Velde (eds.), *Intersubjectivity and Intersubjectification in Grammar and Discourse: Theoretical and Descriptive Advances*, 1–5. Amsterdam: John Benjamins.

Casad, Eugene H. and Ronald W. Langacker. 1985. 'Inside' and 'outside' in Cora grammar. *International Journal of American Linguistics* 51(3): 247–281.

Cienki, Alan. 2015. Spoken language usage events. *Language and Cognition* 7(4): 499–514.

Croft, William. 2009. Toward a social cognitive linguistics. In V. Evans and S. Pourcel (eds.), *New directions in cognitive linguistics*, 395–420. Amsterdam: John Benjamins.

Croft, William and D.A. Cruse. 2004. *Cognitive Linguistics*. New York: Cambridge University Press.

Dancygier, Barbara and Eve Sweetser (eds). 2012. *Viewpoint in Language: A Multimodal Perspective*. Cambridge, UK: Cambridge University Press.

Deckert, Mikołaj. 2017. Construing temporal magnitudes: Implications for event conceptualisation. *Cognitive Semantics* 3(2): 217–237. Available at https://doi.org/10.1163/23526416--00302005.

Di Paolo, Ezequiel A., Elena Clare Cuffari and Hanne De Jaegher. 2018. *Linguistic Bodies: The Continuity Between Life and Language*. Cambridge, MA: MIT Press.

Etelämäki, Marja and Laura Visapää. 2014. Why blend conversation analysis with cognitive grammar? *Pragmatics. Quarterly Publication of the International Pragmatics Association (IPrA)* 24(3): 477–506.

Fauconnier, Gilles. 1994. *Mental Spaces: Aspects of Meaning Construction in Natural Language*. Cambridge, UK: Cambridge University Press.

Foolen, Ad. 2012. The relevance of emotion for language and linguistics. In A. Foolen, U.M. Lüdtke, T.P. Racine and J. Zlatev (eds.), *Moving Ourselves, Moving Others*, 349–368. Amsterdam: John Benjamins.

Gallagher, Shaun and Dan Zahavi. 2012. *The phenomenological mind* (2nd ed.). London: Routledge.

Gärdenfors, Peter. 1999. Some tenets of cognitive semantics. In J. Allwood and P. Gärdenfors (eds.), *Cognitive Semantics: Meaning and Cognition*, 19–36. Amsterdam/Philadelphia: John Benjamins.

Garfinkel, Harold. 1967. *Studies in Ethnomethodology*. Englewood Cliffs: Prentice-Hall.

Geeraerts, Dirk and Hubert Cuyckens. 2007. Introducing Cognitive Linguistics. In D. Geeraerts and H. Cuyckens (eds.), *The Oxford Handbook of Cognitive Linguistics*, 3–21. Oxford: Oxford University Press.

Górska, Elżbieta. 2014. Why are multimodal metaphors interesting? The perspective of verbo-visual and verbo-musical modalities. In M. Kuzniak, A. Libura and M. Szawerna (eds.), *From Conceptual Metaphor Theory to Cognitive Ethnolinguistics. Patterns of Imagery in Language*, 17–36. Frankfurt am Main: Peter Lang.

Górska, Elżbieta. 2020. *Understanding Abstract Concepts Across Modes in Multimodal Discourse: A Cognitive Linguistic Approach*. New York: Routledge.

Górska, Elżbieta. 2021. Analysing language and multimodal discourse by means of the NEAR-FAR image schema. *Prace Filologiczne* 76(1): 129–150.

Grady, Joseph. 1997. *Foundations of meaning: Primary metaphors and primary scenes*. Berkeley: University of California Berkeley.

Harrison, Simon. 2018. *The Impulse to Gesture: Where Language, Minds, and Bodies Intersect*. Cambridge: Cambridge University Press.

Hauser, Eric. 2011. Generalization: A practice of situated categorization in talk. *Human Studies* 34(2): 183–198. Available at https://doi.org/10.1007/s10746--011--9184-y.

Haviland, John B. 2000. Pointing, gesture spaces, and mental maps. In D. McNeill (ed.), *Language and Gesture*, 13–46. Cambridge, UK: Cambridge University Press.

Heinämaa, Sara. 2013. Merleau-Ponty: A phenomenological philosophy of mind and body. In A. Bailey (ed.), *Philosophy of Mind: The Key Thinkers*, 59–83. London: Bloomsbury.

Heritage, John. 1984. A change-of-state token and aspects of its sequential placement. In J. Maxwell Atkinson and John Heritage (eds.), *Structures of Social Action*, 299–345. Cambridge: Cambridge University Press.

Herlin, Ilona and Laura Visapää. 2016. Dimensions of empathy in relation to language. *Nordic Journal of Linguistics* 39(2): 135–157. Available at https://doi.org/10 .1017/S0332586516000111.

Husserl, Edmond. 1960. *Cartesian Meditations: An Introduction to Phenomenology*. Dorion Cairns (transl.). Dordrecht: Springer.

Ishino, Mika. 2007. Intersubjectivity in gestures: the speaker's perspective towards the addressee. In S. Duncan, J. Cassell and E.T. Levy (eds.), *Gesture and the Dynamic Dimension of Language: Essays in Honor of David McNeill*, 243–250. Amsterdam: John Benjamins.

Jensen, Thomas Wiben, Sarah Bro Trasmundi, Marie Skaalum Bloch and Sune Vork Steffensen. 2019. "You know it, how I feel, I mean you just did it:" The emergence of we-ness through re-enactment in psychotherapy. *Cognitive Semiotics* 12(2): 20192017. Available at https://doi.org/10.1515/cogsem-2019--2017.

Johnson, Mark. 1987. *The Body in the mind: The bodily basis of meaning, imagination, and reason*. Chicago: University of Chicago Press.

Johnson, Mark. 2007. *The Meaning of the Body: Aesthetics of Human Understanding*. Chicago: University of Chicago Press.

Kendon, Adam. 2004. *Gesture: Visible Action as Utterance*. Cambridge: Cambridge University Press.

Kimmel, Michael and Christian R. Rogler. 2018. Affordances in Interaction: The Case of Aikido. *Ecological Psychology* 30(3): 195–223. Available at https://doi.org/10.1080/ 10407413.2017.1409589.

Kok, Kasper I. and Alan Cienki. 2016. Cognitive grammar and gesture: Points of convergence, advances and challenges. *Cognitive Linguistics* 27(1): 67–100.

Ladewig, Silva H. 2014. The cyclic gesture. In C. Müller, A. Cienki, E. Fricke, S. Ladewig, D. McNeill and J. Bressem (eds.), *Body-Language-Communication: An international handbook on multimodality in human interaction*, volume II, 1605–1618. Berlin and Boston: De Gruyter Mouton. Available at https://doi.org/10.1515/9783110302028.

Lakoff, George. 1987. *Women, Fire, and Dangerous Things: What Categories Reveal about the Mind*. Chicago: University of Chicago Press.

Lakoff, George and Mark Johnson. 1980. *Metaphors We Live By*. London: University of Chicago Press.

Langacker, Ronald W. 1985. Observations and speculations on subjectivity. In J. Haiman (ed.), *Iconicity in Syntax*, 109–150. Amsterdam: John Benjamins. DOI: 10.1075/tsl.6.07 lan

Langacker, Ronald W. 1987. *Foundations of Cognitive Grammar: Theoretical Prerequisites*, volume I. Stanford: Stanford University Press.

Langacker, Ronald W. 1988. A usage-based model. In B. Rudzka-Ostyn (ed.), *Topics in Cognitive Linguistics*, 127–161. Amsterdam: John Benjamins. Available at https://www .jbe-platform.com/content/books/9789027286192-cilt.50.06lan.

Langacker, Ronald W. 1991. *Foundations of Cognitive Grammar: Descriptive Application*, volume II. Stanford: Stanford University Press.

Langacker, Ronald W. 1993. Reference-point constructions. *Cognitive Linguistics* 4(1): 1–38. Available at https://doi.org/10.1515/cogl.1993.4.1.1.

Langacker, Ronald W. 1995. Viewing in cognition and grammar. In P.W. Davis (ed.), *Alternative Linguistics*, 153–212. Amsterdam: John Benjamins. Available at https://www.jbe-platform.com/content/books/9789027276315-cilt.102.06lan.

Langacker, Ronald W. 1999a. Assessing the cognitive linguistic enterprise. In T. Janssen and G. Redeker (eds.), *Cognitive Linguistics: Foundations, Scope, and Methodology*, 13–59. Berlin: De Gruyter Mouton.

Langacker, Ronald W. 1999b. *Grammar and Conceptualization*. Berlin: De Gruyter Mouton. Available at https://doi.org/10.1515/9783110800524.

Langacker, Ronald W. 2001. Dynamicity in grammar. *Axiomathes* 12: 7–33.

Langacker, Ronald W. 2008. *Cognitive Grammar: A Basic Introduction*. New York: Oxford University Press.

Matthews, Justin L. and Teenie Matlock. 2011. Understanding the link between spatial distance and social distance. *Social Psychology* 42: 185–192. Available at https://doi.org/10.1027/1864-9335/a000062.

McNeill, David. 2005. *Gesture and Thought*. Chicago: University of Chicago Press.

McNeill, David. 2016. *Why We Gesture: The Surprising role of hand movements in communication*. Cambridge: Cambridge University Press.

Merleau-Ponty, Maurice. 1968. *The Visible and the Invisible*. Alphonso Lingis (transl.). Evanston: Northwestern University Press.

Merleau-Ponty, Maurice. 2012. *Phenomenology of Perception*. Donald A. Landes (transl.). London: Routledge.

Meyer, Christian, Jürgen Streeck and J. Scott Jordan. 2017. Introduction. In C. Meyer, J. Streeck and J.S. Jordan (eds.), *Intercorporeality: Emerging socialities in interaction*, xv–xlix. New York: Oxford University Press.

Möttönen, Tapani. 2016. Dependence of construal on linguistic and pre-linguistic inter-subjectivity. *Nordic Journal of Linguistics* 39(2): 209–229. Available at https://doi.org/10.1017/S0332586516000093.

Müller, Cornelia. 2016. From mimesis to meaning: A systematics of gestural mimesis for concrete and abstract referential gestures. In J. Zlatev, G. Sonesson and P. Konderak (eds.), *Meaning, Mind, and Communication: Explorations in Cognitive Semiotics*, 212–226. Frankfurt am Mein: Peter Lang.

Núñez, Rafael, Kensy Cooperrider, Dang Doan and Jürg Wassmann. 2012. Contours of time: Topographic construals of past, present, and future in the Yupno valley of Papua New Guinea. *Cognition* 124(1): 25–35.

Núñez, Rafael E. and Eve Sweetser. 2006. With the future behind them: Convergent evidence from Aymara language and gesture in the crosslinguistic comparison of spatial construals of time. *Cognitive Science* 30(3): 401–450. Available at https://doi.org/10.1207/s15516709cog0000_62.

Nuyts, Jan. 2001. Subjectivity as an evidential dimension in epistemic modal expressions. *Journal of Pragmatics* 33(3): 383–400.

Nuyts, Jan. 2014. Notions of (inter)subjectivity. In L. Brems, L. Ghesquière and F. Van de Velde (eds.), *Intersubjectivity and intersubjectification in Grammar and Discourse: Theoretical and descriptive advances*, 53–76. Amsterdam: John Benjamins.

Raymond, Chase W. 2019. Intersubjectivity, normativity, and grammar. *Social Psychology Quarterly* 82(2): 182–204. DOI: 10.1177/0190272519850781.

Rosiński, Maciej. 2018. *Metaphor activation in multimodal discourse. Case studies on the emergence of geometrical concepts*. PhD thesis, University of Warsaw.

Rybarczyk, Magdalena. 2011. My sister vs. your daughter: Perspective changes and their implicit impact on communication. *ANGLICA* 20: 121–136.

Rybarczyk, Magdalena. 2015. *Demonstratives and possessives with attitude: an intersubjectively-oriented empirical study*. Amsterdam: John Benjamins.

Sambre, Paul. 2012. Fleshing out language and intersubjectivity: An exploration of Merleau-Ponty's legacy to cognitive linguistics. *Cognitive Semiotics* 4(1): 189–224. Available at https://doi.org/10.1515/cogsem.2012.4.1.189.

Schegloff, Emanuel A. 1972. Notes on a conversational practice: formulating place. In D. Sudnow (ed.), *Language and Social Context*, 75–119. New York: Free Press.

Schegloff, Emanuel A. 1992. Repair after next turn: The last structurally provided defense of intersubjectivity in conversation. *American Journal of Sociology* 97(5): 1295–1345.

Schegloff, Emanuel A. 2007. *Sequence Organization in Interaction: A Primer in Conversation Analysis*. Cambridge, UK: Cambridge University Press.

Stankiewicz, Ewa. 2010. *Solidarni 2010*. Film Open Group. Available at http://www.youtube.com/watch?v=ulIkNG2vo3I [Accessed: 19 May, 2010].

Stevens, Michael P. and Simon Harrison. 2019. Spectrums of thought in gesture: Using gestures to analyze concepts in philosophy. *Pragmatics & Cognition* 24(3): 441–473. Available at https://doi.org/10.1075/pc.17024.ste.

Stevens, Michael P., Yu-Hua Chen and Simon Harrison. 2020. The EMI campus as site and source for a multimodal corpus: Issues and challenges of corpus construction at a Sino-foreign university. In A. Cermakova and M. Mala (eds.), *Observing the World through Corpora: Variation in Time and Space*, 377–401. Berlin: De Gruyter.

Stevens, Michael P. 2021. *The interactive ecology of construal in gesture: a microethnographic analysis of peer learning at an EMI university in China*. PhD thesis, University of Nottingham.

Streeck, Jürgen. 2009. *Gesturecraft: The Manu-facture of Meaning*. Amsterdam: John Benjamins.

Stukenbrock, Anja. 2017. Intercorporeal phantasms: Kinesthetic alignment with imagined bodies in self-defense training. In C. Meyer, J. Streeck and J.S. Jordan (eds.),

Intercorporeality: Emerging socialities in interaction, 237–263. New York: Oxford University Press.

Talero, Maria. 2012. Joint Attention and Expressivity: A Heideggerian Guide to the Limits of Empirical Investigation. In J. Kiverstein & M. Wheeler (eds.), *Heidegger and Cognitive Science*, 246–275. London: Palgrave Macmillan.

Talmy, Leonard. 1975. Semantics and syntax of motion. In J.P. Kimball (ed.), *Syntax and Semantics*, volume IV, 181–238. Leiden: Brill. Available at https://doi.org/10.1163/9789004368828_008

Talmy, Leonard. 1985. Lexicalization patterns: Semantic structure in lexical forms. *Language Typology and Syntactic Description* 3(99): 36–149.

Talmy, Leonard. 2017. *The Targeting System of Language*. Cambridge, MA and London: MIT Press.

Talmy, Leonard. 2023. Targeting in Language: Unifying Deixis and Anaphora. In F.T. Li (ed.), *Handbook of Cognitive Semantics*. Leiden: Brill.

Tomasello, Michael. 2001. First steps toward a usage-based theory of language acquisition. *Cognitive Linguistics* 11(1–2): 61–82. Available at https://doi.org/10.1515/cogl.2001.012.

Tomasello, Michael. 2003. *Constructing a Language*. Cambridge, MA: Harvard University Press.

Tomasello, Michael. 2008. *Origins of Human Communication*. Cambridge, MA: MIT Press.

Traugott, Elizabeth C. and Richard Dasher. 2002. *Regularity in Semantic Change*. Cambridge: Cambridge University Press.

Trevarthen, Colwyn. 2012. Embodied Human Intersubjectivity: Imaginative Agency, To Share Meaning. 4(1). 6–56. https://doi.org/doi:10.1515/cogsem.2012.4.1.6.

Varela, Francisco J., Evan Thompson and Eleanor Rosch. 1991. *The Embodied Mind*. Cambridge, MA: MIT Press.

Verhagen, Arie. 2005. *Constructions of Intersubjectivity: Discourse, Syntax, and Cognition*. Oxford: Oxford University Press.

Verhagen, Arie. 2007. Construal and perspectivization. In D. Geeraerts and H. Cuyckens (eds.), *The Oxford Handbook of Cognitive Linguistics*, 48–81. Oxford: Oxford University Press.

Verhagen, Arie. 2008. Intersubjectivity and the architecture of the language system. In J. Zlatev, T.P. Racine, C. Sinha and E. Itkonen (eds.), *The Shared Mind: Perspectives on Intersubjectivity*, 307–331. Amsterdam: John Benjamins. Available at DOI: 10.1075/celcr.12.17ver.

Verhagen, Arie. 2015. Grammar and cooperative communication. In E. Dabrowska and D. Divjak (eds.), *Handbook of Cognitive Linguistics*, 232–252. Berlin: De Gruyter Mouton.

Waugh, Linda R., Bonnie Fonseca-Greber, Caroline Vickers, and Betil Eröz. 2007. Multiple empirical approaches to a complex analysis of discourse. In M. Gonzalez-Marquez, I. Mittelberg, S. Coulson and M.J. Spivey (eds.), *Methods in Cognitive Linguistics*, 120–148. Amsterdam: John Benjamins.

Winter, Bodo and Teenie Matlock. 2013. Reasoning about similarity and proximity. *Metaphor & Symbol* 28: 1–14. DOI: 10.1080/10926488.2013.826529.

Zahavi, Dan. 2001. Beyond empathy: Phenomenological approaches to intersubjectivity. *Journal of Consciousness Studies* 8(5–6): 151–167.

Zima, Elisabeth and Geert Brône. 2015. Cognitive Linguistics and interactional discourse: Time to enter into dialogue. *Language and Cognition* 7(4): 485–498. Available at https://doi.org/10.1017/langcog.2015.19.

Zlatev, Jordan. 2008. The co-evolution of intersubjectivity and bodily mimesis. In J. Zlatev, T.P. Racine, C. Sinha and E. Itkonen (eds.), *The Shared Mind: Perspectives on Intersubjectivity*, 215–244. Amsterdam: John Benjamins.

Zlatev, Jordan. 2010. Phenomenology and Cognitive Linguistics. In D. Schmicking and S. Gallagher (eds.), *Handbook of Phenomenology and Cognitive Science*, 415–443. Dordrecht: Springer Netherlands. Available at https://doi.org/10.1007/978--90--481--2646--0_23.

Zlatev, Jordan. 2016. Turning back to experience in cognitive linguistics via phenomenology. *Cognitive Linguistics* 27(4): 559–572.

Zlatev, Jordan. 2017. Embodied intersubjectivity. In B. Dancygier (ed.), *The Cambridge Handbook of Cognitive Linguistics*, 172–187. Cambridge, UK: Cambridge University Press. Available at https://doi.org/10.1017/9781316339732.012.

Zlatev, Jordan. 2018. Meaning making from life to language: The Semiotic Hierarchy and phenomenology. *Cognitive Semiotics* 11(1): 20180001. Available at https://doi.org/10.1515/cogsem-2018--0001.

Zlatev, Jordan and Johan Blomberg. 2016. Embodied intersubjectivity, sedimentation and non-actual motion expressions. *Nordic Journal of Linguistics* 39(2): 185–208. Available at https://doi.org/10.1017/S0332586516000123.

CHAPTER 11

Cognitive Semantics: Conceptualization, Identity (Politics), and the Real World

Peter Harder

1 Introduction

> Identity is the theme that underlies many political phenomena today, from new populist nationalist movements, to Islamic fighters, to the controversies taking place on university campuses. We will not escape from thinking about ourselves and our society in identity terms. But we need to remember that the identities dwelling deep inside us are neither fixed nor necessarily given to us by our accidents of birth. Identity can be used to divide, but it can and has also been used to integrate. That in the end will be the remedy for the populist politics of the present.
>
> FUKUYAMA, 2018: 182–183

As argued by George Lakoff in *The Political Mind* (2008), cognitive semantics can offer a potentially crucial contribution to the understanding of politics. In describing the role of conceptual models and frames, Lakoff shows what is missing in the classic position that Lakoff calls "old enlightenment reason," and why that is a problem especially for progressives who see themselves as the modern champions of the enlightenment: "Old enlightenment reason" is based on a narrow, objective view of rationality, and because it fails to recognize the role of the conceptual frames and narratives that people identify with, it fails to address a crucial factor in people's political choices. (In its full-fledged "political science" manifestation, old enlightenment reason is embedded in the "rational choice" model of democracy, cf. e.g., Olson, 2011).

Since then, issues of identity have steadily grown in political importance, as illustrated by the political developments in Poland and Hungary and the American election in 2020. Rather than being understandable as a dimension among others in democratic politics, it has come to be a rival to the whole institutional framework of democracy, threatening to override the processes of shared participation on which democracy depends. Lakoff's claim (2008: 11) that democracy is in mortal danger would now strike fewer people as a rhetorical exaggeration (cf. also Applebaum, 2020; Levitsky and Ziblatt, 2018; Mounk,

2018). The aim of this paper is to reassess the contribution of identity-oriented conceptual models to the political process in a situation where identity has become a dominant issue. I share Lakoff's agenda in focusing on weaknesses of the ways in which identity is addressed by progressive forces. The urgency of this agenda is underlined by the striking electoral successes of right-wing identity politics across the world.

I argue that an analysis of the role of conceptualizations in this crisis of democracy needs to pay increased attention to the way in which conceptualizations related to identity are anchored in non-conceptual aspects of the political landscape. A key dimension is the grounding of conceptualizations in the social dimension (discussed in depth in *Meaning in Mind and Society*, Harder, 2010).

In pursuing this agenda, I argue for three points:

(1)   The analysis of conceptual aspects of identity politics needs to address the relation between conceptual and non-conceptual factors

(2)   These relations can be understood in the light of the cognitive-semantic notion of grounding, with three forms being central: bodily, social and factual grounding

(3)   Based on grounding relations, one can more revealingly discuss adequacy criteria and strategic implications of conceptualizations invoked in relation to identity-political issues.

The paper aims to contribute to what Lakoff called the "New Enlightenment"— the revised and expanded picture that recognizes the force of conceptualizations while at the same time including strategies to prevent conceptual framing from being used in the service of lying and cheating (2008: 268).

A word on a key civic aspect of this analysis: I try to show why a conceptual model can look just fine based on purely conceptual criteria, and still not provide adequate political guidance. Academics have been trained specially to handle complex conceptualizations, which means that they are liable to the occupational hazard of overestimating the power of purely conceptual models. I regard intellectuals as having important obligations in relation to public debates, also with respect to identity politics, and therefore I think the danger of overestimating the role of favored conceptual models is an important potential hazard in public debates.

In principle, a discussion of identity in a political context would need to be based on a balanced sample of cases from different cultures across the world. The discussion below, unfortunately, does not live up to this requirement, for reasons of space as well as knowledge limitations. The analysis draws on examples from the Danish context, partly because this is my home ground, but partly also because I think that the basic issues I address may stand out more clearly if viewed apart from the specifics of the dominant Anglophone contexts.

The paper is structured as follows: In section 2, I discuss the social and factual grounding of conceptualizations. In section 3, I discuss the conceptual and non-conceptual aspects of identity, focusing on embodied grounding. In section 4, I outline the core dilemma raised by identity politics: the choice between focusing on group identity or common humanity. In section 5, I take up some key conceptualizations associated with the focus on separate group identities, whiteness and intersectionality. In section 6, I address the right wing of identity politics. Section 7 analyses the complex issue of contested conceptualizations in the area of racism. In section 8, I take up the issue of the adequacy of conceptualization from an academic, analytic perspective. In section 9, I analyze the relations between issues of truth and the rival socially grounded conceptualizations for strategic purposes: what problems do they face? Section 10 sums up the conclusions.

2   The Social and Factual Grounding of Conceptualizations

The role of grounding is a centerpiece of cognitive linguistics. The most familiar form is bodily grounding, but grounding also covers other forms of relations with the context, as in Langacker's terminology where it refers to the process whereby a type is anchored in a concrete instance (cf Langacker, 1991). The issue in general also encompasses other relations with the contextual basis for understanding (cf. also Sinha, 1999; Zlatev, 2005). The general framework for understanding foundational relations in terms of grounding is an "ontology of levels," where higher and more complex levels are based on simpler levels without being reducible to them (cf. Køppe, 1990: Verhagen, 2021). Below I am going to discuss the role of two forms of grounding that have not attracted so much attention: *social* grounding and *factual* grounding.

In addressing the topic of the social grounding of conceptual models, especially in a political context, a cognitive semanticist is in the same territory as an analytic approach based on social constructionism. To some extent, the two approaches have overlapping agendas; for instance, the famous Foucault-inspired analysis of orientalism (cf. Said, 2003 [1978]) can be seen as an analysis of the conceptual framing historically imposed upon Asia by the West. Accordingly, many authors (including myself) recruit insights from both traditions, cf. Hart (2007), Hart and Lukes (2007), Charteris-Black (2004) Chilton (1996; 2004).

However, in stressing the importance of grounding, the approach I adopt aligns itself with the tradition of cognitive semantics rather than social constructionism. In pursuing this agenda, I take up some points associated with critical theory in the social constructionist tradition and show how an approach in terms of grounding can enrich the analysis.

Two quotations may serve to illustrate this point. The following passage from a work on terrorism demonstrates that the thrust of social constructionism is to highlight the power of discourse to shape social reality, downplaying the role of any foundational factors:

> Do we perhaps, beyond its fables and follies, pretend to know what terrorism is? No, indeed, we question the very possibility of defining, and thereby giving a satisfactory account of, the facts categorized as terrorism. Our goal is not to elaborate yet another typology, but rather to redirect the study of terrorism into an examination of the very discourse in which it is couched. As is the case with other discourses of the postmodern world we inhabit, the terrorist signifiers are free-floating and their meanings derive from language itself.
>
> ZULEIKA and DOUGLASS 1995

In relation to identity, this orientation manifests itself in an emphasis on the extent to which identity arises in discourse alone. The passage below is part of a social constructionist critique of a range of authors for allowing a role for an identity that is less than completely based on linguistic discourse:

> (....) We find this same lack of consistency in Bauman's article on language and identity (2000). Bauman also begins his text by stating clearly that identity is a linguistic construct. He tries to emphasize the individual's agency by introducing the notion of 'performance', saying that linguistic performances are the loci in which identity is constructed. Nevertheless, Bauman continues to talk about 'performative display' (Bauman 2000:3, my emphasis), thus suggesting an external reality which is only 'displayed' or represented through performance.
>
> VERSLUYS 2007: 94–95

As illustrated above, the kind of social embedding that is central to social constructionism is predicated on the power of ongoing processes of linguistic interaction, stressing the absence of a priori foundations and essences. An analysis based on grounding stands in contrast to this view by highlighting the importance of the ways in which conceptual meaning is understood on a basis that is already there.

Social grounding covers the ways in which conceptualizations are anchored in the previously established community in which an utterance belongs—

relations between conceptualizations and existing people and practices in the community. There are many types of social grounding, some more stable than others; the most stable forms include the operational social constructions discussed below; the most ephemeral include being the momentary subject of attention in a sudden shitstorm on social media.

Social grounding includes a variational dimension (familiar from sociolinguistics): like phonetic variants, conceptualizations are not homogeneously distributed across the community. In addition to this type of "lectal" variation, the variational dimension of conceptualization includes the issue of *contested* concepts. Such concepts are not only understood differently by social groups—the fact that they are contested means that these groups are battling for the same turf. Each group thinks its own conceptualization is the right way of addressing the issue to which it applies, and the others are wrong, cf. Gallie (1956).

Relatively stable forms of social grounding can be analysed based on Searle's notion of "status functions" (cf. Searle, 1995). The assignment of status functions is the uniquely human way of assigning causal power to entities in the social world beyond the causal power that is due to the laws of nature. The status of being a police officer, for instance, endows a person with special powers of arrest, for instance. A key framework (but not the only one) for status function assignments is the law. Institutions based on status assignments are the groundwork of social reality, applying to everyone in the community regardless of conceptualizations at the individual level.

Institutions based on status assignments contain conceptual content that has been woven into the fabric of society, thereby constituting what I have called "operational social constructions." They differ from other forms of social grounding in that here you can use the conceptualizations to draw direct conclusions about causal consequences that go beyond the mental, conceptual level: when a type of action is legally categorized as a felony, perpetrators are liable to a penalty no matter how they may individually categorize their action. Two interdependent properties are essential for an operational social construction:

(1) acceptance: People have to collectively accept them, otherwise they cannot work—if no-one was willing to accept money as a means of payment, we could not have a monetary system.

(2) efficacy: even if people accepted the idea initially, it is only viable if the system actually works in practice. If it was not in fact possible to get goods in return for money (e.g. if there was no reliable retail infrastructure), people would cease to accept money as a means of payment.

In relation to the progressive wing of identity politics, one constituent of collective social life that is particularly salient is the *rights* that individuals can lay claim to—an issue that is crucial to marginalized groups. Some rights are formally and legally enshrined, such the basic rights of democratic societies covered by the rule of law: the right not to be thrown into jail without being put before a judge, etc.

Collective, socially grounded status is crucial to the concept of rights. As an individual you may conceive of yourself as having certain rights, but that is not enough to ensure that those rights are part of social reality. In order for an individual's rights to be real (operational), *other* people will have to accept them, and mechanisms must be in place to ensure what is necessary (the "efficacy" dimension) for the individual to be granted what she has a right to get. In order to have rights, you therefore depend on the pre-established and operationalized conceptualizations of other members of the collective community.

Social grounding is relevant both for assessing the existing state of the world and in relation to forming a strategy for change (to which we return in section 9). In both cases, the key message is that what you are dealing with is a configuration of conceptual models (ideas) and a collective group of people who may or may not subscribe to those ideas; bluntly speaking, the idea is nothing in itself. A conceptual model in your own mind is never a complete blueprint for political action. That would be the case if the only thing necessary for taking the path from individual to collective conceptual models were to put forward your idea and wait for others to accept it. However, several factors operate to make the pathway more complicated.

Other people usually do not take over your ideas by downloading a complete and immaculate copy. For one thing, other people do not necessarily share the *perspective* that is your point of departure—they have perspectives of their own. And while you may feel that other people should accept the truth of the arguments you make (if they are true!), you cannot expect other people to automatically drop their own perspectives in order to view things from the perspective you want them to have. This requires an act of solidarity and empathy on their part (more on this in the discussion of racism below).

This has implications for how to understand the slogan *the personal is political*. As a centerpiece of second-generation feminism it makes the important point that the issues facing women in a male-dominated society should not be seen as a personal problem that each individual has to face on her own. Instead, the structural factors should be identified and be the basis for a political platform. But, crucially, that precisely does not entail that problems as conceived from an individual's perspective can automatically be translated into a blueprint for collective action. The pathway from personal self-understanding to political action necessarily follows via a social process of finding common causes.

A historical example is the gradual process of women's acquisition of equal civil rights. Let us imagine that this social process had been predicated on the personal take that each woman had on the issue, and these personal takes became the political platform—instead of accepting the simplification, conceptually inadequate in many respects, that this was the same cause for all women. It is fairly obvious that the personal (conceptualization) has to be translated into a socially grounded form in order to become politically operational, including efficacious.

Furthermore, when a particular conceptualization acquires collective status, it becomes part of the individual's environment—which means that it exists in *two* places: in the individual's brain, and in the social world around her. It can only be part of the social environment because it is part of the minds of other people—but to this purely mental fact the collective status assignment is needed to add a causal power that does not follow from its presence inside people's minds. We may *think* of tax dodges as crimes, but this only becomes operational (acquires efficacy) when it is collectively recognized and enforced.

Factual grounding covers the relationship between conceptual models and those states of the world that they are meant to apply to (cf. Harder, 2010: 339–346). As will be apparent, it addresses the same agenda as the concept of truth. Truth obviously remains a centerpiece of the issue, but it is too narrow to capture the whole issue of the relation between conceptualizations and reality. A salient feature of Trump's presidency, to which we return below, is the fact that a simple appeal to the moral imperative of telling the truth has turned out to be politically irrelevant to a large part of the American electorate. Factual grounding is meant to capture other, complicating aspects of the issue: to ask about the factual grounding of a conceptual representation is a broader issue than the point-blank dilemma of truth vs falsity of a proposition. The issue of "fake news" can only be understood in the context of a struggle between competing representations and the social forces behind them.

The concept of truth raises an issue that is relevant to the question of identity in a political context in the form of the intercultural variability of core epistemological concepts, including knowledge and truth, cf. the articles in Mizumoto et al (eds., 2020). A conceivable objection to the argument below might be that truth and factuality as I understand them are concepts belonging to the western tradition, and thus are part of the hegemonic configuration that identity politics is rightly challenging.

It would take us too far to go into this argument here, but I can briefly state my own position as follows: it is the epistemological *conceptualizations*, not the *facts* that are subject to intercultural variability. The question of what counts as a belief, and as a justification of it, is fairly obviously variable across different languages and cultures (there is no obvious Danish translation of the word *belief*, for instance). Facts, in contrast, remain what they are across differences of conceptual approaches to them.

To take an example that faced a linguist friend of mine: When he arrived at his hut in the remote Papuan village where he was going to do field work, the frenzied squawking from the chicken coop called for an explanation. It turned out that the trouble was due to a twenty-foot python that was methodically swallowing one chicken after another. Reporting and assessing this piece of information involved a great deal of intercultural difference (my friend lost a great deal of his initial prestige because he did not simply draw his machete and chop up the python in pieces suitable for cooking)—but that did not affect the *factual* question of whether there really was a twenty-foot python in the chicken coop. As I understand the contributions to Mizumoto et al (2020), none of them seriously challenges this distinction, although they rightly emphasize the extent to which cultural variability affects the proper way to assess proffered contributions to understanding and addressing aspects of the situation.

The way in which the issue of factual grounding can complement a discussion of conceptualizations relevant to political choices can be illustrated with an example from Lakoff. The American dream involves a well-entrenched (= socially richly grounded) "rags-to-riches" narrative for Americans who climb the ladder to success, invoked by Barack Obama among others. As discussed above, it is not possible to ask, in a classic logical vein (where there is nothing else than truth and falsehood, because *tertium non datur*) simply whether this narrative is true or false. Truth in a classical logical universe presupposes a model of reality that is fully mapped out, so that the issue reduces to a question of correspondence between a statement and the world. In a messier, political context, where not only propositional statements but also frames, narratives and conflicting perspectives are involved, asking about factual grounding offers a broader approach to the question of the relation between conceptualizations and the world they are put forward as applying to. In this case we may thus ask, what is the factual grounding for rags-to-riches narrative?

In pursuing this question, a salient fact is that there is no "honored narrative for the reality of Americans who work hard and can't climb the ladder of success because there are no rungs on it," as Lakoff (2008:29) observes. Here we see how a well-entrenched conceptualization of life in America can be put in perspective by being confronted with reality, including aspects of reality that are left out of the picture (and this could be illustrated with classic "old-enlightenment" data such as the reduction in social mobility in recent decades, cf. Piketty, 2014).

Social and factual grounding are also both involved in understanding issues where there is a difference of perspectives involved. The variationist dimension implies that perspectives have different social groundings. Immigration may serve as an example. From the perspective of immigrants escaping from poverty and war, a policy that freely accepts immigrants into a new national community comes across in a way that is different from the one that arises naturally from the perspective of many marginalized citizens in the receiving community who are struggling to make ends meet.

I emphasize carefully that I am not arguing for any stand on the issue. The point is that if you only address the issue based on what conceptualization you find inherently most attractive, there are aspects of the political issue that your analysis does not address. Let me try to sum up the position I take in terms of a very simplified three-point trajectory.

(1)   The first stage is primitive objectivism: the human perspective is a source of error

(2)   The second stage involves two institutionally separate corrections to this view: One is the cognitive revolution, which put the role of conceptualization on the agenda. The other is social constructionism which put the role of discourse on the agenda. Because they were out to explore these new perspectives, they did not focus on relationships with (respectively) non-conceptual and non-discursive factors.

(3)   At the third stage, I try to contribute to the "new enlightenment" by using the concept of grounding in the cognitive tradition to include a more detailed account of the relation between conceptual models and the non-conceptual world—and to extend insights recruited from the discourse-based tradition in terms of grounding

For cognitive semantics, this expansion of the perspective adds a form of complexity that cannot be exhaustively addressed within the specific discipline of cognitive semantics. The reason is that the meanings in question have two sources: in addition to involving a cognitive perspective, they are the result of processes of cognitive meaning construction facing (and handling) challenges emerging from the domains of social experience that they address. Conceptualizations that address the field of economics, for instance, must be understood both from the point of view of the human conceptualizing subject and from the point of view of the phenomena that the mind is grappling with, cf. Harder (2021). The challenge can only be met by expanding the cross-disciplinary network in which cognitive semantics belongs.

3   Conceptual and Non-conceptual Aspects of Identity: The Role of Embodiment

Grounding also has implications for the core concept of this paper, identity. As a point of departure, let me use a definition[1] that is cited in the Wikipedia article on 'identity' (https://en.wikipedia.org/wiki/Identity (social_science), accessed Nov 14, 2020):

> A person's identity is defined as the totality of one's self-construal, in which how one construes oneself in the present expresses the continuity between how one construes oneself as one was in the past and how one construes oneself as one aspires to be in the future"; this allows for definitions of aspects of identity, such as: "One's ethnic identity is defined as that part of the totality of one's self-construal made up of those dimensions that express the continuity between one's construal of past ancestry and one's future aspirations in relation to ethnicity.

In this definition, identity is understood entirely in terms of conceptual construal. This idea reflects the social-constructionist approach discussed above, and pervades the notion of "identity construction," which at one time was a central part of the zeitgeist.

But identity is not something one can construct at will. Zahavi (2014: 59) points out that "who I am is isn't exclusively a question of how I understand myself. It is also a question of who I am quite independently of what I decide." As the necessary foundation, there must exist what Zahavi calls an "experiential self," a pre-conceptual basis for construals to operate on. This pre-conceptual basis is the nucleus of the grounding of conceptualizations of identity.

At the individual level, bodily grounding is basic. Whatever else a person may be, their identity is based on the body of the individual person. That body may be conceptualized in different ways, but the body itself is not a concept—

---

1   Source: Weinreich, Peter (1986). "14: The operationalization of identity theory in racial and ethnic relations." In Rex, John; Mason, David (eds.). Theories of Race and Ethnic Relations. Comparative Ethnic and Race Relations. Cambridge: Cambridge University Press (published 1988). pp. 299ff. ISBN 9780521369398. Retrieved 2018-08-30.

and conceptualizations of that body are necessarily understood in relation to the body itself, which is thus an inescapable part of one's identity.

At the collective end, a similarly uncompromising fact about identity reveals itself: any individual is born into a social context that was there before the new individual arrived. The individual may reposition herself, but processes of repositioning oneself also depend on already available sites or contexts which may serve as the parameters in terms of which new positions may be arrived at.

The social dimension, like the individual dimension, also involves bodily grounding. Genetic dispositions towards forming social bonds have multiple dimensions and layers of evolutionary history, back to co-operative foraging. One evolutionarily recent and specifically human feature is particularly relevant to identity formation. As described by Tomasello (2008), human beings are special in having the capacity for joint attention and activity. This means that they are disposed towards seeking an understanding of the world that they can have together with others. As Tomasello argues, this is what enables human beings to have languages: you cannot have a language unless you have the capacity—and disposition—to home in on a shared understanding of the words and utterances you exchange. As already pointed out by Wittgenstein, there can be no such thing as a private language: either *horse* has the shared meaning "horse," or it has no meaning at all.

The non-conceptual baseline on which construals of identity have to be constructed thus has both an individual and a social, community grounding. This imposes a necessary complexity also on the factual grounding of identity categories. This complexity can be illustrated in relation to gender identities.

As generally in the case of construal processes, the process of conceptualizing (construing) an individual (oneself, for instance) in gender-related terms is not guaranteed to be controlled by the baseline of one's actual identity. But the role of grounding means that the end product of such a process of construal— the narrative that the individual decides to identify with—does not have the last word. To give an example, a traditional male narrative of oneself might include the construal according to which one is god's gift to the female sex— and this may not have the necessary factual grounding.

This also has implications for how to understand categories of gender identity and sexual orientation. If we begin by considering the two opposite models, old-fashioned pure objectivism and pure social constructionism, the new gender identities may be understood in two contrasting ways: in objectivist (essentialist) terms, as discoveries of hitherto suppressed-and-oppressed natural kinds, or, alternatively, as an example of the freedom to construct gender categories unconstrained by the heteronormative hegemony. In both cases, by the rules of the game the result is not open to question. On the one hand, objective truth is what it is—and on the other, who can presume to have the authority to challenge a person's own adopted identity?

The account based on grounding, in contrast, can do a little bit more. The question it can ask is about the relationship between the conceptual construal and its grounding. Conceptualization plays an important role, but the issue cannot be addressed adequately without asking about the relationship between the conceptual content associated with the category and underlying reality.

I carefully emphasize that it is not part of my agenda to take any stand on gender issues: the point is to say that it is impossible to address such issues without facing the question of the relation between conceptual content and the non-conceptual basis to which the conceptualizations are applied. As shown by the existence of transgender persons, the question of grounding cannot be resolved by looking purely at objective features of the body. But this does not eliminate the issue of whether a self-construal is more or less securely grounded. A construal may turn out not to be viable—for reasons that depend not just on feedback from the social environment, but also on experiential responses from the body.

This is not just an academic issue. It has implications for the question of how to respond to the desire of adolescents for medical (including surgical) procedures in order to assume a new gender identity. Arguments for instituting such procedures are strengthened to the extent there is a solid experiential basis for the gender (self) categorization, as opposed to the extent to which this is solely a conceptual model that the individual has decided to adopt. I doubt if anyone would seriously claim that, e.g., a trans identity is purely a question of construal, for instance.

More generally, the issue I am raising here involves the risks of assuming a simplified view of the relation between conceptualizations and the wider world in which they belong. From the point of view that takes its point of departure in a conceptualization, the simplest possible relation would be the social-constructionist one in which both physical and social aspects of reality are in principle infinitely malleable. Neither biological nor social "reality" is based on essences, so once a desirable conceptual construal is available, the task is simply to translate it into lived reality. The advantage of this theory is that it leaves maximum scope for individual agency: my gender is something *I* decide. But one of the features that are involved in adopting a gender identity is sexual attraction, and few people would claim that sexual attraction is entirely subject to agentive decisions. Many people will have a clear memory of the occasion when sexual attraction first manifested itself in their personal history, which is not an experience of imposing a construal on oneself.

I now turn from the nature of identity to the political dimension.

4   Identity and Identity Politics: Group Identity vs. Common
         Humanity

The social dimension of identity is central to identity politics. The most important categories of social identity are nationality, religion, ethnic group, race and gender. In order to understand the place of such social identities in politics, one can compare with the political axis that identity politics has to some extent disrupted, namely the spectrum from left to right.

Positions on the left-to-right spectrum are traditionally understood in terms of attitudes to equality and the role of the state. Left-wing parties are in favor of ensuring an equal distribution of rights and resources across social classes. In order to bring that about, the state is necessary as the agency to enforce such redistribution by means of measures including taxation and workers' rights. Right-wing positions are in favor of letting the distribution of wealth and income develop as it may and do not see inequality as a problem. The basic values of right-wing parties are individual freedom and property rights, and measures involving state interference to ensure more equality are seen as a threat to individual freedom and as a form of oppression. To the extent wealth and social success generally is divided unequally among ethnic groups, races and genders, this is something that each individual has to face on her own.

In terms of this scale, identity politics began on the left and involved the demands of marginalized groups in society for rights that had hitherto been the privilege of the hegemonic majority. In the West, the hegemonic majority roughly speaking comprised white, Christian, heterosexual males. Against this hegemonic majority, groups of people of color, ethnic and religious minorities, women, and people with other sexual orientations began to state their claims for recognition on an equal basis.

Taking race as the example, up to a point the "Black Lives Matter" movement may be regarded as a continuation of the struggle of Martin Luther King as expressed in his *I have a dream* speech and the march to Washington. It puts on the agenda discrimination against people of color, this time focusing on the way they are treated by the police. For many international sympathizers, this is probably still the way they think about the movement.

Martin Luther King's argument was that Blacks are Americans just like everybody else and therefore have a claim to have equal rights and be treated on the basis of "the content of their character," rather than on the basis of their skin color. This is a classic humanist, universalist cause—arguing against illegitimate privilege and in favor of inclusion in the same collective body of citizens. In stressing the claim for rights to apply to everybody regardless of what group they belong to, they echo a famous feature of enlightenment visions of citizenship as defined in the French revolution, famously argued by count de Clermont-Tonnerre in his speech on Dec 23, 1789, in relation to Jews: As citizens, they have the same rights as everybody else—but they cannot at the same time assert privileges due to belonging to their own, Jewish nation.

However, the new, specifically identity-oriented aspect of the movement consists in the definition of the aims in terms of the *difference* between people of color and the majority. The movement is conceived specifically in terms of the rights of the black population. This is relevant in relation to Black Lives Matter movement. The universalist aim of achieving a state of "color-blindness" (as reflected in Martin Luther King's hopes for the future) is viewed as involving a risk of making racial injustice invisible. If the fact is that privilege is unjustly assigned on the basis of race, then forgetting about race would mean hiding injustice rather than doing away with it.

It is important to emphasize that this is still a valid point also from the traditional left-wing, universalist perspective—both at the level of purely conceptual understanding and as part of a political agenda. If privileges are distributed unequally on the basis of membership of categories of race, gender, etc., then we have to stay aware of those categories as part of social reality, otherwise we cannot address the issue of injustice in a transparent and accountable way. This can be understood as including a "group identity"-oriented *conceptual* component that at the same time remains within the purview of a collectively shared *value* system. To the extent that the identity category serves only to mark off those individuals whose unfair treatment (by universal standards) we are at the moment focusing on, they can (and should) be accommodated within a politics based on a struggle for collective shared values.

To that extent, identity politics can still be about ensuring fairness on an equal basis, not about being divisive. From a purely conceptual point of view, we can shift back and forth between two fully compatible construals: the right of an individual (to be judged as an individual human being, rather than as a member of a particular race)—and the rights of the whole race.

However, the emphasis on group rights becomes potentially divisive when the agenda based on this conceptual understanding acquires a group-based *social grounding*. When it comes to the social grounding of the "black lives matter" issue, there is a choice involved: who "owns" the conceptualization—is it a common, Martin-Luther-King-like cause, or is it the property of the Black community alone?

The Black Lives Matter movement resonated enough to attract 15,000 demonstrators at the height of the corona lockdown in Copenhagen (June 7, 2020). However, it caused dismay amid the Danish public sympathy when the organizers instructed white demonstrators to stay in a separate group, and later rejected a plea from a Danish group of sympathizers, including an Amnesty International group, to be co-organizers of another demonstration in Aalborg.

The issue can be related to the struggle in critical theory against the "us vs. them" discourse as applied to the issue of immigration (= in cognitive terms, a conceptual model viewing immigrants and "native" citizens as separate groups). At one time it was often claimed that the widespread use of this "discourse" was the principal reason for discriminatory and prejudiced treatment of immigrants; if only "natives" would desist from this practice, immigrants would be seen simply as people just like "us." In the new climate, the shoe is on the other foot: Those who do not respect the separate group identity of a marginalized group are viewed as part of the problem.

This reflects a position also found in other identitarian contexts, according to which it is only permitted for people who have personal experience of a type of injustice to address the question. A male colleague in the social sciences who took up the question of discrimination against women, afterwards received a message from a student saying that it was hardly appropriate for a privileged male professor to make pronouncements on this issue.[2]

The rejection of what is called "cultural appropriation" reflects the same emphasis on group identity. The idea is that if a white majority person adopts features associated with minority cultures (such as dreadlocks), this is a form of stealing. According to this injunction, white people ought to stay within their own cultural group identity. This attitude may be contrasted with the strand of critical (postcolonial) theory whose key concept is the notion of "hybridity," pointing out that essentialism in the study of culture and society is untenable: rather than being "pure," all social and cultural identities are subject to processes of admixture, variation and change. A frequently invoked quotation may be used to illustrate the difference of perspective: *all forms of culture are continually in a process of hybridity* (Rutherford, 1990: 211).

5   Whiteness and Intersectionality

The emphasis on group identity is also reflected in the concept of "whiteness." On a purely conceptual level, it has the important agenda of addressing the implications for the white majority of living in racially divided world. As a fore-

---

2   There is a distinction that should be kept in mind between "addressing the issue" and "speaking for the victims," in terms of which only the latter is regarded as wrong (for instance, people of color can speak for themselves and should be allowed to do so). While one can sympathize with this rationale, the point remains: group identity overrides common humanity.

runner, one may mention Orwell's dismay (while serving as a police officer in Burma) at finding himself in the role of a "sahib," described in his essay *Shooting an elephant*. However, this impeccable agenda imperceptibly shifts into something more problematic when whiteness is turned around and applied programmatically as a rationale for social division, and based on that imposed on individual human beings. When that happens, the identity category of whiteness is seen as indelibly associated with the physical property of skin color, cf. the following quotation from Nichols (2010):

> Linda Alcoff (1998) warns that it is impossible for whites to disavow whiteness. Even when a white person is completely committed to antiracist efforts, no amount of individual work renders whites ineligible for privileges (p. 12). In other words, there is no escaping the discomfort of being white.

Viewed from this perspective, predicated on racial categorization, any white individual is automatically assigned to a particular social group, with no possibility of being socially constructed in any other way, with the discomfort that it (quite properly, as understood in the extract quoted) entails.

This may be compared with the role of embodiment for one's gender identity, as discussed above. But while it is difficult to wholly deny any role of one's body for gender identity, assumptions about the role of race or skin color for who one "really" is have long been discredited. There is thus no basis for assuming any necessary relation between skin color and personal identity. To the extent this nevertheless turns out to occur, so that white individuals come to feel an inescapable discomfort, this is wholly a social construction that has become internalized. In contrast to identity viewed as self-construal, this is a construal that starts with other people. We return to identity formation imposed by others in section 7 (what people are racists?).

The differentiation may be taken further. The principle of "standpoint theory" (Anderson, 2020) is that it is necessary to take one's point of departure in understanding oppression as it applies to the specific combination of identity categories that each individual belongs to. The situation of black women cannot be understood by referring to categories of feminist theory predicated on white women. Continuing along this path, the situation of black gay women has features not captured by referring to generic gay experience or generic black experience; each group has to be considered on its own. The term "intersectionality" epitomizes this point.

Again, it is important to stay aware both of the conceptually valid points made by the differentiation and the issue that arises with differential social grounding in progressively more subdivided social groups. To repeat: one can argue for intersectionality as a tool for a progressively more fine-tuned *conceptual* understanding of issues of injustice and oppression (cf. e.g., Mattson, 2014) without necessarily being in favor of translating this conceptual understanding into an isomorphic *social fractioning* of the grounding of these conceptualization, where each conceptually separate case is the autonomous territory of separate social groups. The point is the ease with which a justified focus on *conceptualizing* a specific form of injustice can slide into an argument against seeing this issue as part of a jointly shared *social* movement.

In terms of key narratives, the complexity of the picture can perhaps be summed up in relation to an image of the transition from modernity to postmodernity, as one of Lyotard's grand narratives that is being transformed into a multiplicity of sub-narratives. The grand narrative, which has an honored place in classic enlightenment, is that of the gradual victory of liberty, equality and fraternity over oppression and inherited privilege. The question discussed above is the choice of appropriate social grounding for the sub-narratives.

6   Right-Wing Identity Politics

The focus in this paper is on analyzing the issues that are relevant to the progressive, left wing of the identity-based agenda. However, for comparison it is useful also to look at the right-wing side of the issue. Just as in 2008, one feature of the political landscape that is striking also today is the success of right-wing appeals to identity-based political agendas. While we have yet to see a takeover by identity-based agendas on the left, across the world a range of nations have acquired governments that align themselves with right-wing identity-based values. What are the reasons for this success story?

One factor is that the right wing of the identity movement is associated with national, hence nationwide identity appeals, rather than race and gender. Moreover, along with the emphasis on national identity, it involves an association with national traditions understood in relation to conceptual models associated with hegemonic configurations of culture, religion, race, and ethnic identity. The nation can thus be regarded as a metonym for "our traditional national beliefs and ways of life." Electorally, it is not surprising that appeals based on well-entrenched, collective narratives of identity tend to more powerful than appeals based on behalf of unjustly marginalized minorities.

But the social grounding of right-wing narratives also includes widespread interpretations of aspects of the modern world. In an atmosphere of insecurity due to new threatening developments in modern life, the appeal to "good old days" get added attraction. Slogans such as "making America great again" and "taking our country back" are typical of white identity movements, associated with protests against immigration and globalization. If things are going the wrong way, it is also tempting to blame old political elites. The right-wing identity movement is very roughly synonymous with populism, pitting the well-educated 'elite' that is metonymically associated with new developments against the "people" (cf. Müller 2016). This is the feature that more than anything else has unsettled the traditional left-right political axis, because many old-style centre-left voters have shifted their loyalty to new, identity-based parties that promise to bring back the good old days.

Although it operates with the whole nation as its target of identification, in terms of social grounding right wing identity politics clearly operates as a divisive factor (just like the left wing versions). This is seen most clearly in the way it uses the concept of the "people"—which defines the people as those who support the populist position, as expressed in the proverbial retort of populist rulers against their opponents: "we are the people—who are you?"

In terms of the core narrative, the American version has been the subject of a compelling empirical investigation, cf. Hochschild (2016).[3] The so-called "deep story" involves the following basic setup:

> You are patiently standing in a middle of a long line leading up a hill, as in a pilgrimage. Others beside you seem like you—white, older, Christian, predominantly male. Just over the brow of the hill is the American Dream, the goal of everyone in line. Then, look! Suddenly you see people cut ting in line ahead of you! As they cut in, you seem to be being moved back.
>
> quoted from https://globaldialogue.isa-sociology.org/the-american-right-its-deep -story/ accessed 2020.11.16.

The story is much more elaborate, but this already illustrates the way this narrative builds on the "master narrative" of the American Dream, and enacts an interpretation of present-day American reality as involving a disruption of that. It is in fact a bid for an "honored narrative," in Lakoff's terms, for those who do not make it, cf. above—one that embodies an explanation of why the American Dream no longer works and a corresponding attribution of guilt. The main guilty party is this narrative is the political elite that has allowed this to happen. They no longer represent the American people as we know it.

---

3 For an account of the same polarization problem as it manifests itself in Great Britain, cf. Goodhart (2017).

For cognitive semantics, a significant way of understanding this "deep story" was given by one of Hochschild's informants, to whom she turned for assessment of her formulation: "I live your metaphor." This resonates with cognitive semantics but in one respect it takes a different path. Cognitive semantics put on the map the realization that we live by metaphors; but in contrast to metaphors we live by as understood in the cognitive semantics tradition, the informant here inhabited a story that was not predicated on primary embodied experience, but on a particular interpretation of injustices involved in the way American social experience was going.

This conceptual metaphor, with the *social* grounding among white groups who feel let down in terms of the American dream, therefore calls for an investigation in terms of *factual* grounding. Here we may briefly invoke the account of macro-level economic developments in recent decades provided by Piketty (2014). The most salient aspect of his large-scale empirical investigation is the massive rise in inequality. Economic growth in recent decades has chiefly benefited the wealthy minority, leaving the lower half of the middle classes no better off than they were. This suggests that the "deep story" does not address the full factual basis for the sense of being let down for which it provides a conceptual interpretation and framing.

In one respect, the right-wing narrative has a social grounding which may be in danger of being overlooked by progressives: the real, socially grounded role of national identity. As pointed out above, this is a cornerstone of right-wing identity politics in America, Hungary, and Poland among others. I have addressed this issue in relation to the British case, cf. Harder (2014), and one point that is often overlooked is that the foundation of national identity is a classifying, rather than a descriptive property: membership of the collective that constitutes the nation. This feature does not depend on deconstructible narratives of the *Land of Hope and Glory* type. Membership of the national community constitutes the social grounding of a body of rights that underpin the lives of citizens. Resistance to the consequences of globalization is to some extent motivated by a sense that these rights are being eroded. To that extent, one cannot lightly dismiss the tendency to rally round the nation as merely clinging to an ideologically suspect and outmoded illusion.[4]

As an illustration case, to the extent that being (e.g.) a Danish citizen endows you with the right to the assistance of the welfare state, the classic left-wing orientation towards subverting established institutions is not an unambiguous

---

4 But naturally there are also examples in British politics of the influence of national narratives with questionable factual grounding, as illustrated by the Brexit process.

guide to improving the world. In stressing the importance of the social, collective grounding of key conceptualizations, I am arguing that the struggle for recognition of marginalized groups in fact *depends on* the ability to establish (improved) institutions at the collective level—which in democratic societies has to include acceptance by the majority. This is a key reason why grounding the core issues in separate social sub-groups is problematic (more on this in section 9).

7   Contested Conceptualizations of Racism

The conceptual landscape of identity politics has two sides. Above, the focus has been on the nature of the identities that people are fighting for. I now turn to conceptualizations of the enemy. Salient among such conceptualizations is the concept of racism.[5] Here, too, an approach in terms of social and factual grounding can throw light on important aspects of the issue.

Conceptualizations are ways of grasping reality, which is why it is necessary to explore their factual grounding. This applies to racism in two ways. First of all, it needs to be clear to what extent there is a factual basis for racist conceptualizations. I assume, with almost everybody, that this is now a discredited position. But secondly, if racism is the chief adversary, it is important to know what exactly is subsumed by the concept. It is necessary to know what one is up against—including the relationship between racism and other aspects of the (unsatisfactory) social condition.

Racism is a contested concept, which means that there are attitude-based differences in the way this concept is understood. There are two main variants: the oldest refers to a conceptualization (an ideology) according to which persons of color are inferior to white people. The newer variants include not only ethnic and religious differences, but also refer chiefly to the social practice of discrimination, rather than to an individual's belief in a particular conceptualization. This second variant thus does not assume that racism is necessarily associated with an explicit racist ideology. One can be a racist without intending to be. When discriminatory treatment of minorities is not a matter of explicit ideology or personal beliefs, the terms "systemic" or "structural" racism are used. The left wing of the identity movement typically operates with this new definition of racism, while the older definition in terms of ideology is

---

5   Racism used to be understood as covering only issues involving races defined chiefly in terms of skin color, but it has come to cover, by metonymic extension, also issues involving ethnic or religious minorities. For reasons of space I do not go into these subcategories.

more widespread in the population and especially in the more conservative segments. As is typical for contested concepts, each group regards their own understanding of the concept as the right one. Discussions about whether Denmark is a racist country or not typically involve different senses of the term.

The concept of systemic racism has given rise to some public controversy, because what it entails is not entirely clear (especially to those who prefer the older definition based on personal prejudices). It has been argued, for instance, that for racism to be truly systemic it must be enshrined in the way the system officially works, as in the days of South African apartheid. I base the discussion below on a definition in terms of which racist patterns can continue to drive the way the system works, even if they are no longer explicitly present in laws or in mentally represented attitudes. In terms of Bourdieu's concept of *habitus* (Bourdieu, 1977), the inferior treatment of people of color can be automatized so that it appears to be just "the way things are." As an example, in a social condition where people of color only have low-grade jobs, one may automatically disregard their applications for high-level jobs without ever considering why: this is simply not where they belong in terms of the way the world works (cf. also Bargh and Chartrand; 1999: on "the unbearable automaticity of being").

Recently yet another conceptual variant has arisen, a further development of the systemic variant. It is associated with a position that has been voiced by Ibram Kendi (cf. *How to Be an Anti-Racist*, 2019), in terms of which one is classified as a racist unless one is explicitly anti-racist. This is motivated by the fact that passivity underpins the systemic racism that is built into the status quo, and thus anybody who is not engaged in rooting out racism is implicitly supporting it. In terms of social grounding, this variation is even more narrowly associated with the anti-racist left.

This gradual development involves two metonymic processes. The first extends the concept from covering an explicit conceptual model to covering a societal configuration that has effects similar to those of the explicit conceptualization, namely treating people of color as inferior. The second extension metonymically transfers the sense back from the system to the individuals in the system, classing them as racist because they do not take an oppositional stance to the system's racism.

Metonymic change is part of the everyday life of languages and as such there is not much point in criticizing it. However, because of its consequences for the public discussion of racism, it needs to be handled with care. The concept of racism has been extended from a limited but well-defined domain of application to a wider and more complex range of phenomena. These processes have not spread equally across the population, and so have variational social grounding, which has strategic implications discussed in section 9.

From the perspective of the struggle against racism, they have also extended the spectrum of possibilities with respect to who or what the enemy is. In the oldest sense of the concept of racism, the enemy is well-defined: it is the conceptual model (ideology) that class people of color as inferior. Since that ideology exists in the minds of people who are racists, they are also the enemy. In the case of "systemic" racism, the target of the anti-racist struggle is the way in which the system works, and people are no longer equally central. In the last, specifically anti-racist extension of the concept, people come into the picture again, because of their lack of active resistance to the system.

When different meanings are in play, a natural response is to try to settle what the right one is. Linguists know that there is no answer to that question, especially in the case of contested concepts. Instead I am going to address the issue from the point of view of the adequacy of the spectrum of conceptualizations of racism for the jobs that are in play. The adequacy issue has two dimensions, an academic and a strategic one. From the academic point of view, we want to get an adequate grip on the topic; from the point of view of political action, I view the issue from the perspective that we want to address the issues in a way that gives the best possibilities to take democratic action for redressing injustices. These two issues form the topics of the next sections.

8   The Question of Conceptual Adequacy: Metonymy, Prototype Effects, and Polarization

From the academic point of view, adequacy is chiefly predicated on the question of factual grounding. In addressing the question of injustices, the aim must be to get a grip on the way the world works, thereby hopefully helping members of the public to make it work better. We saw how factual grounding provides a vantage point from which to asses the adequacy of conceptualizations without limiting oneself to the dichotomy between truth and falsehood.

We have also seen that in order to practice the new enlightenment we need to keep track of three complicating aspects: We need to address the question of variation and its distribution across the population; we need determine the differential relations between the variants of the concept and those realities that they are meant to apply to; and we need to keep track of differences of perspective on the same event.

This imposes a need for caution in relation to some key mechanisms explored in cognitive semantics, for instance to metonymic extension. Recognizing it as part of the way the cognitive world works does not imply that we can take for granted that metonymic extensions can be treated as unproblematic.

A salient example is the risk that if you are critical of Israel's policies, you may come across as being anti-semitic (by metonymic extension). Logically speaking it is perfectly possible to be critical of Israel without being anti-semitic: many Israeli Jews are critical of Israel's policies. But because of the risk of metonymic "contamination," situations will tend to arise when confusions arise (cf. the contested expulsion from the British Labor Party of Jeremy Corbyn, the previous leader, on charges of anti-semitism).

A different case applies to the way in which the category of racism is applied to the analysis of social problems. Let us take the problematic social situation of immigrants, to which the concept of "systemic" racism is often applied. The problem of metonymic extension then affects one possible part of this view: the assumption that immigrants' lower success rates on the labor market is due to racism.

In terms of elementary scientific methodology, statistical differences in success rates do not automatically show that racial or ethnic prejudice is the critical factor. As pointed out by Necef (2008), potential reasons for lower success rates include factors like transaction costs and education levels. In terms of the way we understand the key concept of racism, we therefore have to decide whether we are going to speak of systemic or structural racism in *all* cases of discrimination, or we want to investigate empirically whether the specific factor that triggers the discrimination practiced by the system is race. If we choose the first option, we have severed the analytic connection between social conditions and racially based habitual attitudes. In most debates about the issue, however, this connection is likely to be taken for granted. There are two reasons for that.

There is a core left-wing narrative about racism, in which ideology is crucial: people of marginalized groups are the victims of power unfairly exerted against those groups, due to ideologies (personal or systemic) that unjustly favor whites, based on a historical configuration that goes back to slavery. In terms of the new enlightenment, however, the question that we must ask in relation to racism is: exactly how much of reality does that narrative and the conceptualization it embodies cover in present-day non-conceptual social reality?

The need for asking this question is obvious if we try to understand the situation in different countries. One would not expect the situation to be exactly the same in South Africa, the USA, and Denmark, for instance. But even in cases where a diagnosis pointing to the role of systemic racism may seem obvious, such as the USA, the empirical dimension is crucial, for instance in order to assess whether things are moving in the right direction (cf. Hughes, 2020). On the level of "new enlightenment" principles, if we want to criticize the right-wing narrative of the "deep story" where ordinary Americans are being pushed aside by queue-jumpers from minority groups, for lacking factual grounding, we have to submit the left-wing narrative to the same critical procedure.

The second reason is the mechanism of prototype effects. In the case of racism, racial prejudice is clearly part of the prototype. Prototype effects (cf. Dahlmann et al., 2016) have an effect on generalizations, so that in understanding what *racism* means, understanding will tend to prioritize the prototype case—just as in understanding what *mother* means, one will tend to think first of the core case, the one that has all the attributes (birth, nurture, married-to-father, etc). When a person, an institution or a society is accused of racism, prejudice is part of the image that will be activated by prototype effects.

The risk of miscommunication because of differences of perspective and different variational conceptualization is enhanced in the case of polarization (cf. Harder, 2005; 2021). When polarization sets in, at the end of the line there is no shared middle. Instead, two opposing extremes gradually take over the field and give rise to conceptualizations that are more and more dissimilar, with less and less overlap. An approach in terms of grounding can also throw light on this phenomenon: Although polarization can be described in terms of conceptualizations, it has a non-conceptual grounding.

The social grounding of conceptual polarization is in a conflict between two groups. This in turn triggers embodied responses in the individuals involving group loyalty. Group loyalty may appear to be a form of conceptual construal, but although loyalty may be linked to a construal of what one is loyal towards, its basic nature is pre-conceptual; in-group bias has experimentally been shown to operate even in the absence of any conceptual specification of the nature of the group (cf. Dunham, 2018). Evolutionarily, the relation between polarization and conflict can be related to the fact that in a conflict, the interesting thing is whether you win or you lose—the middle ground is irrelevant: in a war, guns can only point in one out of two relevant directions. Because this is more basic than the conceptual level, you cannot meaningfully address the situation conceptually before the conflict has subsided. Group loyalty trumps (as it were) both conceptualization and truth.

This is relevant for understanding the nature of the "us-vs.-them" conceptual-model-cum-discourse. It is true that imposing an "us-vs.-them" model on a situation can cause a potentially peaceful situation to deteriorate. But it may also work the other way round: it is a (pre-conceptual, pre-discursive) conflict that drives the conceptualizations. This is likely to be the most basic case, e.g. when war breaks out (cf. Stefan Zweig's description of the climate of opinion after the outbreak of WWI in *Die Welt von Gestern*/The World of Yesterday).

The polarization factor is also the key to the differential success rates of right-wing populist parties in different countries. The division between the "elite" and "the people" feeds on the sense of conflict and resentment against the powers-that-be. The more angry people are, the more voters are likely to be driven to the extremes, including right-wing populism. The impact on the conceptual level is seen in the understanding of the two key concepts, "the people" and the "elite." In a polarized climate, populist heads of state can speak out against the 'elite' and talk about giving the government back to "the people" while systematically enriching themselves and their cronies; because the conflict is predicated on the polarized political situation, this is not felt to be a contradiction.

Polarization is also relevant to what is happening to the discussion on racism. There is little overlap between racism as involving an ideological position viewing colored people as inferior (the sense with the widest social grounding) and racism as involving a lack of commitment to the cause of anti-racism (the radical anti-racist sense). Saying that anyone who is not an active anti-racist is really a racist is structurally similar to Bush's statement after 9/11 that "if you are not with us, you are with the terrorists." The polarization is also evident in the anti-racist use of the concept of "white supremacy" (previously used mainly in relation to Nazi fringe groups) about the people who do not actively enter into the anti-racist struggle. (In the case of the Danish "Black Lives Matter" demonstrations, those who did not understand why a white group could not be accepted as a co-organizers were called white suprematists). The risk also goes for the concept of "whiteness"—as discussed above, the concept can be used to put all white people in a position that is antithetical to the interests of black people—independently of their own personal stance. This is an identity that is justified only by the anti-racist perspective, not by the social or embodied experience of the people themselves.

The key conclusion for the issue of how conceptualizations relate to the world outside conceptual universes is that if you use the concept "racism" to indicate what the adversary is, there is a great deal of uncertainty both about how addressees will understand it, and also about the targets in social reality that you are aiming at in different cases.

There is an element of economy of effort in the problem of operating with a too direct relationship between one's favorite conceptualizations and the facts to which these conceptualizations are meant to apply. Invoking a concept in its prototype variety is the easiest option. Since racism and sexism obviously are issues that need to be addressed, we have to accept that this is a practice that we are not going to be able to avoid. But as language persons, we have to know when language is a blunt instrument—and have something to say about what is missing.

9   Truth and the Strategic Issue

It is not the purpose of an academic article to prescribe a course for political activism. Although it is not hard to guess what the main tenor of my advice would be, the discussion about strategy below should be understood as another part of the analysis, addressing the "applied" perspective on the issue. How can one rationally (in a way consistent with the new enlightenment) use conceptualizations and their social grounding to pursue the struggle for improving the status of oppressed groups, including marginalized majorities?

The crucial aspect here is the relation between conceptualizations in themselves and their community-level status. For democratic states, the key political conceptualizations are those that are collectively grounded as foundations of the processes of democratic decision-making. There cannot be a democratic government unless there is enough social trust that citizens accept the government that is the outcome of a collective process of "status-assignment," even if they did not vote for it. Democratic changeovers can only happen if we assign (collectively) the status of legitimate government to duly elected officials. Like all collective status assignments this process depends on mutual trust—just as the only reason we accept paper money is trust in the collective processes that sustain the value of money.

A concept whose society-level status is of special importance for rational, enlightened action is *truth*. A main point for the new enlightenment is that truth, like all other concepts, is dependent on social processes of acceptance if it is to become operational in the way the world works. This is, in a sense, to take the point argued by social constructivists and turn it on its head.

Social constructionists observed correctly that the things that we take to be true arrive at that status by means of social processes. (Education and scientific discussion are also social processes). This discovery (temporarily?) took attention away from the issue of how to assess whether the statements that achieve the *status* of facts are *actually* true or not. For the new enlightenment to become operational, however, it is an essential presupposition that some descriptions are better approximations to truth (have better factual grounding) than others, and some statements are completely false (have no factual grounding), even if influential people may claim otherwise.

Hence, truth is crucially dependent both on the social process and on the facts of the matter; both relations are essential. The *concept* of truth is essential as a starting point, but truth understood as one of two possible values assigned to propositions is not enough; only an extended account that includes the issues of social and factual grounding will suffice to understand how truth can be made to sustain the social role for which it is needed.

One way of putting it is that truth needs to be *properly* socially constructed. This requires that, at the collective level, we need to co-operate about getting as adequate a picture of the way the world works as we can, as the basis for deciding what rational-and-democratic decisions to make. To the extent that collaboration breaks down due to polarization, and people cling to their separate truths, the chances of enlightened collective political action deteriorate.

The name that will occur to most people here is probably Donald Trump, but it is important to maintain an awareness of the structural aspect of the problem. The fact that the problem also affects the other pole can be illustrated with a Danish case of manslaughter that was caught up in an international discussion about racism (it was covered by New York Times). The victim was black, and one of the two brothers who confessed to the crime had a tattoo with a swastika and the legend "white power," so it clearly conformed to a familiar pattern of violent racism. However, both the prosecutor and the defense pointed out publicly that the three people had in fact been close friends for several years, and the crime was due to a claim by the mother of the two brothers to have been sexually molested by the victim. This did not stop the discussion, however; the head of the Danish Black Lives Matter movement as well as a number of other left-wing debaters maintained that the crime had to be understood as due to structural racism in Denmark (cf. the Danish newspaper *Politiken*, Nov 30, 2020), and the Black Lives Matter spokesperson used the term *lynching* about the case.

For the point I would like to highlight here, it is irrelevant if in fact the killers were secretly motivated by racial prejudice or not. The point is to do with the relation between the status of the narrative (including the conceptual construal) of racial injustice and the status of the legal institution, i.e. the collective "operational social construction" of the law. Those who criticized the police for not including a charge of racially motivated violence have not offered concrete evidence that the motivation had to do with race. To put pressure on the legal system for including a charge for which no evidence has been found is to put a preferred conceptual construal above the workings of the collective, institutional framework. In this very specific sense, it is analogous to Donald Trump claiming that his defeat was due to voter fraud without offering evidence for his claim.

Let me try to be quite clear here: it is of course entirely permissible to point to those features of the event which make it natural to place it within a pattern of racially motivated violence, and also to point to evidence that the Danish police have generally been too averse to addressing the racial aspect of violent crime. The red line I want to point to is the attempt to let the narrative of racial injustice interfere with the workings of the collectively shared judicial system.

That this was the intention was clear from the fact that although racism was not included in the charge, it was claimed as a victory for the Black Lives Matter demonstration that the punishment was set at the maximum level.

This raises the question of what the collectively recognized processes for the proper social construction of truth should be. Previously, there was a pattern whereby assumptions of the elite gradually percolated through the system, cf. Zaller (1992). This pattern was no guarantee that the truth would win out; there is a clear similarity with Marx's observation that the thoughts of the rulers become the ruling thoughts (Marx/Engels, 1932: 35). Nevertheless, the widespread loss of faith in science and traditional media that is collateral damage from the polarization between traditional elites and populists leaves us with the question of how in future we are going to socially construct the truth together. Social media can hardly pretend to be a plausible alternative solution.

As already pointed out, status assignments that grant rights to citizens also depend on collective social construction. Among them are constitutional rights like the rule of law and property rights. When it comes to rights, marginalized minorities thus depend on establishing a state of "operational" acceptance-cum-efficacy in collaboration with the majority.

It is easy to see why this is infuriating. Why should it depend on the hegemonic majority to grant rights that minorities should have as a matter of course in the eyes of all right-minded people? But from the point of view of the new enlightenment, this annoying situation is due to the constitutive status of rights: there has to be a collective community that is strong and operational enough to grant rights so that they acquire the necessary "efficacy"—and there has to be enough mutual trust and co-operation so that rights can be extended beyond the hegemonic majority who could in principle afford to ignore the marginalized groups. If everybody is fighting for themselves only, the question of minority rights does not arise. The baseline for the process of struggling for improved rights for minorities sets up a strategic imperative: success for the goals of identity groups fighting for recognition depends on successful relations with the overall collective community, including the infuriating majority.

This creates a strategic quandary for the situation whereby identity groups have increasingly operated with a social grounding of their identity struggles in their separate communities, instead of seeking to ground their struggle in a common, collective-level movement for equal rights. One can understand and sympathize with the idea that minority groups need to work out their own conceptualizations of experiences and perspectives that the majority can never share, rather than beginning with abstract overall categories that do not fit their own lived reality. But this does not entail that the *social* groundings must necessarily be separate.

Let us go back to the argument presented in the introduction, claiming that it is simplistic to try to change the world by just producing the right conceptualization and then wait for the world to adjust to that conceptualization. What, in principle, is the difference between that simple model and a model based on social grounding?

The crucial difference is that the social world does not run on conceptualizations alone.

It is not just a matter of installing a new conceptualization in people's minds. The conceptualizations that people operate with are grounded in their non-conceptual reality. Change by means of new and better conceptualizations thus interferes not just with people's minds, but with their whole lived reality. First of all, this is something that takes work to do—and secondly, if you want to change people's lived reality, you cannot expect to be able to do that without involving them in the process. This is true both for elementary human reasons and for reasons that are bound up with democracy.

This is a problem for a strategy predicated on each unjustly treated group setting up its own preferred conceptual model, rejecting attempts from external sympathizers, requiring instead the world to simply adjust. The hegemonic majority is not the only obstacle. Let me mention the unhappy case of the quarrel between groups representing what may be called "traditional" lesbians as opposed to transgender females, acronymically known as the TERF wars. This has been an exceptionally acrimonious confrontation; but in this context the point is not who is to blame, but the fact that conceptualizations of identity are not something each segregated group can simply expect other people to accept. Nobody can know in advance what the response of lesbians will be in a situation when the question is how to define the status of persons who identify as women but who have male genitals. Their mutual status relations in collective life have to be worked out in a social process whose precise outcome cannot be stipulated based on each group's conceptual criteria alone.

This issue of course does not magically disappear if the struggle for recognition is grounded in a shared social process. However, it is framed differently—and in a way that leaves room for addressing potential difficulties—when the goal is to include all groups in a collective "we" (the Martin Luther King model). There is work to be done, as pointed out above. This takes patience, but it is worth pointing out that such struggles are not hopeless. In identity politics in the US, a fairly recent example of progress is the achievement for gay people of the right to marriage and the right to serve in the American army. At the time of writing, the first black woman vice president in American history has just been elected. Majorities are not necessarily intransigent (but they sure take their time!)

This is relevant for the use of the term racism, as analyzed above; conceptual adequacy has implications for strategic adequacy. Metonymic extensions and prototype effects militate against shared understanding of the issue, when the term is used in communication with people who are not part of the variational segments that are familiar with the concept of structural or systemic racism. If they do not entertain any conceptualization of people of color as inferior, they will feel unjustly treated if their community is described as racist. The prototype effects will be reinforced by the mechanism Fauconnier calls "achieving human scale" (Fauconnier and Turner, 2002: 312): racism in human scale involves *people* who are racists—systemic racism is more abstract and less tangible. Appeals to "converging evidence" are part of the same pattern: all indications are taken to support one overarching factor conceptualized as "racism" as the target.

A similar strategic issue arises in connection with the concept of whiteness, especially in the form in which a white person who subscribes to this race-based identity category must feel uncomfortable. As pointed out by Tajfel (1981), it is a pervasive feature of human life that people want to feel good about the group to which they belong. A consequence of that is also that forming stereotypes about other groups in order to profile your own group to advantage is also a pervasive feature of social life. This may sound unpleasantly jarring in relation to ideals of universal humanity, but Tajfel can perhaps assert this without suspicion of promoting racial profiling, since his entire family was wiped out in the holocaust. Tajfel's observations suggest that a conceptualization of white majorities as people who ought to be ashamed of themselves is ill positioned to gain universal social acceptance.

The conceptualization of racism according to which it applies to all people who do not actively join the anti-racist struggle has the same problem. The social action that the movement takes by calling people racists for not taking active part in their cause makes sense only from their own committed anti-racist perspective, not from the point of view of people who are just minding their own business. It is likely to further alienate those who may feel they have enough to struggle with on their own, such as the people who feel they live in Hochschild's "deep story." It is worth considering the reaction of the Black community in general: they might be expected to join forces with the Black Lives Matter movement, but in 2020 the Black community gave more votes to Trump than in 2016.

In an academic context, the issue surfaced in the confrontation that ensued when a paper was published by two anti-racists (Howell and Richter-Montpetit, 2019) that characterized the influential "securitization theory" in international relations by Ole Wæver and Barry Buzan as racist. The key point of this theory is that governments can introduce measures that restrict civil rights while imposing barriers against legitimate criticism by classing these measures as matters of "national security" (which are traditionally exempt from transparency). The point is directed against abuse of power and would therefore normally be classed as belonging on the critical side of the political spectrum. The categorization as "racist" rested only on the argument that the theory did not actively pursue racial justice. The conclusion of the paper was that the whole securitization theory had to be rejected for that reason (cf. the rebuttal by Wæver and Buzan, 2020).

Many commentators have dismissed this simply as absurd. But that would underestimate the problem. The authors make two choices that make perfect sense in terms of the anti-racist position as described above. They give a description whose justification is predicated on their own perspective (antiracism) and use that to reject the legitimacy of descriptions from other perspectives. This relies on assuming the right to demand that the collective institution of science reconfigures itself so as to base its practice on their specific perspective only. By doing so they lay down a division in terms of social grounding that splinters off their definition of "good science" from the collective institution. Once again, the collectively upheld status of shared institutions is rejected in favor of the pursuit of justice from a particular perspective.

Both science and democracy are institutions that depend on collective acceptance. Without collective trust, they cannot do their jobs. If only scientific theories that reflect one's own particular agenda are to be admitted, and the rest are "cancelled," there can be no collectively shared institution of scientific pursuit of truth. If each group pursues its own agenda, while members of other groups are not allowed to enter into democratic deliberation with it, there can be no process towards a collective granting of rights to those who need them. If we visualize the position of identity politics on the left in the form of a map, the divisive strategy where each group fights for itself may be pictured as a series of colored dots in the upper left hand corner. As against that, right-wing identity groups cut a wide swath across the map, covering all those who feel that in recent decades something has been taken from them that was rightfully theirs.

To repeat, I am not in the business of telling oppressed minorities what they should do. What I try to do is to present an analysis of conceptualizations and their relations with facts outside the concepts in themselves that is of relevance to understanding the issues involved in identity politics—especially the dependence of the struggle of relatively powerless groups on securing acceptance from the collective as a whole.

10   Conclusions

Identity politics is an influential agenda, both on the political left and on the political right. The upsurge of identity politics contributes to a global situation in which liberal democracy, which seemed at one time to be universally victorious, is under threat. I address in particular the notion of racial issues of identity, but I also touch on gender and national identity.

Cognitive Semantics has previously contributed to enriching understanding of politics in support of democracy. This paper is intended as an attempt to pursue the same agenda. Taking my cue from a slogan launched by Lakoff (2008), I have used the idea of a "new enlightenment" for the approach I try to contribute to.

The fundamental point of the argument above involves the need to extend the analysis from the conceptualizations themselves—the narratives, frames, and cognitive models—to an analysis that focuses on the way conceptualizations are anchored in non-conceptual aspects of reality.

In continuation of a central aspect of the cognitive linguistic tradition, the emphasis on grounding, I have argued for three types of relations that are important in order to understand the role of conceptualizations in identity politics: bodily grounding, social grounding and factual grounding (cf. Harder, 2010). Focusing on grounding relations is a strategy for steering a middle course between the simplifications of an objectivist picture and unconstrained proliferation of conceptual models as associated with radical social constructivism.

Social grounding is concerned with the kind of conceptualizations that have the status of aspects of collective reality. Only conceptualizations which have collective-level status can support the functioning of democratic governments. Central to the argument, this includes the power to introduce rights of the kind that further the causes that identity groups pursue.

I try to illustrate how the concept of factual grounding can be useful in addressing the issue of fake news in a way that goes beyond the simplifications associated with the objectivism that cognitive semantics showed to be inadequate. Instead of simply asking, "is the proposition p true or false?" factual grounding is about how much of social reality a conceptualization arguably subsumes and what particular perspectives it may reflect. This also involves a discussion of the need for caution in analyzing the mechanisms of extension and simplification, and the general variability of conceptual models as understood in cognitive semantics. One may recognize the limitations of a strictly truth-conditional account of meaning and at the same time be aware that metonymic extensions have implications for "enlightening" applications of the concept.

Finally, I suggest that these findings have implications for the strategic issue of how to address the pursuit of identity-political goals. Central in this regard are the relations between the tendency for identity groups to pursue their agendas as jealously separate groups as opposed to pursuing them as groups engaged in pursuing the common grand narrative of equality.

At the end, returning to the overall motif of distinguishing between conceptual models per se and their social grounding of these ideas, one point is the most central: while the differentiated *conceptual* agendas may be both revealing and sympathetic, pursuing them as *socially* segregated agendas may not give the desired results. To the extent identity groups are instrumental in reducing the possibility of collectively shared notions of truth, equality and social justice, they are at risk of promoting the same trajectory of social disintegration as Donald Trump.

References

Anderson, Katherine. 2020. Feminist epistemology and philosophy of science. Available at https://plato.stanford.edu/entries/feminism-epistemology/ (accessed Nov 28, 2020).

Applebaum, Anne. 2020. *Twilight of Democracy—The Failure of Politics and the Parting of Friends*. London: Allen Lane

Bargh, John A. and Tanya L. Chartrand. 1999. The unbearable automaticity of being. *American Psychologist* 54(7): 462–479.

Butler, Judith. 2004. *Undoing Gender*. New York: Routledge.

Charteris-Black, Jonathan. 2004. *Corpus Approaches to Critical Metaphor Analysis*. Basingstoke: Palgrave MacMillan.

Chilton, Paul. 1996. *Security Metaphors. Cold War Discourse from Containment to Common House*. New York: Peter Lang.

Chilton, Paul. 2004. *Analysing Political Discourse. Theory and Practice*. London: Routledge.

Dahlman, Christian, Farhan Sarwar, Rasmus Bååth, Lena Wahlberg and S. Sikström. 2016. Prototype effect and the persuasiveness of generalizations. *Review of Philosophy and Psychology* 7: 163–180.

Dunham, Yarrow. 2018. Mere membership. *Trends in Cognitive Sciences* 22(9): 780–793.

Fauconnier, Gilles and Mark Turner. 2002. *The Way We Think. Conceptual Blending and the Mind's Hidden Complexities*. New York: Basic Books.

Fukuyama, Francis. 2018. *Identity: The Demand for Dignity and the Politics of Resentment*. New York: Farrar Straus and Giroux.

Gallie, W.B. 1956. Essentially contested concepts. *Proceedings of the Aristotelian Society*, New Series 56: 167–198.

Goodhart, David. 2017. *The Road to Somewhere: The Populist Revolt and the Future of Politics*. Oxford: C. Hurst and Company.

Harder, Peter. 2005. Blending and polarization: Cognition under pressure. *Journal of Pragmatics* 37: 1636–1652.

Harder, Peter. 2010. *Meaning in Mind and Society: A Functional Contribution to the Social Turn in Cognitive Linguistics*. Berlin: Mouton de Gruyter.

Harder, Peter. 2014. National identity: Conceptual models, discourses and political change. 'Britishness' in a social cognitive linguistics. *Cognitive Linguistics Studies*: 22–54.

Harder, Peter. 2021. Rationality in economics and politics: a case study in the importance of adequate conceptual analysis. *Cognitive Semantics* 7(1): 31–53.

Howell, Alison and Melanie Richter-Montpetit. 2019. Is securitization theory racist? Civilizationism, methodological whiteness, and antiblack thought in the Copenhagen School. *Security Dialogue*. Available at https://doi.org/10.1177/096701061986 2921

Hochschild, Arlie R. 2016. *Strangers in Their Own Land: Anger and Mourning on the American Right*. New York: The New Press.

Hughes, Coleman. 2020. A better anti-racism. Available at https://www.manhattan -institute.org/a-better-anti-racism (accessed Nov 21, 2020).

Kendi, Ibram X. 2019. *How to be an Antiracist*. New York: Random House.

Køppe, Simo. 1990. *Virkelighedens niveauer. De nye videnskaber og deres historie*. Copenhagen: Gyldendal.

Lakoff, George. 2008. *The Political Mind. Why You Can't Understand 21st-Century American Politics with an 18th-Century Brain*. London: Viking.

Langacker, Ronald W. 1991. *Foundations of Cognitive Grammar*, volume II: *Descriptive Applications*. Stanford: Stanford University Press.

Levitsky, Steven and Daniel Ziblatt. 2018. *How Democracies Die*. New York: Crown.

Marx, Karl and Friedrich Engels. 1932. *Die Deutsche Ideologie*. Erste Abteilung, Band 5. Berlin: Marx-Engels Verlag GMBH.

Mattsson, Tina. 2014. Intersectionality as a useful tool: Anti-oppressive social work and critical reflection. *Affilia* 29(1): 8–17.

Merritt, Anna C, Daniel A. Effron and Benoît Monin. 2010. Moral self-licensing: When being good frees us to be bad. *Social and Personality Psychology Compass* 4/5 (2010): 344–357.

Mizumoto, Masaharu, Jonardon Ganeri and Cliff Goddard (eds.). 2020. *Ethno-Epistemology New Directions for Global Epistemology*. London: Routledge.

Mounk, Yascha. 2018. *The People vs. Democracy: Why Our Freedom Is in Danger and How to Save It*. Cambridge, MA: Harvard University Press.

Müller, Jan-Werner. 2016. *What is Populism?* Philadelphia: University of Pennsylvania Press.

Necef, Mehmet Ü. 2008. Forskellige fortællinger om danskere og indvandrere, in P. Gundelach, H.R. Iversen and M. Warburg (eds.), *I hjertet af Danmark: institutioner og mentaliteter*, 249–255. Copenhagen: Hans Reitzels Forlag.

Nichols, Dana. 2010. Teaching critical whiteness theory. *Understanding & Dismantling Privilege* 1(1): 1–12.

Olson, Mancur. (2011). (Originally published in 1965). *The Logic of Collective Action: Public Goods and the Theory of Groups* (Second Printing with a New Preface and Appendix). Cambridge, MA: Harvard University Press.

Piketty, Thomas. 2014. *Capital in the 21st century*. Cambridge, MA: Belknap Press.

Rutherford, Jonathan. 1990. *A Place Called Home: Identity and the Cultural Politics of Difference*. London: Lawrence and Wishart.

Said, Edward W. 2003. (Originally published 1978). *Orientalism* (With a new preface). London: Penguin.

Searle, John R. 1995. *The Construction of Social Reality*. Harmondsworth: Penguin.

Sinha, Chris. 1999. Grounding, mapping and acts of meaning. In T. Janssen and G. Redeker (eds.), *Cognitive Linguistics: Foundations, Scope, and Methodology*, 223–255. Berlin: Mouton de Gruyter.

Tajfel, Henri. 1981. *Human groups and social categories. Studies in social psychology*. Cambridge, UK: Cambridge University Press.

Tomasello, Michael. 2008. *Origins of Human Communication*. Cambridge, MA: MIT press.

Verhagen, Arie. 2021. *Ten Lectures on Cognitive Evolutionary Linguistics*. Leiden: Brill.

Versluys, Eline. 2007. The notion of identity in discourse analysis: Some 'discourse analytical' remarks. *RASK: internationalt tidsskrift for sprog og kommunikation*: 89–99.

Wæver, Ole and Barry Buzan. 2020. Racism and responsibility: The critical limits of deepfake methodology in security studies. A reply to Howell and Richter-Montpetit. Available at https://doi.org/ 10.1177/0967010620916153.

Zahavi, Dan. 2014. *Self and Other. Exploring Subjectivity, Empathy, and Shame*. Oxford: University Press.

Zaller, John R. 1992. *The Nature and Origins of Mass Opinion*. Cambridge, UK: Cambridge University Press.

Zlatev, Jordan. 2005. What's in a schema? Bodily mimesis and the grounding of language. In B. Hampe and J. Grady (eds.), *From Perception to Meaning: Image Schemas in Cognitive Linguistics*, 313–341. Berlin: Mouton de Gruyter.

Zulaika, Joseba and William Douglass. 1995. *Terror and Taboo: The Follies, Fables and Faces of Terrorism*. London: Routledge.

Volumes Overview

© KONINKLIJKE BRILL NV, LEIDEN, 2023 | DOI:10.1163/_013

PART 2
Basic Issues

VOLUME 2

PART 3
Essential Concepts

VOLUME 4

PART 10
Force and Causation

PART 11
Attention

PART 12
The Targeting System of Language